"Copan and Stewart have chosen a wonderful lineup of relevant topics in the forefront of contemporary discussions about Christianity. These include difficult objections to the Bible and Christianity, scientific and historical evidence supporting God's existence and the truth of Christianity, and sex and gender hot button issues. Moreover, the editors have chosen excellent contributors to address each of these important topics. Highly recommended!"

—MICHAEL LICONA, professor of New Testament studies, Houston Christian University

"This is an extraordinary collection of vigorous essays defending Christianity against historical and contemporary objections. Especially recommended for critics of Christianity and open-minded inquirers."

—CHARLES TALIAFERRO, Emeritus Overby Distinguished Professor, St. Olaf College

"This excellent volume tackles the most challenging questions confronting the Christian faith, offering deeply insightful and well-argued responses from a distinguished group of world-class scholars. A must-read for anyone—scholar or layperson—seeking to engage thoughtful answers to difficult questions."

—JOHN C. PECKHAM, research professor of theology and Christian philosophy, Andrews University

"This intelligent and well-crafted book draws together a range of different experts to address the most pressing objections to Christianity on the market today. All thoughtful Christians will benefit from considering these high-quality essays so that they are 'prepared to make a defense' (I Peter 3:15). Highly recommended!"
—Gavin Ortlund, theologian-in-residence, Immanuel Nashville

"There's virtually no topic in the contemporary debates that's not covered in this terrific volume. What's more, each essay is written accessibly but also embedded in the current scholarly literature. Consequently, the reader will be well-equipped to contend for the faith. This is now my top recommendation for those who wish to go deeper than what the popular-level literature has to offer."
—Travis Dickinson, professor of philosophy, Dallas Baptist University

Christianity Contested

Christianity Contested

Replies to Critics' Toughest Objections

EDITED BY
PAUL COPAN
STEWART E. KELLY

CASCADE *Books* · Eugene, Oregon

CHRISTIANITY CONTESTED
Replies to Critics' Toughest Objections

Copyright © 2024 Wipf and Stock Publishers. All rights reserved. Except for brief quotations in critical publications or reviews, no part of this book may be reproduced in any manner without prior written permission from the publisher. Write: Permissions, Wipf and Stock Publishers, 199 W. 8th Ave., Suite 3, Eugene, OR 97401.

Cascade Books
An Imprint of Wipf and Stock Publishers
199 W. 8th Ave., Suite 3
Eugene, OR 97401

www.wipfandstock.com

PAPERBACK ISBN: 978-1-6667-4325-8
HARDCOVER ISBN: 978-1-6667-4326-5
EBOOK ISBN: 978-1-6667-4327-2

Cataloguing-in-Publication data:

Names: Copan, Paul [editor]. | Kelly, Stewart [editor].

Title: Christianity contested : replies to critics' toughest objections / edited by Paul Copan and Stewart E. Kelly.

Description: Eugene, OR: Cascade Books, 2024 | Includes bibliographical references and index.

Identifiers: ISBN 978-1-6667-4325-8 (paperback) | ISBN 978-1-6667-4326-5 (hardcover) | ISBN 978-1-6667-4327-2 (ebook)

Subjects: LCSH: Apologetics. | Christianity and atheism. | God (Christianity). | Christianity—Controversial literature. | Christian ethics.

Classification: BT1102 C67 2024 (paperback) | BT1102 (ebook)

02/13/25

"Scripture quotations are from the ESV Bible (The Holy Bible, English Standard Version), 2001 by Crossway, a publishing ministry of Good News Publishers. Used by permission. All rights reserved."
Scripture quotations taken from The Holy Bible NIV ® Copyright© 1973, 1978, 1984, 2011 by Biblica, Inc.™ Used by permission of Zondervan. All rights reserved worldwide.
Scripture quotations taken from the (NASB® New American Standard Bible®, Copyright© 1960, 1971, 1977, 1995, 2020 by The Lockman Foundation. Used by permission. All rights reserved. lockman.org)
The Holy Bible New King James Version© copyright © 1982 by Thomas Nelson.
Quotations designated (NET) are from the NET Bible® copyright© 1996, 2019 by Biblical Studies Press, LLC. All rights reserved.
[Scripture quotations are from] New Revised Standard Version Bible, copyright© 1989 National Council of the Churches of Christ in the United States of America. Used by permission. All rights reserved worldwide.

Paul: To the Evangelical Philosophical Society: How good and pleasant it has been for us to dwell together in unity.

Stewart: *in memoriam*: John Lachs: Teacher, Mentor, Friend

Contents

Contributors		ix
Introduction STEWART E. KELLY AND PAUL COPAN		1
1	The Problem(s) of Evil STEWART E. KELLY	9
2	"Genocide" in the Bible PAUL COPAN	34
3	"Slavery" in the Bible PAUL COPAN	65
4	"Except Through Me": The Scandal of Christian Exclusivism RICHARD BRIAN DAVIS	98
5	Divine Hiddenness: Epistemic and Soteriological JAMES K. BEILBY	120
6	An Historical Case for the Resurrection of Jesus of Nazareth GARY R. HABERMAS AND BENJAMIN C. F. SHAW	148
7	Faith and Science ROBIN COLLINS	168
8	Christianity and Human Flourishing GREGORY E. GANSSLE	193

CONTENTS

9 Gender and Christianity — 215
   PRESTON SPRINKLE

10 Christianity and Women — 240
   LYNN H. COHICK

11 Sexual Apologetics Through a Covenantal Lens — 274
   PAUL RHODES EDDY

12 Religious Apathy — 299
   KYLE BESHEARS AND TAWA ANDERSON

Index — 321

Contributors

Tawa Anderson (PhD, Southern Baptist Theological Seminary), professor of philosophy and apologetics, New Orleans Baptist Theological Seminary.

James K. Beilby (PhD, Marquette University), professor of biblical and theological studies, Bethel University, St. Paul, Minnesota.

Kyle Beshears (PhD, Southern Baptist Theological Seminary), pastor, Mobile, Alabama.

Lynn H. Cohick (PhD, University of Pennsylvania), distinguished professor of New Testament and director of Houston Theological Seminary, Houston Christian University.

Robin Collins (PhD, University of Notre Dame), distinguished professor of philosophy, Messiah University.

Paul Copan (PhD, Marquette University), professor of philosophy and Pledger family chair of philosophy and ethics, Palm Beach Atlantic University.

Richard Brian Davis (PhD, University of Toronto), professor of philosophy, Tyndale University.

Paul Rhodes Eddy (PhD, Marquette University), professor of biblical and theological studies, Bethel University, St. Paul, Minnesota.

Gregory E. Ganssle (PhD, Syracuse), professor of philosophy, Talbot School of Theology.

CONTRIBUTORS

GARY R. HABERMAS (PhD, Michigan State University), distinguished research professor of apologetics and philosophy, Rawlings School of Divinity, Liberty University.

STEWART E. KELLY (PhD, University of Notre Dame), professor of philosophy emeritus, Minot State University

BENJAMIN C. F. SHAW (PhD, Liberty University), president of Core Apologetics.

PRESTON M. SPRINKLE (PhD, Aberdeen), president of the Center for Faith, Sexuality, and Gender.

Introduction

Stewart E. Kelly and Paul Copan

WHETHER BELIEF IN HISTORIC Christianity is rationally justified is a matter of no small controversy. One can appeal to Aquinas, Luther, Calvin, Descartes, Leibniz, and Kant as thinkers who affirm the epistemic respectability of belief in the Christian faith. On the other hand, one can appeal to Spinoza, Locke,[1] Hume, Marx, Nietzsche, and Freud as intellectuals who view traditional Christianity with deep suspicion and who argue that there are more than ample reasons for rejecting Christianity. The question arises, "Whom are we to believe, and why?" To affirm there is a lack of consensus is to engage in serious understatement. There is a plethora of "enlightened contemporary intellectuals" who see serious Christian belief as the province of the "naïve and foolish." What sort of objections do they bring against historic Christianity? There are many, and they are typically presented as defeaters of Christian belief, where a "defeater for a belief A is another belief B such that once you come to accept B, you can no longer continue to accept A without falling into irrationality."[2] This volume is a defeater-dedicated work; a number of prominent defeaters will be carefully analyzed and examined to see if

---

1. John Locke is read by many to be a Christian, but this is mistaken. In his *The Reasonableness of Christianity* he clearly affirms that Jesus is the Messiah. But he carefully and consistently avoids addressing the divinity of Jesus, probably because he could no longer affirm it. See Marshall, "Locke, Socinianism, 'Socinianism,' and Unitarianism." Locke is better seen as a Socinian, at least as the term is broadly understood—namely, belief in God and the Scriptures while denying the deity of Christ and, by implication, the Trinity.

2. Plantinga, *Warranted Christian Belief*, x–xi.

they succeed in undermining the epistemic rationality of Christian belief. There are numerous potential defeaters, not all of which can be adequately addressed in a book of manageable length. So, in this work we have selected what we take to be the twelve most serious objections to affirming Christian belief. The twelve consist of the following:

God and the problem of evil: There is too much evil for it to be rational to believe there is an omnipotent, omniscient, and omnibenevolent being as captured in both the Holy Bible and in Christian tradition. This is sometimes referred to as the Evidential Problem of Evil. Chapter 1 addresses this issue.

The practice of genocide in Old Testament war texts: The God of the Old Testament is guilty of commanding genocide—the intentional, mass killing of thousands of undeserving Amalekites, Canaanites, and others. Chapter 2 addresses the claims and purported evidence in support of the charge that God is some sort of moral monster.[3]

The Old and New Testament support of slavery: The Bible fails to condemn slavery as a serious moral injustice. Both the Old and New Testaments speak of slavery, but neither condemns the practice as modern moral sensibilities require. Whether this is a sustainable charge is the focus of chapter 3.

Christianity's narrowness and exclusivism: Traditional Christianity is salvifically exclusive. It would have us believe that faithful followers of Jesus are the only people to enjoy an afterlife in the presence of the one creator God. This is an insult to devoted Muslims, practicing Jews, and Hindus and Buddhists of serious commitment. Christianity affirms Religious Exclusivism, and this offends modern moral sensibilities, which are decidedly Pluralist. Whether Pluralists are rationally justified is the focus of chapter 4.

The problem of divine hiddenness and the question of the unevangelized: There are many humans who have never heard the claims of Christianity. For them and for many others, the true God seems hidden from them. Should we conclude that such people, after death, are eternally separated from the love of God? Is it consistent with historic Christianity to affirm some sort of postmortem opportunity? Chapter 5 investigates the case for it.

The impossibility of miracles, including Jesus' bodily resurrection: There are seemingly compelling reasons for rejecting belief in miracles.

---

3. Atheist Richard Dawkins makes such claims in Dawkins, *God Delusion*.

More specifically, the arguments against belief in the bodily resurrection of Jesus succeed in showing there was neither an empty tomb nor a risen Lord. Does the evidence support the claim that Jesus truly died and his body rotted in the tomb—or other such naturalistic theories? Chapter 6 seeks an answer to such questions.

The conflict between science and the Christian faith: The success of modern science is incompatible with the truth of Christian belief. As Richard Dawkins and others have argued, if the integrity of science is affirmed, then traditional Christianity must be rejected. Chapter 7 carefully examines how faith and science should be understood.

The Christian faith's undermining of human flourishing: Friedrich Nietzsche and others argue that Christianity is inconsistent with human flourishing and happiness. Nietzsche claims that the death (irrelevance/realized non-existence) of God opens up the possibility of humanly created values that focus on the will to power and make genuine happiness possible. Evaluating Nietzsche's claim is front and center in chapter 8.

Christianity's narrow view of gender: Christianity affirms there are two fundamental genders, male and female, rooted in concepts developed in the Bible. The last thirty years or so have seen an explosion of new gender categories and an implicit argument that the biblical account needlessly (and cruelly) limits the options to two. Chapter 9 examines the arguments for a multiplicity of genders.

Christianity's misogyny and oppression of women: In the last one hundred years or so, a number of feminists have claimed that Christianity oppresses women and is also guilty of a thoroughgoing misogyny. Chapter 10 seeks to ascertain what Christianity teaches about the nature and value of women.

Christianity's restrictiveness regarding human sexuality and marriage: Human sexuality is an area where there is little contemporary consensus, and the biblical view of sexuality and marriage is often seen as overly restrictive and too judgmental. Chapter 11 offers a systematic and nuanced reply to various non-Christian perspectives.

Apatheism and the irrelevance of Christianity: Some thinkers nowadays argue that it no longer matters whether God exists or whether Christianity is true. *Apatheism* sees God and religious faith as essentially irrelevant for the modern human condition. The core claims of Apatheism are examined in chapter 12.

CHAPTER SUMMARIES

In chapter 1 Stewart Kelly addresses what is broadly known as the problem of evil. In reality, it is a family of issues brought together under a single heading. The topics addressed in this chapter include the following:

1. The Logical Problem of Evil: this is the idea that the existence of evil (e.g., undeserved pain and suffering) is logically inconsistent with a being who is all-powerful, all-knowing, and all-loving.[4] It is widely acknowledged there is no explicit contradiction between God's goodness and power and the existence of evil; so we need to add the claim that God has no morally sufficient reason to allow the evil he does. Whether the objection is successful hinges on the epistemic acceptability of the additional premise.

2. The Evidential Problem of Evil: the existence of gratuitous or pointless evil, such as a fawn suffering horribly in a forest fire or a girl brutally murdered, seems to morally implicate the God of Christianity. The success of this challenge hinges on whether belief in the *apparent* lack of a justifying good (for some particular horrific evil) is sufficient to justify belief in an *actual* lack of a justifying good.

3. Two other issues addressed are first, an argument by Paul Draper that there is a moral principle that, if true, shows God to be unjustified in allowing certain evils. Draper's argument is examined in order to see if God is indeed culpable. Secondly, the view known as Skeptical Theism is examined. Suppose God did indeed have reasons for allowing Rowe's fawn and the young girl to suffer. Should we, as epistemically limited beings, believe that we would have access to such reasons? This chapter examines whether Skeptical Theism is a viable option for the committed theist.

Paul Copan tackles the issue of God and genocide in chapter 2. Critics ranging from Richard Dawkins to Joshua Bowen have claimed that the Old Testament God looks a vindictive bully and a bloodthirsty ethnic cleanser. There could not be a good God if this being has sanctioned obviously immoral acts. Copan argues at length that a careful analysis of the relevant Old Testament texts does not support the charge of genocide. He further argues that the Old Testament never glorifies war. He also makes clear that, contrary to a number of critics, we should not play off the God

---

4. These qualities describe the God of historic Christianity.

INTRODUCTION

of the Old Testament against the God of the New Testament. The Old Testament God is not vengeful and villainous while the New Testament one is loving and kind. The God of the Bible is gracious and longsuffering, in addition to being a God of justice. Copan argues that the commands to kill others (e.g., the Canaanites or Amalekites) are given only reluctantly and in response to the persistent wickedness of those people.

Chapter 3 examines the issue of the Bible and slavery. Critics such as Hector Avalos and Sam Harris, among others, claim that the Mosaic law endorses slavery. Given the obvious immorality of slavery, if true, this would reflect rather badly on the Mosaic law, the authority of the Old Testament, and the trustworthiness of Scripture. If the challenge of Avalos and Harris is successful, then the Mosaic law can be fruitfully compared to the antebellum United States South. The specter of four million slaves at the beginning of the Civil War looms large as we examine the Mosaic law. Copan meticulously examines the relevant Old Testament texts to show that slavery-endorsement charges cannot be sustained.

In chapter 4 Rich Davis addresses the issue of Religious Exclusivism. Brian McLaren and other non-traditionalists charge evangelical Christianity with promoting a narrow and intolerant view of salvation. Historic Christianity has advanced the view that faith in Jesus Christ is the only genuine path to salvation. The arguments of McLaren, religious pluralist John Hick, and others are carefully presented and then evaluated in light of some central texts in Scripture. Davis believes that if we take the claims of Jesus seriously, then we cannot in good conscience concur with Religious Pluralists such as McLaren and Hick. Whether or not Exclusivism is fashionable, it does seem to be the view of Jesus and the New Testament.

Chapter 5 asks the question, "What is the fate of the unevangelized?" Those who are Christians have both heard the gospel and responded to it in faith. But there are millions of people who have never heard the gospel, let alone respond to it in faith. We could add that God seems hidden from a still-larger swath of humanity. What is the fate of the observant Jew, the devout Muslim, and the serious Buddhist who have never had the opportunity to consider the claims of Jesus? Are they to be subject to eternal separation from God, or is there perhaps another alternative? Jim Beilby mounts a sustained argument for Postmortem Opportunity, the idea that all humans who have never heard the gospel will get that opportunity after their earthly life is over. Arguing that Scripture never explicitly rules out such an option, Beilby states that this postmortem possibility is logically consistent with the loving and gracious God found in the Scriptures.

The resurrection of Jesus of Nazareth is the lynchpin of the Christian faith. If Jesus did not rise from the dead, then our faith is in vain and Christianity collapses, as the apostle Paul makes clear in 1 Corinthians 15. In chapter 6 Gary Habermas and Ben Shaw argue that belief in Jesus' resurrection is the best explanation of a number of widely accepted facts. The majority of critical scholars accept that the tomb was empty and that the disciples believed that the risen Jesus appeared to them. There are a limited number of options here. To mention but three possibilities, the first is the idea of a collective or group hallucination. A second possibility is the Swoon Theory, the idea that Jesus fainted (but did not die), and then revived in the coolness of the tomb. The third possibility is that Jesus rose bodily from the dead, thus providing an explanation of both the empty tomb and the post-mortem appearances to the disciples.

Many intellectuals believe that the success of modern science functions to undermine the rationality of belief in God. The (believed) truth of naturalistic Darwinian evolution, the incompatibility between faith and reason, and the belief that the scientific method disallows belief in transempirical realities (such as God) are individually and/or collectively sufficient to undercut belief in God. In chapter 7 Robin Collins carefully examines these and other objections to see whether they succeed in making Christian theism irrational. Collins also looks at the apparent fine-tuning of the universe (so as to permit human life) and the fact that the universe is intelligible to determine whether these factors genuinely point toward the existence of the God of Christian theism.

Friedrich Nietzsche was strongly opposed—and even hostile—to historic Christianity. He fervently believed that Christianity was a life-denying faith and that it radically undermined genuine human flourishing and the possibility of human happiness. In chapter 8 Greg Ganssle examines Nietzsche's concerns to see whether he succeeds in portraying Christianity as a life-denying system of thought. Nietzsche shares with Marx and Freud the conviction that embracing Christianity ensures one's unhappiness and guarantees that an individual will never flourish. While the Christian ethic centers on God's self-giving love for us that inspires our love and service to others. Nietzsche is partial to what is sometimes called "expressive individualism," where each of us pursues and creates her own meaning and she rejects God's desired purpose for each human life as anti-human and contrary to our deepest needs. Ganssle considers Nietzsche's alternative conception of flourishing and finds it wanting.

The last twenty to thirty years have witnessed a revolutionary sea-change on the topic of gender. Traditional views of gender have come under withering assault from a wide variety of sources. In chapter 9 Preston Sprinkle expertly and sympathetically gives the reader a detailed map and guide to this largely uncharted terrain. He focuses on a few specific issues. One deals with the role our sexed bodies play in shaping human sexuality. To what extent, if any, does sex determine who we are? Another asks the question whether gender stereotypes are reducible to biological sex. Sprinkle argues that the biblical categories should guide our understanding of gender, as they provide us with the ethical foundation for our discussion and for understanding the complex issues surrounding gender roles, human sexuality, and the complicated interplay between the two.

Historically, Christianity has often been guilty of the oppression or marginalization of women. Whether this fact is somehow grounded in or justified by Scripture is far from clear. Chapter 10 tackles the tough and thorny issues arising out of the treatment of women in Scripture. Lynn Cohick helps us navigate the territory of Scripture and writings in the early church. She argues that both Scripture and early church practice hold women in high regard, and that no cogent case supporting oppression or misogyny from either source is sustainable.

Human sexuality is a hotly contested topic today. It's also an area where there is little consensus as to how we should think about these issues. Paul Eddy carefully constructs a view of sexuality and marriage that is faithful to historic Christianity and clearly at odds with modern moral sensibilities. In a highly nuanced chapter, Eddy argues that we must appeal to Scripture if we are to construct a view of human sexuality that does justice to both our being divine image-bearers and the truths of Scripture.

Finally, chapter 12 examines a fairly recent phenomenon known as *Apatheism*. This is the belief that the question of God's existence is fundamentally irrelevant for modern human beings. As such, we should not care one iota about it. Similarly, the question about the truth of Christianity is also a matter of profound indifference. Tawa Anderson and Kyle Beshears critically examine the arguments offered in support of Apatheism and find them wanting. They make a case that the question of

God's existence has massive significance for both the beliefs and the lives of modern-day people.

The scholars working on the above topics are all evangelical Christians. But it should be noted that they represent a wide range of views under the broad umbrella of Evangelicalism. On intramural matters there exist a number of substantive differences: eschatology, the nature of Jesus' atoning death, the details of biblical Christology, the extent of the noetic effects of sin, whether the husband-wife relationship is egalitarian or complementarian, and the relationship of divine sovereignty and human freedom (to mention just a few of the areas of disagreement). What binds us together is a common commitment to Jesus Christ as Savior and Lord as well as to the epistemic rationality of historic Christian theism.

It should be noted this commitment is a defeasible one: if any of the twelve defeaters examined is successful, then historic Christian theism requires either modification or in some cases (say, if Jesus did not rise bodily from the dead) outright rejection. The authors write with a sense of confidence and humility. We are confident in the deliverances of reason and in the responses to the challenges considered. We also write with a keen awareness of our own human frailty and the limits of our cognitive situation. We both encourage and welcome carefully considered replies to what we offer in this volume, and we look forward to engaging in critical and charitable discussions in the future.

BIBLIOGRAPHY

Dawkins, Richard. *The God Delusion*. New York: Mariner, 2008.
Locke, John. *The Reasonableness of Christianity*. Vol. 6 of *The Works of John Locke in Nine Volumes*. 12th ed. London: Rivington, 1824.
Marshall, John. "Locke, Socinianism, 'Socinianism,' and Unitarianism." In *English Philosophy in the Age of Locke*, edited by Michael Alexander Stewart, 111–82. New York: Oxford University Press, 2000.
Plantinga, Alvin. *Warranted Christian Belief*. New York: Oxford University Press, 2000.

I

The Problem(s) of Evil

Stewart E. Kelly

INTRODUCTION

ELIE WIESEL (1928–2016), A Jewish survivor of Auschwitz and Buchenwald, wrote about the suffering and death endured by his family during World War II. He and his family were loaded on boxcars and then shipped to the camps. He writes,

> The cherished objects we had brought with us thus far were left behind in the train, and with them, at last, our illusions.
> Every two yards or so an SS man held his tommy gun trained on us. Hand in hand we followed the crowd. An SS noncommissioned officer came to meet us, a truncheon on his hand. He gave the order, "Men to the left! Women to the right." Eight words spoken quietly and indifferently, without emotion. Eight short simple words. . . . I had not had time to think, but already I felt the pressure of my father's hand: we were not alone. . . . Tzipora held mother's hand. I saw them disappear into the distance; my mother was stroking my sister's fair hair as though to protect her, while I walked on with my father and the other

men. And I did not know that in that place, at that moment, I was parting from my mother and Tzipora forever.[1]

By the end of the war, Wiesel's parents and Tzipora had all perished in the camps. At sixteen years of age he was alone, without family, and not knowing where to turn. Wiesel's personal suffering borders on the unimaginable, the horrific.[2] Other accounts of horrific suffering come to mind. Ivan Karamazov's poignant description of the fate of babies at the hands of the Turks,[3] and Alexander Solzhenitsyn's epic saga of life in the gulags.[4] And in the literature on the problem of evil are two oft-noted instances: (a) a baby fawn suffering horribly in a fire and its aftermath; (b) a young girl in Michigan being brutalized and eventually killed.[5]

We not only have these horrific evils to consider but also have reports of one genocide after another, especially in the twentieth century. A few of the better-known examples:

- Stalin's Purges and the murder of some twenty million Soviets;
- Mao's slaughter of millions during the so-called Great Cultural Revolution in China (estimates of sixty to eighty million killed);
- The carnage of the two World Wars, with fatalities approaching seventy to eighty million;
- The Armenian Genocide: The mass killing of one to two million Armenians by the Turks during and after World War I.[6]

If Christians believe in a God who is omnipotent, omniscient, and perfectly good, and yet there are staggering amounts of evil, the question presents itself: "Can I be mature both intellectually and spiritually, be aware of the enormous and impressive amounts of suffering and evil in the world, be aware also of the best atheological arguments [arguments supporting atheism] starting from the facts of evil, and still be such that Christian belief is rational and warranted for me"?[7]

1. Wiesel, *Night*, 27.
2. See the fine work by Marilyn Adams, *Horrendous Evil*.
3. See Fyodor Dostoyevsky's *Brothers Karamazov*.
4. See Alexander Solzhenitsyn's *Gulag Archipelago*.
5. For a while the two victims were referred to (in the literature) as "Bambi" and "Sue." I find these terms rather objectionable, because they can be read as trivializing or objectifying the victims, and I shall myself use the terms "the fawn" and "the girl."
6. See Naimark, *Genocide*.
7. Plantinga, *Warranted Christian Belief*, 460.

Alvin Plantinga's point can be easily summarized: If a traditional Christian is well-informed concerning the facts of evil and suffering, is it yet reasonable for that person to embrace Christian belief? Most of this chapter is dedicated to these issues confronting the informed Christian.

In spite of the examples given above, evil and suffering are ultimately a deeply personal experience. We know from reading, being aware of others' lives, and recalling vivid experiences in our own lives that evil confronts us all individually. A few of the countless examples are mentioned here:[8]

- Woody Guthrie: Guthrie, a prominent folksinger, contracted the disease known as Huntington Chorea, one of the worst diseases known to humanity. It causes both physical and mental suffering; then, after years of torture, it inevitably brings death.
- Buddy Holly: Famous rock and roll/rockabilly star whose plane crashed and killed him in Iowa in 1959. He was twenty-two years old.
- Evan Sullivano: A boy from Middletown, New Jersey[9] who waged a five-year battle against leukemia before dying at age eighteen. Along the way, his father died of a heart attack and, shortly after his death, his mother was diagnosed with advanced breast cancer.

So there it is—one of the fundamental realities of human existence is the fact of suffering, in some cases unimaginable suffering. Yet as Christian theists who accept the Bible as the inspired and authoritative Word of God, we passionately believe that an all-loving, all-powerful, and all-knowing God exists. Can we simultaneously—and with rational justification—affirm both the reality of evil/suffering and the reality of God? J. L. Mackie and William Rowe, two eminent philosophers working from a tradition extending back through David Hume to Epicurus, are convinced that the evil and suffering are undeniable, and in some important sense epistemically overwhelming. They claim we can no longer rationally defend Christian theism but should face the facts and embrace either agnosticism[10] at best or atheism at worst. We now turn to presenting and evaluating the arguments offered by Professors Mackie and Rowe.

---

8. This list is massively selective. I make no claim that these examples are somehow more worthy of mention than the billions not named.

9. The author's home town.

10. Agnosticism is often characterized by the lack of sufficient evidence to support either (G) (God exists) or (~G) (God does not exist).

THE LOGICAL PROBLEM OF EVIL

In 2000 the Christian author Lee Strobel commissioned the pollster George Barna to conduct a national survey, one that included the question, "If you could ask God only one question ... what would you ask?"[11] The most popular response (given by 17 percent of the respondents) was "Why is there pain and suffering in the world?" As Michael Peterson has noted, "Something is dreadfully wrong with our world."[12]

There are at least two ways in which Christian theism might be shown to be epistemically unjustified: First, the sheer weight of the evils in the world makes it epistemically unlikely that the statement "God exists," is true. The other way is if it can be shown that the existence of (any) evil is logically inconsistent with the God of Christian theism.

In the 1950s J. L. Mackie posed what has come to be called the *Logical Problem of Evil*. Mackie believed "it can be shown, not that religious beliefs lack rational support, but that they are positively irrational, that several parts of the essential theological doctrine [of God] are [logically] inconsistent with one another." Mackie claims it is impossible for all of the following propositions to be true at the same time:

(M1) God is omnipotent.

(M2) God is omniscient.

(M3) God is perfectly good.

(M4) Evil exists.

The initial question that arises is, "Where exactly is the supposed contradiction?" It certainly is not an *explicit* contradiction. For example, let's say Barney said two things are true:

1. Fred is married to Wilma.

2. Fred is not married to Wilma.

Either (1) can be true or (2) can be true, but (1) and (2) cannot simultaneously be true; they are mutually exclusive claims. So, if Fred states both (1) *and* (2) to be true, he is being logically inconsistent (and contradicting himself).

---

11. Beebe, "Problem of Evil."
12. Peterson, *God and Evil*, 1.

THE PROBLEM(S) OF EVIL

Mackie himself acknowledges that the logically inconsistency is not of the Flintstone variety elucidated above, but rather an *implicit* contradiction. This means that Mackie needs to add one or more claims to the initial set of four claims above so as to make what is implicit now explicit. Mackie proposes[13] we add the following two propositions to the set of four:

(M5) If God is all powerful, then he can create any world whatever.

(M6) If God is morally good, then he prefers a world without evil over our current world (and all its evil).

From (M5) we get the idea that God could have created a world with humans who always freely choose good. And from (M6) we learn that God wants such a world. Combining (M5) and (M6) we see both that God *can* create and that he *wants* to create a perfect world. So, if we take (M1)–(M6) together, we see there should be a world with no moral evil[14] whatever. But clearly the following proposition is false:

(M7) There is no evil.

There is now an *explicit* contradiction between (M4) and (M7).

What shall we say to Mackie? Given that (M7) is entailed by the conjunction of (M5) and (M6), Mackie's two additional premises, we need to ask ourselves whether the Christian theist is committed to accepting (M5) and (M6)? Here the answer is a resounding *no!*

Neither proposition (M5) nor proposition (M6) is necessarily true. To rebut the charge of logical inconsistency, all the Christian theist need do is to show (M5) and (M6) are possibly false.[15] This is because a necessary truth cannot possibly be false; so, if it is possible for a proposition to be false, then it is not necessarily true. More formally,

Premise 1: If a proposition is necessarily true, then it is impossible for it to be false.

Premise 2: But both propositions (M5) and (M6) are possibly false.

---

13. The following is indebted to J. L. Mackie, *Miracle of Theism*.
14. The issue of natural evil still needs attention, though that takes us rather far afield.
15. Remember that logical inconsistency requires an airtight (logically speaking) case, with *no possibility* of being false.

Conclusion: The propositions are not necessarily true.[16]

Alvin Plantinga has developed the best-known reply to the challenge presented by Mackie here. He points out that if the view of human free will known as Compatibilism[17] were (necessarily) true, then God could guarantee a world with free creatures and no moral wrongdoing.[18] But, Plantinga, notes, Compatibilism is not only not necessarily true; it is in fact false.[19] Plantinga thinks a superior understanding of human free will is captured by the view known either as Libertarianism[20] or as Agent Causation Libertarianism.[21] On a Compatibilist view, free actions are compatible with causal antecedents, while the Libertarian thinks such causal antecedents makes the action in question unfree. Is Libertarianism a possible view of human free will? It is widely accepted that the answer is yes, even by those who think the Compatibilist take on free will is superior. So, if Compatibilism is not necessarily true, and logical inconsistency requires the relevant propositions to be necessarily true, then Mackie's claim of logical inconsistency is fatally undermined.

A little further reflection shows that (M6) is no better off than (M5). It also is not necessarily true. Consider the following:

1. We allow for pain and suffering to occur if some greater good (e.g., the peace that passes all understanding, Phil 4:7) is made possible with the experience of difficult times.

2. There is also a modicum of wisdom in the popular dictum, "No pain, no gain." What does not kill you (often) makes you stronger.

3. Many people, Christian and otherwise, would testify that some of the greatest growth in their lives was made possible by a period of pain and suffering.

16. *Modus Tollens* is the relevant argument pattern here.

17. Compatibilism is the view of human free will that states that free actions are compatible with being causally determined by antecedent states of affairs.

18. This presumably would apply to angels also.

19. This is a matter of no small controversy. The dominant view among Christian philosophers is some form of Libertarianism, though a number of committed Compatibilists also exist.

20. Libertarianism regarding free will has almost nothing to do with the political view by the same name (other than they both are fond of freedom in some sense). Plantinga defines "libertarianism" as "the view that a person is free with respect to a given action if and only if that person is both free to perform that action and free to refrain from performing that action . . ." (Plantinga, "Free Will Defense").

21. Roderick Chisholm was one of the better-known advocates of this position.

The above makes clear that, just as with (M5), (M6) is also not necessarily true, and is in fact false. Given we have shown neither (M5) nor (M6) is necessarily true, Mackie and his fellow atheologians have failed to produce a set of propositions which demonstrate the logical inconsistency between the existence of God and the existence of evil.

THE EVIDENTIAL PROBLEMS OF EVIL:

In the popular mind, atheism is often seen as a reasonable alternative to Christian theism, and a number of atheists have led the way: Richard Dawkins (1941–), Sam Harris (1967–), Christopher Hitchens (1949–2011), and Daniel Dennett (1942–2024), sometimes collectively known as the Four Horsemen of Atheism. These four, and a plethora of others,[22] have championed the cause of atheism over the past thirty years or so. One could make a respectable case that the best of the arguments offered from this select group come from Dennett (a professional philosopher)[23] or Dawkins (a biologist of some note). But the strongest arguments come not from the above thinkers, but from two professional philosophers: William Rowe (1931–2012) and Paul Draper (1960–). In 1979 Rowe published a seminal article, "The Problem of Evil and Some Varieties of Atheism."[24] This is widely regarded as the single most influential atheological argument[25] in the last fifty years.[26] In the next few pages we will closely examine three particular examples of the *Evidential Argument from Evil*:

1. William Rowe's First Evidential Argument from Evil (1979);
2. William Rowe's Second Evidential (Bayesian) Argument from Evil;
3. Paul Draper's Evidential Argument from Evil.

We focus on these arguments because they are the strongest and most sophisticated evidential arguments for atheism in the past fifty

---

22. Ayaan Hirsi Ali, Jerry Coyne, John Loftus, P. Z. Myers, Dan Barker, Richard Carrier, Michael Martin, Keith Parsons, Victor Stenger, Steven Pinker, Quentin Smith, and Peter Singer all come to mind.

23. See his book co-authored with Plantinga: Dennett and Plantinga, *Science and Religion*.

24. Rowe, "Problem of Evil," 12–29.

25. "Atheological" arguments are ones intended to establish the rationality of belief in God's non-existence.

26. This article has been cited in the literature over four hundred times.

years.[27] Their arguments are clearly laid out and engaged in the ongoing dialogue between atheism and theism.

Rowe's First Evidential Argument

Taking both human and animal suffering as clear examples of evil, Rowe offers the following argument:

(R1) There exist instances of extreme suffering which an omnipotent, omniscient being could have prevented without thereby preventing the occurrence of any greater good.

(R2) An omniscient wholly good being would prevent the occurrence of any intense suffering it could, unless it could not do so without thereby preventing the occurrence of some greater good.

──────────────────-

∴ (R3) There does not exist an omnipotent, omniscient being

The rough idea is very simple:

Pointless evils exist.[28]

God would not permit pointless evils.

──────────────────-

∴ God does not exist.

What should we say regarding this argument? Taking a close look at the argument, three things can be noted. First, the initial premise is what might be called the "factual premise"—it is a claim about how the world is. It has two components:

A. The claim that evils occur;

B. The claim that some/many of these evils have no greater good attached.

Second, God would prevent any horrific evils unless it was necessary to allow them so as to make possible a greater good. This can be

27. Other impressive arguments have come from Michael Tooley, Bruce Russell, Graham Oppy, and others. We are clearly being selective in choosing just three, but we suggest a good case can be made for choosing these three. The arguments most worth analyzing are the most impressive evidential arguments from evil.

28. Pointless or "gratuitous," where the basic idea is an evil for which no greater good occurs. Pointless evils do allow for goods, just not greater goods.

termed the "theological premise"—it is a claim about the nature of God. Third, the conclusion is logically entailed by the two premises—it is a valid (truth-preserving) argument.

If one (e.g., a Christian theist) is not inclined to accept the conclusion, then one had better find something objectionable about one or both of the premises. Most theists[29] will readily grant the truth of the theological premise. As Rowe writes,

> The second premise of the argument expresses a belief about what a morally good being would do under certain circumstances. According to this belief, if a morally good being knew of some intense suffering that was about to occur and he was in a position to prevent its occurrence, he would prevent it unless he could not do so without thereby losing some greater good of which he was aware.[30]

Given the obvious plausibility of the second premise, we agree with Keith Yandell when he writes that "the crucial question is whether it is certain, or at least more probable than not, that there is unjustified evil, whether natural or moral."[31] Rowe acknowledges that a Christian can justifiably reject the Evidential Argument if they are successful in finding "some fault with its first [factual] premise."[32]

So how exactly does Rowe defend premise 1? He begins by presenting the story of a suffering animal. He writes,

> Suppose in some distant forest lightning strikes a dead tree, resulting in a forest fire. In the fire a fawn is trapped, horribly burned, and lies in terrible agony for several days before death relieves its suffering. So far as we can see, the fawn's intense suffering is pointless, leading to no greater good. Could an omnipotent, omniscient being have prevented the fawn's apparently pointless suffering? The answer is obvious, as even the theist will insist. . . . Since no greater good, so far as we can see, would have been lost had the fawn' intense suffering been prevented, doesn't it appear that premise 1 of the argument is true, that there do exist instances of intense suffering which an

---

29. There are some notable exceptions, which we will not pursue in this chapter.
30. Rowe, *Philosophy of Religion*, 80–81.
31. Yandell, "Theism and Evil," 1–7.
32. Rowe, "Problem of Evil," 4. To be clear, the fault found would have to be of substance.

omnipotent, omniscient being could have prevented without thereby preventing the occurrence of any greater good?[33]

What is the Christian theist to say in response to Rowe's challenge? Here it needs to be clear that Rowe's argument for premise 1 amounts to the following:

1. It *appears* there is no sufficient reason for God to allow the suffering of the fawn.[34]
2. There *probably is* no sufficient reason to justify God's allowing the fawn to suffer.

Based on the horrific suffering of the fawn, Rowe believes the (*apparent*) truth of (1) clearly justifies our inference to the (*probable*) truth of (2). What are we to think about Rowe's inference? There is a massive literature on this very particular question, and we can only highlight a few of the salient points.

Rowe's inference demands that we think of the evidence that might justify the inference. Suppose, as Plantinga has written, "I look inside my tent: I don't see a St. Bernard, it is then [highly] probable that there is no St. Bernard in my tent. That is because if there were one there, I would very likely have seen it; it's not easy for a St. Bernard to avoid detection in a small tent."[35] Suppose then we look again inside the tent: "I don't see any noseeums (very small midges with a bite out of all proportion to their size); this time it is not particularly probable that there are no noseeums in my tent . . ." So now the Big Question: is our perception of the reasons for God allowing horrific evils more like the St. Bernard in the tent (where reality corresponds with initial appearances) or more like the noseeums (where reality may well not correspond with initial appearances)? Rowe's answer is the former—if there were such justifying reasons for God allowing the evils, then we would spot them. And since we don't see the possible justifying reasons, there are good reasons to think they are not there. Based on this reasoning, God's existence, epistemically speaking, is in serious trouble.

---

33. Rowe, *Philosophy of Religion*, 80–81.

34. Stephen Wykstra points out that Rowe's use of "appears" is akin to a promissory note of sorts. If something "appears" to be true, then there are, all things considered, very good reasons to think it is true. Given his take on this word, he objects to Rowe using the word when there is no good reason to make the inference (crucial for the success of Rowe's argument) from "It appears" to "It probably is."

35. Plantinga, *Warranted Christian Belief*, 466.

Plantinga, William Alston, Stephen Wykstra, Michael Bergmann, and many other Christian philosophers do not share Professor Rowe's conviction that if greater goods (correlated with particular horrific evils) existed, we humans would recognize them.[36] At a deeper level, they fundamentally question (and reject) Rowe's confidence in human cognitive powers.[37]

In the early 1980s Stephen Wykstra responded to Rowe in his "The Human Obstacle to Evidential Arguments from Suffering: On Avoiding the Evils of 'Appearance.'"[38] Here Wykstra develops the central Christian intuition that Rowe's premise 1 is not true, because humans lack the general cognitive abilities to discern and/or appreciate the greater good correlated with some specific horrific evil. Wykstra's position, which has been dubbed "Skeptical Theism,"[39] develops a position heartily endorsed by the Christian philosophers mentioned above.[40]

Wykstra questions why (*contra* Rowe) we should believe that humans have the general cognitive capacity to discern God's purposes. He rejects Rowe's claim that if such purposes/reasons existed, we humans would be able to know them. Wykstra's basic principle here, captured by the acronym CORNEA (Conditions Of ReasoNable Epistemic Access), undercuts Rowe's premise 1. Wykstra defines CORNEA as follows:

> On the basis of cognized situation s, human H is [epistemically] entitled to claim "It appears that p" only if it is reasonable for H to believe that given her cognitive faculties and the use she has made of them, if p were not the case, s would likely be different than it is in some way discernible by her.[41]

The question quickly arises, "What exactly does Wykstra mean by this principle?" Does this principle entail that Rowe cannot legitimately make the move (jump) from the claim

---

36. It is true that we might well recognize a few of the greater goods. For a nuanced development along these lines see Stump, "Problem of Suffering," 12–25.

37. Rowe's confidence in human reason is broadly representative of the view of human reason in many branches of the European Enlightenment. Alister McGrath has called this the "omnicompetence of reason." See McGrath, *Historical Theology*, 233.

38. Wykstra, "Human Obstacle," 73–94.

39. So labeled by Draper. The label is a bit of a misnomer, as skeptical theists are not skeptical about God's existence (the core meaning of "skeptical" here), but only of our cognitive abilities in this particular epistemic situation.

40. It seems fair to say that Skeptical Theism is the dominant view among Christian philosophers on this matter, though there are numerous notable exceptions.

41. Wykstra, "Human Obstacle," 85.

"It *appears* there is no sufficient reason for God to allow this evil"

to

"There *probably is* no sufficient reason for God to allow this evil"?

This move (or inference) assumes that if there were a sufficient reason for God to allow this evil, we would probably know it. Such a reason would be within our cognitive range rather than beyond our ken.

Wykstra and others have doubts, massive doubts, that Rowe's assumption is true. Why, he asks, should we think it is true? As Greg Ganssle notes, we might well discern why God allows certain (generally not horrific) evils to happen.[42] Some possible reasons include an increased dependency on God and a more serious prayer life. But given that God is omniscient and humans are radically limited both in how much we know and in our capacity to know, we recognize there is a massive epistemic gap between God and us.[43] Given this fact, why would we expect to know God's reasons for allowing evils, especially particularly horrific instances? Who would be confident (or arrogant) enough to think we could discern why God allowed the Holocaust to occur?! I have absolutely no idea, and I see no reason to think anyone else does either. We are all rowing in the same epistemic boat. The suffering of Rowe's fawn and many other awful evils is inscrutable. In a 1991 essay, William Alston expands upon the position developed by Wykstra. In defending *Skeptical Theism*, Alston writes, "I am by no means the first to suggest that the atheological argument from evil is vitiated by an unwarranted confidence in our ability to determine that God could have no sufficient reason for permitting some of the evils we find in the world."[44]

Skeptical Theism

"Even the very wise cannot see all ends"

GANDALF, LORD OF THE RINGS

---

42. Ganssle and Lee, "Evidential Argument from Evil."18.

43. It is *very* difficult to overstate the magnitude of this gap. As the Christian singer Susan Ashton puts it (speaking about God), "There is a Grand Canyon between you and me." We may well know of a number of goods, but to think they are representative of the entire set of goods (and how they interrelate) is unjustified.

44. Alston, "Inductive Argument from Evil," 35.

THE PROBLEM(S) OF EVIL

In making the case for Skeptical Theism (ST), Alston argues that a number of cognitive limits can be delineated. He mentions all of the following:

> Lack of Data—This includes, *inter alia*, the secrets of the human heart, the detailed constitution and structure of the universe, and the remote past and future, including the afterlife, if any.
> 1. **Complexity Greater Than We Can Handle**—Most notably there is the difficulty of holding enormous complexes of fact (e.g., different possible worlds or different systems of natural law) together in the mind sufficiently for comparative evaluation.
> 2. **Difficulty of Determining What Is Metaphysically [Logically] Possible or Necessary**—Once we move beyond conceptual or semantic modalities (and even that is no piece of cake), it is notoriously difficult to find any sufficient basis for claims as to what is metaphysically possible, given the essential nature of things, the exact character of which is often obscure and virtually always controversial. This difficulty is many times multiplied when we are dealing with total possible worlds or total systems of natural order.
> 3. **Ignorance of the Full Range of Possibilities**—This is always crippling when we are trying to establish negative conclusions [e.g., there are no sufficient reasons for God to allow]. If we don't know whether there are possibilities beyond the ones we have thought of, we are in a very bad position to show that there can be no divine reasons for permitting evil.
> 4. **Ignorance of the Full Range of Values**—When it is a question of whether some good is related to E [the particular evil] in such a way as to justify God in permitting E, we are for the reason mentioned in (4), in a very poor position to answer the question if we don't know the extent to which there are modes of value beyond those of which we are aware. For in that case, so far as we can know, E may be justified by virtue of its relation to one of those unknown goods.
> 5. **Limits to Our Capacity to Make Well Considered Value Judgments**—The chief example of this we have noted is the difficulty in making comparative evaluations of large complex wholes.[45]

Alston's list and all it contains gives us more than adequate justification for blocking Rowe's inference and eliminating any plausible reason for

---

45. Alston, "Inductive Argument from Evil," 29.

accepting premise 1 of Rowe's Evidential Argument. We have no reason whatever to agree with Rowe that we can legitimately make the move from

"It *appears* there is no sufficient reason for God to allow this evil"

to

"There *probably is* no sufficient reason for God to allow this evil."

The considerable evidence for Skeptical Theism combined with the Christian theist's belief in the omnipotence and perfect goodness of God is more than enough to block Rowe's crucial inference. There is enough evidence not only to withhold judgment for Rowe's first premise; indeed, there is enough to justify the stronger claim that the denial of that premise is epistemically justified.

Remember that even if we do not see any morally sufficient reason for God allowing the fawn to suffer (it is a "noseeum" inference), we know that this is entirely in keeping with the massive epistemic distance between humans and God. This can be captured by the (very) catchy phrase:

(N) "*Noseeum*" does not mean "*Nobeeum*"[46]

No apparent sufficient reason neither entails nor makes probable the actual non-existence of sufficient reasons.

Some critics of Skeptical Theism (ST) have argued that ST entails a thoroughgoing Moral Skepticism, and since Moral Skepticism is clearly an untenable philosophical position, then Skeptical Theism itself is untenable in light of this *reductio ad absurdum* argument. Michael Almeida and Graham Oppy claim the commitment to Skeptical Theism undermines our ordinary moral practice. They claim, for example, that if you see a young child being kidnapped in a supermarket and you can easily (and at no personal risk) prevent the dastardly deed from occurring, then it would be morally reprehensible for you to refrain from intervening.[47] This failure to intervene is grounded in our not knowing whether the abduction might result in some exceptional greater good which would allow it. Thus our skepticism about greater goods leads to a sort of moral paralysis concerning moral intervention here. Their argument can be summarized as follows:

1. If Skeptical Theism is true, then Moral Skepticism is true. (If A, then B.)

---

46. The spelling is intentional.
47. Almeida and Oppy, "Sceptical Theism," 96–116.

2. If Moral Skepticism is true, then we will generally lack knowledge whether any particular action will lead to a greater good. (If B, then C.)

3. If we lack this knowledge, then we suffer from Moral Paralysis. (If C, then D.)

4. If we have Moral Paralysis, then we will not intervene here. (If E, then F.)

5. If we do not intervene, the result is clearly unacceptable and radically undermines everyday moral practice. (If F, then G.)

6. ∴ Daily moral practice is undermined. (∴ G)

This is clearly a valid argument, and since most Christian theists are committed to Skeptical Theism, the question arises whether the Skeptical Theist can escape the force of the Almeida-Oppy claim. Michael Bergmann and Michael Rea argue, convincingly I believe, that the answer is clearly, "Yes, we can escape it." They argue that when theists consider the bearing of Skeptical Theism on our everyday moral practices, "they will inevitably and quite sensibly do so in a way that takes account of other things that they believe."[48] Thus we should reject Premise 1 of Almeida and Oppy's argument. But when we do this, we realize that our everyday moral intuitions are completely untouched by the truth of Moral Skepticism.[49] This is because God has clearly laid out moral guidelines in Scripture,[50] and we have every reason to prevent the child's abduction and none to refrain from intervening. Skeptical Theism is a very particular (and in some ways narrow) kind of skepticism. So, very briefly:

1. Yes, on being skeptical regarding God's purposes regarding horrific evils;

2. No, on being skeptical regarding moral principles or on actions flowing from those principles;

3. No, on any other relevant sort of skepticism (such as skepticism regarding epistemic justification or skepticism regarding truth–metaphysical skepticism).

---

48. Bergmann and Rea, "In Defence of Sceptical Theism," 44.
49. Bergmann and Rea, "In Defence of Sceptical Theism," 244ff.
50. As well as what is referred to as elements of common grace (conscience, for example)

So, despite the vociferous protestations of Almeida and Oppy, we confidently reject their claim that Skeptical Theism entails Moral Skepticism, and reiterate the falsity of premise 1. (It is false that, if A, then B.) And once we block that entailment, we see that our ordinary moral practices are very much intact, and we can now ride to the rescue of the young child while leaving Almeida and Oppy in our rearview mirror.

Given the above considerations, we are now in a position to summarize why the lynchpin of Rowe's Evidential Argument from Evil, namely the factual premise, is richly deserving of rejection:

1. There is no general epistemic principle that requires the move from "it appears there is no morally sufficient reason" to "there is probably no morally sufficient reason." Sometimes, as with the St. Bernard in the tent, we can make the epistemic move in question. In the case of the suffering fawn, the relevant example is the noseeum one. Though we see no reason (or no noseeums), it hardly follows there is no reason.

2. The underlying reason here is that Skeptical Theism is true—it corresponds with a state of affairs in the world. Given the epistemically staggering gap between God (the eternal, omniscient creator) and humans (the temporal, finite knowers), we heartily concur with Wykstra that something similar to CORNEA is true. We do well to cite Plantinga here:

> Given that God *does* have a reason for permitting these evils, why think we would be the first to know? Given that he is omniscient and given our very substantial epistemic limitations, it isn't at all surprising that his reasons for some of what he does or permits *completely escapes us*. But then from the fact that no goods we know of are such that they justify God [serve as his reasons for] permitting E1 or E2, it simply doesn't follow that it is probable with respect to what we know, that there aren't any such goods, or that God has no reason for permitting those evils.[51]

It may not surprise some, given the frequent and broadly persuasive criticisms of Rowe's Evidential Argument, that Rowe himself came to believe that his original (1979) argument was a failure. He writes that, "I now think this argument is, at best, a weak argument." He continues, "I propose to abandon this argument altogether . . ."[52]

---

51. Plantinga, *Warranted Christian Belief*, 467, emphasis added.
52. Rowe, "Evidential Argument from Evil: A Second Look," 267.

It should be pointed out that we did not choose to evaluate this argument from Rowe because he himself eventually came to acknowledge its shortcomings. It was rightly chosen because it was widely considered to be one of the strongest atheological arguments in the literature. The huge number of responses to Rowe attest to the widespread respect accorded both Rowe and his work.

In acknowledging the shortcomings of his original argument, it should be noted that Rowe developed a second evidential argument that he considered more promising than the first. We now turn to that second argument.

Rowe's Bayesian Argument

Bayes's Theorem is a mathematical theorem used for determining the probability (P) of X given some background information. Rowe is interested in determining the probability of God existing relative to our background knowledge (K) and the existence of horrific evils (E). We initially determine the probability of God's existence relative to our background knowledge, then we factor in the existence of horrific evils and see how that affects the probability of God existing. Rowe desires to approach this issue without giving either the atheist or the theist an unfair advantage. Rowe appeals here to what can be called the Level Playing Field Assumption, a *neutral* starting point of sorts. Rowe suggests that both atheism and theism be assigned an antecedent probability of .50 (or 50 percent probability). Thus neither view, Rowe believes, is unduly favored.[53] We are now in a position to ask two pertinent questions:

1. Is Pr (G/E & K) > Pr (G/K) ?

2. Is Pr (G/E & K) > 0.50 ?[54]

53. The question lurking is unduly favored "with respect to what?"

54. OK, so what does all this mean? The formula [Pr(G/K)] deals with the probability (Pr) of God (G) existing given our current knowledge (K). The formula [Pr (G/E & K)] deals with the probability (Pr) of God (G) existing given our current knowledge (K) and the existence of evil (E). Rowe and other atheists see the antecedent probability of God's existence (the probability of God prior to considering the issue of evil[s]) as .50 (and .50 for atheism). And then they see the existence of evil as lowering the probability of God below .50, making it clearly irrational to believe in God's existence. As the below argument makes clear, the theist has excellent reasons not to grant atheism a probability equivalent to theism, and she also has no good reason to think the existence of evil does much, if anything, to lower the probability of God's existence. Bayes's Theorem can get quite complex, but the above captures the gist of it.

Rowe believes that this Bayesian version of the evidential argument, compared to his first version, is now both new and improved. But wait ... there's more! Rowe also argues that "it must be acknowledged that (E) does lower the probability of (G)." Secondly, "if we start with our judgments about the probability of (G) on (K) and the probability of (E) on (G) & (K), (E) lowers (G)'s probability significantly, making (~G) twice as likely as (G)." Thus atheism is rationally superior to theism, and Rowe's second attempt is vindicated. It also shows that the Christian theist cannot possibly be justified in affirming (G), as the existence (E) given (K) lowers the probability of (G) below .50.

What should we say to Rowe here? He clearly thinks (E) is a genuine defeater for (G) and that atheism is an epistemically more viable option than theism for the genuine seeker after truth. But as with his first argument, there are serious problems lurking. Here are a few of them:

Why would any sensible Christian grant that the antecedent probability of atheism equals the antecedent probability of Christian theism?! Christians, even epistemically charitable Christians, don't see much reason to assign atheism a probability much above 0.00 (maybe 0.01 during Christmas season). Sensible Christians have plenty of reasons to affirm the Christian faith and virtually none to affirm atheism.[55] Rowe's assignment of probability seems to assume that some sort of neutral starting point is possible, when none is.[56]

It is puzzling why Rowe resurrects (P) in his Bayesian Evidentialist Argument. Remember that (P):

(P) No good we know of [that is apparent to us] justifies God in permitting E1 and E2

is simply a restatement of (1), where the argument amounted to Rowe's "it does not appear" claim. Remember that the Christian critic agrees with (P) as stated, but given the truth and relevance of Skeptical Theism, sees no reason to go beyond (P). If both (P) and Skeptical Theism are true, then (P) by itself continues to be a nonstarter for the Christian. (P) obtaining is *exactly* what we would/should expect given the conjunction of

---

55. It should be noted that many Christians have doubts, and though this may weaken their epistemic confidence in (G), it does nothing to strengthen the justificatory chances of (~G).

56. The classic here is Thomas Nagel's work. See Nagel, *View from Nowhere*.

(G) God exists.

and

(ST) Skeptical Theism is true.

Rowe is not reintroducing (P) because he agrees with the Christian critic that it is an innocuous claim, but because he makes the epistemic move from

The appearance claim

to

The probability claim.

But remember that Rowe's inference is not justified; so reintroducing it here is of no value.

(3) Skeptical Theism is still undefeated by any and every argument Rowe offers. We readily grant that (P) is true, but as they say in New Jersey, "So what!" If you were trying to drive across the United States and (P) was akin to a map, it wouldn't get you out of the county.

(4) Not only is (P) *not* a threat of any sort (its truth fails to make [G] less likely), but the conjunction of (G) and (ST) *make (P) likely*, given God created humans as free creatures and the fact of our severe cognitive limits.

(5) Given the above considerations, our view of (P) is the following:

Pr (P/G & ST) > Pr (~G)

The supposed danger for Christian theism is genuine if and only if (P) is true *and* Rowe's inference from "appears" to "probably is" goes through. All this shows that Rowe's Second Evidential Argument from Evil fares no better than the first, with Plantinga noting that "it is, if anything, weaker than the first."[57]

Draper's Evidential Argument from Evil

Paul Draper, a noted contemporary philosopher, has offered a number of Rowe-inspired Evidential Arguments. One of his most recent (and most challenging) is found in "Pain and Pleasure: An Evidential Problem for

---

57. Plantinga, *Warranted Christian Belief*, 467.

Christianity Contested

Theists."[58] Draper, in an ingenious argument, asks us to consider the pattern of pain and pleasure in the world. Draper seeks to answer the question of whether "any serious hypothesis that is logically inconsistent with theism explains some significant set of facts about evil or about good and evil much better than theism does." Draper is convinced the answer is an emphatic *yes*. He then sets out to compare the explanatory power of theism versus the power of what he calls the Hypothesis of Indifference (HI). The various elements of his argument are as follows:

- (HI) neither the nature nor the condition of sentient beings on earth is the result of benevolent or malevolent actions performed by non-human persons.
- (C) HI explains O reports much better than theism does.
- (O) represents the observation reports concerning pain and pleasure.
- (CH) is the claim that Christianity is true.

Draper believes that with respect to observation reports (O) about both human and animal pain, and the testimony one has encountered concerning the observations others have made, that HI explains the facts O reports much better than theism does.[59]

Should we be persuaded by Draper's argument? We agree with Plantinga that Draper's claim is both subtle and sophisticated; giving it a nuanced reply would require more space than we can give it here. Having said that, there are some concerns that come to mind:

1. Draper claims that "the antecedent probability of (O) (the relevant observation reports about pain and pleasure) is much greater on the assumption that (HI) is true than on the assumption that theism is true." We suggest, it is not clear *why* anyone would want to engage in such a comparison. When we Christians come to comparing (CH) with (HI), we are bringing to bear *all the reasons* we are theists. Why think a theist would prefer (HI)? Draper has nothing to say here.

2. Plantinga argues elsewhere that (C) is false.[60] A theist has a much richer metaphysical toolbox to handle concerns regarding pain and pleasure.

---

58. Draper, "Pain and Pleasure," 14.
59. Draper, "Pain and Pleasure, 14.
60. See Plantinga, "On Being Evidentially Challenged."

THE PROBLEM(S) OF EVIL

3. Skeptical Theism again bubbles to the surface here. How much would we have to know before we could meaningfully compare atheism and theism with respect to explaining pain and pleasure? Working with Alston's list of human cognitive challenges, we see the answer is "quite a bit." Why think, let alone seriously entertain the possibility, that we are in a good epistemic position to do this? As Ganssle notes, "The probabilities of atheism and theism respectively explaining our observations about pain and pleasure are not related to one another."[61] It is entirely possible that the observations are surprising on both views! Furthermore, there is no neutral or mutually agreed upon framework for grounding the needed comparison.

4. Ric Otte argues that even if (C) were true here, "it would have no consequences for the rationality of most theist's religious beliefs,"[62] especially if they are Christian theists. If (C) is true, is the evidence for Jesus' bodily resurrection somehow undermined? Is the Design Argument now impugned? May it never be! Both lines of evidence are intact, and the Christian theist can stop holding her breath—the rationality of Christian theism still endures.

5. Draper's argument, admittedly impressive in many ways, is not investigating reality in all its breadth and depth. He is laser focused on a very narrow slice of reality. Suppose you went to MetLife Stadium for a New York Giants football game, and fifty thousand people were attending the game. Then all the fans, using high powered binoculars, spot a large ant[63] at the 2-yard line (no doubt heading for the end zone). You then write a nice news story that focuses only on the ant (let's call her Ethel). We may learn something about ants in general, Ethel in particular, or even their foot speed on natural grass fields. No matter how well we come to know Ethel (a very fine ant, I'm sure), we have learned nothing about the two teams playing in the game, the referees, the fans, or the game of football. Draper's argument "fails because it looks only at a narrow subset of a religious person's beliefs."[64] By focusing more on theism than on

---

61. Ganssle and Lee, "Evidential Problems of Evil," 22.
62. Otte, "Draper's Evidential Argument," 26–40.
63. A Giant ant, no doubt!
64. Otte, "Draper's Argument."

29

Christian theism (or Muslim theism) "Draper's argument loses all relevance."[65]

6. Christians have no good reason to think (CH) is less probable than (HI). What does it mean that CH "is intrinsically much less probable than (HI)?" No sensible Christian is going to agree proceeding with Mere Theism, which is but a truncated, cheap knockoff of the real thing—full-orbed Christian Theism.

7. The Logical Argument from Evil begins with premises that traditional Christians heartily acknowledge. Draper's argument, on the other hand, "depends on probabilistic reasoning that is suspicious at best, and Christians have no reason to accept this form of reasoning."[66] Why not begin the argument with a set of claims to which the Christian theist is amenable? Such an argument's chances are massively superior to Draper's offering.

CONCLUSION

We have now finished examining four of the leading arguments intended to undermine the rationality of Christian Theism and to promote Atheism as an epistemically superior alternative. We looked at:

1. The Logical Argument from Evil
2. Rowe's First Evidential Argument from Evil
3. Rowe's Second/Bayesian Argument from Evil
4. Draper's Evidential Argument from Evil

We have found, after careful analysis, all four to be wanting. None of them should cause the Christian Theist to be anxious about the justification

---

65. Otte, "Draper's Argument," 31.

66. Otte, "Draper's Argument," 31. A fundamental problem can be identified in Draper's argument and the arguments of many who have advanced evidential arguments such as his. Here is the question: "Why should we think that someone (here, Draper) has found a rather esoteric moral principle that no one has thought of before, that God is answerable to, and shows God to be morally deficient?' The answer is that we are well within our epistemic rights in being plenty skeptical of such principles, and careful analysis shows our skepticism to be amply justified. Both the book of Job and Skeptical Theism justify our having doubts about (1) there being such a principle; and (2) our having the cognitive capacity to recognize the existence of such a principle. Draper needs *both* (1) and (2), but he has neither (1) or (2).

of her most cherished beliefs. Dawkins, Harris, Hitchens, and Dennett have all foamed and fulminated against Christian Theism, but their arguments (with the occasional exception of Dennett) are vastly inferior to the ones we have examined. Dawkins, for example, is generally not taken seriously in the professional philosophical literature, as his arguments are more vitriol than substance. Given that the strongest arguments for atheism are arguments based on the existence of evil,[67] to defuse all four arguments removes some of the biggest intellectual obstacles to Christian theism. The fact that these arguments fail to establish the non-existence of God does not guarantee that God *does* exist, but our opponents have hit us with their best shot, and we have more than weathered the storm. We look to the future, confident that Christian Theism will continue to meet the various and sundry challenges that come its way successfully.

BIBLIOGRAPHY

Adams, Marilyn. "Horrendous Evils and the Goodness of God." *Proceedings of the Aristotelian Society, Supplementary Volumes* 63 (1989) 297–310.

Adams, Robert. "Must God Create the Best?" *Philosophical Review* 81 (1972) 317–32.

Ahern, M. B. *The Problem of Evil*. London: Routledge, 1971.

Almeida, Michael, and Graham Oppy. "Sceptical Theism and Evidential Arguments from Evil." *Australian Journal of Philosophy* 81.4 (2003) 96–116.

Alston, William. "The Inductive Argument from Evil and the Human Cognitive Condition." *Philosophical Perspectives* 5 (1991) 29–67.

———. "Some (Temporarily) Final Thoughts on Evidential Arguments from Evil." In *The Evidential Argument from Evil*, edited by Daniel Howard-Snyder, 311–32. Bloomington, IN: Indiana University Press, 1996.

Basinger, David. "Evil as Evidence Against God's Existence." *Modern Schoolman* 58 (1981) 175–84.

Beebe, James R. "Logical Problem of Evil." *Internet Encyclopedia of Philosophy*, 2003. https://iep.utm.edu/evil-log.

Bergmann, Michael. "Commonsense Skeptical Theism." In *Science, Religion, and Metaphysics: New Essays on the Philosophy of Alvin Plantinga*, edited by Kelly Clark and Michael Rea, 9–30. New York: Oxford University Press, 2012.

Bergmann, Michael, and Michael Rea. "In Defence of Sceptical Theism: A Reply to Almeida and Oppy." *American Philosophical Quarterly* 83 (2005) 241–51.

———. "Skeptical Theism and Rowe's New Evidential Argument from Evil." *Nous* 35.2 (2001) 278–96.

Christlieb, Terry. "Which Theisms Face an Evidential Problem of Evil?" *Faith and Philosophy* 9 (1982) 45–64.

Chrzan, Keith. "God and Gratuitous Evil: A Reply to Yandell." *Religious Studies* (1991) 99–103.

---

67. Rowe and most other atheists would acknowledge this point.

Davis, Stephen. "The Problem of Evil in Recent Philosophy." *Review and Expositor* 82 (1985) 535–48.
Dawkins, Richard. *The God Delusion*. New York: Mariner, 2008.
Dennett, Daniel C., and Alvin Plantinga. *Science and Religion: Are They Compatible?* Oxford: Oxford University Press, 2010.
Draper, Paul. "More Pain and Pleasure: Reply to Otte." In *The Evidential Problem of Evil*, edited by Daniel Howard-Snyder, 41–54. Bloomington, IN: Indiana University Press, 1993.
———. "Pain and Pleasure: An Evidential Problem for Theists." In *The Evidential Problem of Evil*, edited by Daniel Howard-Snyder, 12–29. Bloomington, IN: Indiana University Press, 1993.
———. "Probabilistic Arguments from Evil." *Religious Studies* 28 (1993) 303–17.
Gale, Richard. *On the Nature and Existence of God*. New York: Cambridge University Press, 1991.
Ganssle, Gregory, and Yena Lee. "Evidential Problems of Evil." In *God and Evil*, edited by Chad Meister and James K. Dew, 14–25. Downers Grove, IL: InterVarsity, 2011.
Hare, Peter H., and Edward H. Madden. "Evil and Inconclusiveness." *Sophia* 11 (1972) 8–12.
Howard-Snyder, Daniel. "Introduction." In *The Evidential Problem of Evil*, edited by Daniel Howard-Snyder, xi–xx. Bloomington, IN: Indiana University Press, 1993.
Jordan, Jeff. "Does Skeptical Theism Lead to Moral Skepticism?" *Philosophy and Phenomenological Research* 72.2 (2006) 403–17.
Kelly, Stewart E. "The Problem of Evil and the Satan Hypothesis." *Sophia* 2 (1997) 29–47.
Mackie, J. L. *The Miracle of Theism: Arguments for and against the Existence of God*. Oxford: Oxford University Press, 1982.
McGrath, Alister E. *Historical Theology: An Introduction to the History of Christian Thought*. Oxford: Wiley Blackwell, 2022.
Nagel, Thomas. *The View from Nowhere*. Rev. ed. Oxford: Oxford University Press, 1989.
Otte, Richard. "Probability and Draper's Evidential Argument from Evil." In *Christian Faith and the Problem of Evil*, edited by Peter van Inwagen, 26–40. Grand Rapids: Eerdmans, 2004.
Peterson, Michael. "God and Evil: Problems of Consistency and Gratuity." *Journal of Value Inquiry* 13 (1979) 305–13.
Plantinga, Alvin. "The Probabilistic Argument from Evil." *Philosophical Studies* 35 (1979) 1–53.
———. "Tooley and Evil: A Reply." *Australasian Journal of Philosophy* 60 (1982) 66–75.
———. *Warranted Christian Belief*. New York: Oxford University Press, 2000.
Rowe, William L. "The Evidential Argument from Evil: A Second Look." In *The Evidential Problem of Evil*, edited by Daniel Howard-Snyder, 262–85. Bloomington, IN: Indiana University Press, 1993.
———. "Evil and the Theistic Hypothesis: A Response to S. J. Wykstra." *International Journal for Philosophy of Religion* 16 (1984) 95–100.
———. "Evil and Theodicy." *Philosophical Topics* 16 (1988) 119–32.
———. *Philosophy of Religion*. 2nd ed. Belmont: Wadsworth, 1993.
———. "The Problem of Evil and Some Varieties of Atheism." *American Philosophical Quarterly* 16 (1979) 335–41.

Russell, Bruce, and Stephen Wykstra. "The Inductive Argument from Evil: A Dialogue." *Philosophical Topics* 16.2 (1988) 133–60.
Tooley, Michael. "The Argument from Evil." *Philosophical Perspectives* 5 (1991) 89–134.
Trakakis, Nick. "The Evidential Problem of Evil." *Internet Encyclopedia of Philosophy*, n.d. https://iep.utm.edu/evil-evi.
———. *The God Beyond Belief: In Defence of William Rowe's Evidential Argument from Evil.* New York: Springer, 2006.
Wiesel, Elie. *Night.* New York: Bantam, 1982.
Wykstra, Stephen J. "The Human Obstacle to Evidential Arguments from Suffering: On Avoiding the Evils of 'Appearance.'" *International Journal for Philosophy of Religion* 16.2 (1984) 73–93.
Yandell, Keith E. "Theism and Evil: A Reply." *Sophia* 11 (1972) 1–7.

2

"Genocide" in the Bible

Paul Copan

FOUR APPROACHES

PERHAPS THE LEADING PARADIGM test case for the reliability of our moral intuitions—along with the wrongness of torturing babies for fun or rape—would be our revulsion at acts of genocide.[1] And one of the leading challenges against "the God of the Bible" is that he allegedly commands the Israelites to commit genocide against the Canaanite peoples: "You shall utterly destroy them, the Hittite and the Amorite, the Canaanite and the Perizzite, the Hivite and the Jebusite, as the LORD your God has commanded you" (Deut 20:17). So, the argument continues, we should *reject the God of the Bible* because he mandates acts that are grossly immoral—a point highlighted by "New Atheists" such as Richard Dawkins.[2]

---

1. Thanks to Stewart Kelly and Linnea Clay for their helpful comments on an earlier draft of this essay.

2. Dawkins, *God Delusion*, 31. The fourfold taxonomy I am setting forth here is from Trimm, *Destruction of the Canaanites,* 50.

A second approach maintains that these Old Testament commands are genocidal; however, we must *reject that a good God could have commanded this*. The "actual" God of love and kindness didn't do the commanding. Rather, it was the "textual" God—the fictitious, literary deity in the mind of the fallen, violence-prone biblical narrators or prophets, who misinterpreted the "actual" God's message due to their corrupted ancient Near Eastern worldview.[3] This approach is taken by theologian Greg Boyd and Old Testament scholar Eric Seibert. When the Old Testament declares, "Thus says the Lord," these thinkers say, "It depends." The true ("actual") God and Father of our Lord Jesus Christ loves his enemies and commands us to turn the other cheek. Any harsh or violent-sounding command couldn't come from the one true God.

A third alternative is that, for justifiable reasons, *God did command what one could call "genocide" (or approximating it), but this was a unique, highly specified, unrepeatable situation for a brief period in biblical salvation history*. This event was connected to ancient Israel's receiving the land that God had promised to them and, simultaneously, the Israelites carried out a divinely mandated judgment against a wicked people who engaged in ritual prostitution, incest, bestiality, and infant sacrifice—acts that would be considered criminal in any modern society.

Elsewhere I offer critiques of these three approaches—especially the first two.[4] A fourth view, which I (along with many other scholars) take, *rejects that any genocide took place*. Indeed, the more I have explored this topic of Old Testament warfare, the less I see language of "genocide." Increasingly, I have come to see these are simply stock ancient Near Eastern rhetorical, hyperbolic devices commonly utilized in war texts—along with other textual indicators. Furthermore, the greater emphasis in the biblical text is on driving out or dispossessing the Canaanites, which presupposes their ongoing existence in another location. When we understand these commands in their proper context, we see something much more like ordinary, ancient fighting between combatants.

One could, of course, *remain agnostic about this question*. But lest we think that Jesus is not severe, think again: both testaments assume *both* "the kindness and severity of God" (Rom 11:22; cf. Exod 34:6–7). While Jesus reveals the loving heart of God (John 14:9), this is not opposed to wrath and judgment—a sign of God's justice as well as his care and

---

3. See Boyd, *Warrior God*; Seibert, *Violence of Scripture*.

4. See Copan, *Moral Monster?*; *Vindictive Bully?*; Copan and Flannagan, *Did God Really Command Genocide?*

concern about violence and dehumanization. Jesus himself is described as *kind*: "A bruised reed he will not break, and a smoldering wick he will not quench" (Matt 12:20 ESV). But he is also *severe*: his sovereign rule is associated with "a rod of iron" (Rev 12:5). As we read the Old Testament with a Trinitarian and Christological lens, this same Jesus who led the Israelites out of Egypt through the Re(e)d Sea struck down disobedient Israelites in the wilderness. According to our most reliable Greek manuscripts, the latest critical edition of the Greek New Testament (Nestle-Aland 28) uses the name "Jesus" in Jude 5: "*Jesus*, having saved the people out of the land of Egypt, later destroyed those who did not believe" (Jude 5 NET; also ESV; cf. 1 Cor 10:4).[5] As we will see, the triune God doesn't show favoritism, whether Canaanite or Israelite; the "wrath of the Lamb" comes against those who defy divine goodness (Rev 6:16).

In this chapter, we point out that genocide is not in view. It is more like standard ancient Near Eastern warfare texts, though with some qualifications. In approaching these texts, we want to do so as the Old *and* New Testament authorities do. As it turns out, neither the Old or New Testament views the Canaanite wars as morally troubling. In unpacking a number of interrelated issues on Old Testament warfare, I'll make a number of statements and elaborate on them.

Wars Against the Canaanites: Ethically Rather Than Ethnically Motivated

Some have charged that the Old Testament promotes segregation, fear, and hostility toward different races and religions,[6] not to mention genocide and ethnic cleansing.[7] Kenton Sparks charges that Israel drove out the Canaanites "simply because they were pagans."[8] As we'll see below, this is not at all the case. Also, the modern term "genocide" is often used loosely in today's discourse about the Canaanite wars. But today's more technical, nuanced definitions of "genocide" don't easily fit with ancient Near Eastern practices and what we see in Scripture.[9] For instance, David

---

5. See the most recent critical Nestle-Aland edition (28th) of the Greek New Testament text.

6. Jenkins, *Laying Down the Sword*.

7. Dawkins, *God Delusion*, 51.

8. Sparks, *God's Word in Human Words*, 297–98.

9. Charlie Trimm states: "Upon closer examination it is difficult to find examples of genocide in the ancient Near East due to very different cultural ideas. While mass killing

Firth argues that emotive terms such as "ethnic cleansing" or "genocide" are "inappropriate" because "only combatants are killed and an alternative way was always available."[10]

First, theologically speaking, *the Canaanites were God's enemy because of their immoral practices* (incest, bestiality, infant sacrifice, ritual prostitution). Moreover, the *Israelites themselves* would become God's enemy if they imitated those practices and broke covenant with him: "I will act with wrathful hostility against you" (Lev 26:28). God would vomit or drive out the Israelites just like he did the Canaanites (Lev 20:23). God was far more concerned with the corrosive Canaanite moral and religious *identity* than with its *ethnicity*—a pernicious influence that could infect Israel and obstruct her own mission and identity.

Second, as we argue below, *the language of "extermination" is mistaken*. Sweeping terms such as leaving "no survivor" or anything "that breathes" are exaggerated (e.g., allegedly obliterated Canaanites remain in the land of Israel for generations), and Judahites who are to be "utterly destroyed" (cf. Jer 25:9–11) really just go into exile or are defeated in battle—not exterminated.

Third, *the biblical text makes much more of "driving out" or "dispossessing" the Canaanites than of killing*. The emphasis is on displacing Canaanites so that they would relocate elsewhere. This is supported by the fact that these peoples remained in Israel's midst into the reigns of David (Hittites) and Solomon (Canaanites)—eleventh and tenth centuries BC—and even beyond the Babylonian exile (Jebusites) of the sixth century BC.[11]

Fourth, *throughout the Old Testament, plenty of other nations are singled out for judgment for acting wickedly—not simply Canaanites*. Furthermore, *this judgment extends to God's people as well* (e.g., Amos 1–2).

Fifth, *the New Testament attests to divine judgment on national Israel*. Though Jesus loves and weeps over Jerusalem, he curses it for its hard-heartedness, hypocrisy, and nationalism: "May no one ever eat fruit from you again!" (Mark 11:14). Jesus does this with other Israelite cities as well (e.g., Luke 10:13–15), on whom judgment fell in AD 70 by the Romans. And Jesus himself struck down unbelieving, idolatrous Israelites in the wilderness (Jude 5).

---

certainly happened, the core element of killing people because of their group identity is missing, especially related to ethnic or religious identities" (Trimm, "Causes," 49).

10. Firth, *Message of Joshua*, 27.

11. See 2 Sam 5:6–8; 24:7; 1 Kgs 9:16, 20–21; Ezra 9:1.

Essentially, ethnicity or tribal identity is irrelevant—so, not "genocide." From the outset, God made clear that judgment would fall on the Canaanites when their sin had fully ripened (over half a millennium)—not before (Gen 15:16; cf. Amos 2:9–10). And that hallowed city of Jerusalem had pagan (Amorite and Hittite) roots (Ezek 16:3). The very tribes God would drive out of Canaan (Gen 15:18–21) had a history of being friendly at various points in Israel's history and were even incorporated into the Israelite community.[12] The later-hostile Amalekites were Abraham's descendants (Gen 36:12).

Even Joshua includes the Canaanite Rahab's rescue and incorporation into Israel (Josh 6); Canaanite "strangers" from Shechem in a covenant-renewal ceremony (Josh 8:33, 35); Israel's treaty with the Gibeonites (Josh 9). This illustrates the fact that Canaanite cities could have attempted to make peace with Israel, but they refused (Josh 11:19).

No, it was not ethnicity but rather Canaanite disobedience (Heb 11:31), its "unclean" practices, its "abominations" and "impurity" (Ezra 9:11; cf. Lev 18:30; Deut 13:5; 18:9; 1 Kgs 21:26) that brought about the Canaanite expulsion. And Israel, too, would be expelled from the land for imitating these practices (Deut 18:10; 2 Kgs 16:3; 17:17; 21:6; 2 Chr 33:6; cf. Ps 106:35–39; cf. Lev 18:27–28; 20:22–24). So God doesn't simply throw out the Canaanites from the land, he gives them "lots of time to turn from their waywardness before Yahweh will be able to say, 'That's it.'"[13] It would have been wrong to drive out the Canaanites before the time was ripe.

God's Severe Actions in the Short-Term, Universal Blessing in the Long-Term

God's long-term strategy was to bless humanity through Abraham (Gen 12:1–3), but there were immediate obstacles—namely, hostile opposition that hindered or interfered with the achievement of that divinely commissioned final goal.

First, as God's covenant people, *Israel needed to preserve its identity in order to fulfill its mission to bring universal blessing,* but it faced a pernicious Canaanite threat. The fledgling nation of Israel easily slipped into

---

12. See Num 32:11–12; Josh.2:1–11; 8:33–35; Judg 1:16; 1 Sam 7:14; 26:6; 2 Sam 1:3, 13; 6:10–11; 11:3; 23:34 (cf. Josh 13:13; Jer 40:8; 23:39; 24:16–18; 1 Chr 2:55; 12:4; Neh 3:7.

13. Goldingay, *Genesis,* 252.

idolatry, covenant-breaking, and sexual immorality; repeatedly, God's global saving mission through Israel was under threat (Exod 32; Lev 17:7; Num 25:1, 3; 31:16; Josh 24:23; Amos 5:26; cf. Acts 7:43). Thus the strong language of Deuteronomy "was only being realistic in recognizing the power of Canaanite temptation when Israelite faith in Yahweh was a newly budded flower."[14]

Second, *God's redemptive plan for the world had to begin somewhere at some time, and it was a messy, broken world with which God started.* God accommodates the situation by getting his hands dirty. At times he must bring judgment, but he is a God who is always willing to relent and show mercy to those who recognize their wickedness and waywardness and repent, whether Israelites or pagans (Exod 34:6–7; Gen 18:32; Jer 18:7–8; Jonah 3:10–4:2). John Goldingay writes:

> The fate of Canaan is subordinate to the promise of Israel. But the promise to Israel is in turn subordinate to the fate of the whole world. A temporary unfairness that discriminates for Israel and against Canaan is designed to give way to a broader fairness. Election is exclusive in the short term, but it is designed in due course to benefit others [beyond] its short-term beneficiaries.[15]

In the end, God's intent is for Israel's long-standing enemies to become united with his people in a redeemed community (Ps 87:4; Isa 19:25; Zech 9:2–7). Even during Israel's efforts to take the land, the fact that there "was not a city which made peace with the sons of Israel" except the Gibeonites (Josh 11:19) suggests *the possibility of a negotiated peace with any willing Canaanites.*[16] Indeed, God was always willing to relent from threatened judgment; this includes Sodom and Gomorrah (Gen 18:32), Rahab (Josh 2), Canaanite strangers (Josh 8:33, 35), Nineveh (Jonah 4:2), and so on. And in addition to God's waiting patiently for over half a millennium (Gen 15:16), the Canaanites had forty years of warning—including astonishing signs, wonders, and the visible presence of God, such as the pillar of cloud by day and fire by night in the midst of the Israelite camp. Canaanites could have fled the land or simply aligned themselves with the powerful God of Israel. Death was certainly not inevitable.

---

14. Goldingay, "Justice and Salvation," 186.
15. Goldingay, "Justice and Salvation," 184.
16. Beal, *Joshua*, 254.

Third, God's action in the world meant divine "counter-violence" for Israel to be freed from Egyptian bondage and Canaanite temptation. Without God's intervention against these threats, Israel would not exist. As Daniel Hawk notes: "Israel would not exist apart from the application of divine power and the execution of divine violence to liberate and conquer. No exodus, no conquest. No violence, no Israel."[17] Likewise, John Goldingay adds:

> God had made the destiny of the entire world depend on Israel—not on what Israel would do but on what God would do through Israel. This might seem a weird action on God's part, but it is an action affirmed by testaments. As Jesus put it in John 4, salvation is from the Jews. Therefore, no Jews, no salvation. One can see why this is so: "Jesus is Jewish. No Jews, no Jesus."[18]

Though God hates violence and is not described as violent in the Old Testament (1 Chr 22:8; Ps 11:5; Prov 6:16–17), he reluctantly enters into the power-structures of this world. This involves a kind of reluctant, last-resort "counterviolence" (Lam 3:33). The unfolding biblical story of God's interaction with humans "tells what this decision costs God."[19] Indeed, "if God commands violence, it is part of a whole concessionary scheme of operation, an accommodation to the fact of rampant evil which he detests but has not abolished."[20]

Israel's High-Stakes Fighting: Spiritual Warfare Against Forces Threatening to Undermine God's Global Redemptive Purposes

Some critics will construe Israel's battles against the Canaanites as an "us vs. them" or "good guys vs. bad guys" scenario. What about the feelings of the hapless Canaanites? How would we like it if another nation invaded ours?[21]

In response, first, the critic typically dismisses key features of the biblical story. In doing so, he refuses to allow its interlocking pieces to

---

17. Hawk, *Violence of the Biblical God*, 165.
18. Goldingay, *Numbers and Deuteronomy*, 85.
19. Hawk, *Violence of the Biblical God*, xiv.
20. McConville and Williams, *Joshua*, 112. Likewise, see Carroll R., "Reflections of the Violence," 120–21.
21. Seibert, *Violence of Scripture*, 101.

hold together in a coherent divinely directed narrative, and, thus, the moral and theological case for judgment against the Canaanites will be lost. This is much like removing Gandalf from the *Lord of the Rings* or Jack Bauer from the TV series *24*. To get rid of them means the story lacks integrity and unity. So even for just the sake of argument, let us allow for the following:

(a) God uniquely chose Israel as a vehicle of blessing to the nations;

(b) God delivered them from bondage in Egypt with many signs and wonders;

(c) the Canaanites were genuinely wicked people who engaged in abhorrent, pernicious practices and whose time for judgment had finally come;

(d) Israel's military and numerical inferiority required trusting in God to drive out the Canaanites;

(e) Israel's battles represented a cosmic struggle in which evil forces threatened to undermine Israel's identity, integrity, and mission to bring blessing to the world; and

(f) the land of Israel would be the place of arrival of the Messiah, whose redemptive work would bring the promise of Abraham to fulfillment—namely, the blessing of all the nations.

To reject these affirmations leaves us with an effete, meager patchwork of claims that no longer have any explanatory power or narratival force.

Second, *if the Scriptures are God's revelation, then we actually have a God's-eye view of the Canaanites*. Unlike the critics who ask, "How would you like it if another nation invaded yours?," even Canaanites like Rahab recognized that God was clearly fighting on Israel's behalf, and when the Canaanites heard about God's mighty acts in Egypt and beyond, their "hearts melted" and "no courage remained" in anyone (Josh 2:10–11); other Canaanites did as well (5:1; 9:9–10; cf. 1 Sam 4:6–8). As such, the Canaanites had forty years to contemplate the greatness of Israel's God. They were well-informed about Yahweh, and some of them even turned to the God of Israel (e.g., Josh 8:33, 35). So when we read Deuteronomy or Joshua, we are "reading with God"—from God's perspective. Furthermore, the New Testament authorities also affirm without apology that God was behind the driving out of the Canaanites (Acts 7:45; 13:19; Heb 11:30–34; Jas 2:25). Goldingay points out: "If there is a contradiction between loving your enemies and being peacemakers, on one hand, and Joshua's undertaking this task at God's command, on the other, the New Testament does not see it."[22]

Third, contrary to the idea that Israel was just one nation invading another, *God's work through Israel's battle was that of the divine "warrior" engaged in a cosmic battle against dark powers* (Exod 12:12; 15:3). Israel's fighting was not against hapless, helpless Canaanite tribes. Rather, the Canaanites had well-fortified cities and were numerically and militarily superior to Israel (Deut 1:28; 9:1–2; 20:1–2). Fighting against the Canaanites naturally inspired fear in the hearts of Israel and so required trust in God (Deut 1:21; 20:1–4). Eventually, in light of Israel's sustained existence, its Messiah would emerge and rise up to cast down "the ruler of this world" (John 12:31).

The notion that Israel was just one tribal people driving out another tribe contradicts the biblical narrative and leaves us without a coherent and compelling story.

Israel's Warfare Accounts: High Degree of Hyperbole and Other Rhetorical Devices from the Ancient Near East

Deuteronomy 20:16–18 reads:

> Only in the cities of these peoples that the LORD your God is giving you as an inheritance, you shall not leave alive anything that breathes. But you shall utterly destroy [*haram*] them, the Hittite and the Amorite, the Canaanite and the Perizzite, the Hivite and the Jebusite, as the LORD your God has commanded you, so that they may not teach you to do according to all their detestable things which they have done for their gods, so that you would sin against the LORD your God.

What are we to make of this language? Perhaps it would first be helpful to see how this *exaggerated* language was utilized in both the ancient Near East and the Old Testament itself—and then see how the verb *haram* (sometimes translated "utterly destroy") ought to be translated. Then we can examine other indicators of hyperbole and exaggeration.

---

22. Goldingay, *Joshua, Judges, and Ruth*, 3.

"GENOCIDE" IN THE BIBLE

Ancient Near Eastern Warfare Hyperbole

The ancient Near Eastern world commonly resorted to a kind of "trash talk" akin to our sports jargon: "We totally destroyed that team"; "we annihilated those guys"; "our team slaughtered yours." The ancient Near Eastern "trash talk" included phrases like "left alive nothing that breathes"; "man and woman, young and old"; "no survivors"; "utterly destroyed [*haram*]"; "perished." Just as no one takes sports trash talk literally today, back then, no one took this ancient trash talk literally either.

Here is a sampling of what this looks like:[23]

Ancient Near Eastern "Trash Talk" (Exaggeration)	The Historical Reality
Egypt's Thutmose III (late fifteenth century BC) proclaimed he had overthrown Mitanni's "great army" in "the twinkling of an eye"; it had "perished completely, as though they never existed, like the ashes."[24]	Mitanni's forces lived to fight beyond this in the fifteenth and fourteenth centuries.[25]
The Bulletin of Rameses II reads: "His majesty slew the entire force . . . as well as all the chiefs of all the countries that had come with him. . . . His majesty slaughtered and slew them in their places . . . and his majesty was alone, none other with him."[26]	Rameses II exaggerated Egypt's less-than-decisive victory at Kadesh against Syria (1274/1273 BC), which was far from an overwhelming victory.
Pharaoh Rameses III boasted about the Battle of the Delta and the invading Sea Peoples (1175 BC): "I slew the Denyen in their islands, while the Tjeker and Philistines were made ashes. The Sherden and the Washesh of the sea were made nonexistent."[27]	This "victory" actually led to Egypt's economic devastation and to its eventual decline. In fact, Philistia would later colonize eastern Egypt—despite the pharaoh's boast.
King Mesha of Moab (840/830 BC) claimed that "Israel has utterly perished for always."[28]	This was a premature judgment—by one hundred years! Actually, the Assyrian invasion in 722 BC devastated the Northern Kingdom of Israel.

23. This chart is taken from Copan, *Vindictive Bully?*, 201.
24. Kitchen, *On the Reliability*, 174.
25. Younger, *Ancient Conquest Accounts*, 190–92.
26. Younger, *Ancient Conquest Accounts*, 245.
27. Pritchard, *Ancient Near Eastern Texts*, 262.
28. Kitchen, *Reliability*, 174.

The same is true of Assyria's, Egypt's, and Susa's war texts as well. There we read of taking lands or cities in a "single day"—which is what Joshua does in 10:13, where victory is achieved in a "single day" or "whole day."

Hyperbole in Biblical War Texts

When we read Joshua and Judges, we see two sides of the ancient warfare ledger: one side refers to wasting the enemy while the other side mentions an abundance of Canaanite survivors. What's more, the biblical accounts' inclusion of survivors presents a *more realistic* scenario than that of other ancient Near Eastern nations, which didn't mention survivors in their annals.

Here is a biblical sampling of both "annihilation" and "no annihilation"—the idealistic and the realistic—side by side:

> Joshua 10:33: Joshua "defeated" the king of Gezer and "left him no survivor." (Annihilation)
>
> Judges 1:29: "Ephraim did not drive out the Canaanites who were living in Gezer; so the Canaanites lived in Gezer among them." King Solomon would eventually capture Gezer (1 Kgs 9:16). (No annihilation)
>
> Joshua 10:39: All the inhabitants of Debir were "utterly destroyed." (Annihilation)
>
> Joshua 11:21: Then Joshua "utterly destroyed" Anakites in Debir. (No annihilation earlier)
>
> Joshua 11:11: At Hazor, Joshua left alive "no one who breathed"; he "burned Hazor with fire." Cities like Hazor were "utterly destroyed." (Annihilation)
>
> Judges 4:3: Jabin the king of Hazor fights against Israel with nine hundred chariots. This and other Canaanite cities were cleared out and then reinhabited.[29] (No annihilation earlier)
>
> Judges 1:8: "Then the sons of Judah fought against Jerusalem and captured it and struck it with the edge of the sword and set the city on fire." (Annihilation)
>
> Judges 1:21: "But [the Benjamites] did not drive out the Jebusites who lived in Jerusalem; so the Jebusites have lived with [them] in Jerusalem to this day." (No annihilation)

---

29. Firth, *Joshua*, 202.

Critic Joshua Bowen, with whom I will occasionally be interacting in this essay, makes the argument that the Israelites were commanded to *devote to destruction* (*haram*) the cities of Canaan—that these were "divine commands for violence and genocide."[30] He insists the sweeping language of Joshua is not hyperbolic. But he ignores very clear and repeated indications of hyperbole, including the juxtaposed texts listed above. Indeed, many more such "annihilation"/"no annihilation" contrasts could be added, thus illustrating hyperbole and indicating that no "genocide" took place.[31]

What's more, the biblical text unequivocally states that Joshua did all that Moses commanded (i.e., "utterly destroy [*haram*]" in Deuteronomy 7 and 20). But if Joshua's strict obedience did not entail total-kill actions, then driving out Canaanites from their cities and leaving many survivors are not a violation of Moses's command. As we'll see, God's chief concern is that the Israelites did not destroy Canaanite religious articles as over against merely killing Canaanites (Judg 2:1; cf. Deut 7:5)—thus allowing the pernicious, immoral Canaanite identity to continue.

Indeed, Israel's taking of the land was gradual and could be characterized as "*disabling raids*," according to Egyptologist Kenneth Kitchen, after which the Israelites moved back to their base camp at Gilgal—without holding those places (Josh 10:15, 43)[32]—"so there was no sweeping take over and occupation of this region at this point. And no total destruction of the towns attacked."[33]

So, despite critics like Bowen who claim that Joshua depicts a "massive invasion" by the Israelites and that this allegedly "contradicts" the findings of archaeology,[34] this "massive invasion" notion is contestable for several reasons:

(a) These attacks, we've seen, were disabling raids, after which the Israelites returned to their base camp at Gilgal without holding those cities.

(b) God himself told the Israelites that they would take the land "little by little" (Deut 7:22), as they numbered only around twenty thousand people (rather than, say, two million).[35]

---

30. Bowen, "Your Eye Shall Have No Pity," 183.
31. For more such parallel verses, see Copan, *Vindictive Bully?*, 202.
32. Josh 6:24; 8:19; 11:11.
33. Kitchen, *On the Historical Reliability*, 162, emphasis original.
34. Bowen, "Your Eye Shall Have No Pity," 178.
35. Humphreys, "Number of People," 196–213, esp. 203–4.

(c) They would *not destroy cities*, except for Jericho, Ai, and Hazor; they would merely *occupy* cities and homes that they did not build (Deut 6:10–11; 9:1).

(d) Judges 1 reinforces this point by affirming that the Israelites couldn't drive out Canaanites from a number of cities.

(e) On at least three occasions, the Canaanites attacked the Israelites (Josh 9:1–2; 10:1–5; 11:1–5).

(f) Even though the Canaanites knew of God's immense power and thus had ample warning (2:9–11; 5:1; 9:1, 3; 10:1; 11:1; cf. 1 Sam 4:8), they hardened their hearts and fought against Israel anyway.

Furthermore, the chief objective of the Israelites was to *drive out* or *dispossess* the Canaanites; the ratio of driving out language to killing language is 3:1.[36] Indeed, since the Canaanites were aware of Yahweh's supremacy and power over Egypt and the Amorite kings and his pillar-of-cloud-and-fire presence in Israel's midst, they could have departed the land without any life being lost.

Disabling these Canaanite cities was the main objective in Israel's warfare (Deut 20:16). And, to reinforce the fact that non-combatants were not involved in these battles, Richard Hess notes that during the late Bronze Age, these Canaanite cities were military forts with a "king" (military commander), especially at Jericho and Ai. By contrast, civilians lived in hamlets and would flee to the hills when their citadels were attacked.[37] All other cities were left intact rather than "utterly destroyed." Egyptologist James Hoffmeier notes that this was a "limited conquest of key sites in strategic areas," adding, "clearly the Bible does not claim a maximal conquest and demolition of Canaan."[38] Likewise, Daniel Hawk comments: "To read Joshua as extermination is to misread the text."[39]

---

36. Miller, "How Could a God of Love?"

37. See Richard Hess's argument in "Appendix 2" of Groothuis, *Christian Apologetics*. For a further defense against challenges from Charlie Trimm, see Hess's review of Trimm's book, *Destruction of the Canaanites*.

38. Hoffmeier, *Archaeology of the Bible*, 67, 68.

39. Hawk, *Violence of the Biblical God*, 167.

Haram: "Utterly Destroy"?

Here we come to the verb *haram* ("utterly destroy," "place under the ban") and its cognate *herem* (sometimes translated "utter destruction"). This word-group is applied to Joshua's taking of the land in obedience to Moses's earlier command (Josh 11:12, 15, etc.; see Deut 7:1–6; 20:16–18). However, we have noted that many Canaanite survivors continued in the land. That is, the continuing existence of Canaanites in the land is by no means indicative of disobedience.[40] Thus, Joshua's "utter destruction" makes better sense as hyperbole.

Indeed, John Walton and Harvey Walton insist that *herem* is "commonly mistranslated" as "utter destruction."[41] So what does it mean then? Its various shades of meaning will depend on respective literary contexts.

"Comprehensive Victory"

David Firth claims that *herem* means, roughly, "comprehensive victory,"[42] although in various extrabiblical warfare accounts listed above, victories may only be minimal or even pyrrhic. In Joshua, the decisive-sounding total-kill language is far less so than what most readers have typically imagined.[43] In examining the word *nashal*—"destroy"—which can also mean "dislodge" or "clear out" (2 Kgs 16:6), Markus Zehnder points out: "The use of the word *nāšal* implies that the conquest of the land of Canaan will be accomplished with little violence."[44]

Firth's observation that the "standard element" of hyperbole in this war-text genre mitigates against rendering *haram* as "totally destroy" but rather as "defeat comprehensively."[45] Wray Beal likewise notes Joshua's primary emphasis on *a preliminary victory*, which includes many Canaanites still remaining in the land.[46]

---

40. Hawk, *Violence of the Biblical God*, 26.
41. See Walton and Walton, *Lost World of the Israelite Conquest*, 167–94.
42. Firth, *Joshua*, 207–8.
43. Firth, *Joshua*, 55.
44. Zehnder, "Annihilation of the Canaanites," 269.
45. Firth, *Joshua*, 56.
46. Beal, *Joshua*, 254.

"Consecrated"—Not Killed

Haram can also mean "set apart," though *not* destroyed or killed. For example, a *servant*, an *animal*, or a *field* is *haram* (Lev 27:21–28). The terms "consecrated" (*qadash*) and "most holy" (*qodesh qodeshim*) to the Lord (i.e., priestly use) are terms parallel to *haram*. These denotes a new status from which someone or something cannot be released. Similarly, the city of Jericho was *herem* (Josh 6:17) even though its gold, silver, bronze, and iron *weren't destroyed* but put into the treasury of the Lord's house (6:24). Here, *haram* means "giving something over to God," not "slaughtering people."[47] Even Israelite soldiers fighting against Ai were *herem* until they dealt with disobedient Achan; they weren't targeted for death.[48]

Identity-Removal

Bowen writes that the "logic of . . . Deuteronomy 7" clearly means absolute destruction of the Canaanites.[49] Yet Bowen ignores other considerations that militate against this claim. Joshua tells us "the land had rest from war" (Josh 11:23) and that Joshua had "utterly destroyed" and "left nothing undone" that "Moses commanded" (Josh 11:12, 15, 20). The same book makes clear that Canaanite nations still remained, that Israel shouldn't make covenantal alliances with them (Josh 23:12), and that Israelites were to purge themselves of any foreign gods and serve the Lord (24:1–28).

As we consider Deuteronomy 7, it becomes clear that Canaanite *peoples* themselves are not the central focus, but rather *Canaanite idolatry, immorality, and the potential threat to Israel's identity through breaking covenantal allegiance to Yahweh*. Deuteronomy 7:1–5 refers to the Canaanite nations having been *cleared away, defeated,* and *utterly destroyed*. And *then* the text adds that the Israelites should not intermarry with the Canaanites or make religious alliances with them—a very strange thing if the Canaanites had already been obliterated. John Walton and Harvey Walton likewise note that "the prohibition . . . against intermarriage would be unnecessary."[50] Iain Provan comments about the logic of this text—which moves from removal to destruction to not intermarrying and

---

47. Goldingay, *Old Testament Ethics*, 269.
48. Firth, *Message of Joshua*, 21.
49. Bowen, "Your Eye Shall Have No Pity," 182–83.
50. Walton and Walton, *Lost World of the Israelite Conquest*, 193.

making alliances with the Canaanites—makes no sense if taken literally. And as we move on to Joshua and Judges, we encounter plenty of Canaanite survivors: "All of this, already, raises real questions about the proper understanding of [*haram*], long before we get to the matter of the typical [hyperbolic] language of ancient Near Eastern conquest accounts."[51]

We see something strikingly similar in a previous parallel scenario outlined in Exodus 23. There, God first threatens to wipe out or "completely destroy [*kahad*]" the Canaanites (v. 23)—a term that closely resembles *haram*. But what does this look like? The text adds that God will send his "terror" on ahead of Israel in the form of "hornets" to "drive out [*garash*]" the Canaanites ahead of the Israelites' coming (vv. 27–28). What's more, he will drive them out "little by little," adding that "I will deliver the inhabitants of the land into your hand, and you will drive them out before you" (vv. 30–31). We have both "wipe out" and then "drive out" language.

Likewise, Deuteronomy 7 is much less straightforward than Bowen claims. Gordon Wenham rightly observes that what we have here appears "more rhetoric than literal demand. . . . It is evident that destruction of Canaanite religion is more important than destroying the people."[52] That is, Israel must destroy their religious artifacts, shrines, and altars—a central point of identity for the Canaanites: "But thus shall you deal with them: you shall break down their altars and dash in pieces their pillars and chop down their Asherim and burn their carved images with fire" (v. 5 ESV). These identity-markers of the Canaanites could be removed without removing Canaanites.

Walton and Walton emphasize that *haram* as "utter destruction" is a mistranslation; rather, it means "removal of identity or removal from use."[53] They illustrate with the analogy of Nazi Germany:

> After World War II, when the Allies destroyed the Third Reich, they did not kill every individual German soldier and citizen, they killed the leaders specifically and deliberately (compare to the litany of kings put to the sword in Josh 10–13) and also burned the flags, toppled monuments, dismantled the government and the chain of command, disarmed the military, occupied the cities, banned the symbols, vilified the ideology, and

---

51. Provan, *Seriously Dangerous Religion*, 421n52.

52. Wenham, *Guide to the Pentateuch*, 137. (We could add that this would fit the strong "utterly destroy" language of Deuteronomy 13:12–18.)

53. Walton and Walton, *Lost World of the Israelite Conquest*, 167–94.

persecuted any attempt to resurrect it—but most of the people were left alone, and most of those who weren't were casualties of war. This is what it means to *herem* an identity.[54]

As we've seen, apart from three cities, other *herem* cities were left intact. This simply means that everyone who lived there had to go away— that is, be "driven out":

> Killing them is one way to make them go away, of course, but it is not the only way and probably not the preferred way (especially if they are fighting back). The terror that goes before the Israelite army (e.g., Exod 23:27; also Deut 2:23; 11:25) is probably intended to encourage [the Canaanites] to flee rather than fight. Nowhere in the conquest account does the army systematically hunt down fleeing refugees; nowhere are urban citizens trapped in protracted sieges.[55]

Of course, if any destruction took place, it was against those who "engaged in armed resistance, since later chapters will show many alive and well in these regions" (e.g., Hebron and Debir in both Josh 10:36–39 and five years later in 15:13–15). Destruction—not random violence— would only come to "those who continued to oppose what God was doing and would themselves have chosen to destroy Israel," with the result that "only combatants are killed and an alternative way was always available."[56]

In my debate with Randal Rauser, I drew on this Nazism-German people analogy. I noted how God called Israel to de-fang the Canaanites by destroying their religious objects, which grounded their religious identity. I referred to the Allies removing Nazi "religion" or ideology from the nation of Germany. Strangely, Rauser (who was following modern definitions) called the Allies work of Nazi identity-removal "genocide."[57] So much the worse for modern definitions! They negate the great good brought to humanity by dismantling Nazism—a pernicious, destructive ideology ("religion") that threatened global peace.

In this Canaanite religion–Nazism parallel, we clearly see a distinction between a people-group that need not be obliterated so long as their harmful religious identity was quashed. So Canaanites could continue to

---

54. Walton and Walton, *Lost World of the Israelite Conquest*, 177.
55. Walton and Walton, *Lost World of the Israelite Conquest*, 176–77.
56. Firth, *Message of Joshua*, 127.
57. See Copan and Rauser, "Can the Canaanite Conquest be Reconciled?"

live in the land if they shed their pernicious, immoral practices that were inspired by their deities, religious objects, and rituals. To remove these from the land was to de-fang the Canaanites—just as the Allies de-fanged Germany of Nazism.

Exile

Sometimes *haram* simply refers to *exile*. For example, God promises to bring the Babylonians "against this land [of Judah] and against its inhabitants," and "I will utterly destroy [*haram*] them and make them a horror and a hissing, and an everlasting desolation" (Jer 25:9 ESV). Interestingly, this is an "everlasting desolation" that lasts "seventy years" (v. 11); Babylon itself would afterwards become "an everlasting desolation" (v. 12). Of course, Judah continued to survive the Babylonian exile. Yes, *the Babylonians disabled Judah's social, religious, economic, military, and political structures*, and Judahites were killed. The nation, however, survived.

In Deuteronomy, God warns: "Like the nations that the LORD makes to perish before you, so shall you perish [*abad*], because you would not obey the voice of the LORD your God" (8:20 ESV). "Perish" is sometimes parallel to *haram* and in this Deuteronomic context refers to simply to "exile"—an exile mentioned later in the book: "Outside the sword will bereave, and inside terror—both young man and virgin, the nursling with the man of gray hair" (32:25). Verse 26 uses hyperbole in God's threat to "remove the memory" of Israel from history (v. 26). Thus *haram*-as-exile language builds on Deuteronomy 8:20;[58] Israel's perishing (*abad*) was "like the nations" of Canaan, which weren't obliterated. And as the Canaanites were "spewed out" of the land (*no genocide*), so God's people would be spewed out (*no genocide*) (Lev 18:24–28).

Merisms (Totalizing Language)

God created "the heavens and the earth" (Gen 1:1)—that is, the *entire* physical world. The Old Testament uses the expression "from Dan to Beersheba"—that is, the *entire* land from northernmost city to its southernmost city 160 miles away (Judg 20:1; 1 Sam 3:20; 2 Sam 3:10; etc.). This universalizing or sweeping language is called a "merism."

---

58. See Ford, "'Dispossessing' the Canaanites," 57, 61.

Likewise, in various warfare texts, we have totalizing or comprehensive language covering all of a city's or nation's demographic. The passage in the previous section (Deut 32:25) mentions *young man/virgin* and *nursling/man of gray hair*. This language gives the impression that the future will bring *total destruction*. But as we've seen, the reality is simply Judah's *military defeat* and *exile*. True, defeat and exile affect everyone—young and old, male and female (e.g., 2 Chr 36:17; cf. Jer 6:11; 44:7; Lam 2:21; Ezek 9:6). But clearly this wasn't "genocide."

Furthermore, merisms like *man/woman* and *young/old* may be used of battle scenes even if non-combatants like women and children are *not* present—the more typical scenario in warfare (e.g., Jer 4:29).

We'll look at 1 Samuel 15—the war with the Amalekites—as one such example. Before doing so, we'll consider two biblical texts about the same battle—one is a more straightforward account and the second is a hyperbolized reading.

> "Do to [Og] what you did to Sihon king of the Amorites, who reigned in Heshbon." So they struck him down, together with his sons and his whole army, leaving them no survivors. And they took possession of his land. (Num 21:34–35 NIV)

> We completely destroyed them, as we had done with Sihon king of Heshbon, destroying every city—men, women, and children. (Deut 3:6 NIV; see also 2:33–34)

Bowen claims that Deuteronomy 2 and 3 clearly refer to the annihilation of all persons, including non-combatants.[59] However, Deuteronomy's typically *intensified rhetoric* surrounding the word *haram*[60] needs to be viewed against the backdrop of Numbers 21's *on-the-ground reportage* (i.e., only adult male combatants were killed, though even this, too, is hyperbolized, "leaving no survivors"). Deuteronomy uses totalizing language of *women* and *children* (3:6) and piles on further merisms: "no survivors" (v. 3), "all his cities" (v. 4), "not one of the sixty cities" (v. 4), "the whole region" (v. 4), "completely destroyed" (v. 6), and so on. In other words, non-combatants appear to be targeted in Deuteronomy though the Numbers 21 narrative makes clear that only a male army was defeated.

---

59. Bowen, "Your Eye Shall Have No Pity," 178–79.

60. I argue elsewhere that similar ramped-up rhetoric in Deuteronomy intensifies the plainer language of Exodus 24 and 32. See Copan, *Is God a Vindictive Bully?*, 214–16, 219–21.

In addition, King Sihon marched with his army and military gear about *twenty miles*—"from the Arnon [River] to the Jabbok [River]" up to Ammonite territory (vv. 23–24 NIV). This military march obviously *excludes* women, children, and the elderly.[61] Joshua as well as 1 Samuel will pick up this sweeping language of Deuteronomy, even though noncombatants are not present.

The clarity of this hyperbolic interpretation is even further evident toward the end of Numbers 21, where the text clearly differentiates between the dispossessed civilians and the combatants that were killed. Consider the sequence of *driving out* the Amorite civilians and then *killing* King Og and his army: (a) first, Moses sent spies to Jazer and Israel "captured its surrounding settlements and dispossessed [*yarash*] the Amorites who were there" (v. 32 NIV); (b) then, the Israelite army went to Bashan to fight against King Og and his army. The LORD told Moses, "Do not be afraid of him, for I have delivered him into your hands, along with his whole army and his land.... So they struck him down [*nakah*], together with his sons and his whole army, leaving them no survivors" (vv. 34–35 NIV). Old Testament scholar David Howard observes that this is a strong indicator that the focus of the annihilation was any king and army opposing God's people, *not* a generalized, sweeping mandate to annihilate every last living Amorite. The majority of those people in Jazer and its villages were driven out, not annihilated.[62] Again, the more closely we look, the more we see that nothing like genocide is involved.

Lesser, Localized Battle Plus "Universal Conquest"

We've seen that *haram/herem* can refer to decisive defeat, consecration (without killing), exile, and identity-removal. We have also seen that hyperbole and merism dominate these war texts. Another rhetorical device that reinforces the exaggeration theme is a *local battle–universal conquest* pairing. We see this in 1 Samuel 15—but first some context.

Following Amalek's attack on Israel (1 Sam 14:48), Samuel issued a command to Saul that utilizes the totalistic language of war rhetoric (v. 3): men, women, young, old, cattle, sheep, and donkeys. But it is no more so than the language of Deuteronomy and Joshua (e.g., Josh 6:21):

---

61. Webb and Oeste, *Bloody, Brutal, and Barbaric?*, 196–97 (see footnotes also).

62. Personal correspondence, April 14, 2023. Howard sent me an excursus on *herem* ("utter destruction"), which would be part of the second edition of his *New American Commentary* on Joshua.

though only combatants fight and are killed, the rhetoric of the war text includes non-combatants.

Bowen claims that Yahweh demanded "complete wholesale destruction" of Amalek. And "because Saul did not slay everyone—including the king" of Amalek, he is rebuked by the prophet Samuel for not killing choice animals and king Agag.[63] What is going on in this text? It will become clear that *haram* here doesn't mean *utterly destroy* or *annihilate*.

First, Bowen's phrasing, "did not slay everyone," is misleading. He ignores an important verse here: the narrator tells us that, *except for king Agag*, Saul *had indeed* "utterly destroyed all the people" (v. 8).

Second, Bowen ignores the fact that women and children can be included in the hyperbolic language even if they are not present—as we have seen when comparing the battles with the Amorite kings in Numbers 21 with the rhetorical retelling of this event in Deuteronomy 2–3.

Third, *women and children would not have been present at the pitched battle against Amalek*. We know there simply were no women or children there at this battle site—something Bowen misses or obscures.[64] So why think there were no non-combatants there? Clearly, Saul was fighting a *combatant* battle at "the city of Amalek" (v. 5) and Saul had sent a message to Israel's friends there—the Kenites—to leave the anticipated battle scene (which Bowen acknowledges); so the Kenites "departed" (v. 6). If the Kenites left the anticipated battle scene, surely women and children would not be present either.

One side-note here: although the choice animals from a "the city of Amalek" (v. 5) were taken and kept alive by Saul,[65] we know that the Amalekites had other animals that David later took when fighting them (1 Sam 27:8–9). And this suggests that the problem was less that Saul killed all the animals from battle than that he kept these animals as a kind of status symbol for himself—as he did with keeping Agag alive and also building a monument to honor himself (v. 12)

Fourth, to make the hyperbole even clearer, *David ends up fighting against an Amalekite army in 1 Samuel 27 and 30*. This is another indication that Saul's *haram* simply indicated a limited military victory over Amalek, not obliteration.

Fifth, the hyperbole becomes more apparent with *an additional ancient Near Eastern indicator of exaggerated language in war texts*: localized

---

63. Bowen, "Your Eye Shall Have No Pity," 184.
64. Bowen, "Your Eye Shall Have No Pity," 184.
65. Firth, *1 & 2 Samuel*, 173.

battle plus universal conquest. Both Saul and David fought against the Amalekites in (a) a localized battle followed by (b) rhetorical language of universal conquest.

Saul:

> *Localized battle:* "Saul came to the city of Amalek and set an ambush in the valley" (v. 5)
>
> *Universal conquest:* "Saul defeated the Amalekites, from Havilah as you go to Shur, which is east of Egypt" (v. 7). This region is vast, extending from Arabia to Egypt.[66]

David:

> *Localized battle:* In sweeping language similar to 1 Samuel 15, David "did not leave a man or a woman alive" (1 Sam 27:8–9). Clearly this was not literally so. Even so, the Amalekites then raided David's camp, and he and his men "slaughtered" them, and "not a man of them escaped," except four hundred Amalekites (30:10, 17).
>
> *Universal conquest:* After the initial fighting, David was said to have fought in the same vast (exaggerated) territory as Saul did—"as far as Shur, to the land of Egypt" (27:8).

Hoffmeier notes that "lofty assertions of universal conquest side by side with sober statements about taking individual cities" are hyperbolic indicators in ancient war texts.[67] As Ralph Klein argues, "It is impossible to imagine the battle actually traversed the enormous distance from Arabia almost to Egypt."[68]

These 1 Samuel war texts reveal hyperbolic rhetoric in triplicate: *exaggeration by merism* ("man and woman, child and infant") plus *exaggerated "total-kill language"* ("utterly destroyed") plus *exaggerated "universal conquest" rhetoric* following a localized battle.

DEUTERONOMY 20 AND NUMBERS 31 ON FURTHER EXAMINATION

A couple of additional passages are worth examining in this discussion.

66. The fact that Amalekites were nomads doesn't undermine the hyperbole bound up in the "universal conquest" motif, contra Webb and Oeste, *Bloody, Brutal, and Barbaric?*, 210–11.

67. See Hoffmeier, *Israel in Egypt*, 1–42.

68. Klein, *1 Samuel*, 150.

Deuteronomy 20

The relevant portion reads:

> When the LORD your God delivers [the city] into your hand, put to the sword all the men in it. As for the women, the children, the livestock and everything else in the city, you may take these as plunder for yourselves. And you may use the plunder the LORD your God gives you from your enemies. This is how you are to treat all the cities that are at a distance from you and do not belong to the nations nearby. However, in the cities of the nations the LORD your God is giving you as an inheritance, do not leave alive anything that breathes. (vv. 13–16 NIV)

This chapter gives instructions regarding warfare with two groups:

1. Surrounding nations "very far from you" (vv. 10–15), which are *outside* the land; if peace terms are rejected, then the men are to be killed (v. 13). Women and children would be assimilated into Israel. War rape, common among other ancient Near Eastern nations, is clearly ruled out by Israel's laws of marriage and sexuality (e.g., Gen 2:24) as well as protocols for marriageable foreign women in a post-war setting in the very next chapter (Deut 21:9–14).[69]

2. Canaanite cities "nearby" are *within* the promised land (vv. 16–20)—and the warfare language sounds more severe: "Do not leave alive anything that breathes."

We have made certain observations about battles against "utterly destroyed" cities *within* Canaan mentioned in Joshua.

- The language of "utter destruction [*herem*]" typically means "decisive victory" or can mean "exile" or "removal from ordinary use"; it clearly does not refer to "annihilation" or anything close to this but simply fits within the ancient Near Eastern totalizing war-text conventions of hyperbole and merism.

- Plenty of survivors dwell within the land after Israel's disabling raids, and only three Canaanite cities are burned; the rest remain intact.

- The existence of these survivors does not contradict Joshua's strictly obeying the injunctions of Moses in Deuteronomy 7 and 20.

---

69. Furthermore, the battlefield was off-limits for sexual activity (1 Sam 21:4–5; 2 Sam 11:7–13).

As with other biblical texts, Bowen ignores the hyperbolic language concerning warfare against Canaanite cities, as is evident in Joshua's mention of many survivors; so he takes Deuteronomy 20's "rules of engagement" and its reference to *haram* as meaning utter obliteration.[70] But, as we've seen, the text tells us something else.

The chief point here is this: Given the factors listed above, we can say that if clear indications of hyperbole are present *within* the "sacred space" of the land of Canaan, then *all the more* would hyperbolic language apply to cities *outside* of Canaan. As William Webb and Gordon Oeste write, "If this hyperbole is clear about those who dwell within the land of Canaan, clearly we have reason to think this is the case for cities outside the land where the threat of idolatry and covenant-breaking is removed from the Israelite nation."[71] Further, in most cases of Israel's battles outside the land of Canaan, the adult males are left alive and are pressed into forced labor or paying tribute to Israel.[72]

Numbers 31

What I summarize elsewhere concerning Numbers 31 I treat here in brief.[73] This text relates to the treatment of Midianite women and children after Israel's battling against the Midianite army. Keep in mind that the Midianite women, through the instigation of Moabite king Balak and the pagan prophet Balaam (Num 31:16), seduced Israelite men into adultery and idolatry; Israelites abandoned their covenant with Yahweh and aligned themselves with Baal (Num 25). It was a malicious act by Midian that led Israel into treachery and treason. God sent a punishing plague into the Israelite camp, which was eventually stayed by Phineas the priest's intervention.

Six chapters later, God commanded the Israelites to fight against the Midianite army: "They fought against Midian, as the LORD commanded Moses, and killed every man" (Num 31:7 NIV). Then Moses adds the

---

70. Bowen, "Your Eye Shall Have No Pity," 181–83.

71. Webb and Oeste, *Bloody, Brutal, and Barbaric?*, 194.

72. See Judg 3:7–11; 2 Sam 8:2, 11–14; 10:1–14//1 Chr 19:1–15; 2 Sam 10:15–19//1 Chr 19:16–19; 2 Sam 12:29–31//1 Chr 20:1–3; 1 Kgs 11:15–17; 22:29–40; 2 Kgs 3:1–27; 8:20–22//2 Chr 21:8–10; 2 Kgs 8:28//2 Chr 22:5–6; 1 Chr 5:10, 19–22; 18:1–2, 3–9, 12–13; 2 Chr 20:7; 25:11–12, 14–15//2 Kgs 14:7; 2 Chr 27:5; Isa 11:14. These references come from Webb and Oeste, *Bloody, Brutal, and Barbaric?*, 193.

73. See Copan, *Vindictive Bully?*, 216–18.

injunction to kill the *women* (nonvirgins) and *young boys* too (vv. 15–18). What are we to make of this? Below are two possible interpretive approaches.

Scenario 1: *Totalizing Language Applied to Deliberate Midianite Seduction*

The traditional understanding is that this seduction was a particularly malevolent act—a wilful assault on Yahweh's electing purposes and on Israel's covenantal integrity: Israel played the harlot and joined themselves to Baal (Num 25:1–3); it was a deliberate strategy to undermine Israel's covenant, its national identity, and its mission to bring blessing to the world. Thus, a severe response to Midianite subterfuge is appropriate. Why include the boys? To prevent their rising up in the next generation to continue the attempted overthrow of Israel.[74] Furthermore, this brought a curse on Israel for covenant violation—the very goal the Moabite king Balak had intended all along (Num 22–24)—and Israel was the victim of this attack, not the aggressor. Thus, God's and Moses's commands are motivated by justice.

Now if we assume that men, women, and boys were wiped out in this retaliation and any others were assimilated into Israel, *then we apparently have no more Midianites nation left over*—and thus no remaining Midianite threat. However, we have indicators that hyperbole is rearing its head once again.

For one thing, within a generation or two, "innumerable" Midianite soldiers fought against Israel (Judg 6:5). John Goldingay notes: "Midian's appearing in strength later in the Old Testament . . . would be odd if they were annihilated in the wilderness."[75] Indeed, Midianites lived on for generations; they are mentioned in the apocryphal book of Judith (2:25–26), whose events took place in the fourth century BC. Also, that every Midianite man was killed without a single Israelite fatality appears to be another exaggeration (Num 31:49)—the flip-side of "we left no survivors" talk.

---

74. For example, Naylor, "Numbers," 194. Thanks to David Firth (July 29, 2021) and Lissa Wray Beal (August 2, 2021) for their insights on this question through personal correspondence. Thanks to Mark Awabdy for sending me a pre-published material on Numbers 31 from his then-unpublished *Numbers* commentary. In addition, see Firth, *Including the Stranger*.

75. Goldingay, *Numbers and Deuteronomy*, 86.

Scenario 2: Moses's (Not God's) Own Command That Apparently Goes Unheeded

In my estimation, Scenario 2 makes better sense in light of the biblical text. The LORD specifically *commands* (*tsavah*) retribution for this seduction—*against Midianite men*: "[Israel] fought against Midian, as the LORD commanded Moses, and killed every man" (Num 31:7 NIV). Israel obeyed, but Moses proceeds to add *his own command*—to kill the women (nonvirgins) and young boys too (vv. 15–18).[76]

Why think this is just Moses's and not God's command? First, the Israelite army had *already* carried out the LORD's specific command (v. 7). There is nothing slipshod in their obedience; they fully accomplished their mission. Second, Moses appears to give a non-authoritative order, much like the prophet Nathan's urging David to build the temple (2 Sam 7:3), which had to be rescinded. Or we could compare this to an "old prophet" who tests another (a "man of God") by lying to him (1 Kgs 13:7–26, esp. v. 18), which is an obvious departure from God's original command to the man of God. These are instances of off-the-cuff, non-authoritative prophetic assertions. Here, Moses *reformulates* what divine "vengeance" (*neqamah*) calls for (Num 31:2, 3). Third, *nothing happened after Moses's command was issued*. The focus at the end of the chapter is on the distribution of material spoils and permission for Israelite men to take Midianite *wives* for themselves if they chose to (cf. Deut 21:10–14). But *there was no actual implementation of those orders*.[77] Fourth, we have seen that the total-kill language used throughout the Old Testament is typically laden with hyperbole.

Finally, in light of Moses's anticipated death (Num 31:2), he plays a more transitional and secondary role here—in contrast to the heightened role of the priesthood at this juncture (cf. 25:7–8; 27:19–22; 31:6, 21–24, 25, 31, 41, 47, 51–54). This fact is borne out as we look at the literary framework of Numbers 31. The very structure of Numbers 31 presents Moses's command (v. 16) as an outlier—a superfluous command that goes beyond what God had ordered.[78] As I note elsewhere, Numbers 31 focuses on two sets of divine commands (vv. 1–4 and vv. 25–31); two

---

76. See Brown, "Vengeance and Vindication," 65–84; Brown cites other scholars (e.g., Horst Seebass) sympathetic to this second scenario. See also Goldingay, *Numbers and Deuteronomy*, 85–86.

77. Goldingay, *Numbers and Deuteronomy*, 85.

78. Brown, "Vengeance and Vindication," 67.

acts of obedience in response to the divine commands (vv. 5–12 and vv. 31–47), and two nonauthoritative extensions of those commands (vv. 31:13–18 and vv. 48–54); these two sections are then bisected by a singular section on purification in order to emphasizes the key role of the priesthood (vv. 19–24).[79] Again, I refer readers to the structural details of Numbers 31 that I outline elsewhere.

CONCLUSION: THE REALITY OF WAR AND TRAJECTORY OF PEACE IN BIBLICAL CONTEXT

The Reality of War and the Mission of Israel

We have considered the question of Israelite "genocide" against the Canaanites. Moving beyond a superficial "Sunday school" reading of the text, we see that nothing like "genocide" applies. In the ancient Near East, fighting for survival was very real. A nation fought or aligned itself with another nation to protect itself—or else it disappeared from the scene.

As we have seen, the Old Testament's battles were not racially motivated. The Canaanites engaged in wicked practices (incest, bestiality, ritual prostitution, infant sacrifice), but God waited over half a millennium until they were ripe for judgment. In other words, God is reluctant to bring judgment, and it is only as a last resort—when God finally says, "That's enough!" Israel, being militarily and numerically outmatched, had to trust in God to drive out the Canaanites. Making peace with Israel was always an option, not to mention fleeing from—rather than fighting against—Israel, whose God had a track-record of mighty deeds that were well known in Canaan. In other words, Canaanites were killed only if they resisted, and this would have been in combatant areas—namely, the "cities" of Canaan, which were military citadels and administrative centers. Even so, the Canaanites several times attacked Israel, which had to act defensively.

Despite the critics, the word *herem* clearly does not mean literal "utter destruction" Along with other rhetorical devices, this word is used *hyperbolically* alongside mentions of an abundance of survivors. Israel's key mission was to remove the religious/moral identity of the Canaanites—much like Germany needed to be de-Nazified. The problem was not the ongoing presence of Canaanites in the land but rather Israel's

---

79. Brown, "Vengeance and Vindication," 69.

refusal to destroy Canaanite idols and making covenantal alliances with them and their gods, which threatened to undermine Israel's mission and identity.

THE OLD TESTAMENT'S IDEAL AND TRAJECTORY OF PEACE

Though we see a great deal of war in the Old Testament, this is not God's ideal. He is a *reluctant* "warrior" who engages in battle on behalf of the oppressed (Exod 15:3) and against those who oppose God's righteous and redemptive purposes. The Old Testament does *not* describe God as "violent [*hamas*]." Rather, this is said of evil *human beings*. God opposes the violent (e.g., Ps 11:5) and those who shed innocent blood (Prov 6:17). If we may say it, God responds with a kind of "counterviolence" to oppose human beings who harm, oppress, and tyrannize others. God delights in peace (Isa 2:4; Mic 4:3), and he blesses those who make peace (Matt 5:9)—not war, which is a last resort.

Though war may be necessary (e.g., in Exod 17, when vulnerable Israel was attacked by the Amalekites after crossing the Red Sea), it was to be carried out by trust in God (Deut 20:1) and even with prayer (e.g., Moses's praying with Aaron and Hur holding up his arms while Joshua fought against Amalek). God routinely reminds Israel that military might cannot ultimately be trusted (Ps 20:7) and that victory belongs to the LORD, even if weapons are used (1 Sam 17:47). God will at times surprise his people by granting them victory against armies, even without the use of weapons, through a clear demonstration of God's power (Deut 17:6; Judg 7:2, 4, 20; 2 Kgs 6:22–23).

Furthermore, we see no glorification of war and certainly not army-building (Judg 7:3; Deut 20:1); trust in developing weaponry and horsepower is forbidden (Deut 17:16). In fact, if an Israelite man has just gotten married, acquired a new house or vineyard, or is afraid to fight, he didn't have to participate in war (Deut 20:5–8). Furthermore, even where instructions for fighting in Canaan are given in Deuteronomy 20, there is nothing about land-grabbing, no expansionist vision. The task is limited to the land God is giving Israel—a land whose inhabitants are extremely wicked and violent. The Old Testament downplays warfare, even if God commands it. Even though David fought battles to protect

Israel, he was not permitted to build a temple because he was a man of bloodshed (1 Kgs 5:3; 1 Chr 28:3).

God's long-term ideal is that even Israel's enemies will be redeemed and eventually included among the people of God (e.g., Ps 87:4–6; Isa 19:25; Zech 9:7). Despite the messiness of divinely mandated wars, which God *reluctantly* commands, God's ideal is peace and reconciliation, even with Israel's enemies. God desires to bring the blessings of peace and reconciliation to all the nations (Gen 12:3; Rev 12:9–17). Indeed, God's reconciling work through Jesus the Messiah is directed at us humans, who have been God's enemies and rebelled against his righteous rule over us (Rom 5:5–11). War is neither the ideal nor the ongoing reality for God's people. God's ideal is that, through the nation of Israel, peace and blessing would come to all the nations. This has begun through God's reconciling work of redemption through Christ's self-sacrificial, atoning death and whose lasting peace will be realized in the new heavens and new earth in which righteousness dwells (2 Pet 3:13).[80]

BIBLIOGRAPHY

Awabdy, Mark A. *Numbers*. Grand Rapids: Baker Academic, 2023.
Beal, Lissa Wray. *Joshua*. Grand Rapids: Zondervan, 2019.
Bowen, Joshua. "'Your Eye Shall Have No Pity': Old Testament Violence and Modern Evangelical Morality." In *Misusing Scripture: What Are Evangelicals Doing with the Bible?*, edited by Mark Elliott et al., 177–99. London: Routledge, 2023.
Boyd, Gregory. *The Crucifixion of the Warrior God*. Minneapolis: Fortress, 2017.
Brown, Ken. "Vengeance and Vindication in Numbers 31." *Journal of Biblical Literature* 134.1 (2015) 65–84.
Carroll R., M. Daniel. "Reflections of the Violence of God in Amos." In *Wrestling with the Violence of God: Soundings in the Old Testament*, edited by M. Daniel Carroll R. and J. Blair Wilgus, 113–32. Bulletin for Biblical Research Supplement 10. Winona Lake, IN: Eisenbrauns, 2015.
Copan, Paul. *Is God a Moral Monster?* Grand Rapids: Baker, 2011.
———. *Is God a Vindictive Bully?* Grand Rapids: Baker, 2022.
Copan, Paul, and Matthew Flannagan. *Did God Really Command Genocide?* Grand Rapids: Baker Academic, 2014.
Copan, Paul, and Randall Rauser. "Can the Canaanite Conquest Be Reconciled with a God of Love?" *Unbelievable?* (podcast), October 7, 2022. https://podcasts.apple.com/gb/podcast/can-the-canaanite-conquest-be-reconciled-with-a/id267142101?i=1000581941546.
Dawkins, Richard. *The God Delusion*. Cambridge: Black Swan, 2001.

---

80. Special thanks to the kind friends at the Lanier Theological Education Centre in Yarnton, England for their hospitality at Manor Farm, where my wife Jacqueline and I were able to stay and where I worked on writing this chapter.

Firth, David G. *Including the Stranger: Foreigners in the Former Prophets.* Downers Grove, IL: IVP Academic, 2019.

———. *The Message of Joshua.* Downers Grove, IL: IVP Academic, 2015.

Ford, William. "Dispossessing the Canaanites in Deuteronomy." In *Map or Compass? The Bible on Violence,* edited by Michael Spalione and Helen Paynter, 56–71. Sheffield, UK: Sheffield Phoenix, 2022.

Goldingay, John. *Genesis.* Grand Rapids: Baker Academic, 2020.

———. *Joshua, Judges, and Ruth for Everyone.* Louisville, KY: Westminster John Knox, 2011.

———. "Justice and Salvation." In *Theological and Hermeneutical Studies,* edited by Wolin Kim et al., 168–87. Vol. 1 of *Reading the Hebrew Bible for a New Millennium.* Harrisburg, PA: Trinity 2000.

———. *Numbers and Deuteronomy for Everyone.* Louisville, KY: Westminster John Knox, 2010.

———. *Old Testament Ethics: A Guided Tour.* Downers Grove, IL: IVP Academic, 2019.

Groothuis, Douglas. *Christian Apologetics.* 2nd ed. Downers Grove, IL: IVP Academic, 2021.

Hawk, L. Daniel. *The Violence of the Biblical God: Canonical Narrative and Christian Faith.* Grand Rapids: Eerdmans, 2019.

Hess, Richard. "Appendix 2." In *Christian Apologetics,* by Douglas Groothuis, 717–31. 2nd ed. Downers Grove, IL: IVP Academic, 2021.

———. Review of Charlie Trimm, *Destruction of the Canaanites. Denver Journal* 25 (2002). https://denverjournal.denverseminary.edu/the-denver-journal-article/the-destruction-of-the-canaanites-god-genocide-and-biblical-interpretation.

Hoffmeier, James K. *The Archaeology of the Bible.* Oxford: Lion, 2008.

Humphreys, Colin J. "The Number of People in the Exodus from Egypt: Decoding Mathematically the Very Large Numbers in Numbers I and XXVI." *Vetus Testamentum* 48 (1998) 196–213.

Jenkins, Philip. *Laying Down the Sword: Why We Can't Ignore the Bible's Violent Verses.* New York: HarperOne, 2012.

Kitchen, Kenneth A. *On the Reliability of the Old Testament.* Grand Rapids: Eerdmans, 2006.

Klein, Ralph W. *1 Samuel.* Word Biblical Commentary 10. Waco, TX: Word, 1983.

McConville, J. Gordon, and Stephen N. Williams. *Joshua.* Grand Rapids: Eerdmans, 2010.

Miller, Glenn M. "How Could a God of Love Order the Massacre/Annihilation of the Canaanites?" *Christian Thinktank,* February 8, 1997. https://www.christian-thinktank.com/qamorite.html.

Naylor, Peter John. "Numbers." In *The New Bible Commentary,* edited by D. A. Carson et al., 158–97. Downers Grove, IL: InterVarsity, 1994.

Pritchard, James B., ed. *Ancient Near Eastern Texts Relating to the Old Testament.* 3rd ed. Princeton: Princeton University Press, 1969.

Provan, Iain. *Seriously Dangerous Religion: What the Old Testament Really Says and Why It Matters.* Waco, TX: Baylor University Press, 2014.

Seibert, Eric. *The Violence of Scripture: Overcoming the Old Testament's Troubling Legacy.* Minneapolis: Fortress, 2012.

Sparks, Kenton. *God's Word in Human Words: An Evangelical Appropriation of Critical Biblical Scholarship.* Grand Rapids: Baker Academic, 2008.

Trimm, Charlie. "Causes: Genocide in the Ancient Near East." In *The Ancient World*, edited by Tristan Taylor, 31–49. Vol. 1 of *The Cultural History of Genocide*. London: Bloomsbury, 2021.

———. *The Destruction of the Canaanites: God, Genocide, and Biblical Interpretation*. Grand Rapids: Eerdmans, 2022.

Walton, John H., and J. Harvey Walton. *The Lost World of the Israelite Conquest: Covenant Retribution and the Fate of the Canaanites*. Downers Grove, IL: IVP Academic, 2017.

Webb, William J., and Gordon K. Oeste. *Bloody, Brutal and Barbaric*. Downers Grove, IL: IVP Academic, 2019.

Wenham, Gordon J. *A Guide to the Pentateuch*. Vol. 1 of *Exploring the Old Testament*. Downers Grove, IL: InterVarsity, 2003.

Younger, K. Lawson. *Ancient Conquest Accounts: A Study in Ancient Near Eastern and Biblical History Writing*. Journal for the Study of the Old Testament Series 98. Sheffield, UK: Sheffield Academic, 2009.

Zehnder, Markus. "The Annihilation of the Canaanites: Reassessing the Brutality of the Biblical Witnesses." In *Encountering Violence in the Bible*, edited by Markus Zehnder and Hallvard Hamelia, 263–90. Sheffield, UK: Sheffield Phoenix, 2013.

3

"Slavery" in the Bible

Paul Copan

INTRODUCTION: A BRIEF HISTORY AND DEFINITION OF "SLAVERY"

SLAVERY HAS BEEN A universal feature of human history—extending from antiquity up to the present. University of Oxford's Nigel Biggar furnishes thorough documentation of this phenomenon in his excellent, balanced book *Colonialism: A Moral Reckoning*.[1] The history of slavery includes ancient Mesopotamians, Greeks, Carthaginians, Romans, Chinese, Japanese, Koreans. Incas and Aztecs subjugated peoples and imposed forced labor on them from the fifteenth century onward. In North America, Comanches (from the eighteenth century and beyond) ran a slave economy.[2] From Muhammad onward, slavery was common in the Muslim world. And in the eighth and ninth centuries, Vikings provided white slaves from Eastern Europe and the British Isles to slave markets in Arab Spain and Egypt (eighth and ninth centuries)—*white slaves*—from

---

1. See Biggar, *Colonialism*.
2. Biggar, *Colonialism*, 47–48.

Eastern Europe and the British Isles.[3] From the sixteenth to the mid-eighteenth centuries, raiders from Tunis, Algiers, and Tripoli alone "enslaved between 1 million and 1.25 million Europeans."[4] Another estimate reckons that Muslim slave trade as a whole (lasting until 1920) transported about seventeen million slaves, mostly African. This exceeds the estimated eleven million shipped by Europeans across the Atlantic.[5]

Biggar adds: "Meanwhile Africans had been enslaving other Africans for centuries, mostly by capturing them in war or raids" and would be exported "first to Roman markets and then to Arab ones." This was in addition to "local uses," which included supplying victims for human sacrifices—a common practice in West Africa, which was "attested as early as the tenth century by Ibn Hawqal, and by Europeans four hundred years later."[6] Most commonly, their fate was to be buried alive. In 1797, one report was that between 1,400 and 1,500 people were sacrificed at royal funerals in Asante.[7]

Biggar then asks a question that is relevant to the topic of this chapter: What features of slavery are simply evil? He points out that at different times and places, the condition of the slave *differed*, and the right to ownership was not always absolute. Some work can be laborious and even "soul-destroyingly tedious, without amounting to slavery."[8] He continues:

> Sometimes laborious work is performed under the terms of an unfair indenture or contract, to which the employee has consented only under duress—and yet an exploited employee does not quite make a slave. Even "forced labour" can fall well short of slavery. There is nothing necessarily wrong with requiring members of a community, by law or custom, to spend some of their time and energy on public works or in public service.
>
> What distinguishes and specifies slavery as the simple evil that we now understand it to be is not hard labour, or an unfair contract, or legal compulsion. What specifies it is that the slave's time and employment are owned, not voluntarily under certain conditions for certain purposes and for a certain length of time, but absolutely. The slave is the slave-owner's disposable

---

3. Biggar, *Colonialism*, 48.
4. Biggar, *Colonialism*, 48.
5. Biggar, *Colonialism*, 48.
6. Biggar, *Colonialism*, 48.
7. Biggar, *Colonialism*, 48.
8. Biggar, *Colonialism*, 46.

property, to be put to whatever use the owner decides, and to be bought and sold—and perhaps even killed—at will. That is the pure form or "paradigm" of slavery, and it is the treatment of another human being as absolutely disposable property that makes it categorically worse than other forms of unjust employment.[9]

Biggar reminds us: "It is important to remember that, historically, not everything that went by the name 'slavery' lived down to this simply evil form."[10]

This evil kind of slavery characterized the antebellum South. Harriet Beecher Stowe (1811–1896), author of *Uncle Tom's Cabin*, wrote that Southern masters had absolute control over every aspect of their slaves' lives: "The legal power of the master amounts to an absolute despotism over body and soul," and "there is no protection for the slave's life."[11]

Many modern readers associate certain texts in the Mosaic law with antebellum slavery. After all, aren't humans called "property" (literally, "silver") in Exodus 21? Aren't foreigners "acquired" to be slaves in Israelite households in Leviticus 25? And don't our modern translations of the Old Testament routinely use the term "slave" or "slavery"?

In this chapter, I both summarize material from previous works as well as add new material on servitude.[12] First, I examine the Old Testament's humanizing vision of personhood and equality—in contrast to other ancient views about servitude. I then compare this vision to the brutal practices of slavery in the antebellum South. I argue that the assumption that Old Testament servitude laws are (near-)identical to the brutality of Southern slavery is a massive mistake, though a common one made in our day. Thirdly, I examine the misleading and emotion-laden terms "slave" and "slavery"—renderings common in many modern translations. I show this neutral term should be rendered "servant" or "worker." Fourth, I examine miscellaneous servitude texts in the Old Testament raised by critics. Fifth, I look specifically at Leviticus 25—probably the servitude text critics most often cite. Finally, I give a brief overview of servitude in the New Testament.

---

9. Biggar, *Colonialism*, 46.
10. Biggar, *Colonialism*, 46.
11. Stowe, *Key to Uncle Tom's Cabin*, 139.
12. This chapter condenses material on servitude from Copan, *Is God a Moral Monster?* and (especially) *Is God a Vindictive Bully?*

THE OLD TESTAMENT WORLDVIEW AND VISION

A covenant in the ancient Near East is between two partners or parties, and in most cases they are *not* equals. Even so, God's covenant with Israel and his law code given to them was quite distinct from other ancient Near Eastern nations. The "Ten Commandments" passage in Exodus 20 draws out some of these distinctions:

- A personal God initiates a loving covenant with Israel ("I am the LORD your God").
- It is not the king (e.g., as in Babylon or Assyria) who is the legislator.
- New kings in the ancient Near East would make new law codes that canceled out previous covenants—unlike Israel's law code, which remained permanent for Israel.
- Along with priests, the king is subject to the law, just as every Israelite is (Deut 17:19; cf. 2 Sam 12:1–14).
- The Mosaic law code is a democratized one (note the common reference to "your brother/s" therein); it does not assume a social or political hierarchy with corresponding laws and punishments according to class distinction. Each Israelite is subject to God's law, which is evidenced by God's addressing the Israelites in the second-person singular in Exodus 20.
- The covenant springs from God's gracious activity ("who brought you up out of the land of Egypt"; cf. Deut 7:7–8) rather than being the result of forceful subjugation or conquest, which was the common form of covenant between suzerain and the vassal nation, who makes a covenant of loyalty.
- God blesses Israel in particular so that all nations could be blessed through Israel (Gen 12:3; Deut 6:4–6; Ps 67).[13]

The God who creates the universe and makes all persons in his image has a plan to redeem all the nations through the one nation he has chosen. God begins with the particular and moves to the universal.

What then are some of the implications of this as it relates to servitude in the Old Testament? For one thing, God permits certain *non-ideal* laws because of human fallenness, sin, and hard-heartedness (e.g., Matt 19:8). These laws take into account that God's people will sin. Thus, God

---

13. See Lalleman, *Celebrating the Law?*, 15–41.

"will start where people are and point out specific steps that lead toward where they should be," writes John Goldingay.[14] Furthermore, certain laws address the moral *floor* of Israelite life, not its ethical *ceiling*. Israel's laws often regulate suboptimal behavior rather than present the moral ideal. That is why it is important to keep focused on the broader vision of the Old Testament's worldview (e.g., the creational ideals of Genesis 1–2) rather than focusing on particular non-ideal laws that address the brokenness of the post-Edenic world.

For example, in the ancient book of Job, we read of Job's assumption that he and his servants are equal in status—that they have come from the same place.

> If I have rejected the cause of my manservant or my maidservant,
> when they brought a complaint against me,
> what then shall I do when God rises up?
> When he makes inquiry, what shall I answer him?
> Did not he who made me in the womb make him?
> And did not one fashion us in the womb?
> (Job 31:13–15 ESV)

Job here reflects the vision of humanity in Genesis 1:26–28 in that *all* humans are God's image-bearers. This non-hierarchical, democratized equality stands in contrast to other ancient Near Eastern cultures, in which *the king* alone bore the image of the gods. The Greco-Roman world was also strongly hierarchical. And when it comes to servitude, philosophers like Plato and Aristotle took a negative view of manual labor. For Aristotle, some people were simply born to be slaves. He considered a slave to be an "animated tool"; the "natural slave" is without human reason.[15]

Moreover, Athenian "democracy" was highly aristocratic and was built on the institution of slavery.[16] During the first century, approximately 10 percent of the Roman Empire was comprised of slaves.[17] Unlike ancient Israel, Rome's infrastructure was supported by slavery.

These hierarchical structures are akin to ancient Near Eastern societies outside Israel. Moreover, ancient Near Eastern cultures were typically divided into two categories: the exploiter and the exploited; those

---

14. Goldingay, *Theological Diversity*, 153.

15. Aristotle, *Nicomachean Ethics* 8.11.

16. Berman, *Created Equal*, 160; Ferry, *Brief History*, 72–73. A particularly helpful essay on Old Testament servitude is Williams, "'Slaves' in Biblical Narrative," 441–52.

17. British Museum, "Slavery in Ancient Rome."

who demanded or extracted tribute (i.e., the political nobility) and those who paid it (e.g., workers, slaves). Joshua Berman notes that a chasm existed between "the *dominant tribute-imposing class* and *the dominated tribute-bearing class.*"[18] By contrast, he observes, Israel's creational vision of fundamental human equality (Gen 1:26–28) shaped its "more egalitarian" and democratized society in contrast to the rigid social division in other ancient Near Eastern nations.[19] We'll see more of these moral ideals illustrated as we look more closely at servitude in Israel.

THE MOSAIC LAW VS. SOUTHERN SLAVERY

Abraham Lincoln's Second Inaugural Address (March 4, 1865) addressed the North and South regarding their attitudes toward slavery.

> Both read the same Bible and pray to the same God, and each invokes His aid against the other. It may seem strange that any men should dare to ask a just God's assistance in wringing their bread from the sweat of other men's faces, but let us judge not, that we be not judged. The prayers of both could not be answered. That of neither has been answered fully. The Almighty has His own purposes.

Commenting on this era, historian Mark Noll's book *The Civil War as a Theological Crisis* observes that in the antebellum South, defenders of slavery quoted servitude texts from the Bible, while abolitionists appealed to the fundamental equality of human beings as God's image-bearers. Yet Noll points out that Southerners *read into* the biblical text their own attitudes of racism. Furthermore, abolitionists themselves attempted to show how biblical servitude was radically different from Southern slavery. In addition, Southerners failed to distinguish questions about (a) the Bible and *servitude* and (b) the Bible and *race*. For the pro-slavery side, race and slavery simply became intertwined as the default position with no attempt to treat these as distinct questions.[20]

Whether then or now, critics like Hector Avalos or Sam Harris have claimed that the Mosaic law endorses slavery akin to the antebellum South with all of its brutality and the absence of any rights, for the slavemaster or his foremen could inflict any physical harm he wished—the

---

18. Berman, *Created Equal*, 4, emphasis original.
19. Berman, *Created Equal*, 5, 168.
20. Noll, *Civil War*, 52, 54.

slave was to be treated like "farm equipment."[21] We make plain below that if Southerners had actually applied the servitude texts from the Mosaic law, the United States would not have borne the ugly stain of slavery in its history. Indeed, the mandates regarding servitude in Israel's law collection actually prohibited kidnapping, injury, return of runaway slaves to masters, and so on. Many of Israel's provisions were radical, humanity-affirming, and liberating when compared to the backdrop of ancient Near Eastern servitude.

Another critic, Joshua Bowen, has claimed that, though Southern slave laws on the books may have technically offered protections for slaves, those laws were often ignored. Likewise, the same could be said about the Old Testament in which abuses were prohibited but not upheld in practice.[22] One problem here is that if the Old Testament's laws are humane, then what is the argument? One could say this about *any* humane law in *any* land: good laws can be ignored or grossly violated without law enforcement. Secondly, if we have indications of servants in Israel being treated as humans with dignity, rights, and agency, then this further weakens Bowen's argument.

As for Southern slavery, it's true that *overseers* on a plantation could be punished for excessively harsh treatment of slaves. Southern legislators and judges ignored common law practice in its application to slaves; while certain anti-abuse laws on the books applied to slave owners and slave hirers, the laws allowed for loopholes concerning the brutal actions of overseers or foremen. But so much the worse for Southern slavery! The Old Testament shouldn't be lumped in with such abuses. Furthermore, the modern practices of kidnapping slaves—the very foundation for modern slavery—as well as implementing the fugitive slave laws (1793 and 1850) are a clear violation of the Mosaic law. The contrast will become clear. Christopher Wright's observation remains unchallenged: the servant in Old Testament law "was given human and legal rights unheard of in contemporary societies."[23]

---

21. For a general overview, see Avalos, *Slavery*. Sam Harris simply asserts without justification that "slaves" in the Old Testament were treated as "farm equipment" (*Letter to a Christian Nation*, 14).

22. Assyriologist Joshua Bowen raised this in a conversation with me on October 3, 2020, when he and Skylar Fiction interviewed me on Old Testament slavery. For some reason, this video is no longer available on YouTube.

23. Wright, *Walking in the Ways*, 124.

Provisions for Servants in Israel

What were some of the benefits and provisions for servants in Israel? They include the following:

Provision 1: Harsh physical treatment of Israelites or aliens was forbidden[24]

The Israelites' experience in Egypt shaped a good deal of Mosaic legislation. Israelites were prohibited from mistreating both *fellow Israelites* as well as *aliens* (i.e., immigrants) who were living in the land.[25] If an employer ("master") caused his servant/worker permanent injury (e.g., loss of eye or tooth), the servant would be released, and his debt canceled (Exod 21:27). The law gave servants legal recourse to press for freedom—a similar theme found in Job 31:13–15. As David L. Baker writes, "Thus it is another indication of Old Testament law treating marginal people as human beings, with many of the rights accorded to full members of the covenant community."[26]

Critics like Avalos have treated such texts both incorrectly and uncharitably. Avalos has made the claim that Exodus 21:21 allows for an employer ("master") to physically abuse his (Israelite) servant to within an inch of his life. But just as long as the servant didn't die immediately, the employer is not liable ("he survives a day or two").[27]

Now, this is a rather silly claim. For one thing, any fair-minded judge in Israel could see through such a charade. Secondly, servants had rights, and in the preceding verse, we read that the employer who struck a servant and *killed* him would be liable to the death penalty—that is, "avenged" (v. 20 ESV), which is language typical of capital punishment. Thirdly, we've seen that if there is a permanent injury (loss of eye or tooth), the servant gets to go free. This isn't damage to a piece of furniture or farm equipment here. The text clearly affirms (and presupposes) the servant's humanity.

Furthermore, consider three relevant matters:

---

24. On the brutality and dehumanization of antebellum Southern slavery, see Berlin, *Many Thousands Gone*; Baptist, *Half Has Never*.

25. "Immigrant" is an appropriate translation of the Hebrew word *ger* ("sojourner" or "alien") according to Gowan, "Wealth and Poverty," 345.

26. Baker, *Tight Fists or Open Hands?*, 129.

27. Avalos, *Slavery, Abolitionism*, 80–81.

(a) *An employer's permanent eye or tooth injury to his servant meant release from servitude*, as we've seen. The employer would have to absorb the debt of the servant because of his harsh actions (Exod 21:26–27).

(b) *This passage concerns accidental injury/death*; so even if the employer wasn't capitally punished ("avenged"), this doesn't mean he isn't liable to *some* penalty (e.g., monetary payment, which is what was standard for accidental deaths [e.g., Exod 21:28]).

(c) *The immediate context of Exodus 21:21 often goes unnoticed—paying one's medical bills during recovery from accidental injury*: "He ... shall take care of him until he is completely healed" (vv. 18–19). I point out elsewhere that a judge would show leniency to the employer if he paid the injured servant's medical bills, even if the servant dies a few days later.[28] The text is making plain that the intent was not to kill. Hittitologist Harry Hoffner has rendered Exodus 21:21 as "that [medical payment] is his silver," not that the *servant* is the employer's silver.[29] But even if the latter rendering *were* the case, this would simply be a statement about the foolishness of undermining one's own assets in the form of paying for human work. Why injure your own hired help? That is only to your financial detriment.

Provision 2: Kidnapping was expressly condemned in Israelite and other ancient Near Eastern law (e.g., Babylonian and Hittite)[30]

Two passages figure in here. Exodus 21:16 is a more *generic* prohibition: "He who kidnaps [*ganab*] a man [*ish*]." Deuteronomy 24:7 focuses on kidnapping a fellow Israelite. But even regarding the latter, "the absence of a prohibition does not amount to permission. The exhortations concerning the rights of resident aliens indicate that this would also be considered wrong."[31] In contrast to the antebellum South, kidnapping for Israelites was not a matter of taking *property*; it was a *person* offense. This is illustrated in Genesis 40:15, where Joseph himself was "kidnapped [*ganab*] from the land of the Hebrews" (Gen 40:15). As various scholars

---

28. See chapter 13 in Copan, *Is God a Moral Monster?*
29. Hoffner Jr., "Slavery and Slave Laws," 150–51.
30. Babylonian: "Hammurabi Code," §14; Hittite: §§19–21.
31. Baker, *Tight Fists or Open Hands?*, 117.

have noted, the Mosaic law focused on the "law of persons," which was distinct from the more dominant "law of things" in other ancient Near Eastern law collections.[32]

Provision 3: Foreign runaway slaves who came to Israel seeking refuge were protected from harsh masters (Deut 23:15–16)

Ancient nations such as the Babylonians, Egyptians, Hittites, and Amurru had extradition treaties for the return of foreign fugitive slaves to their masters. Also, Hittite, Mari (Syria), and Nuzi (Mesopotamia) documents—along with the Code of Hammurabi—call for severe punishments (e.g., gouging out the eyes) of returned fugitive slaves.[33] Babylon legislated the death penalty for anyone harboring runaway slaves.[34] These sound more like America's Fugitive Slave Act of 1850 and very much *unlike* the Mosaic law, which prohibited sending foreign runaway slaves back to their harsh foreign masters.

Provision 4: Israel had fixed six-year term limits on servitude

After six contracted years (Exod 21:2), once-impoverished (indentured) servants were required to be released with debts resolved. This time-limit was "a fundamental departure from the norms of the ancient Near East," Berman writes.[35] Now someone may respond that some ancient kings may have released slaves within a comparable time span. But what often goes unmentioned is that the kings' offering release was merely haphazard or arbitrary; it was not mandated by law, as it was for Israel. And what's more, the ideal would be that Israelite servants were treated well so that they would voluntarily continue in lifelong service (Exod 21:6: "serve him permanently [*olam*]").

---

32. See chapter 8 in Copan, *Vindictive Bully?*
33. Baker, *Tight Fists or Open Hands?*, 132.
34. For example, Hammurabi states: "If any one receive into his house a runaway male or female slave of the court . . . the master of the house shall be put to death" ("Hammurabi Code," §§16; 19).
35. Berman, *Created Equal*, 99.

Provision 5: Israel's laws made provisions to prevent people from slipping into poverty and thus into servitude

As I note elsewhere, Israel's worldview and moral framework set forth in the Mosaic law stands out as ethically superior in many ways. For one thing, the laws of surrounding nations did not show concern for foreigners in the land. Nor did those nations make provisions for the poor. By contrast, Israel had gleaning laws for the poor of the land (Lev 19:9–10), restricted the time of servitude to six years (as we've seen), prohibited interest on loans to the poor (Exod 22:25). And when servants completed their term of service and paid off their debts, those who hired them were to send them off with abundant provisions (Deut 15:7–10). There was also the Year of Jubilee, which called for further assistance for the poor (Lev 25). This speaks very powerfully against the institutionalization of slavery in Israel.[36]

We have already seen that servants had rights in Israel. This was true of other vulnerable persons as well: female war captives (Deut 21:10–14), foreign runaway slaves (23:15–16), or the oft-repeated triad of orphans, widows, and aliens (14:28–29; 26:12–13). All of these had rights and were to be treated as *free agents* (e.g., 30:19). They were not considered *things* or *objects*. In other parts of the ancient world, no such rights existed for, say, war captives, criminals, or slaves. Baker writes: "It is characteristic of Old Testament law that the beneficiaries are not the elite but those at the margins of society."[37]

In addition to these provisions, another difference between Israel's laws and those of the antebellum South is that servitude in Israel is not race-based. Neither racial *inferiority* nor racial *differentiation* was the basis of servitude. Rather, it was *poverty* that drove Israelites into contracted service ("selling" oneself for hire) for six years (Lev 25:39).[38] The main argument driving Southern slavery was the alleged inferiority of "Hamitic" (i.e., African) people.[39] In addition to the fact that all human beings are bearers of God's image (Gen 1:26–28), the Israelites' experience of slavery in Egypt further provides warrant for caring for the alien

---

36. A number of these differences between Israel and other ancient Near Eastern nations are documented in Baker, *Tight Fists or Open Hands?*
37. Baker, *Tight Fists or Open Hands?*, 135.
38. Meyers, *Exodus*, 35.
39. Williams, "'Slaves' in Biblical Narrative," 444.

(*ger*) who lives in Israel (e.g., Lev 19:34; Deut 24:14–15)—something the Mosaic law mentions three dozen times.[40]

Some critics may raise the question about Leviticus 25:44–46, which may give the impression that foreign servants can be treated as property. We address that matter later. But before doing so, we should take a closer look at the words *ebed* ("worker," "servant," "slave"?) and *ebedim* ("servitude," "slavery"?).

"Slave" vs. "Servant" or "Worker"

The *Concise Oxford English Dictionary* defines "slave" as "a person who is the legal property of another or others and is bound to absolute obedience, human chattel [i.e., property]."[41] That's what Southern slavery was like, and that's the definition some Bible readers impose on the Old Testament text. But we should first ask: how did the Old Testament authors and the original audience understand the term *ebed*? We can fill out the answer with the following considerations.

First, *modern translations of the Old Testament use "slave" and "slavery" far more often than earlier translations.*[42] The King James Version (1611) has the word "slave" only *once* in the Old Testament: "Is Israel a servant? is he a homeborn slave?" (Jer 2:14 KJV). What's more, the term "slave" isn't even in the Hebrew text of Jeremiah but was inserted by the translator. With all the negativity and emotion related to modern race-based slavery—not to mention the Civil War, slavery's abolition, Jim Crow laws, the passage of the Civil Rights Act (1964)—it's surprising that *modern* Bible translations frequently use the emotion-laden words ("slave"/"slavery") in the Old Testament. For example, New King James Version (1982): "slave" 42 times, "slavery" once; New International Version (1984): "slave" 104 times, "slavery" 17 times.

In addition to similar English translations, this is true of a Jewish translation into English (Jewish Publication Society) as well as more recent German, Spanish, and Dutch translations. These all follow the same pattern of using stronger, emotion-laden language of "slave" as over against their earlier versions.[43]

---

40. Baker, *Tight Fists or Open Hands?*, 188.
41. *Concise Oxford English Dictionary*, s.v. "slave."
42. On this, see Peter Williams's helpful essay "'Slaves' in Biblical Narrative."
43. Williams, "'Slaves' in Biblical Narrative," 444.

Second, *the term* ebed *is not inherently negative; it is neutral in Hebrew, meaning "worker" or "servant," and to render it "slave" guarantees a negative association.* In addition to the word *ebed*, the *female* servant is called a "handmaid" (*amah*, e.g., Ps 86:16); there is no female equivalent to *ebed*.[44] So to associate adjectives like "degrading," "oppressive," or "owned" with *ebed* is a great distortion.[45] *The context must make clear whether the word is used positively, neutrally, or negatively.* Israel's servitude in Egypt was "bitter" (Exod 1:14), a matter of "hard labor" (Exod 1:11, 14), and likened to an "iron furnace" (Deut 4:20). On the other hand, *ebed* could be honorific: "the servant [*ebed*] of the Lord," which is used of Moses (Deut 34:5) and Joshua (Josh 1:1; 24:29). To ignore the context will lead to distortion.

Third, the basic meaning of this word is "worker," and it refers to a dynamic dependency relationship. The word *ebed* is related to the verb *abad*—"work" or "serve" or even "worship" (e.g., Exod 8:1; 20:5; Josh 24:15), and the noun form (*ebed*: worker, servant) covers a range of meanings:

- *non-Israelites who are lifelong servants*, though they may become persons "of means" in Israel and even hire Israelites to work as servants for them (Lev 25:47)
- those who are *temporary servants for incurring debt*
- *those who serve God* ("servant of the Lord")

Biblical scholar Peter Williams notes certain translational concerns: "To render the term [*ebed*] sometimes as 'slave' and at other times as 'servant' fails to represent the fact that there really is no clear distinction between the various occurrences of the word."[46] There are two dangers in automatically assuming the translation "slave": (a) *doing so infuses each usage with negativity* (conjuring up modern slavery); (b) *doing so creates a false binary* (one is either "slave" *or* "free"). The same is true about using the corresponding term "master [*adon*]" instead of, say, "employer": (a) *the term "master" conjures up the negativity of Southern slavery;* (b) *it creates another false binary* ("master" versus "slave"). So a temporary worker's entering into a six-year contract with an employer now looks like being permanently owned by an absolute despot.

---

44. Wright, "*Ebed/Doulos*," 85.
45. Ringgren, "*abad*," 383–85, 390.
46. Williams, "'Slaves' in Biblical Narrative," 451.

So how to proceed? In each of the three *ebed* categories above, they suggest a person *in a subordinate role in a dynamic dependency relationship*. This relationship could be compared to an athlete, who is "traded" to a team that has an "owner." It would be wrong to slap the term "slave" on this player in a dynamic dependency relationship. To do so would be like taking a neutral term like *melek* ("king") and rendering it "puppet king."[47]

So, using the term "servant" is a better overall translation for *ebed*: "The word 'servant' . . . has less-definite associations, and a great deal of semantic flexibility. It may pain modern consciences to use the word 'servant' for any worker whom we regard as having in fact been in slavery, but such consciences may not in fact be the best guides to translation."[48]

Fourth, *we can illustrate our point by examining the word "servant"* (ebed) *or "servants"* (ebedim) *in the book of Exodus*. We can see just how neutral the term is when we compare Israel's servitude to Pharaoh in Egypt and to serving God in the wilderness. The Israelites are called Pharaoh's oppressed "servants" (Exod 5:15, 16), yet even *the Egyptians* themselves were called Pharaoh's "servants" (5:21). But notice that Israel is to engage in service to God in a liberated state: God commands Pharaoh to let Israel go "that they may serve [*abad*] me in the wilderness" (7:16). That is, Israel moves from one state of servitude to another, from bondage to freedom, from bitter oppression to life under Yahweh's good rule (Exod 4:23; 7:16; 8:1, 20; 9:1, 13; 10:3, 7, 8, 11, 24, 26). We have two kinds of servitude.

We see a similar parallel to this in 2 Chronicles 12:8. There, Shemaiah the prophet gave God's message to the unfaithful king Rehoboam: "They [Judahites] will become his [Egyptian king Shishak's] slaves [(l)ebadim] so that they may learn the difference between my service [*abodah*] and the service [*abodah*] of the kingdoms of the countries." To serve God is freeing; serving a foreign king is oppressive.[49] Indeed, an Israelite king could even "serve" his people by creating conditions that allow them to flourish (1 Kgs 12:7; cf. 2 Chr 35:3, where Levites are called to "serve" the LORD *and* his people Israel).

The Old Testament *takes a generally negative attitude* of one person's being in the service of another and *attempts to remedy this*. Baker writes, "One of the primary motivations for obedience in the laws on care for

---

47. Williams, "'Slaves' in Biblical Narrative," 452.
48. Williams, "'Slaves' in Biblical Narrative," 451.
49. Williams, "'Slaves' in Biblical Narrative," 452.

the poor and oppressed is the exodus, God's liberation of his people from slavery in Egypt." And Israel's highly democratized structure enabled it to engage in strategies to alleviate poverty: "Unlike neighbouring countries, Israel had no social stratification, and all Israelites were considered brothers and sisters (cf. Lev 25:39–43; Deut 15:7–11; 17:15, 20)."[50]

Baker makes this insightful comment: the "Hebrew word translated 'slave' means literally a 'worker,' whereas the [ancient Near Eastern] Akkadian equivalent means 'one who has come down' in social position."[51] The implication? Servitude "did not fit well with the ideals of Israelite society, and laws were designed to reduce the number of people" in servitude and also protect servants who were actually not freed.[52]

SOME MISCELLANEOUS TEXTS RELATED TO SERVITUDE

In this section, we'll look at some servitude texts in hopes of bringing illumination about servitude in Israel.

> *Exodus 21:2–6*
> If you buy a Hebrew servant, he is to serve you for six years, but in the seventh year he will go out free without paying anything. If he came in by himself he will go out by himself; if he had a wife when he came in, then his wife will go out with him. If his master gave him a wife, and she bore sons or daughters, the wife and the children will belong to her master, and he will go out by himself. But if the servant should declare, "I love my master, my wife, and my children; I will not go out free," then his master must bring him to the judges, and he will bring him to the door or the doorposts, and his master will pierce his ear with an awl, and he shall serve him forever.

This text raises several questions.[53] Why is the male servant's departure emphasized? What about the female servant, who *does* get mentioned in a later parallel text (Deut 15:12–17)? And isn't this text allowing for the fragmentation of servant families? Are the wife and children required to stay behind with the employer while the husband/father gets to depart?

---

50. Baker, "Humanisation of Slavery," 14.
51. Baker, "Humanisation of Slavery," 14.
52. Baker, "Humanisation of Slavery," 14.
53. Here I follow Douglas K. Stuart's treatment of this text in his *Exodus*, 476–81.

In response, we can say that this text is not being gender-specific, and Deuteronomy 15 makes this point explicit. If a person is to serve out a contracted six-year term, this applies to both men and women, and judges would know how to apply the case in a sex-neutral way. We could read it this way: "If you buy a Hebrew servant, *she* is to serve you for six years. But in the seventh year, *she* will go out free. . . . If *her* master *gives her a husband*, and they have sons or daughters, *the husband and the children will belong to her master, and she will go out by herself.*"

But what about the seeming harshness of this scenario? If we see what the *three* basic options would have been available for an Israelite servant, we can realistically think about this situation rather than attempting to impose our own modern cultural expectations on what simply would not have been feasible in an ancient setting.

Option 1: Delay: Let's assume we are dealing with a male servant who marries. He has already begun his six-year term of service: he must wait for his wife, whom he has married during his term service ("if his master gave him a wife"). She would only be free to leave after her six-year term. Now if there are children born during his term, these children would be under the official protection of the employer in whose home they are living until the wife's term is completed. Obviously, this arrangement, which would involve family separation, would be very impractical. Debts still must be paid off, and marriage (or having children) does not exempt them from paying their debts.

Option 2: Pay: It is possible that the male who leaves after his service then pays his former employee for his wife's release ("redemption"). However, given that after having been set free from debt, this redemption would not be feasibly achieved for most people.

Option 3: Stay: Verses 5–6 indicate the optimal scenario: the servant could commit himself to working permanently in the household of his employer ("I love my master"). This voluntary act would be ceremonially sealed, and the man/husband would permanently live with family under the roof of his employer. This would be the more feasible scenario.

Goldingay argues that it was not a bad arrangement for a servant—alien or native—to find refuge in an Israelite home: "Perhaps many people would be reasonably happy to settle for being long-term or lifelong servants. Servants do count as part of the family."[54] For example, 1 Chronicles 2:34–35 mentions the Egyptian servant Jarha; he is

---

54. Goldingay, *Israel's Life*, 465.

part of the family such that his employer, Sheshan, gives his daughter to him in marriage. Foreign servants could also achieve high positions in Israel: Ebed-Melech, an Ethiopian servant in the royal palace, is also given a particular divine promise of protection encompassing his entire household (Jer 39:7–17). King Hezekiah has a foreign servant as his secretary—Shebna (an Egyptian name) (1 Kgs 19:2).

> *Leviticus 19:28*
> You shall not make any cuts in your body for the dead nor make any tattoo marks on yourselves: I am the Lord.

This has been a curious text, and not a few students have asked me about whether having a tattoo today would be "unbiblical." Though we won't comment extensively on this text, we can get clarity about what the text means and what it says about servitude.

In terms of the history of interpreting this text, one interpretation about the prohibition against tattoo marks is its connection with pagan mourning practices in the ancient Near Eastern world. After all, it seems connected to mourning because the verse also mentions "cuts on your body for the dead" (cf. Deut 14:1, "You shall not cut yourselves or shave your forehead for the sake of the dead").[55] However, Leviticus 21:5 prohibits Israelites from making "cuts in their flesh," but there is no mention of mourning here.

A second interpretive option is that tattoos represent idolatry and thus paganism in general. The earliest rabbis and then later Jewish interpreters in the Middle Ages connected tattoos with idolatry in that they purportedly signified one's belonging to a pagan deity.

However, the third interpretive alternative is the more likely. John Huehnergard and Harold Liebowitz make a strong case that the tattoo was a mark of ownership and that it was connected to slavery—namely, being owned by another human being. In ancient Egypt, tattoos were found on females, though not exclusively so. These women were identified as dancing girls or slaves or members of a harem, though high-ranking women might have been tattooed. In Mesopotamia, slaves were branded or tattooed on the forehead or hand. The purpose of marking the slave was that, if she ran away, she could be returned to her "rightful owner."

By contrast, Israel was prohibited from tattooing because of the degradation involved in owning another human being (i.e., treating him

---

55. Here I follow Huehnergard and Liebowitz, "Biblical Prohibition," 59–77.

as property). As we have seen, Exodus 21 allows for the *voluntary* piercing of an ear for the servant who freely chooses to remain in lifelong servitude in his employer's home. This is not forced servitude.

One text that may be of interest (and could perhaps offer those desiring biblical justification for sporting a tattoo on their body!) is Isaiah 44:5, "This one will say, 'I am the LORD's'; and that one will call on the name of Jacob; and another will write on his hand, 'Belonging to the LORD,' and will name Israel's name with honor." Note that this action of a person's writing the LORD's name on his hand is not used pejoratively. And God himself—as if in reciprocal fashion—attaches himself to his people by writing their name on his hand indicating that he is their God (cf. Isa 49:16, where the stronger verb "engrave [*haqaq*]" is used).

> *Exodus 21:28–33*
> If an ox gores a man or a woman to death, the ox shall surely be stoned and its flesh shall not be eaten; but the owner of the ox shall go unpunished. If, however, an ox was previously in the habit of goring and its owner has been warned, yet he does not confine it and it kills a man or a woman, the ox shall be stoned and its owner also shall be put to death. If a ransom is demanded of [owner of a goring ox], then he shall give for the redemption of his life whatever is demanded of him. Whether it gores a son or a daughter, it shall be done to him according to the same rule. If the ox gores a male or female slave, the owner shall give his or her master thirty shekels of silver, and the ox shall be stoned.

I discuss this "goring ox" passage in greater detail elsewhere.[56] I mention this text because of a potential misunderstanding regarding servitude. In this passage, one might get the impression that the servant is of lesser value in Israel. After all, why doesn't the owner of the killing ox pay with his life for a servant just as he would with a free person?

In response, first, if the ox kills a servant, the goring ox must still put to death—a heavy financial loss for the ox's owner. Second, such injuries could be commuted to monetary payment. Commenting on Numbers 35:31, Walter Kaiser points out a wide consensus amongst commentators that fifteen out of sixteen potential death penalty cases (except murder) could be commuted to monetary payment: "This [text] has widely been interpreted to imply that in all the other fifteen cases the judges could commute the crimes deserving of capital punishment

---

56. Copan, *Vindictive Bully?*, 76–77.

by designating a 'ransom' or 'substitute.' In that case, the death penalty served to mark the seriousness of the crime."[57] And this is exactly what we see here. Verse 29 mentions that the owner "shall be put to death," but the ransom option immediately appears: "If a ransom is demanded of [the ox's owner], then he shall give for the redemption of his life whatever is demanded of him" (v. 30).

Thirdly, Desmond Alexander notes that the ransom amount for the free person was not pre-set; it was only fixed in the law for the servant. In the case of a free person, the plaintiff, defendant, and judge would have to settle on a ransom price that was not established by law: "The figure of thirty shekels is probably the minimum value that was to be placed upon a human life [for ransom].... This suggests that for the author ... there was little fundamental difference between a free person and a slave. The main distinction lay in the fact that it was easier to calculate the amount of the ransom to be paid for causing the death of a slave."[58]

Gordon Wenham reminds us that, according to Leviticus 27:2–8, a sliding payment scale existed for a contracted servant. This depended on the servant's age, skills, and sex (which also suggests physical strength). This wasn't a matter of intrinsic worth.[59]

FOCUSING ON LEVITICUS 25

The most challenging-sounding text critics bring up—and that leaves believers puzzled too—is Leviticus 25:42–51. However, as you keep reading to the end, certain redemptive themes and broader considerations arise and help give important perspective:

> For they [Israelites] are My servants whom I brought out from the land of Egypt; they are not to be sold in a slave sale. You shall not rule over him with severity, but are to revere your God. As for your male and female slaves whom you may have—you may acquire male and female [servants] from the pagan nations that are around you. Then, too, it is out of the sons of the sojourners [ha-toshabim] who live as aliens [ha-garim; sing. ger] among you that you may gain acquisition, and out of their families who are with you, whom they will have produced in your land; they also may become your possession. You may even bequeath them to

---

57. Kaiser, *Toward Old Testament Ethics*, 91–92; "God's Promise Plan," 293.
58. Alexander, *Exodus*, 491; Wenham, "Leviticus 27:2–8," 264–65.
59. Wenham, "Leviticus 27:2–8," 264–65.

your sons after you, to receive as a possession; you can use them as permanent [servants]. But in respect to your countrymen, the sons of Israel, you shall not rule with severity over one another.

Now if the means of a stranger [*ger*] or of a sojourner [*toshab*] with you becomes sufficient [*nasag*], and a countryman of yours becomes so poor with regard to him as to sell himself to a stranger [*ger*] who is sojourning [*toshab*] with you, or to the descendants of a stranger's family, then he shall have redemption right after he has been sold. One of his brothers may redeem him, or his uncle, or his uncle's son, may redeem him, or one of his blood relatives from his family may redeem him; or if he prospers [*nasag*], he may redeem himself. He then with his purchaser [*qanah*] shall calculate from the year when he sold himself [*makar*] to him up to the year of jubilee; and the price of his sale shall correspond to the number of years. It is like the days of a hired man that he shall be with him. If there are still many years, he shall refund part of his purchase price [*miqnah*] in proportion to them for his own redemption.

Introductory Remarks

The context of this passage is the Year of Jubilee, which is another provision to help impoverished Israelites stave off deepening poverty. As we read Leviticus 25, we see three stages:

(a) an Israelite mortgages his land (vv. 25–28); if that fails,

(b) he can receive an interest-free loan (vv. 35–38); if this doesn't resolve the problem,

(c) he can contract himself—"sells himself" (v. 41)—and other family members within their own tribal or clan territory. The hope is that once the contracted work is complete and debts are resolved, the person and his family can return to normal life.[60]

There was no social security or welfare system for Israelites in the ancient Near East. One scholar observes: "Like many employees in the modern world, although legally free, a servant may have nowhere else to go and no alternative but to stay."[61]

---

60. Baker, *Tight Fists or Open Hands?*, 162.
61. Goldingay, *Israel's Life*, 465.

In the *Dictionary of the Old Testament: Pentateuch*, Gene Haas refers to this text that mentions gentile servants ("slaves"), and he makes clear that they "are considered human beings" with various safeguards and protections in place that come with living in Israel, which is to be a haven and refuge for runaway foreign slaves.[62] He adds that *all Mosaic law passages on servitude* assume these three basic principles:

Principle 1: "All humans, even slaves and bondslaves, have rights and privileges under the law and before God."

Principle 2: It is better to live in the security and provision that servitude in Israel affords than to live in poverty and destitution, especially when one can come to love his employer/"master" (Exod 21:5–6).

Principle 3: "Family is important and must be maintained even in the condition of poverty and bondservice."[63]

Whether a foreign or Israelite servant, humans were not commodities—a marked contrast to other ancient Near Eastern nations.

As for Leviticus 25, it *does not encourage* acquiring foreign servants; the law only *permits* this and is not promoting the creation of an underclass of servitude. Indeed, foreign runaway slaves had reassurances from the Mosaic law that they could find refuge in Israel. There they could find a relatively stable life by attaching themselves to Israelite households. On top of this,

(a) kidnapping was prohibited;

(b) "acquiring" foreigner servants *was not forcible*; and

(c) these "acquired" persons *were not free people suddenly put into servitude*; indeed, these foreign persons "are already slaves, or are offered by sale by their families."[64]

That is, as within Israel, economic deprivation might lead foreigners to "sell" a family member to an Israelite household in order to get out of debt and poverty.

Unlike surrounding nations, which showed "relatively little concern" for foreigners[65] and made no provision for them, Israel provided benefits to vulnerable foreigners in their midst:

---

62. Haas, "Slave, Slavery," 781.
63. Haas, "Slave, Slavery," 782.
64. Baker, "Humanisation of Slavery," 14.
65. Baker, *Tight Fists or Open Hands?*, 177.

- gleaning laws, from which a foreigner like Ruth was able to benefit;
- a Sabbath rest to the entire household—including servants—which was a provision that surrounding nations did not have;
- equal rights under the law for both foreigner and native (Exod 12:49; Lev 24:22);
- the story of Israel's history of deliverance from harsh servitude in Egypt informing Israel's gracious treatment of aliens living in the land.

Duke University professor emerita Carol Meyers writes:

> [These] laws provide significant protection for slaves [or, better translated, "servants"]. For example, masters must not abuse their slaves, fugitive slaves are to be given asylum rather than returned to their masters, and slaves are entitled to holidays. Elsewhere in the ancient Near East slaves are subject to property law, which focuses on the rights of slave-owners over their property. In Israel, slaves themselves have rights, and the laws are concerned with the slave as a person, emphasizing compassion for someone in a vulnerable position.[66]

So, simply because Israelites weren't to treat their fellow Israelites harshly (v. 43), this didn't imply that the foreigner was to be treated with severity. In fact, just a few chapters earlier, the law demands that the alien in the land was to be loved and treated with kindness: "When a stranger resides with you in your land, you shall not do him wrong. The stranger who resides with you shall be to you as the native among you, and you shall love him as yourself, for you were aliens in the land of Egypt; I am the LORD your God" (Lev 19:33–34). To what does this "severity [*perek*]" against the Israelite servant refer? It is likely the forcible or manipulative attempt to keep him beyond the six-year term limit (e.g., Jer 34:12–16). And whereas Israelite servant had "term limits" of six years, there were no specific restrictions for alien servant. And as for aliens in the land, the Mosaic law condemned taking advantage of them:

> Cursed is he who distorts the justice due an alien, orphan, and widow. (Deut 27:19)

---

66. Meyers, *Exodus*, 308.

> You shall not oppress a hired servant who is poor and needy, *whether he is one of your countrymen or one of your aliens who is in your land in your towns.* (Deut 24:14, emphasis added)

The simple fact is: foreigners were to be well-treated in Israel. Goldingay writes about foreign as well Israelite servants in the land: "their advantage is that as servants they are part of the master's household; they get fed, sheltered, and looked after like members of the family. Possibly they also get some sort of wage."[67]

We have also noted that acquiring these foreigners as servants is *permissible*, not demanded. Also, we have here a kind of *legal* or *contractual* language that we use of sports team "owners" who "buy" or "trade" players, even though the humanity of the players isn't questioned. In addition, although informed critics often recognize that Israelite servants had basic human rights, these critics tend to assume that foreign servants are property rather than rights-bearing persons in Israel. Given all of this background, we can now look at the specific language of this text.

"Acquiring" and "Bequeathing"

The language pertaining to acquired *foreign* servants turns out to be language applied to *Israelite* servants or Israelites in general. The first apparent trouble-spot in Leviticus 25 is reference to *acquiring* (*qanah*) non-Israelite servants. But notice that such "acquisition" language is used of *persons*—whether individual Israelites, the Israelite nation, or non-Israelites—for example:

- "that [or 'he'] is his silver" (Exod 21:21)[68]
- "acquire" (*qanah*) (Gen 47:23; Ruth 4:5; cf. Gen 4:1)
- "possession" (*ahuzzah*) (Lev 25:45; cf. Exod 19:5, which uses *agullah* ["(God's) own possession"]; Deut 26:18, God's "treasured possession")
- "sells himself" (*makar*) (Lev 25:39; cf. Exod 21:7), which is different from the context of the prohibition against kidnapping, where one "sells" another as property (Exod 21:16).

---

67. Goldingay, *Israel's Life*, 465.
68. Again, this rendering is from Hoffner Jr., "Slavery," 150–51.

Furthermore, in the chart below,[69] notice that identical language used of *both* Israelite servants and non-Israelite servants—that is, the "sons of the sojourners [*hatoshabim*] who live as aliens [*hagarim*] among you" (Lev 25:44–46).

Chart: Terms Associated with Israelites and Non-Israelites (Mostly) from Leviticus 25

Term	Used of Israelites	Used of Non-Israelites
"sojourner" (*toshab*) and "alien" (*ger*)	In the land, Israelites are "*aliens* [*gerim*] and *sojourners* [*toshabim*] with [God]" (v. 23).	Non-Israelites are "the *sojourners* [*hatoshabim*] who live as *aliens* [*hagarim*]" in the land (v. 45).
"servant" (*ebed*)	An Israelite can be a "servant" (*ebed*) (Deut 15:17).	A non-Israelite "male" servant (*ebed*) and female servant (*amah*) may be acquired (v. 44).
"acquire" (*qanah*)	The Israelite servant "must calculate with the one who bought [*qanah*] him . . ." (v. 50 NET). The Israelites were "purchased" (*qanah*) by God, who brought them out of Egypt (Exod 15:16; cf. Isa 11:11). In a legal transaction, Boaz was able to "acquire" (*qanah*) Ruth as his wife (4:5, 10). In Genesis, Eve "acquired" (*qanah*) a son with the Lord's help (Gen 4:1), and Joseph "acquires" the people and the land of Egypt (Gen 47:23).	Israelites "may acquire" (*qanah*) servants "from the pagan nations that are around [them]" (v. 44).

---

69. This slightly modified chart is taken from Copan, *Vindictive Bully?*, 178.

"prosper" (*nasag*)	If an Israelite servant "grows rich" (ESV) or "prospers [*nasag*], he may redeem himself" (v. 49; cf. v. 26).	"If a stranger [*ger*] or sojourner [*toshab*] with you [Israelites] becomes rich [*nasag*], and your brother beside him becomes poor and sells himself to the stranger [*ger*] or sojourner [*toshab*] with you or to a member of the stranger's [*ger*] clan..." (v. 47 ESV).
"permanently" (*olam*)	If the servant declares his love for his employer (master) and declares that "I will not go out free," then after a formal public ceremony, "he shall serve him forever [*olam*]" (Exod 21:5–6 NET).	Israelites can have "permanent" (*olam*) non-Israelite servants (v. 46).

To summarize the vocabulary associated with both *Israelite* servants and *foreign* servants:

- *Both* are called "sojourner" (*toshab*) and "alien" (*ger*) (Lev 25:23, 45);
- *Both* are referred to as "servant" (*ebed*) (Exod 21:5; Lev 25:44).
- *Both* may be "acquired" as a servant (*qanah*) (Lev 25:50, 44).
- *Both* can improve themselves and "prosper" (*nasag*) (Lev 25:49 with 47).
- *Both* the Israelite and non-Israelite may be in service to another "permanently" (*olam*) (Exod 21:5–6; Lev 25:46).
- *Both* may be "acquired" as a servant (Lev 25:44; 25:50); note that *Israelite* could potentially *sell* himself/be voluntarily "sold" (*makar*) to a resident alien (Lev 25:47).

Unfortunately, critics like Hector Avalos seem to stop reading at Leviticus 25:46. If Avalos had included 47–50 in his discussion, this would have gutted many of his negative arguments on Leviticus 25. If we keep reading, we see that the foreign servant potentially rising to prosperity, the Israelite servant "selling" himself to the prosperous foreigner, the poor Israelite's being "acquired" by a foreigner, and so on.[70] As one reviewer noted, Avalos's overall tone is both hostile and uncharitable.[71]

70. See Avalos, *Slavery*, 2011).
71. For instance, Avalos says that Israel had a "whole class of temple slaves"—namely,

What about the matter of giving as an inheritance or "bequeathing" (*nachal*) foreign servants to one's children "permanently"? We could add that God considers his own people his "inheritance": "My own people and My inheritance [*nachalah*], Israel" (Joel 3:2; cf. Isa 19:25). Furthermore, according to Egyptologist James Hoffmeier, typically foreign workers in Israel, who could not possess land, would nevertheless only remain within a household for a generation—maximum, two—before getting assimilated into the host culture. For example, Egypt's pharaohs might bring back foreign prisoners of war, who would then work for the state. But within a generation or two, they would become thoroughly Egyptianized through intermarriage, cultural assimilation, taking on Egyptian personal names and social practices, and identifying as thorough Egyptians. The same would be true in Israel. The modern notion that servitude continues generation after generation just didn't exist in the ancient Near East.[72]

What is most illuminating here is that the text of Leviticus 25 makes clear that the foreigner who is a servant in an Israelite household could become a "person of means [*narag*]" and even potentially "acquire [*qanah*]" or hire an Israelite to work for him (Lev 25:47). If an *Israelite* servant can be "acquired" and "sell [*mokar*] himself" to a prosperous foreigner (v. 47), then what is the actual problem with "acquiring" *foreign* servants—persons with dignity and worth—who may become economically successful in Israel? On closer inspection, we just don't have the language of oppression and tyranny here—merely the language of legal transaction. The Mosaic law actually "takes into account the potential prosperity of immigrants ('If a stranger or sojourner with you becomes rich . . .' Lev 25:47)."[73]

---

the Levites (84), But this is a rather strange claim, as serving in the Lord's house was considered a great privilege (e.g., Ps 84:2, 3, 10).

In a review of Avalos's book, J. Albert Harrill writes: "this new book reads more like a manifesto of a political ideology than a serious study of historical interpretation" (547). He adds: "Avalos has done little to elevate or enlighten the discussion" (549).

72. Hoffmeier, "Slavery and the Bible," panel discussion at Lanier Theological Library, Houston, Texas, October 30, 2015, https://vimeo.com/144318832, 9:15 to 22:00. In personal correspondence with Hoffmeier (Feb. 9, 2022), he noted the work of anthropologist and Egyptologist Stuart Tyson Smith on this assimilation question. See Hoffmeier, "Egyptian Religious Influences," 3–35. In this work, Hoffmeier engages with Smith's scholarship, especially on pages 7-17. I am grateful for Hoffmeier's resourcefulness in providing material on this topic.

73. Gowan, "Wealth and Poverty," 345.

Moreover, the foreign servant is not inevitably stuck in poverty and servitude. We earlier noted Goldingay's observation: "Perhaps many people would be reasonably happy to settle for being long-term or lifelong servants. Servants do count as part of the family."[74] He adds that a servant's situation "could be secure and reasonably comfortable, and one can even imagine people who started off as debt servants volunteering to become permanent servants because they love their master and his household, and it is good for them to be with their master (Deut 15:12–18)."[75] And once again, "Even a foreigner can do well as a servant."[76]

In Leviticus 25:46, God issues this command to the Israelites: "In respect to your countrymen, the sons of Israel, you shall not rule with severity over one another." Does that mean that foreigners, by contrast, *could* therefore be mistreated? Absolutely not! The book of Exodus makes this clear: "You shall not oppress a stranger [ger], since you yourselves know the feelings of a stranger, for you also were strangers in the land of Egypt" (Exod 23:9). And again: "You shall not wrong a stranger [ger] or oppress him, for you were strangers in the land of Egypt" (Exod 22:21). These commands not to oppress apply not just to *foreigners*, but also to *foreigners who are servants* since *the Israelites themselves had once been foreigners in servitude in Egypt*.

Deconstructing Old Testament Servitude

The late noted Old Testament scholar D. J. A. Clines pointed out that the Mosaic law ultimately *deconstructs* servitude and the institutionalization of it in ancient Israel. How? By the twofold consideration of (a) *runaway* and (b) *voluntary servitude*. How so? Clines notes that the unique and extraordinary Israelite provision for runaway slaves (Deut 23:15–16) ultimately undermines the institution of servitude altogether. Slaves can run away from a harsh *foreign* master and find refuge in Israel. And if *Israelite* servants happened to be oppressed *in Israel*, then running away would be a ready option for them as well. Clines continues: "What is amazing about the law of the fugitive slave is that it enables a slave to

---

74. Goldingay, *Israel's Life*, 465.

75. Goldingay, *Israel's Life*, 465–66.

76. Goldingay, *Israel's Life*, 467. For another perspective on the topic of servitude, see Bowen, *Did the Old Testament?* See also the debate between Bowen and Jewish-Christian scholar Michael Brown in Bowen and Brown, "Was Slavery in the OT Morally Permissible?"

acquire his or her own freedom—by the relatively simple expedient of runaway. A slave can choose not to be a slave."[77] Clines adds: "If a slave can choose not to be a slave," then "the concept of slavery does not exist as it once was thought to exist."[78]

Although we looked at this passage earlier, Exodus 21:6 adds another dimension to the deconstruction of servitude in Israel: if an Israelite servant *loves* his employer ("master"), he may *freely choose* to attach himself *permanently* to that household. Clines comments: "Slavery is in a sense abolished when it ceases to be a state that a person is forced into against his will." With this blurring of the lines between *freedom* and "servant" (or "slave"), the institution has "lost its conceptual force."[79]

Servitude in Israel was nothing like the antebellum South. Israel's servants, foreign or national, were to be treated with dignity as those bearing the image of God—not as dehumanized objects of ownership over whom there was an "absolute despotism of body and soul," as Harriet Beecher Stowe wrote. The Old Testament's humanizing spirit toward Israelite and gentile, toward servant and employer alike, is borne out in Isaiah 58:6: "Is this not the fast which I choose, to loosen the bonds of wickedness, to undo the bands of the yoke, and to let the oppressed go free and break every yoke?" Thus, if foreigner servants in Leviticus 25 were oppressed and under a dehumanizing yoke by an Israelite, then this would utterly violate spirit of the LORD's chosen fast in Isaiah 58.

In closing this section, we could add yet another angle from which to view gentile servitude in the Old Testament.[80] However democratized certain Mosaic laws were compared to parallel laws in other ancient Near Eastern law collections, Jesus himself acknowledged that Moses issued some *non-ideal* laws because of the hardness of human hearts (Matt 19:8). Nevertheless, the Old Testament eschatological vision proclaims that the law externally given to Moses on stone tablets would be written on the hearts of God's people under the new covenant:

> But this is the covenant which I will make with the house of Israel after those days," declares the LORD, "I will put my law within them and on their heart I will write it; and I will be their God, and they shall be my people." (Jer 31:33)

77. Clines, "Ethics as Deconstruction," 78.
78. Clines, "Ethics as Deconstruction," 79.
79. Clines, "Ethics as Deconstruction," 81.
80. Thanks to Esau McCaulley for suggesting this idea to me while in Yarnton, England (February 2024).

In the latter days, *the Mosaic law's purport would be realized or fulfilled with both Jews and gentiles alike streaming to Israel and obeying God's law* (Isa 2:2–3; Mic 4:1–2). Whether one is an Egyptian, Assyrian, or Israelite, these are all people of God, whom God (respectively) calls "My people," "the work of My hands," and "My inheritance" (Isa 19:23–25).

So even though both alien and Israelite, "the stranger as well as the native," were to live under "one standard" in the land (Lev 24:22), the new covenant era anticipated *within the Old Testament itself* a fundamental negation of Jew-gentile distinctions (e.g., Zech 9:7). So even a servitude text like Leviticus 25—however harshly the critic may judge it—cannot be taken as ideal even by Old Testament standards themselves. Isaiah makes this clear:

> Let not the foreigner who has joined himself to the LORD say, "The LORD will surely separate me from his people." Nor let the eunuch say, "Behold, I am a dry tree." . . . Also the foreigners who join themselves to the LORD, to minister to him, and to love the name of the LORD, to be his servants, every one who keeps from profaning the sabbath and holds fast my covenant; even those I will bring to my holy mountain and make them joyful in my house of prayer. Their burnt offerings and their sacrifices will be acceptable on my altar; For my house will be called a house of prayer for all the peoples. (Isa 56:3, 6–7)

A POSTSCRIPT ON NEW TESTAMENT SERVITUDE

Although I more fully address the New Testament treatment of slavery elsewhere,[81] I can briefly note the following here about the New Testament and servitude:

(a) The nature of Roman servitude depended on the priorities of the head of the household (*paterfamilias*) and the roles he designated for servants (e.g., educating his children till they were of age; doing secretarial/scribal work; managing household affairs). Slavery could also involve more menial work such as working in mines. Slavery was not necessarily for a lifetime; many slaves could be freed (manumitted) by purchasing their own freedom. Paul himself urged slaves to gain their freedom if they were able to do so (1 Cor 7:21).

---

81. Copan, *Vindictive Bully?*, 184–86.

(b) The New Testament opposes any kind of oppression and tyranny (Luke 4:17–19). This includes kidnapping (1 Tim 1:10) as well as treating humans as cargo (Rev 18:13).

(c) In the Christian "house rules" Paul sets forth in Ephesians 5–6 and Colossians 3–4, he *first* addresses those would typically be *ignored* in such letters—wives, children, and slaves—and Paul exhorts them as responsible human agents rather than appendages or property in the household. Paul reminds masters that they have a "Master in heaven" to whom they are responsible and will give an account (Col 4:1; cf. Eph 6:9). This Master will reward everyone according to his deeds, "whether slave or free" (Eph 6:8).

(d) Galatians 3:28 makes clear that in Christ there is "no slave or free." All social distinctions are irrelevant before the cross of Christ. This is why Philemon is to receive Onesimus back as a "brother" and "no longer as a slave" (v. 16, which sounds like the language used of *all* Christians in Galatians 4:7: "no longer a slave but a son"). And there is some question about the exact relationship between Onesimus and Philemon and whether Onesimus was an actual slave, let alone a runaway slave, as there are no "flight" verbs in Paul's address to Philemon.[82]

(e) In Romans 16, Paul indicates partnership in ministry with *slaves* like Andronicus and Urbanus, which were two common slave names in the Roman empire. Andronicus and Junia (a female) are even called "apostles" or church-planting missionaries (v. 7: "outstanding among the apostles" NIV]). Paul calls them "kinsmen" and "fellow prisoners," and he calls Urbanus his "fellow worker" (v. 9).

(f) Romans 16 also reminds us that slaves have a prominent place within the congregation alongside wealthy persons like Priscilla and Aquila, who had a "church in their house" in Rome (vv. 3–5). All of them—slave and free—were commanded to "greet one another with a holy kiss" (v. 16), which was a sign of affection and family belonging for both slave and free.

(g) Churches comprised of slave and free believers would share in the Lord's Supper together (e.g., 1 Cor 11:18–34). This was a regular event celebrated with a meal preceding it; such meal-sharing represented the warmth and acceptance of spiritual family at which master and slave ate and drank together.

---

82. For a discussion of Philemon, see chapter 14 in Copan, *Moral Monster?*

Paul is subversive and radical in addressing attitudes concerning class distinctions. While Christians were powerless to change the Roman social structure of slavery—an institution protected by Roman power in which slaves were confined to households without the ability to gather any momentum outside their homes to mount a protest movement—Christians could begin within the household of faith to set the pattern of how redeemed masters and slaves in Christ were to relate to one another.

CONCLUSION

What we can say is that the Old Testament's laws regarding servitude are radically different not only from modern slavery but also slavery in other parts of the ancient Near Eastern world. The vision of the Old Testament presents servants as persons rather than property, and the Mosaic laws makes many provisions for those in poverty to stay afloat economically so that they would not have to enter into servitude. Whether an Israelite servant or a foreign servant, she could improve her lot and become economically successful. Laws regarding Old Testament servitude were worlds—and *worldviews*—apart from the practice of slavery in the ancient Near Eastern world as well as in the antebellum South and other places where the brutality of modern slavery was practiced—and is even practiced today.[83]

BIBLIOGRAPHY

Alexander, T. Desmond. *Exodus*. Downers Grove, IL: IVP Academic, 2019.
Aristotle. *The Basic Works of Aristotle*. Edited by Richard McKeon. New York: Random, 1941.
Avalos, Hector. *Slavery, Abolitionism, and the Ethics of Biblical Scholarship*. Sheffield, UK: University of Sheffield Press, 2011.
Baker, David L. "The Humanisation of Slavery in the Old Testament Law." In *The Humanisation of Slavery in the Old Testament*, edited by Thomas Schirrmacher, 13–20. Bonn: Verlag für Kultur und Wissenschaft, 2015.
———. *Tight Fists or Open Hands? Wealth and Poverty in Old Testament Law*. Grand Rapids: Eerdmans, 2009.
Baptist, Edward. *The Half Has Never Been Told*. New York: Basic, 2016.
Berlin, Ira. *Many Thousands Gone*. Cambridge, MA: Belknap, 2000.

---

83. Special thanks to the kind friends at the Lanier Theological Education Centre in Yarnton, England (in Oxfordshire), for their hospitality at Manor Farm, where my wife Jacqueline and I were able to stay and where I worked on writing this chapter. Thanks also to Stewart Kelly and Linnea Clay for their suggestions for improving this essay.

Berman, Joshua. *Created Equal: How the Bible Broke with Ancient Political Thought.* Oxford: Oxford University Press, 2008.

Biggar, Nigel. *Colonialism: A Moral Reckoning.* London: Collins, 2023.

Bowen, Joshua. *Did the Old Testament Endorse Slavery?* No loc.: Digital Hammurabi Press, 2021.

Bowen, Joshua, and Michael Brown. "Was Slavery in the OT Morally Permissible?" *Modern-Day Debate,* May 11, 2019. https://www.youtube.com/watch?v=32y7rbiiRos.

British Museum. "Slavery in Ancient Rome." n.d. https://www.britishmuseum.org/exhibitions/nero-man-behind-myth/slavery-ancient-rome.

Clines, D. J. A. "Ethics as Deconstruction, and the Ethics of Deconstruction." In *The Bible in Ethics: The Second Sheffield Colloquium,* edited by J. W. Rogerson et al., 77–106. Journal for the Study of the Old Testament Supplement Series 207. Sheffield, UK: Sheffield Academic, 1995.

Concise Oxford English Dictionary. 12th ed. Oxford: Oxford University Press, 2011.

Copan, Paul. *Is God a Moral Monster?* Grand Rapids: Baker, 2011.

———. *Is God a Vindictive Bully?* Grand Rapids: Baker Academic, 2022.

Ferry, Luc. *A Brief History of Thought: A Philosophical Guide to Living.* New York: Harper Perennial, 2011.

Goldingay, John. *Israel's Life.* Vol. 3 of *Old Testament Theology.* Downers Grove, IL: IVP Academic, 2009.

———. *Theological Diversity and Authority of the Old Testament.* Grand Rapids: Eerdmans, 1987.

Gowan, Donald E. "Wealth and Poverty in the Old Testament: The Case of the Widow, the Orphan, and the Sojourner." *Interpretation* 41 (1987) 341–53.

Haas, G. H. "Slave, Slavery." In *Dictionary of the Old Testament: Pentateuch,* edited by T. Desmond Alexander and David W. Baker, 778–79. Downers Grove, IL: InterVarsity, 2003.

Harrill, J. Albert. Review of *Slavery, Abolitionism, and the Ethics of Biblical Scholarship* by Hector Avalos. *Biblical Interpretation* 21 (2013) 547–49.

Harris, Sam. *Letter to a Christian Nation.* New York: Knopf, 2006.

Hoffmeier, James K. "Egyptian Religious Influences on the Early Hebrews." In *Did I Not Bring Israel Out of Egypt? Biblical, Archeological, and Egyptological Perspectives on the Exodus Narratives,* edited by James K. Hoffmeier et al., 3–35. Winona Lake, IN: Eisenbrauns, 2016.

———. "Slavery and the Bible." Panel discussion at the Lanier Theological Library, Houston, Texas, October 30, 2015. https://vimeo.com/144318832.

Hoffner, Harry A., Jr. "Slavery and Slave Laws in Ancient Hatti and Israel." In *Israel: Kingdom or Late Invention?,* edited by Daniel I. Block, 130–55. Nashville: B & H Academic, 2008.

Huehnergard, John, and Harold Liebowitz. "The Biblical Prohibition against Tattooing." *Vetus Testamentum* 63.1 (2013) 59–77.

"The Hammurabi Code (ca. 1780 BCE)." *Hanover College, History Department.* https://history.hanover.edu/courses/excerpts/211ham.html.

Kaiser, Walter C. "God's Promise Plan and His Gracious Law." *Journal for the Evangelical Theological Society* 33.3 (1990) 289–302.

———. *Toward Old Testament Ethics.* Grand Rapids: Zondervan, 1983.

Lalleman, Hetty. *Celebrating the Law? Rethinking Old Testament Ethics*. 2nd ed. Milton Keynes, UK: Paternoster, 2016.
Meyers, Carol. *Exodus*. Cambridge: Cambridge University Press, 2005.
Noll, Mark. *The Civil War as a Theological Crisis*. Chapel Hill, NC: University of North Carolina Press, 2006.
Ringgren, Helmut. "*abad*." In *Theological Dictionary of the Old Testament*, edited by G. Johannes Botterweck, 10:982–85. Grand Rapids: Eerdmans, 2000.
Stowe, Harriet Beecher. *A Key to Uncle Tom's Cabin: Presenting the Facts and Documents upon Which the Story Is Founded, Together with Corroborative Statements Verifying the Truth of the Work*. Boston: John P. Jewett, 1853.
Stuart, Douglas K. *Exodus*. New American Commentary 2. Nashville: B & H, 2008.
Wenham, Gordon. "Leviticus 27:2–8 and the Price of Slaves." *Zeitschrift für die Alttestamentliche Wissenschaft* 90 (1978) 264–65.
Williams, Peter. "Slaves in Biblical Narrative and in Translation." In *On Stone and Scroll: Essays in Honour of Graham Ivor Davies*, edited by James K. Aitken et al., 441–52. Berlin: de Gruyter, 2011.
Wright, Benjamin G., III. "*Ebed/Doulos*: Terms and Social Status in the Meeting of Hebrew-Biblical and Hellenistic-Roman Culture." In *Slavery in Text and Interpretation*, edited by Richard Horsley et al., 83–111. Semeia 83/84. Atlanta: Society of Biblical Literature, 2001.
Wright, Christopher J. H. *Walking in the Ways of the Lord*. Downers Grove, IL: InterVarsity, 1995.

4

"Except Through Me"

The Scandal of Christian Exclusivism

Richard Brian Davis

INTRODUCTION

CHRISTIANITY IS A RELIGION; it is also a conceptual system. It not only prescribes a way of living (Christians were originally referred to as "people of the Way"[1]), but also includes a set of doctrines to be believed—teachings essential to Christianity that cannot be denied without abandoning the system. Since the first century, Christians have almost without exception claimed that these doctrines are true—and objectively so. They're not "cleverly invented stories,"[2] products of wish fulfillment, or true "for us" simply because that's how we "self-identify." They're true, rather, because that's the way the world *is*, and we know that it is because these doctrines are supported by the publicly available historical facts.[3]

---

1. See Acts 9:2; 24:14.
2. 2 Pet 1:16.
3. After reporting his encounter with the resurrected Jesus, the apostle Paul says to Festus: "What I am saying is true and reasonable. The King is familiar with these things. ... I am convinced that none of this has escaped his notice, because it was not done in a corner" (Acts 26:25–26).

In a culture that virtually mandates diversity and inclusion, it is nothing short of scandalous to claim that Christianity is factually and objectively true. Consider, for example, what the vast majority of Christians have believed—what is commonly termed "the gospel."

God is holy, loving, and just. He made the world and everything in it, and everything he created was good. Human beings were created in God's image with the power of choice: to obey him or not. In a primordial act, our ancestors freely rebelled against God. In doing so, they corrupted themselves, forfeited God's favor, and brought ruinous calamity upon the human race. We human beings, each of us, have inherited a "fallen" condition: a condition inclining us *to* sin and *away from* God. We sin because it is our inherited propensity to do so—and we do so. We thus find ourselves guilty before God, our good works of no effect, and in dire need of a savior.

In his mercy and grace, however, God has instituted a plan of salvation whereby the just penalty for our sins (i.e., death and separation from God) is voluntarily borne by a substitute: his Son, Jesus Christ, whom he sent into the world to be "the atoning sacrifice for our sins."[4] God has given proof of this by raising him from the dead. Those who repent of their sin and place their faith in Christ (and Christ alone) for salvation are forgiven, reconciled to God, and inherit eternal life. Those who do not stand condemned. Since they have rejected God's one and only Son, they will be shut out from God's presence forever.[5]

The term "gospel" literally means "good news." But can we really say the Christian gospel is good news if it declares there is *only* one true religion or worldview, *only* one way of salvation, and that Jesus Christ is that *only* way? Is this what our devout Hindu, Muslim, and Buddhist friends are to be told? How does that help build bridges and reduce hostility?

Not surprisingly, these *only*-claims have met with stiff opposition. On the moral level, this attitude of exclusion is said to be prideful,[6] judgmental,[7]

---

4. 1 John 2:2.

5. Thanks to my colleague Scott Masson for his helpful comments here.

6. "Natural pride . . . becomes harmful when it is elevated to the level of dogma and is built into the belief system of a religious community . . . implying an exclusive or a decisively superior access to the truth or the power to save" (Hick, *Interpretation of Religion*, 194).

7. The doctrine of original sin "promotes a dualistic judgmental, accusatory mindset . . . [which] in turn breeds hostility and rivalry. . . . [It] often aids in the expansion of sin" (McLaren, *Why Did Jesus*, 133).

hostile,[8] dangerous,[9] and "the stuff of empire and exploitation."[10] Still further, there is the epistemic or intellectual complaint. Since the doctrines of the other great world religions are "as epistemologically well based"[11] as belief in the gospel, it is plainly arbitrary or egotistical to insist on the alethic superiority of Christianity and, on that basis, attempt to convert people of other faiths.

In this chapter, I critically assess both of these objections. I first sketch a case for Christian exclusivism. I argue that both logic and Jesus' teachings about himself require it. Next, I explore specific versions of the moral and epistemic objections to Christian exclusivism. None of these, I contend, presents an insuperable obstacle to belief in an exclusive gospel. Nor is consolation likely to be found in the embrace of pluralism, according to which there are many paths to God, so that salvation may be appropriated by those outside the Christian faith.

A CASE FOR CHRISTIAN EXCLUSIVISM

Logic of the Whole

You are a Christian exclusivist, as I use the term, if you believe (a) that the individual propositions making up the gospel are true, and (b) that no religious system whose core teachings contradict the gospel is true. And, naturally enough, if (a) is true, (b) is as well. That's just a matter of logic. Contradictions cannot be true. If there is *just one* way to God (as the gospel teaches), there can't be *many* ways to God (contrary to what the Bahá'í faith teaches). According to Islam, Jesus never died.[12] But that's

---

8. You are a hostile Christian, says McLaren, if you strongly agree with this statement: "I see other faiths as wrong, false, or evil, and I maintain a posture of opposition to all faiths but the Christian faith" (McLaren, *Why Did Jesus*, 69).

9. "Here ... we come to the ethical bedrock for why we must recognize the diversity of God's ways: if Jesus and the God he embodied warned against the dangers of empire, they would also warn against the danger of only one way" (Knitter, "Many Ways to God," 513).

10. "Any nation or any religion or any ideology that claims to be the 'only truth', or that feels it has been divinely designated as the final truth for all other truths, is open to the temptation, if not the necessity, of allowing such claims to justify or necessitate power over others. Such power is the stuff of empire and exploitation" (Knitter, "Many Ways to God," 513).

11. This is John Hick's expression. See the excerpt from his letter to Alvin Plantinga reproduced in the latter's "Ad Hick," 295.

12. Quran 4:157–58.

a false doctrine if the gospel is true. For the gospel teaches that "Christ died for our sins."[13] And if so, then he died. The thing to see is that there is nothing unseemly or improper for a Christian who believes the gospel to think of all those religions whose (core) doctrines contradict her own as being in the wrong. Indeed, that is what she *must* think—at least if she is thinking logically.

But why think the gospel *is* true in the first place? Here the exclusivist's reply is likely to be complex and many-sided. Consider, for example, the nature of the claims included in the gospel. They are of vastly different kinds. Some are arguably subject to proof. That there is a God, says Thomas Aquinas, has "been proved demonstratively by the philosophers, guided by the light of the natural reason."[14] That some things are in motion, that the universe had a beginning, that the material world doesn't exist by a necessity of its own nature—these are facts about the world to which one might appeal as furnishing grounds for believing in God. Other propositions—for example, that we are guilty of sin or wrongdoing—are such that they can be known by way of introspection as we reflect on our thoughts, motivations, and desires. Still others will be thought of as the product of special revelation: what God has revealed to us in Scripture.[15] The specifics of God's plan of salvation—in particular, that salvation is available through Christ alone—no doubt fall into this class.

So, the Christian exclusivist is an exclusivist on two levels. With respect to the gospel as a whole, she thinks of it as true and every religious system incompatible with it as false. But she also believes the parts of the gospel, and some of these are exclusivistic just in themselves. To say, for example, that Jesus is the only way to God is to deny that there is any other way—not Krishna, Zoroaster, Lao-tze, Buddha, or the Prophet Muhammad. It means that Rumi, the thirteenth-century Sufi poet and mystic, was in error when he taught, "There are as many paths to God as there are souls on the Earth."[16] So why do Christians reject the idea of many paths in favor of only one? Fundamentally, it is because they believe (and think they have good reasons for believing) that this is what Jesus himself taught.

---

13. 1 Cor 15:3.

14. Chapter 3 in Aquinas, *Summa Contra Gentiles*.

15. According to Aquinas, God has chosen to reveal even those truths about himself that can be reached by natural reason. For otherwise, few of us—e.g., those lacking the time or disposition to work through the arguments—would have knowledge of God. See chapter 4 in Aquinas, *Summa Contra Gentiles*.

16. Cited in Sägesser, "Freedom of Belief," 65.

Logic of the Parts

In the Gospel of John, the fourteenth chapter, Jesus tells his disciples that he will soon be leaving to prepare a place for them in his Father's house. Anticipating their distress, he offers this assurance: "You know the way to the place where I am going." Their reply indicates that they don't:

> Thomas said to him, "Lord, we don't know where you are going, so how can we know the way?" Jesus answered, "I am the way and the truth and the life. No one comes to the Father except through me. If you really knew me, you would know my Father as well. From now on, you do know him and have seen him. . . . Do you not believe that I am in the Father and the Father is in me?"[17]

Set within this passage is an implicit argument—an argument directed, in the first place, to Jesus' disciples, but also by extension to us. Its foundational premise is

1. Jesus is in the Father, and the Father is in Jesus

which is then used to underwrite two theses:

2. If you know Jesus, then you also know the Father

and

3. Jesus is the only way to the Father.

Now (2) actually follows from (1)'s right conjunct alone: that the Father is in Jesus. That by itself guarantees that to know Jesus is to know the Father. The argument makes no use of (1)'s left conjunct. But it also has an interesting implication, namely,

4. If you know the Father, then you also know Jesus

from which we can validly infer:

5. If you don't know Jesus, then you don't know the Father.

But if knowing God the Father is a precondition for going to be where Jesus is (namely, his Father's house), then if you don't know Jesus, you won't be where he is. You won't be in a place Jesus went to prepare for you.

---

17. John 14:5–7, 10.

Naturally, this raises the all-important question of what it means to *know* Jesus in this context. Fortunately, the biblical text makes that clear. When Philip asks Jesus to settle the question of how they might know the way to the Father, Jesus replies:

> Don't you know me, Philip, even after I have been among you such a long time? Anyone who has seen me has seen the Father. How can you say, "Show us the Father"? Don't you believe that I am in the Father, and that the Father is in me? The words I say to you are not just my own. Rather, it is the Father, living in me, who is doing his work.[18]

This passage is initially perplexing. In philosophers' talk, Philip clearly knew Jesus *by description*. He knew many true propositions (facts) about him: that he was from Nazareth, that he cared about the poor, that he believed we should love our enemies. He also knew him *by acquaintance*; he was related to him in a direct and personal way—not merely by description from afar. He had followed him for three years. And yet Jesus still says, "Don't you know me, Philip?" Translation: "Philip, you *don't* know me." You don't know me, if you don't recognize who I am; and you don't know who I am if you don't believe (1).

The first stage in Jesus' argument, then, is that if you don't believe (1), you don't know God the Father. The second is that if (1) is true, then "No one comes to the Father except through me." Upon reflection, however, it is (1)'s right-conjunct, namely,

(1-Right) The Father is in Jesus.

that is doing all the logical work here. If (1-Right) is Jesus' reason for the conclusion "No one comes to the Father *except* through me," he is clearly intending his listeners to interpret it as the stronger claim

(1-Right') The Father is *only* in Jesus.

For if the Father were in other religious teachers, then (by the logic of the argument), Jesus wouldn't be the *only* way to the Father. He would be one among many ways—the number of ways being determined by how many others the Father was in. But that's not what Jesus says. And if, as he does say, "The words I say to you are not just my own" but those of the Father, then if (1-Right') is true, the Father is speaking authoritatively only through Jesus, but not Buddha, Confucius, or Muhammad. God isn't in them, so their words aren't from God. The Father lives in, does his work, and teaches solely through his Son.

---

18. John 14:9–10.

All of this follows from that initial premise—a premise, we might be surprised to learn, Jesus doesn't leave unsupported. The disciples are told that they should believe (1) "on the evidence of the miracles themselves."[19] If the Christian exclusivist has reason to believe that John's Gospel is historically reliable on this point,[20] she too will be justified in believing (1) and therefore that Jesus is the only way to God despite what all the other religious teachers have to say. These are the things a Christian will (naturally) believe. Why should she believe otherwise?

OBJECTIONS TO CHRISTIAN EXCLUSIVISM

Moral Objections

I turn first to the moral complaints. Many arguments have been proposed for the impropriety of believing the gospel to be exclusively true. Here I'll restrict myself to those that seem to me the most persuasive and important.

Hate and Hostility

According to Brian McLaren, these moral complaints have a common root. They can all be traced to the fact that Christian exclusivists have carved out their identity in opposition to non-Christian religions. This, he thinks, is a bad thing:

> The stronger our Christian commitment, the more we emphasize our differences in terms of good/evil, right/wrong, better/worse. We may be friendly to individuals of other religions, but our friendship always has a pretext: we want them to switch sides. ... This kind of pseudo friendship expresses the "love the sinner, hate the sin" mind-set: love the Hindu but hate his Hinduism.[21]

And again, "When religions develop an oppositional identity—we oppose, therefore we are, or we know who we are because we know whom we oppose—their strong identity comes at a high cost."[22]

---

19. John 14:11.
20. This isn't the place to go into the details. But see Blomberg, *Reliability of the Gospels*. See also the Habermas and Shaw chapter in this volume on the evidence for God's raising Jesus from the dead, which plays an important epistemic role in attesting the content of Jesus' teaching.
21. McLaren, *Why Did Jesus*, 9–10.
22. McLaren, *Why Did Jesus*, 20.

The cost is hostility, which McLaren equates with opposition:

> By hostility I mean opposition, the sense that the other is the enemy.... Hostility makes one unwilling to be a host.... Hostility is an attitude of exclusion, not embrace; of repugnance, not respect; of suspicion, not extending the benefit of the doubt; of conflict, not conviviality.[23]

To find out just how hostile you are—in particular towards other religions—you can respond to the following statement (on a scale of 0–5, where 0 = "absolutely untrue" and 5 = "strongly agree"): "I see other faiths as wrong, false, or evil, and I maintain a posture of opposition to all faiths but the Christian faith."[24] The higher your score, the more hostile you are. It goes without saying, of course, that opposition in this sense (treating others as repugnant, suspicious enemies)—let's call it *personal opposition*—is generally deplorable and something Christians should do their best to avoid.

Still, it wouldn't automatically follow that a Christian shouldn't seek to develop an oppositional identity. For consider *propositional opposition*. Two propositions P and Q are propositionally oppositional, we might say, just in case P and Q have opposing truth-values (one is true, the other false). In fact, McLaren himself agrees that hostility extends to the world of ideas; for we can be "hostile toward science and learning, hostile toward honest questions and new ways of thinking."[25] And here he is surely right: we can indeed be hostile (i.e., rationally opposed) to these things.

Let's think for a moment in terms of Aristotle's famed "Square of Opposition." The opposite corners on his "Square" have opposing truth values—and necessarily so since they are contradictories. Suppose, then, that I believe some specific proposition—the "A" corner pictured on the top left in Figure 1. I believe "All human beings are sinners."

---

23. McLaren, *Why Did Jesus*, 19.
24. McLaren, *Why Did Jesus*, 69.
25. McLaren, *Why Did Jesus*, 20.

A: All human beings are sinners

E: No human beings are sinners

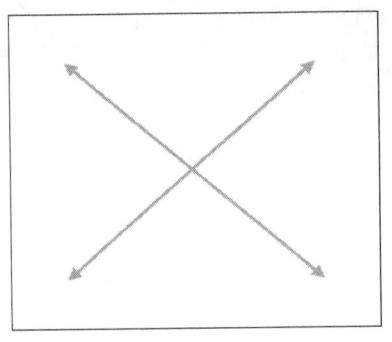

I: Some human beings are sinners

O: Some human beings are not sinners

Figure 1

And then let's say you believe its opposite, its contradictory—the "O" proposition: Some human beings are not sinners. It's just a matter of elementary logic that if I believe A—perhaps because I read it in my Bible (Rom 3:23)—I must oppose the truth of O, the thing you believe. I have to *exclude* that in my thinking; I have to see us as differing in terms of right/wrong. For if I don't, then as we've said, I'll find myself believing contradictions. Moreover, if it is better to hold true beliefs than false ones, I should think that my A belief is alethically *better than* your O.[26] It scarcely follows that I won't shake *your* hand or have *you* over for dinner. Propositions and people are not the same thing. I can love and respect you without believing what you believe.

Now here, I'm afraid, McLaren muddies the waters considerably. This is mere "pseudo friendship," he says. For the friendship has a pretext: "We want them to switch sides." But this line of reasoning is deeply flawed. If we think about it carefully, the "love the sinner, hate the sin" argument is both logically invalid and its conclusion (very probably) a strawman. From the fact that

(6) We should love the sinner but hate his sin

it hardly follows that

---

26. "Alethically," from the Greek word for truth, *alētheia*.

(7) We should love the Hindu but hate his Hinduism.

For (7) is not a substitution instance of (6), and this for the simple reason that Hinduism—taken as a collection of doctrines—isn't the right sort of thing to count as a sin (along with lying, cheating, stealing, and the like). It's a set of propositions. You don't hate propositions; you believe them or disbelieve them. What McLaren is doing here is uncharitably shoehorning an emotionally loaded term ("hate") into the equation where it has no business. (7) doesn't follow from (6); at best it's a strawman imputed to the Christian without justification. No sensible believer will take responsibility for it.

What she will no doubt affirm in its place, however, is

(7′) We should love the Hindu but *disagree* with his Hinduism.

The left side of the conjunction follows from Matthew 22:39: "You shall love your neighbor as yourself." The right-side is required by the law of non-contradiction. Since Christianity and Hinduism are contradictories, a thinking Christian *must* disagree with Hinduism—just as a thinking Hindu must disagree with Christianity. So it seems perfectly possible for the Christian to emphasize her differences with other religions in terms of true/false and right/wrong without that spilling over to personal animosity and opposition.

Exploitation and Empire

The Exploitation Argument

Theologian Paul F. Knitter contends that to endorse Christian exclusivism—or exclusivism of any strain—is open to the charge of exploitation and empire building:

> I believe the historical record is clear: any nation or any religion or any ideology that claims to be the "only truth," or that feels it has been divinely designated as the final truth for all other truths, is open to the temptation, if not the necessity, of allowing such claims to justify or necessitate power over others. Such power is the stuff of empire and exploitation.[27]

The question at once arises: *are* "only truth" religions and ideologies invariably tied to exploitation? Knitter apparently thinks so. The Buddhist scholar, Rita Gross, goes a step further here:

27. Knitter, "Many Ways to God," 513.

> The track record of religions that claim exclusive and universal truth for themselves is not praiseworthy or uplifting. How much empire building, how many crusades and religious wars, big and small, have gone on in the name of defending the "*one true faith*"? There seems to be a cause-effect link between claims of exclusive truth and suffering; or to say it more strongly, the main result of exclusive truth-claims has been suffering, not salvation.[28]

We can cull from these quotations. The first has to do with exploitation. There is a *correlation*, Knitter suggests, between an ideology's claiming of itself that it is the "only truth," and that claim leading to the exploitation and mistreatment of others. And if so, Gross seems to say, we have reason to believe that it is those exclusive truth claims that are the culprit. They have been the *cause* of "suffering, not salvation."

This argument is doubly defective. Consider, first, its basic premise:

> CORRELATION: Every "only truth" religion is accompanied by the mistreatment of others.

Why should we believe such a sweeping generalization? Knitter doesn't give us a lot to go on here. He does say that "only truth" religions are subject to "the temptation, if not the necessity" of exploiting others. This initially suggests that CORRELATION is to be understood as an analytic truth: one true by virtue of the meanings of its terms. We know that triangles are three-sided because that's part of the definition of a triangle. In like manner, perhaps Knitter is using the expression "'only truth' religion" to mean "a religion that involves mistreating others." If so, CORRELATION would be a tautology and, as such, would require no proof.

Unfortunately, nothing is settled by a definition. The question of how many moons orbit the earth can hardly be settled by announcing that we've agreed to use the term "the earth" to mean "the third planet from the Sun with only one moon." For the original (astronomical) question remains. Likewise, if someone wants to know whether "only truth" religions are accompanied by exploitation, they're not asking for a definition of terms. Their concern is *factual*; they want to know whether CORRELATION is true *as a matter of historical fact and record*. Here Knitter apparently concedes the point. It's not that "only truth" religions "must

---

28. Gross, "Excuse Me," 80, cited in Knitter, "Many Ways to God," 513.

lead to the demeaning and mistreatment of others." Rather, he says, "I am simply observing that they do."[29]

Here we immediately run into problems having to do with the scope of Knitter's observations. CORRELATION says that *every* "only truth" religion *was* attended, *is* attended, and always *will be* attended by exploitation. But, of course, Knitter's limited personal experience doesn't support anything remotely like that. For her part, Gross will only say that "many crusades and religious wars" have been undertaken to defend "the *one* true faith." She doesn't claim that *every* "only truth" religion (past, present, and future) is attended with its own war or crusade. As far as Knitter's and Gross's personal observations go, therefore, CORRELATION doesn't rise above the level of an unproven, hasty generalization.

This defect aside, we can still ask how Gross's conclusion, that is,

> CAUSATION: Every "only truth" religion causes the mistreatment of others.

follows from Knitter's CORRELATION. "Only truth" religions may well be correlated with exploitation, but why think they're responsible for it? How is that even possible? A religious system, as we've said, is an abstract set of doctrines or propositional claims. As such, it is causally impotent. Doctrinal *systems* don't mistreat people; it's *people* that do that. Religious doctrines can be true or false, believed or disbelieved. What they can't do is succumb to temptation. Nor can they cause their proponents to do anything—e.g., to cancel or persecute those who disagree. You might as well argue that the number 7 could single out for mistreatment those who insist that it is an even number, or that its being added to 5 comes to 13 and not 12.

You might reply that what Gross really means to say is that "only truth" religions inevitably include members who persecute others in the name of their religion. Well, perhaps so; but even if so, what would that prove? Would it show, for example, that proponents of the gospel have mistreated others *because that's what the gospel requires of them*? Clearly not. For the gospel, as we've stated it, contains no proposition to the effect that *if you believe this gospel is solely true, you are justified in demeaning and mistreating those who reject it*. Those who have done so have acted of their own accord and on false pretenses. The gospel in no way sanctions such reprehensible behavior.

---

29. Gross, "Excuse Me," 80.

It might be said that while the gospel *in itself* doesn't cause exploitation and suffering, nevertheless *believing of it* that it's the sole truth does. But this doesn't follow either. For consider: Jesus believed that the gospel was true, and yet he mistreated no one at all. He had compassion on the sick, the poor, and the marginalized regardless of whether they agreed with his exclusive message. More than that, he prayed for those who crucified him. His "except through me" truth claims didn't result in his exploiting others; precisely the opposite was the case. Jesus' teachings about himself led to *his own* arrest and crucifixion. And a similar fate befell some of his closest followers.

The upshot is that the argument from CORRELATION to CAUSATION isn't logically sound. Accordingly, it doesn't supply us with a sufficient reason for thinking Christian exclusivism is "the stuff of" exploitation.

The Empire Argument

Still, the Knitter-Gross quotations hint at a separate line of thought, this one centering on the so-called dangers of empire. When human beings take the place of God, Knitter informs us,

> they are enabled and entitled to take whatever else they want. *Idolatry prepares the way for empire.* This, as contemporary scripture scholars are making clear, is what animated and aroused the Jewish prophets, especially the prophet Jesus of Nazareth: they were opposed to the empires that tried to take the place of God, whether such empires were found in the royal courts of Babylon, Jerusalem, or Rome.[30]

Knitter adds that since "Jesus and the God he embodied warned against the dangers of empire, they would also warn against the danger of only one way."[31] But just how does my proclaiming that Jesus is the only way make me guilty of empire building? The basic idea is this. Those who claim that their religion (paradigm, worldview) is uniquely true take the place of God. They adopt a "God's-eye-point-of-view" (GPV). Thomas Nagel calls it "the view from nowhere,"[32] in which one presumes to speak

---

30. Knitter, "Many Ways to God," 513.
31. Knitter, "Many Ways to God," 513.
32. See Nagel, *View from Nowhere*.

from a neutral vantage point "over and above" all religions or paradigms. We do this whenever we issue unqualified, universal declarations such as

- No religion can be true if it is internally inconsistent.
- Any religion that teaches there is no God is false.
- Every worldview that teaches that Jesus never existed contradicts the historical facts.
- All those who reject Christ are not saved.

Those who speak this way do so for the purpose of gaining the upper hand and controlling others. It's a blunt power move—an act of aggression designed to build an empire. And if Knitter is right, "Jesus and the God he embodied" sternly warned against this. The only remedy is to apply a hermeneutic of suspicion to what they say. We must deconstruct their language, expose their power motives, and regard their "truth claims" with suspicion. Their GPV pronouncements are flatly immoral, and their moral wrongdoing is only compounded, if they have adopted this perspective, knowing full well that it doesn't exist. Thus, according to the postmodernist thinker, James K. A. Smith,

> If we consider . . . the reality of deep *moral* [or religious] diversity and competing visions of the Good, postmodern society is at a loss to adjudicate the competing claims. There can be no appeal to a higher court that would transcend a historical context or language game, no neutral observer or "God's-eye-view" that can *legitimate* or *justify* one paradigm or moral [or religious] language game above another. If all moral [religious] claims are conditioned by paradigms of historical commitment, then they cannot transcend those conditions.[33]

In short, due to our situatedness (ethnic, historical, and otherwise), our religious claims are always made from within a perspective. There is no such thing as transcending one's paradigm, in which case there is no such thing as truth *simpliciter*. There is only truth-in: truth in a paradigm, or a language game, or a religious system.

Well, straightaway this poses a serious problem for the Christian exclusivist. For Jesus' declaration (JD) "No one comes to the Father except through me" is clearly made from a GPV. It clearly implies that there is only one correct path to God. If we declare that JD is true *simpliciter*,

---

33. Smith, "Little Story about Metanarratives," 131.

we assume a GPV on the matter. We raise JD "over and above" its rivals. And if our postmodern critic is right, that means we should be *suspicious* of Jesus' claim; we should *doubt* whether it's true. For what Jesus is doing here, we shall have to say, is shameless empire building. This claim Jesus makes about himself—that he is the *only* way to the Father—is nothing more than a brazen power grab. This is hardly a pretty picture.

But here, perhaps, Knitter and Smith would reply that Jesus is perfectly entitled to adopt a GPV for the simple reason that he is God. But in *that* case, surely the Christian exclusivist can happily follow suit, confidently asserting JD from a GPV in inter-faith dialogue. Naturally, this will imply that she takes Christianity to be the only true religion, placing it alethically "above" all the rest in her thinking. Still, if it's right and proper for Jesus to issue JD from a GPV, it's hard to see how the Christian exclusivist can be faulted for bearing witness to Jesus' claim from that same standpoint.

At any rate, before she can denounce the exclusivity of the gospel, the postmodern perspectivalist has her own moral hurdle to clear. For in rejecting Christian exclusivism, she must assert the following:

- No claim made on behalf of any religion can be true from a God's-eye-view.
- Anyone who claims her religion is the "only truth" is guilty of empire building.
- There is no way to adjudicate between competing religious systems.
- All truth claims are power moves designed to control the hearer.

These declarations she enjoins upon us as the settled truth of the matter. Those who accept these pronouncements have got it right. Those who don't—well, they're in the wrong. But here the postmodernist is hoist on her own petard. For in dismissing the exclusivist in this way, she has adopted the very "God's-eye" point of view she assured us could never be occupied. She has thereby raised her paradigm "above" the exclusivist's. By her own dictates, therefore, we must regard her GPV declarations with suspicion, since they are guilty of no less a sin than the one she is so anxious to impute to the Christian exclusivist: empire building.

Epistemic Objections

According to Wilfred Cantwell Smith, in the face of religious diversity, it is no longer possible to "go out into the world and say to devout, intelligent, fellow human beings: . . . 'We believe that we know God and we are right; you believe that you know God, and you are totally wrong.'"[34] John Hick puts his finger on the difficulty:

> [We cannot] reasonably claim that our own form of religious experience, together with that of the tradition of which we are a part, is veridical whilst others are not. We can of course claim this; and indeed virtually every religious tradition has done so, regarding alternate forms of religion either as false or as confused and inferior versions of itself. . . . Persons living within other traditions, then, are equally justified in trusting their own distinctive religious experience and in forming their beliefs on the basis of it. . . . Let us avoid the implausibly arbitrary dogma that religious experience is all delusory with the single exception of the particular form enjoyed by the one who is speaking.[35]

The difficulty here isn't *alethic*; it's *epistemic*. It has to do with my justification for taking the gospel to be true to the exclusion of the other religious options. Hick's contention is that no religion is ever justified in claiming it is the "only truth." This isn't because religious truth claims can't be justified—say, because they lack a truth value.[36] It's because they're all "equally justified"; each is "as epistemologically well based"[37] as the others. But then, Hick declares, "The only reason for treating one's tradition differently from others is the very human but not very cogent reason that it is one's own!"[38] To treat any one religion as superior to its "equally justified" fellows, perhaps insisting that everyone convert to one's own religion, is thus wholly arbitrary and unjustified.

Well, what has the Christian exclusivist to say for herself? There are a few things to note. First, Hick's parity argument assumes that *religious experience* is the only relevant source of justification for religious beliefs. But this is highly doubtful. As we noted above, the doctrinal claims

---

34. Smith, *Religious Diversity*, 14.
35. Hick, *Interpretation of Religion*, 235.
36. A position known as noncognitivism and defended by A. J. Ayer. See chapter 6 in Ayer, *Language, Truth, and Logic*.
37. See Plantinga, "Ad Hick," 295.
38. Hick, *Interpretation of Religion*, 235.

comprising a religious system are vastly different. Some are known by way of sense experience, some by introspection, others by rational argument, and still others by the testimony of eyewitnesses or historical records. If by a "religious experience" Hick means the mystical, often numinous experiences people report having when they are engaged in religious activities (e.g., fasting, praying, meditating, and the like), it is implausible *in excelsis* to think of them as justifying whole doctrinal systems. Hence, with only religious experience to go on, Hick may well be right: every religion is *equally* justified, but only because they're all *inadequately* justified.

Secondly, Hick assumes that all religious experiences are veridical. Christian religious experience justifies Christian belief; Hindu religious experience justifies Hinduism. Neither enjoys an epistemic advantage. One is reminded here of David Hume's claim that miracle reports used to establish Christianity over and against the religions of Rome, Turkey, and Siam are counterbalanced by the reports brought forward to establish those systems.[39] In a similar vein, Charles Hartshorne maintains that the miracle reports in favor of Jesus' resurrection don't tilt the scales in favor of Christianity because their ability to do so is neutralized by the fact that miracle accounts abound in other religions with diametrically opposed doctrines. "I do not feel that I can choose," he says, "among such accounts."[40] But why not? As Gary Habermas observes on this score,

> [Hartshorne's claim] appears to assume that, just because miracle reports abound, they are on similar footing. However, such a view (regardless of whether any miracles have ever occurred) forgoes the process of critical interaction. Are they all to be . . . accepted en masse *simply because a variety of such reports does exist?*[41]

The answer, quite obviously, is that they should not. To be sure, there are miracle reports aplenty. It doesn't follow that they're equally credible. That's not something we can assume *a priori*. These reports must be critically assessed. And the same goes for religious experiences. If they are what justify our religious beliefs, then if all such experiences were veridical, every religion would be on an epistemic par. In that case, it would indeed be arbitrary to declare one's own religion—or worldview, whether

---

39. See Hume, *Dialogues Concerning Natural Religion*, 116.
40. See Hartshorne, "Response to the Debate," 137.
41. Habermas, "Resurrection Claims," 171.

religious or secular—to be the "only truth." But of course the question is: *are* all religious experiences veridical? At the outset, there is simply no reason to suppose they are.

In fact, after careful investigation, we might come to discover that while some religious experiences are undeniable (people do have them), they don't serve to confirm any doctrine. Others we may judge to be nonveridical altogether, since they are being used to justify what we know to be unethical or absurd—idolatry or human sacrifice, let's say, or the worship of extraterrestrials. The thing to see is that we're not obliged to treat these experiences as if they were cut from the same cloth. Hick's charge of epistemic arbitrariness almost certainly rests on a false premise: that we don't have principled reasons for discriminating between the veridical and the nonveridical here. Unfortunately, he doesn't provide us with any reason for thinking so.[42]

PLURALISM TO THE RESCUE?

Perhaps at this point we can agree that Christian exclusivism survives the moral and epistemic objections raised against it. Still, you say, isn't there a better way? Couldn't the Christian gospel be reframed in such a way that it is more *pluralistic*: that it at least be open to the idea that there are many paths to God? Here I wish to consider Brian McLaren's recent proposal—the heart of which is echoed by the Christian philosopher Michael Rea.

According to McLaren, if we begin with a proper doctrine of the Holy Spirit, the Spirit of God, we can see that Christianity is just one truth among many. Here is McLaren's definition: "The Holy Spirit is God-in-us or God-upon-us or God-among-us everywhere and anywhere . . . the Spirit is ubiquitous—everywhere, always, in all creation."[43] We're given a few options here, but the central thrust seems to be this. Since the Spirit is *omnipresent*, we can rightly say that he is "in" us, "upon" us, and "among" us. And the idea, I take it, is that this follows if he is *everywhere*. According to McLaren, this also "leads to [another] thought, logical and hard to dispute":

> The Holy Spirit pre-exists all religions, cannot be contained by any single religion, and therefore cannot be claimed as private

---

42. On distinguishing veridical from nonveridical religious experiences, see the detailed discussion in Yandell, *Epistemology of Religious Experience*.

43. McLaren, *Why Did Jesus*, 150.

> property by any one religion. That means that Pentecostals don't own the Holy Spirit, nor do Christians, nor do monotheists, nor do theists.... So we can say that the Spirit is open-source rather than proprietary.[44]

In other words, a Christian shouldn't think of herself as having the Holy Spirit in a unique sort of way—for example, based on the relationship she has with God by virtue of having trusted Christ alone for salvation. On McLaren's view, the Holy Spirit is *already* working in and through these other religions, so that the goal of the missionary enterprise isn't to see people *turn* to Christ, but rather *learn* from these non-Christian and pagan religions. Thus McLaren:

> We can understand human religions—all human religions, including our own—as imperfect responses to our encounters with the Spirit who is present in all creation.... Each religion, based on its unique location and history, would have a unique, particular, and evolving perspective from which to encounter the Spirit in a unique way.[45]

Consequently, "we would expect the Holy Spirit to be moving, working, 'hovering' over each religion ... [so that] other religions have something to offer us as well based on their real and unique encounters with the Spirit."[46]

The basic idea, then, is that every religion presents a unique way to God. Different pathways but the same God. In this regard, Michael Rea has championed an "Any God-Same God" principle:

> Christians and Muslims have very different beliefs about God; but they agree on this much: there is exactly one God. This common point of agreement is logically equivalent to the thesis that all Gods are the same God. In other words, everyone who worships a God worships the same God, no matter how different their views about God might be.[47]

From a Christian perspective, there are several things to say about McLaren's and Rea's suggestions. Here I'll highlight a couple of the more glaring deficiencies.

---

44. McLaren, *Why Did Jesus*, 150.
45. McLaren, *Why Did Jesus*, 151–52.
46. McLaren, *Why Did Jesus*, 153.
47. Rea, "On Worshipping the Same God."

First, McLaren's approach is based on a flawed understanding of the relation of the Holy Spirit to those outside the Christian faith. Nowhere in the Bible does it say that the Holy Spirit "hovers" over other religions. This claim is based on a flawed understanding of the Spirit, whom McLaren defines as follows: "God-in-us or God-upon-us or God-among-us everywhere."[48] For McLaren, the "us" here is all of us—Christian believer and non-believer alike.

But this is a loaded definition. It simply assumes without justification that everyone has the Holy Spirit *in* them. From a Christian perspective, that simply isn't true. The Holy Spirit isn't *in* a person unless he or she has received the Spirit. And there are very precise conditions for this to take place: "And Peter said to them, 'Repent and be baptized every one of you in the name of Jesus Christ for the forgiveness of your sins, and you will receive the gift of the Holy Spirit.'"[49] What McLaren has badly confused is the Holy Spirit's *omnipresence* (his being everywhere present) with the Holy Spirit's *indwelling presence*. The former doesn't imply the latter. According to the Bible, the ministry of the Holy Spirit to non-believers is not that of co-creation but rather *conviction*.[50]

Secondly, Rea's "Any God-Same God" principle leads to absurdity. To be sure, if "everyone who worships a God worships the same God," then Muslims and Christians do worship the same God. But shockingly, so do the worshipers of Ra, Baal, Asherah, Molech, Dagon, Zeus, Hermes, the Wiccans, and countless others. Are we really to believe that the worshipers of these false gods were (and are) all worshiping the Christian God, the God of the Bible? If you think so, pause for a moment and consider the story of Gideon. Before he could lead Israel out of the hands of the Midianites, there was something he was told to do:

> That night the LORD said to [Gideon], "Take your father's bull, and the second bull seven years old, and pull down the altar of Baal that your father has, and cut down the Asherah that is beside it and build an altar to the LORD your God on the top of the stronghold here, with stones laid in due order. Then take the second bull and offer it as a burnt offering with the wood of the Asherah that you shall cut down."[51]

---

48. McLaren, *Why Did Jesus*, 150.

49. Acts 2:38.

50. "When he comes, he will convict the world of guilt in regard to sin and righteousness and judgment" (John 16:8).

51. Judges 6:25–26.

The question arises: why would the LORD command a thing like that? It hardly makes sense. Gideon's father was simply worshiping Baal, and in so doing (on Rea's "Any God-Same God" principle), he was worshipping Yahweh! What could be more laudable and praiseworthy than that? Well, you don't need to be a philosopher, a theologian, or even a Christian to see that something has gone horribly awry here. That Gideon is told to pull down the altars to Baal (to whom child sacrifices were routinely offered). And that the apostle Paul later warns the Athenians that "in the past God overlooked such [idolatrous] ignorance, but now he commands all people everywhere to repent,"[52] is a crystal clear indication that (for the Christian at least) "the only true God"[53] is never to be mixed or identified with any other God.

The Oxford philosopher Mary Midgley once said: "An ethical theory which, when consistently followed through, has iniquitous consequences is a bad theory and must be changed."[54] One cannot help but think that Midgley's maxim has an obvious, powerful, and direct application to the "Same God" philosophers.

By way of conclusion then: there are good reasons for the Christian who accepts the gospel to think of it as exclusively true. The moral and epistemic objections to Christian exclusivism pose no obstacles to her doing so. Still further, a recent attempt to construct a more inclusive gospel faces grave objections of its own. In a religiously diverse world, to publicly proclaim an "except through me" gospel is plainly scandalous. There is the threat of remaining silent or being canceled. Here I am inclined to think that the serious Christian should largely disregard these cultural frights, following instead the sage advice of Peter and the other apostles: "We must obey God rather than men!"[55]

BIBLIOGRAPHY

Aquinas, Thomas. *Summa Contra Gentiles, Book One: God.* Translation with an Introduction and Notes by Anton C. Pegis. New York: Image, 1955.

Ayer, A. J. *Language, Truth, and Logic.* 2nd ed. New York: Dover, 1952.

---

52. Acts 17:30.
53. John 17:3.
54. Midgley, "Duties Concerning Islands," 157.
55. Acts 5:29. My thanks to Paul Copan for his helpful comments on an earlier draft.

Blomberg, Craig L. *The Reliability of the Gospels*. 2nd ed. Downers Grove, IL: IVP Academic, 2007.

Gross, Rita. "Excuse Me, but What's the Question? Isn't Religious Diversity Normal?" In *The Myth of Religious Superiority: A Multifaith Exploration*, edited by Paul F. Knitter, 75–87. Maryknoll, NY: Orbis, 2005.

Habermas, Gary. "Resurrection Claims in Non-Christian Religions." *Religious Studies* 25 (1989) 167–77.

Hartshorne, Charles. "Response to the Debate." In *Did Jesus Rise from the Dead? The Resurrection Debate*, edited by Terry L. Miethe, 137–42. San Francisco: Harper and Row, 1987.

Hick, John. *An Interpretation of Religion*. New Haven, CT: Yale University Press, 1989.

Hume, David. *Dialogues Concerning Natural Religion with Of the Immortality of the Soul, Of Suicide, Of Miracles*. Edited by Richard H. Popkin. 2nd ed. Indianapolis: Hackett, 1980.

Knitter, Paul F. "There Are Many Ways to God." In *Debating Christian Theism*, edited by J. P. Moreland et al., 509–19. Oxford: Oxford University Press, 2013.

McLaren, Brian. *Why Did Jesus, Moses, the Buddha, and Mohammed Cross the Road? Christian Identity in a Multi-Faith World*. New York: Jericho, 2012.

Midgley, Mary. "Duties Concerning Islands." In *People, Penguins, and Plastic Trees*, edited by Christine Pierce and Donald VanDeVeer, 156–64. 2nd ed. Belmont, CA: Wadsworth, 1986.

Nagel, Thomas. *The View from Nowhere*. New York: Oxford University Press, 1986.

Plantinga, Alvin. "Ad Hick." *Faith and Philosophy* 14 (1997) 295–97.

Rea, Michael. "On Worshipping the Same God." *Huffington Post: Religion* (blog), December 21, 2015. https://www.huffpost.com/entry/on-worshipping-the-same-g_b_8840936.

Sägesser, Caroline. "The Right to Freedom of Belief: An Historical Perspective on Secular Humanism." In *Routledge Handbook of Freedom of Religion or Belief*, edited by Silvio Ferrari et al., 56–70. London: Routledge, 2021.

Smith, James K. A. "A Little Story about Metanarratives: Lyotard, Religion, and Postmodernism Revisited." In *Christianity and the Postmodern Turn: Six Views*, edited by Myron B. Penner, 123–40. Grand Rapids: Brazos, 2005.

Smith, Wilfred Cantwell. *Religious Diversity*. New York: Harper and Row, 1976.

Yandell, Keith E. *The Epistemology of Religious Experience*. Cambridge: Cambridge University Press, 1994.

5

Divine Hiddenness

Epistemic and Soteriological

James K. Beilby

IF GOD EXISTS, WHY isn't his existence (or love, or providential plan, etc.) more obvious? This question has an ancient pedigree, for it has been asked by generations of God-followers as they experience moments of doubt and trial. These "dark nights of the soul" are not uncommon and are given full voice in the lament psalms in Scripture as the Psalmist cries out to God, "Where are you?" and "Why have you turned your face from me?" The apparent hiddenness of God can also be understood as a feature of God's relationship with humans, a result of the fact that God is transcendent, that humans are finite, sinful, and "see through a glass darkly." But divine hiddenness can also be understood in a very different way, as an objection to or argument against traditional Christian theism. On this understanding, the fact that God seems hidden to many people throughout history is an argument against God's perfect goodness or love. If God is perfectly loving and desires to be in relationship with his creation, why would so many people be in the dark with respect to his existence and purposes? In the words of Friedrich Nietzsche, this objection asks: "Is a god of goodness notwithstanding and merely could not express himself more clearly! Did he perhaps lack the intelligence to do so? Or the eloquence?"[1]

1. Nietzsche, *Daybreak*, 89–90.

Let's call the first of these the *theological* problem of divine hiddenness and the second the *apologetic* problem of divine hiddenness. The first of these focuses primarily on hiddenness as an ontological property of God and the second focuses on the epistemic status of God's revelation. This chapter will focus on the latter of these.[2] Moreover, I will discuss two different senses in which God might be said to be hidden. The first focuses on the claim that *knowledge of God's existence* is hidden from some people, even from some who apparently very much desire to know that God exists. The second sense in which God might be said to be hidden is soteriological in nature. God's plan of salvation is hidden from some people. I will unpack each of these objections, discuss a range of possible responses, and articulate what I take to be the best answer to each of these objections.

Two caveats before proceeding. As a work of Christian apologetics, my discussion of the hiddenness problem will be confined to the Christian religious tradition. Moreover, I am not seeking to provide an answer that the skeptic will take as a refutation of their arguments. Whether such a lofty goal is achievable or not, I have a more minimal goal: to offer a response to hiddenness arguments that might be deemed to be persuasive by those within the Christian tradition.

THE PROBLEM OF GOD'S EPISTEMIC HIDDENNESS

In the contemporary philosophical literature on divine hiddenness, J. L. Schellenberg's work is exemplary. His discussion of divine hiddenness arises out of his experience of the Christian theological tradition, but it is aimed more broadly at personalist versions of ultimism, which he defines as the belief that the ultimate religious reality is a personal being who is the "all-powerful, all-knowing, all-good, and all-loving creator of the universe."[3]

The first version of Schellenberg's divine hiddenness argument appeared in 1993 in *Divine Hiddenness and Human Reason* and in 2007 he made significant revisions to his argument in *The Wisdom to Doubt: A Justification of Religious Skepticism*. While there are important differences

---

2. On the difference between the ontological and epistemological dimensions of this question, see Coakley, "Divine Hiddenness," 230.

3. Schellenberg, *Hiddenness Argument*, 20.

in the arguments developed in these two works, there is a core argument that remains the same.[4] It can be stated as simply as this:

(A1) If a loving God exists, then there are no nonresistant nonbelievers.

(A2) There are nonresistant nonbelievers.

(A3) No loving God exists.[5]

The basic idea is clear enough. God's being perfectly loving entails that he would make himself known to all people. If this was the case, the only nonbelievers would be those who intentionally and explicitly resist the evidence God provides of his existence. Or, on the other hand, if there are nonbelievers who are open to the idea of God's existence—their nonbelief is not born out of epistemic resistance—then that entails that the perfectly loving God of Christianity does not exist. This is not an evidential argument. Schellenberg is not merely claiming that, given God's love, we have reason to believe that reasonable nonbelief would not occur; rather, this is a deductive argument. He claims that God's openness to relationship "is a priori part of the concept of a loving God."[6]

Schellenberg's most recent revision of the hiddenness argument was published in 2015 in *The Hiddenness Argument*. Unlike his previous two books on the topic, this volume was written for a wider audience and is designed to provide both an accessible, updated version of the argument and an autobiographical reflection on how the argument developed as it did. Schellenberg's 2015 version of the argument proceeds as follows:

(B1) if a perfectly loving God exists, then there exists a God who is always open to a personal relationship with any finite person. And,

(B2) if there exists a God who is always open to a personal relationship with any finite person, then no finite person is ever non-resistantly in a state of nonbelief in relation to the proposition that God exists.

---

4. The most significant change is Schellenberg's ceasing to describe nonbelief as culpable/non-culpable, choosing to focus on nonresistant nonbelief. "I now see this focus on culpability and inculpability as a mistake. Nonbelief might conceivably be culpable in many different ways, and by making these moves at the beginning of the argument I was forcing it ultimately to support the view that there is, in the actual world, nonbelief that in *none* of these ways is owed to culpable behavior. I wanted the best developed and most forceful hiddenness argument, but this was not the way to get it" (Schellenberg, *Hiddenness Argument*, 55, emphasis original).

5. I'm drawing on Charity Anderson's simplified version of Schellenberg's argument. See Anderson, "Divine Hiddenness," 120.

6. Anderson, Review of *Hiddenness Argument*, 87.

And,

(B3) if a perfectly loving God exists, then no finite person is ever non-resistantly in a state of nonbelief in relation to the proposition that God exists. But,

(B4) some finite persons are or have been non-resistantly in a state of nonbelief in relation to the proposition that God exists. So,

(B5) no perfectly loving God exists. And,

(B6) if no perfectly loving God exists, then God does not exist.

Therefore,

(B7) God does not exist.[7]

There are a number of revisions in this argument from Schellenberg's earlier versions. Most, such as his reference to "finite persons," are subtle refinements designed to avoid objections raised against the original argument.[8] Schellenberg has also ceased to use the phrase "nonresistant nonbeliever." It was open to misunderstanding because there are two senses to the word belief: "belief that [x exists]" and "belief [or trust] in x." In his 2015 version, Schellenberg replaces "nonresistant nonbelief" with "non-resistantly in a state of nonbelief in relation to the proposition that God exists." This makes it abundantly clear that he is focusing on propositional belief that God exists. He avers that one can only enter into a loving, trusting relationship with God if one believes that God exists. However, because the phrase "non-resistantly in a state of nonbelief in relation to the proposition that God exists" is unwieldy in the extreme, I will continue to use the phrase "nonresistant nonbelief," while keeping in mind Schellenberg's emphasis on propositional belief.

Another change in the 2015 version reflects a shift in Schellenberg's thinking over the years regarding how to construe one of the concepts central to the argument. It involves moving from the claim, "A perfectly loving God would provide evidence adequate for belief that he exists," to, "A perfectly loving God would always be open to personal relationship with any finite person." This change moves Schellenberg's focus away from the availability (or lack) of evidence and toward the

---

7. Schellenberg, *Hiddenness Argument*, 103.

8. For a list of the differences between Schellenberg's 1993 and 2015 arguments, see Jordan, "Divine Hiddenness," 188.

mere fact that some people experience honest doubt about whether a loving God exists.[9]

It is important to note that, for Schellenberg, the concept of non-resistant nonbelievers should not be understood that there will be no development of religious belief or that at every moment humans will experience the deepest possible divine-human communion.[10] He claims only that "we might expect at all times to be in possession of belief, and to have at all times the opportunity to be involved in some level of explicit relationship with God."[11] The key phrase here is "at all times." He is not merely claiming that non-resistant nonbelievers will not exist in the eschaton, he is claiming that if a perfectly loving God exists, non-resistant nonbelievers will *never* exist.[12]

This is a bold and, on its face, dubious claim. How does Schellenberg justify the claim that all nonresistant people will be in possession of the propositional belief that God exists *at all times*? While he acknowledges that humans retain free will in their encounter with evidence for God's existence and that the depth of the divine–human relationship will "vary depending on the response of the human term of the relation,"[13] he holds an involuntarist understanding of belief-formation. On this (not implausible) view, when I am seated in front of a table, I don't choose whether to believe "I am seated" or "there is a table in front of me." Rather, I find myself with those beliefs. Similarly, Schellenberg argues that given that God is all-powerful, he could reveal himself in such a way as to produce the belief "God exists" in all but those who were deliberately closing their eyes to the evidence. Moreover, given the fact that God is perfectly loving, he would do so.

Finally, setting aside the oddness of Schellenberg's "finite persons" language, it is clear that he wants to focus not just on "the skepticism of modern human beings." Schellenberg adds another category of non-resistant nonbelief, a category he calls "pre-doubt"—the lack of theistic belief among those who lived in the distant past, long before the advent of monotheism.[14]

9. Anderson, Review of *Hiddenness Argument*, 86.
10. Schellenberg "Hiddenness Argument Revisited (I)," 208.
11. Schellenberg, "Hiddenness Argument Revisited (I)," 208.
12. Trent Dougherty and Ted Poston develop this distinction in "Divine Hiddenness and the Nature of Belief," 183–98 (see esp. 186–89).
13. Schellenberg "Hiddenness Argument Revisited (I)," 208.
14. Schellenberg, *Hiddenness Argument*, 76–79.

RESPONSE TO THE EPISTEMIC HIDDENNESS ARGUMENT

A response to an epistemic hiddenness argument like Schellenberg's typically proceeds down one of two paths. One can deny the claim that there are nonresistant nonbelievers, or one can deny the claim that God's being perfectly loving is incompatible with there being nonresistant nonbelievers. My critique will address each of these.

On the Idea of Nonresistant Nonbelievers

Are there nonresistant nonbelievers? Schellenberg believes the answer to be, "Obviously, yes," but the question is far more complicated than it may seem on the surface, primarily because there are significant ambiguities in the concept of nonresistance that need to be teased out. What is clear is that there are people who report that they are open to the propositional truth of God's existence but also deem the evidence for God existence to be insufficient. But does this fact by itself suggest that these people are nonresistant? Not at all. A better answer would be to say that we don't know whether they are resistant, or, if they are, the extent to which they are resistant. In most cases, we simply don't have access to the sort of information that would allow us to say with any degree of confidence whether a person was actually resistant to belief in God. Moreover, the first-person perspective here is not as helpful as some might assume, for often we are in the dark about why we believe as we do.

Given human nature, it is uncontroversial to say that there are some nonbelievers whose rejection of the evidence for God's existence is influenced by things other than a desire for the truth, but of course the same thing could be said of the belief of some Christians. While the belief of some Christians is undoubtedly motivated by fear of punishment or desire for control, it is also likely that in some cases religious skepticism is driven by fear of control, that it arises as a teenage rebellion against parental demands, or that it is driven by a desire for greater sexual freedom than allowed by the mores of one's religious tradition. Does that mean that the nonbeliever is resistant in Schellenberg's sense? It depends what sort of freight is loaded onto the concept of resistance. Recall that Schellenberg's new argument involves a shift away from the objective provision of evidence toward a subjective sense of genuine doubts about God's existence. If a person's religious skepticism is based on reasons that are not truth-aimed, all that means is that their beliefs are unlikely to be considered knowledge. But that doesn't imply that their skeptical beliefs are dishonest, insincere, or somehow inappropriate given the experience of the person in question.

Setting all this aside, it seems that charity demands that we take seriously the claims of those who claim to desire relationship with God, but who struggle with the absence of evidence for God's existence. In fact, even if we set charity aside, it is reasonable to believe that there are some whose doubts about God's existence are sincere. Even if I believe that the skepticism of many is not truth-aimed and that some who are skeptical of God's existence, in a very real sense, deep-down don't want God to exist, I find it impossible to say that this is the case with all skeptics. I say this because even though I am a convinced Christian theist who makes a living helping college students confront their doubts and answer their religious questions, there are times when my own doubts are very real. They rarely linger long and, even when they are present, they don't cause me to question my choice of seeking to live like Jesus Christ or my calling to teach theology—in fact, some of my best, most effective teaching has come at times when I share my own doubts and attempt to be transparent about how I process them. But it isn't difficult for me to imagine how people who do not have the academic resources I have benefitted from might have much less ability to dispel the doubts that they encounter. Moreover, it is easy to see how those whose educational opportunities revolved around skeptics like Feuerbach, Freud, and Marx rather than believers like Plantinga, Wolterstorff, and Alston might have a harder time arriving at a theistic interpretation of the evidence for God's existence.

Consequently, I'm willing to accept the notion that there are (or, more minimally, might be) nonresistant nonbelievers. By this I mean that there exist people that want (in some meaningful—even if difficult to fully specify—sense) to believe in God but find themselves unable to do so for epistemic reasons. They believe that the evidence is balanced against God's existence, they believe things that they believe are conceptually incompatible with God's existence, or they believe that there are undefeated defeaters for the belief that God exists. What I question is whether these people truly fit Schellenberg's category of "nonresistant" and whether their existence constitutes a logical barrier to theistic belief.

The primary problem is that Schellenberg's notion of nonresistance seems fairly one-dimensional. A person is non-resistant if they "want" to believe that God exists. However, such a person might be open to the propositional belief that God exists, but not open to what such a belief might require of them. Are they nonresistant nonbelievers? Further, a person might be open in principle to belief that God exists, but is unwilling to accept a certain subset of the available evidence for God's existence. Perhaps they have epistemological commitments that causes them to see such forms of evidence as substandard. For example, a person who adopts a Humean-style empiricist epistemology will be hard pressed to see much of the possible evidence for God's existence and action in the world—just as they will be unable to see the evidence for many other realities (the existence of other minds, the existence of the past, etc.)

The lesson here is this: it is possible to be nonresistant to propositional belief in God, but resistant in other ways that prevent one from actually believing that God exists. In making this claim, I am neither questioning the meaningfulness of nonresistance nor am I claiming that there could not be people who are in some important sense nonresistant nonbelievers. Instead, I am taking the advice of William Abraham. He argued that reflections on Christian belief ought to "fit the complexity and raggedness of human experience." What Abraham said of Christian belief should also apply to skeptical epistemological claims. Speaking in terms of prototypical categories is fine as long as we remain aware of the abstractions we have created. In his invocation of "nonresistant nonbelievers," Schellenberg has lost sight both of the complexity of ordinary nonbelievers and believers who struggle with their nonbelief—"Lord, I believe; help my unbelief" (Mark 9:24 NKJV).

The error in Schellenberg's argument isn't in taking seriously God's perfect love when thinking about the extent and nature of God's revelation. I think that it is true that if God is perfectly loving, he would provide that which is necessary for relationship with him to all who are willing and able to receive it. By "that which is necessary for relationship with him," I am thinking of sufficient evidence of his existence, character, and offer of salvation. Schellenberg's error comes in the assumption that God's provision of that which is necessary for relationship with him implies the truth of each of the following:

1. If God open to relationship and has provided evidence of his existence, then humans are in possession of that evidence.

2. If God has provided evidence, then all nonresistant people will assent to the proposition God exists.

Demonstrating the falsity of each of the above claims is the burden of the next two sections.

Provision of Evidence/Possession of Evidence

Many Christian theists who deny the existence of non-resistant nonbelievers do so because they believe both that God has provided evidence of his existence and that the evidence he provides is available (in principle) to all people—and they often appeal to Romans 1:19–20 to justify this contention. If evidence of God's existence is available, then nonbelievers must be resistant. On the other hand, Schellenberg and his compatriots argue that nonresistant nonbelievers do exist and, on that basis, infer that God has not provided evidence of his existence and, by virtue of that, is not open to relationship.

The mistake made by both sides here is in the assumption that God's provision of evidence necessitates that humans (and nonresistant nonbelievers in particular) will be in possession of that evidence. Charity Anderson has persuasively argued that, despite its initial plausibility, the connection between evidence-providing and evidence-possession fails. She argues that "it is not the case that in order to count as providing evidence to someone, the intended recipient must have the evidence."[15] There are a number of reasons why evidence provision by God might not result in evidence possession by nonresistant nonbelievers, but the most significant reason is that the evidence that God provides is defeated by misleading evidence.[16]

But why might there be misleading evidence regarding God's existence in a world created by a perfectly loving God? The seeds of that answer are in Schellenberg's own argument. While Schellenberg's argument revolves around the concept of nonresistant nonbelievers, he acknowledges that there might be some people who are resistant to the evidence of God's existence. But the very notion of resistant nonbelievers (and the concept of human freedom that explains why some are resistant and some are not) provides an explanation of where misleading evidence regarding God's existence might come from. Misleading defeaters are arguments produced by resistant nonbelievers in an attempt to justify both their nonbelief and epistemic resistance. Hence, as Anderson says,

---

15. Anderson, "On Providing Evidence," 246.
16. Anderson, "Divine Hiddenness," 125–27.

"Just as the free will of agents contributes to an explanation for why God allows (at least some) evil in the world, the free will of agents can explain the introduction of certain defeaters and thus contribute to an explanation of divine hiddenness."[17]

A second reason why people might fail to possess evidence of God's existence despite God's provision of sufficient evidence is that the evidence God provides might be misinterpreted. This is different than having the evidence for God's existence defeated. There is no defeater that rebuts or undercuts the epistemic import of the evidence God provides; rather, the evidence is understood as supporting the truth of something other than God's existence. Rather than pointing to God's existence, the evidence is seen as indicating the majesty of the natural world or the nobility of humans or something else. Notice that misinterpreting evidence doesn't require any sort of epistemic resistance on the nonbeliever's part. But notice also that the possibility of misleading defeaters for divine evidence is also relevant here, because it is possible that one of the causes of the misinterpretation of the evidence God provides is the presence of misleading counter-evidence which discourages or, in some cases, eliminates the possibility of a theistic interpretation of the available evidence.

The general point being made here is that Schellenberg sets up a false either/or when he claims that nonbelievers are either culpably resistant to belief in God or God has provided insufficient evidence. The epistemic situation of many people, whether they be believers or not, is far more complicated than this.[18]

Must the Nonresistant Believe in God?

Suppose Schellenberg grants the complexity of the epistemic situations in which people find themselves. His response seems to be that the situational specifics are overridden by the fact that an all-powerful God could make it such that there wouldn't be any nonbelievers who are nonresistant in the requisite sense. The crucial question is this: Can an all-powerful God make it such that all nonresistant people will become aware of the evidence God provides, will properly interpret the provided evidence, will reject any and all misleading defeaters for that evidence, and will, on the basis of that evidence, assent to the proposition "God exists"?

17. Anderson, "Divine Hiddenness," 127.
18. Anderson, "Divine Hiddenness," 130.

Of course, being omnipotent, God could obliterate the nonbelieving person and replace them a nanosecond later with an identical copy minus all the skeptical beliefs and with a full and detailed set of religious beliefs. But let's set aside explanations that ignore the agency of the person. Let's assume that a necessary requirement of any solution to this problem is that God respects the agency of the believer. Couldn't God make the evidence of his existence so clear and so overwhelming that a person could not misinterpret it and would inevitably believe? For example, whenever a person harbored doubts about God's existence, couldn't God cause a burning bush to pop up out of the ground (or the floor, if one was indoors) and inform the non-resistant, but potentially skeptical, person that she is standing on holy ground and that God loves her and has a wonderful plan for her life? Or whenever they were confronted with a skeptical argument, couldn't God dispatch an angel to provide the clearest possible refutation of that argument? (And, of course, the angel would do so sounding exactly like Morgan Freeman.) Of course, God could do both of these things—his acting in this way is both logically possible (the action does not entail a logical contradiction) and metaphysically possible (it is consistent with the laws of metaphysics). But the more interesting questions are, "Would he?" and, per Schellenberg's claims, does God's love entail that he *must* do so? These are questions that can only be answered with reference to God's purposes in revealing himself to humanity in the first place.

Let's grant that God could in fact reveal himself in a way that would cause a skeptical person to believe that they were in the presence of an all-powerful being. But would such a revelation elicit worship? Would such a revelation even be a genuine revelation of God? Would it make possible that which God actually desires: a relationship? Not necessarily. Even if propositional belief that God exists is necessary for relationship with God, it is not sufficient. Schellenberg's error is that he construes a person's awareness of God as being analogous to a person's awareness of the full moon in the night sky on a clear night. One might miss the moon, but only if one was deliberately directing one's attention away from the night sky. If one looked up, one couldn't avoid the belief that the moon was full without actively resisting the belief. The error here is not epistemological; it is theological. The Christian theist's approach differs precisely because God is not an object, but a subject. The question is not whether God (or, if you wish, "the ultimate") exists, but what kind of God or ultimate being exists? Consequently, God's revelation is not aimed at making it such that more people possess the belief "God exists" but rather at bringing people to the place where they desire to bow a knee to God and enter into loving relationship. This point is powerfully illustrated by James 2:19, which says, "So you believe that God exists? So what! Even Satan and the demons believe that" (my paraphrase). The point being made in this passage is that it is possible to fully affirm the existence of God but wish that it wasn't true, or to wish that the God that existed was different or more consistent with one's philosophical or moral commitments. In terms of theological axiology, *mere* propositional belief that God exists is relatively unimportant.

The theological perspective motivating this response to Schellenberg can be expressed in the form of a pair of conditions on God's self-revelation: (1) God's revelation would respect the agency of the person and (2) the knowledge of God that would result from God's revelation must be knowledge of a person rather than an object, concept, or principle. The implication of the first condition is obvious. God's self-revelation operates within the boundaries of human freedom. The implications of the second condition are equally important. Because God is revealed only as a personal being, knowledge of God can never have the sort of objective status that occurs with knowing about the existence of an object. Rather, knowledge of God requires what Kierkegaard calls "inwardness" or "subjectivity."[19] Notice that even when Scripture speaks about the supposed universal knowledge of God in Romans 1:19–20, it is not the mere facticity of God's existence that is known but rather his "eternal power and divine nature" (ἀΐδιος αὐτοῦ δύναμις καὶ θειότης [*aidios autou dynamis kai theiotēs*]). Knowledge of God is not knowledge of trivia but is intended to be personal knowledge that results in awe or worship. Those seeking the latter will also come to know God's existence, those seeking the answer to the trivia question will possess neither. Of course, the subjectivity of knowledge of God doesn't suggest a theological nonrealism where God isn't real until he is known by a person.[20] Rather, God is not real unless he is known as a personal being and related to with spiritual sensitivity. As C. Stephen Evans says (following Kierkegaard), "When a human being is not spiritually attuned, God is not experienced as real, and in a sense God is not real for that person."[21]

19. Evans, "Can God Be Hidden and Evident," 243.

20. For a critique of anti-realist readings of Kierkegaard, see Evans, "Realism and Anti-Realism."

21. Evans, "Can God Be Hidden and Evident," 244.

Here is another instance in which Schellenberg's language of "nonresistant nonbelievers" gets complicated. The salient question is not merely whether a nonbeliever is resistant or not, but *to what* they might be (or might not be) nonresistant. For instance, I might be wildly nonresistant to receiving a raise from my university, but that doesn't mean that I would accept any conditions associated with such a raise. I would not accept a raise even if that meant I had to teach five times the number of classes I currently teach or if I had to replace my teaching duties with administrative duties. Similarly, a nonbeliever might be nonresistant to coming to know whether God exists, but not be at all open to relationship with the God that exists, and certainly not any relationship with God that places moral expectations or constraints on their behavior.

In summary, while it is clear (to my mind at least) that a loving God would desire to be in relationship with every human person, it isn't clear that a loving God would desire any sort of relationship with humans. For instance, God isn't open to a relationship with humans where humans see themselves as God's moral and intellectual equals. Why? Because that would be to allow humans to believe something that is false and even destructive to our sense of ourselves and our role in the universe. As such, it is important to see that God's openness to relationship is openness to a particular sort of relationship with humans. Consequently, there are actions that are within God's power to perform that could result in there being no nonresistant nonbelievers, but this would result in a problematic relationship with God. Of those actions, riffing on the famous song by Meatloaf, God might say: "I'll do anything for relationship with nonbelievers, but I won't do that."

Evaluating the Epistemic Hiddenness Argument

My response to Schellenberg's hiddenness argument can be summarized as follows: (1) The notion of nonresistance to belief in God is complicated, far more complicated than Schellenberg's argument acknowledges. (2) Schellenberg's argument gives us no good, all-things-considered reason to think that God is not open to relationship and has not provided evidence of his existence, even if there are people who are nonresistant and not (currently) in possession of evidence for God's existence. (3) There are a number of good theological reasons to think that God's self-revelation would not be coercive and would be aimed at those who were not only nonresistant but also possessed a desire for personal and relational knowledge of God, as opposed to mere propositional knowledge.

But there is a crucially important question lurking in the vicinity of this argument. Suppose the nonresistance in question was not mere nonresistance to the proposition that God exists, but nonresistance to relationship with God, and suppose the timing of the question was not "at any moment" but was "at the end of all things." Would a perfectly loving God allow there to be people who were nonresistant to authentic relationship on Judgment Day? This question presses a different version of divine hiddenness question: the problem of soteriological hiddenness.

SOTERIOLOGICAL HIDDENNESS

In the contemporary apologetic literature addressing the hiddenness of God, it is God's epistemic hiddenness that has received the majority of attention. This battle has largely (but not exclusively) been waged at the intersection of theism, atheism, and agnosticism. But reflection on implications of the particularity of the Christian message of salvation has always been a part of the Christian tradition. The soteriological hiddenness of God is an apologetic problem for traditional Christian belief in that it calls into question God's goodness in creating a world and a system of redemption that seems to leave so many without the sort of opportunity that Scripture seems to suggest God desires his lost sheep to receive (Matt 18:12–14//Luke 15:3–7).

From Schellenberg's perspective, the concept of God's epistemic hiddenness is not "evil" per se;[22] it is just a feature of the world in which we live, a feature that he argues should cause us to reject the existence of an all-good, personal God. But from the perspective of Christian theism, the soteriological hiddenness of God is directly parallel to the problem of evil. In its simplest form, the problem of soteriological hiddenness concerns the alleged logical incompatibility of God being all-powerful and perfectly loving and the fact that some people seem to lack an opportunity to be saved. The argument against God's existence from soteriological hiddenness can be expressed as follows:

1. If a loving God exists, then no person will fail to receive a salvific opportunity.

---

22. Schellenberg, *Hiddenness Argument*, 31.

2. There are people who fail to receive a salvific opportunity.
3. Therefore, no loving God exists.

The defense of the first premise often proceeds with an appeal to God's fairness. This appeal is problematic, for it isn't just obvious how the concept of fairness should apply here. In particular, shouldn't the demand be for justice, not mere fairness? However, the justification of the first premise via an appeal to God's fairness is unnecessary, for God's desire for the ubiquity of salvific opportunity is pretty clearly taught in Scripture. The second premise is an expression of the fact that there are some people who, it seems, do not have access to the teachings of a particular religious tradition. From the perspective of that tradition, such people might be said to be "unevangelized" or "lacking salvific opportunity." This concept is more complicated than it appears on the surface and requires some unpacking.

Who Are the Unevangelized?

The description of a "nonbeliever" is relatively straightforward. A person is a nonbeliever if they lack belief in God and take an agnostic stance on God's existence or if they believe that God does not exist and embrace atheism. Matters are more complicated when describing those who lack salvific opportunity, simply because the matter of what it takes to receive a salvific opportunity is hotly debated. For instance, from a Christian perspective, has a person who lives in Mongolia in the ninth century BC received an opportunity to be saved? If hearing and responding to the gospel of Jesus Christ is necessary, then obviously not. But if all that is required for salvation is a faith commitment to God, then perhaps the denizen of Mongolia has received a salvific opportunity. If this person sees the starry night sky and commits himself fully and faithfully to the Creator of the stars, then some in the Christian tradition would argue that his lack of theological knowledge about his Savior doesn't change the fact that he has embraced with faith the God that actually exists.

So there will be disagreement on who is and who is not actually unevangelized, but we can coherently talk about three categories of people who might be seen as lacking a salvific opportunity. The first category is the typical one. Consider the aforementioned example of a person who lives in Mongolia in the ninth century BC. This person is temporally and geographically isolated from any presentation of the Christian gospel message. And, of course, there have been millions of people who have lived after the death of Christ who still have not heard the gospel. Schellenberg makes a big deal of this fact, calling it an example of "pre-doubt." He argues that *Homo sapiens* pre-date the advent of the major theistic religions by at least fifty thousand years, and while they believed in a complex mixture of gods and spirits, they didn't believe in the all-powerful, perfectly loving God of Christian theism.[23]

There are also more complicated examples, such as infants who died before developing the capacity to understand notions of sin and salvation and persons with intellectual disabilities. These examples are controversial for two reasons, because there are some who might argue that intellectual disabilities are no barrier to awareness and commitment to God and because there are many who would argue that infants are already saved. (Most would apply this very same argument to persons with intellectual disabilities.) The proffered means of their salvation vary, whether it be election, baptism, or an "age of accountability" principle, but genuine questions about the salvation of such people remain.

Finally, there is the most controversial category of "unevangelized," a set of people that I have termed the "pseudo-evangelized."[24] If the unevangelized are people who have not "heard" the gospel, the pseudo-evangelized are people whose "hearing" has been complicated, conflicted, or incomplete. Perhaps it is best to say that the pseudo-evangelized either have not truly heard the gospel or have not heard the true gospel. Consider Kunta Kinte, a character in Alex Haley's work of historical fiction, *Roots*.[25] He was born in the Gambia in 1750, enslaved at seventeen, and brought to North America. Kunta hears about the God of his slave-owners, and he rightly rejects this God, because the God worshiped by white slave-owners evidently deems the rape, murder, and torture of Africans to be just fine. Has Kunta heard the gospel? He's heard the name "Jesus," and he's heard some Christian truth-claims, but he hasn't heard the gospel, the good news of Jesus Christ. And here's the central point: from the point of view of Christianity, if God desires that all people be saved, there is no way that God would deem the revelation experienced by Kunta to be satisfactory.[26]

23. Schellenberg, *Hiddenness Argument*, 76–79.
24. Beilby, *Postmortem Opportunity*, 10–15.
25. Haley, *Roots*.
26. There are many subtly different examples which might be called pseudo-evangelized. I discuss three such examples in *Postmortem Opportunity* (11–14), but there are undoubtedly more.

Responses to Soteriological Hiddenness

There are three categories of responses to soteriological hiddenness. The first, which I mention only to set aside, is *Agnosticism*. This response avers that Scripture speaks only to the question of what one must do to be saved, not to the question of what happens to those who do not hear. Consequently, according to Agnosticism, the problem of soteriological hiddenness is a question that we cannot answer and shouldn't even try.[27]

The second category of response is called *Restrictivism*. The hallmark of Restrictivism is an acknowledgement that there are some who do not have an opportunity to be saved—salvific opportunity is restricted in scope. But Restrictivists nonetheless defend the existence and goodness of God as being compatible with the lack of universal accessibility of salvation. As such, the Restrictivist denies the first premise (1) in the above argument: "If a loving God exists, then no person will fail to receive a salvific opportunity." Charles Hodge neatly summarizes this view as follows: "There is no faith, therefore, where the gospel is not heard; and where there is no faith, there is no salvation."[28] Restrictivists do not typically deny the universality of knowledge of God, as they typically affirm that Romans 1:19–20 teaches that all have awareness of God's existence, but they deny that such knowledge is sufficient for salvation. In the words of Bruce Demarest, "General revelation elicits the anxious interrogation, 'What shall I do to be saved?' It prompts the question and poses the difficulty, but it cannot provide the solution."[29] Restrictivism is typically conjoined with (and justified by) a Calvinist soteriology, but it is possible to be an Arminian Restrictivist.

The third category of response to the soteriological problem of divine hiddenness is *Accessibilism*. The Accessibilist seeks to deny the second premise (2) of the above argument, holding that salvation is accessible

---

27. I set this answer aside because even if the soteriological hiddenness question is difficult to answer with complete confidence, it is better to try to answer and be measured about that answer than to have no meaningful response to this important question. The viability of the agnostic answer to soteriological hiddenness depends crucially on the impossibility or invalidity of other answers. If there are good answers, then the agnostic stance is a non-starter. Of course, this does not mean that there will be no remaining unanswered questions; it means only that the attempt to offer at least the framework of an answer is worth the effort.

28. Hodge, *Systematic Theology*, 2:648.

29. Demarest, *General Revelation*, 70.

to all people.[30] There are a number of varieties of accessibilism, each differing in their assessment of how salvation is accessible to all apart from hearing the gospel. *Universal Opportunity* claims that, despite appearances to the contrary, all will receive an opportunity to be saved *in this life*. Those who do not hear the gospel through evangelism and preaching will be provided with a salvific opportunity through a vision or angelic visitation.[31] *Inclusivism* involves the affirmation that it is possible to be saved through general revelation. Using Hebrews 11:6 ("Without faith it is impossible to please God, because anyone who comes to him must believe that he exists and that he rewards those who earnestly seek him") as a template for salvific access, Inclusivists claim that a person who sees the majesty of God's creation and choses to worship the creator of the stars is responding to God's grace. Those who respond affirmatively to the grace God gives them are saved. Finally, *Postmortem Opportunity* is a version of Accessibilism which affirms that those who did not receive a premortem salvific opportunity will receive a postmortem opportunity to hear and respond to the gospel. This postmortem presentation of the gospel will be granted to all whom God knows to be in need of it and could occur in the intermediate state or on the Day of Judgment, depending on one's theological anthropology and eschatology.

One final view should be mentioned, a view that does not fit neatly into either the Restrictivist or Accessibilist categories. This view is called *Molinism*. Through God's middle knowledge, or knowledge of what would have happened, God providentially orders the world such that all people who would respond to the gospel will have an opportunity to hear it.[32] By implication, therefore, all people who do not receive an opportunity are such that they never would have responded to the gospel, even if it had been presented to them. This view has Restrictivist elements in its claim that God is perfectly good even though some do not receive a salvific opportunity, and it is Accessibilist in its affirmation that all who would have responded do, in fact, receive an opportunity.

---

30. As I will argue below, not all versions of Accessibilism are successful in their denial of (2).

31. Geisler, *Sin and Salvation*, 465.

32. Craig, "No Other Name," 172–88. In *Postmortem Opportunity* I characterized Craig's answer to the destiny of the unevangelized problem as a version of Universal Opportunity (92–94). I now view that characterization as a mistake. It is better understood as a hybrid.

An Apologetic Evaluation of these Responses

My evaluation of these answers comes with an important caveat. There is no theologically neutral standpoint from which to evaluate these theories. One's answer to the apologetic problem of soteriological hiddenness will be determined primarily by *theological* commitments, assumptions, and desiderata, not *apologetic*. And while I admit that it is folly to allow theological commitments to be determined solely by apologetic utility, I will nonetheless offer an assessment of the apologetic utility of these answers to the problem of soteriological hiddenness.

Restrictivists respond to the problem of soteriological hiddenness by acknowledging that some lack salvific opportunity, but explaining how God can be perfectly good and loving nonetheless. The Restrictivist acknowledges that God is soteriologically hidden to some and offers a theological explanation, typically in the form of a Calvinistic approach to election. On this view, God chooses to provide irresistible grace to some but not all people, and those who lack salvific access are people whom God has not elected.[33] Theologically speaking, the greatest challenge for Restrictivists is maintaining the lack of lack of salvific opportunity in the face of the many passages that seem to clearly teach that God desires all to be saved. John 3:16, "for God so loved the world that he gave his one and only Son," and 1 Timothy 2:4, "[God] wants all people to be saved and to come to a knowledge of the truth," are commonly cited, but there are many others (e.g., Eccl 3:11; Matt 23:37; Heb 2:9; 2 Pet 3:9; 1 John 2:2). From an apologetic point of view, Restrictivism is a tough sell. This is a problem not because Christian doctrines should only be embraced if they are apologetically plausible—a dangerous and unstable theological mindset, for what is deemed plausible is always changing!—but rather because it is the task of the Christian apologist to present the truths of the Christian faith in their most persuasive form. The difficulty of defending the perfect goodness of God in the face of the claim that God does not desire all to be saved is significant.

The various versions of Accessibilism all argue that salvific opportunity is given to those who do not hear the gospel of Jesus Christ. But the affirmation of Accessibilism is not the same as denying the second premise of the soteriological hiddenness argument. Consequently, while

---

33. This is complicated, because a Calvinist could affirm that people who have not heard the gospel are elect. Moreover, it is certainly possible to be a Calvinist Accessibilist.

each of the above versions of Accessibilism articulates an account of how salvation can be accessible apart from hearing the gospel, these accounts are not all equal as answers to the problem of soteriological hiddenness.

The claim made by the defender of Universal Opportunity that God makes himself and his offer of salvation known to every person in this life (either through a dream or vision or angelic visitation) is utterly implausible. If such widespread revelation was offered, there would certainly have been some historical footprint or account of it. One could try to account for this by claiming that the world religions are a response to God's universal offer of salvation, but such a claim would open the door to religious pluralism. Further, Universal Opportunity has no response to cases of pseudo-evangelism, babies who die in infancy, or the cognitively disabled. Those cases would have to be explained in another way.

Inclusivism is a significant improvement on Universal Opportunity in that it provides a more plausible explanation of the salvation of adults who live in a time and place separated from the gospel.[34] But, like Universal Opportunity, Inclusivism is not a theory of universal accessibility of salvific opportunity. It does not (by itself) have any way to account for the salvation of infants, the intellectually disabled, or the pseudo-evangelized.

The Molinist solution to the problem of soteriological hiddenness is fascinating and controversial. It constitutes a significant improvement on Restrictivism in its ability to affirm that God provides a salvific opportunity to every person who would respond affirmatively. But this response to soteriological hiddenness only works if the concept of middle knowledge is itself viable—which is a matter of significant debate.[35] But even if it is viable, there is something disturbing about the fact that so many of the people who evidently "would have never responded to the gospel under any set of circumstances" are people of color. This objection is complicated, for one might claim in response that the fact that Christianity flourished in the Caucasian West rather than in Africa or Asia is an accidental, contingent fact about Christianity. Nonetheless, given Christianity's dubious history with devaluing persons of color, any theory that

---

34. I am not here taking a stand on the debate whether salvation requires explicit faith.

35. The most significant objection to Molinism is called the "grounding objection." See Adams, "Middle Knowledge," 109–17; Davison, "Craig on the Grounding Objection," 365–69. William Lane Craig's response to the grounding objection can be found in "Middle Knowledge, Truth-Makers," 337–52.

implies that there was a possible scenario in which a large percentage of people of color that have existed would *never* have chosen God is apologetically problematic. Moreover, it is unclear whether the Molinist solution has any answer to the problem of the pseudo-evangelized. How does the Molinist's affirmation that "all who would respond to the gospel will have an opportunity" when dealing with Kunta Kinte? Or does the Molinist have to claim that the pseudo-evangelized all suffer from transworld damnation and that there is no possible world in which they would have responded affirmatively? Hence, the pseudo-evangelized constitute a worrisome counterexample to William Lane Craig's claim that, given the Molinist solution, "no one is lost because of lack of information due to historical or geographical accident. All who want or would want to be saved will be saved."[36]

THE APOLOGETIC UTILITY OF POSTMORTEM OPPORTUNITY

I will close this chapter with a close look at the apologetic utility of the theory of Postmortem Opportunity. I do this for two reasons: it constitutes a meaningful answer to both epistemic and soteriological hiddenness, and it has been commonly (and quite unfortunately) dismissed in contemporary Christian apologetic discourse.

Postmortem Opportunity as Response to Divine Hiddenness

Among all the various answers to the problem of soteriological hiddenness, only Postmortem Opportunity can claim that there is no person who has existed or will exist, whether they be unevangelized, an infant, a cognitively disabled person, or pseudo-evangelized person who will fail to have an opportunity to hear the gospel. There are many ways to imagine what this might look like, but I think that C. S. Lewis's description of Aslan's encounter with Emeth in *The Last Battle* provides a compelling image. Emeth is a young Calormen who spent his entire life serving Tash (a wholly evil being who is the functional equivalent of Satan). However, when walking through the stable door into an eschatological realm of beauty and happiness, he is approached by Aslan (a lion and the Narnian equivalent of Jesus). Emeth falls at his feet and thinks, "Surely this is the

36. Craig, "No Other Name," 185.

hour of death, for the Lion (who is worthy of all honour) will know that I have served Tash all my days and not him."[37] But Aslan embraces him, saying, "Son, thou art welcome," and goes on to explain, "All the service thou hast done to Tash, I account as service done to me." Aslan explains that he and Tash are opposites and therefore, "No service which is vile can be done to me, and none which is not vile can be done to him."[38] As such, despite the fact that Emeth believed that he was seeking Tash his entire life, Aslan informs him that, "Unless thy desire had been for me thou wouldst not have sought so long and so truly. For all find what they truly seek."[39]

Lewis contrasts the postmortem response of Emeth with that of the dwarves, who, despite being Narnians (Aslan's chosen people), had thoroughly hardened their hearts and were unable to see Aslan for who he is. They respond to Aslan's attempt to reach them not with belief but with fear and mockery, and they justify their skepticism, saying, "Well, at any rate there's no Humbug here. We haven't let anyone take us in. The Dwarfs are for the Dwarfs."[40]

It is important to set God's offer of a postmortem opportunity in the correct soteriological context. It is an opportunity for people to see and respond to the God they did not know, but perhaps have been seeking their entire life. There are segments of contemporary Christianity who, in their zealous and understandable efforts to emphasize the importance of a personal decision for Christ, have obscured the fact that following Christ is not solely a decision made at an altar call. It is a decision made every day. Every day our choices become dispositions, which become habits, which become our character. And that character is either formed in a way open to loving God and neighbor, or it is not. Moreover, this is true of all people, whether we call ourselves "believers" or whether we do not. Lewis makes this point powerfully when he says: "The world does not consist of 100 percent Christians and 100 percent non-Christians. There are people (a great many of them) who are slowly ceasing to be Christians but still call themselves by that name: some are clergymen.

---

37. Lewis, *Last Battle*, 164.

38. Lewis, *Last Battle*, 164–65.

39. Lewis, *Last Battle*, 165. Some see the story of Emeth as supportive of Inclusivism, not Postmortem Opportunity. I discuss this argument in *Postmortem Opportunity*, 272–77.

40. Lewis, *Last Battle*, 148.

There are other people that are slowly becoming Christians though they do not call themselves so."[41]

Further, a postmortem opportunity isn't the soteriological equivalent of a pop quiz. There is no need to see the postmortem salvific opportunity offered by God as demanding an immediate and rushed answer. Here's how to make sense of that idea. Suppose there is such a thing is hypertime, where multiple moments can be contained within a single moment—or, more precisely, there are multiple hyper-moments contained in a single temporal slice of time.[42] Given the reality of hypertime, God could provide a person with as much time as they needed to respond to the gospel. I'm not sure the concept of "needing time to make the salvific decision" is theologically sound, but if time was needed, it could be granted.

The theory of Postmortem Opportunity is also an answer to the problem of divine epistemic hiddenness. Those from whom God has been epistemically hidden in this life, whether they live as believers or skeptics, will have an opportunity to know God—not through the clumsy arguments of natural theology, but personally. At this point, whether or not a person is resistant will be revealed and one's motives for seeking knowledge of God will be laid bare. As a result, some people who have, by all outward appearances, followed God for their entire life will find that their religious efforts were directed at something other than God. This is the message of Matthew 7:22–23: "Many will say to me on that day, 'Lord, Lord, did we not prophesy in your name and in your name drive out demons and in your name perform many miracles?' Then I will tell them plainly, 'I never knew you. Away from me, you evildoers!'" On the other hand, there will be those who, for whatever reason, lacked explicit belief in God in this life but nonetheless had a heart that was open to relationship with God and who, upon receiving a postmortem opportunity, choose to bow a knee to the God they were implicitly seeking their entire life.

---

41. Lewis, *Mere Christianity*, 176.

42. On hypertime, see Hudson, *Fall and Hypertime*; "Essay on Eden," 273–86. Thanks to Tom McCall and Hud Hudson for correspondence on this matter.

Biblical and Theological Objections to Postmortem Opportunity

Postmortem Opportunity is an answer to both the epistemological and soteriological forms of the divine hiddenness problem. But the apologetic persuasiveness of these answers depends on the theological viability of the concept of a postmortem opportunity itself. There are a number of objections to Postmortem Opportunity. I will mention five of the most common.[43]

1. Scriptural objections: A common objection to a postmortem opportunity is that Scripture teaches that death is the end of salvific opportunity. Those who make this claim typically appeal to Hebrews 9:27: "People are destined to die once, and after that to face judgment." This passage, it is claimed, teaches that judgment comes immediately after death. Moreover, there is no mention of a postmortem opportunity. At best, this constitutes an argument from silence, but even if this passage could be taken as teaching that judgment follows immediately after death (which is, frankly, dubious), it would not rule out a postmortem opportunity, for the most plausible timing of a postmortem opportunity is on the Day of Judgment itself.

A second scriptural passage used to argue against postmortem opportunity is the parable of Lazarus and the Rich Man in Luke 16:19–31. In this passage, not only is there no mention of postmortem opportunities to hear the gospel; the reference to the "great chasm" dividing the saved and unsaved in the afterlife is often taken to suggest that one's salvific fate is set at death. It is important to note that this is a parable—an odd parable, but a parable nonetheless. This parable speaks not to the details of the eschatological state, but to the salvific irrelevance of worldly wealth. Moreover, the oddness of this parable can be explained by the fact that Jesus, it seems, adapted a common Egyptian story and used it to critique the Pharisees who were "fond of money" (Luke 16:14). Finally, if this passage is taken as a description of the eschatological state, it describes a situation in which believers can view the suffering of unbelievers—a proposal that most people (other than Jonathan Edwards) regard as theologically problematic.

2. Second chance? Does a postmortem opportunity constitute a second chance to be saved, one that decreases the motivation to follow

---

43. A more complete discussion of the objections to postmortem opportunity can be found in my *Postmortem Opportunity*, particularly chapters 4, 6, and 7.

Christ in this life? There are versions of postmortem opportunity that allow for ongoing postmortem chances as a means to universal salvation, but there is also a non-universalistic version of postmortem opportunity. On this view, God provides a postmortem opportunity to those that he knows did not receive a meaningful opportunity in this life. The postmortem opportunity does not secure a second chance for anybody, but rather the universality of a first chance.

3. *Motivation for Missions?* If Christians come to believe that God provides a postmortem opportunity to those who do not hear the gospel in this life, doesn't that eliminate the motivation to tell people about the gospel now? This objection is based on some problematic assumptions. Our motivation for evangelism should not flow from the belief that "we are the only hope for these people" but on the fact that God has commanded that we "go into all the world." We go out of obedience, not because God has no ability to achieve the *missio Dei* without us. Further, the reason why we spread the gospel now is because of the intrinsic, this-worldly value of the Christian way of life. Salvation is not just about punching a ticket to heaven, but as living for Christ now, in this life. Finally, this objection illicitly assumes that all who experience a postmortem opportunity will respond affirmatively. That assumption is not justified, which leads to the next objection.

4. *Who could say no to Jesus?* On this objection, all who experience a postmortem opportunity will be saved. Universalists are unbothered by this claim, but there are good reasons to reject this assumption. While there will be no atheists on Judgment Day, that doesn't mean that all will embrace relationship with God. The obvious precedents for this claim are Lucifer, who was with God in heaven and still rebelled, and Adam and Eve, who joined Satan's rebellion despite walking with God in the garden. Understanding the possibility of people rejecting their postmortem opportunity requires a proper understanding what is and what is not offered in the postmortem opportunity. The question asked by God will not be, "Do you believe I exist?" or, "Would you rather experience joy in heaven or burn in hell?" The question will be the question of Milton's Satan: "Do you want to reign in hell or serve in heaven?"[44]

5. *Why not before?* Regarding the possibility of postmortem opportunity, Schellenberg would undoubtedly press the following question: If such a direct personal encounter was possible on Judgment Day, why

---

44. Milton, *Paradise Lost* 1.263 (22).

isn't it possible in this life? Now, I think there is a good answer to this question, but suppose there was not. Is it a serious problem if we lacked an answer to this question? I don't think it is. My inability to answer this particular question constitutes an epistemic problem for Christianity only if the following is true: "If God has a good reason for not fully revealing himself personally at one time and not at another, then that reason would be apparent to me."[45]

The response to Schellenberg's question forces us to return to the matter of God's purposes in revealing himself. His revelation, whether on Judgment Day or before, is not aimed to produce belief that he exists, but to provide an opportunity to enter into a salvific relationship. Schellenberg's protestations that propositional belief is necessary for relationship and that therefore a perfectly loving God should provide an encounter that provides an opportunity for propositional belief ignores some important theological realities. First, not everything that is necessary but not sufficient is a good thing when taken by itself. The initial incision in a life-saving surgery is necessary, but by itself is harmful. Second, to again utilize a surgery analogy, when a person is on death's door, more aggressive, atypical surgical options become palatable. The provision of a postmortem opportunity to those who God knows have not had an opportunity to hear and respond to the gospel is that sort of last-minute, life-saving intervention. Finally, if God provides a premortem opportunity for salvation to people, it is difficult to see how such a revelation on our part doesn't create a swamping problem for any Christian effort to teach, disciple, and spread the gospel. Per my comments above, I'm not saying that it eliminates our *duty* spread the gospel, but it pretty clearly eliminates the *need* for it.

Ultimately, Schellenberg's claims about what a perfectly loving being would do in the face of nonresistant nonbelief are correct with respect to a postmortem opportunity for the unevangelized and pseudo-evangelized. God, as perfectly loving, would not allow a person who truly did not know about the possibility of relationship with God to be separated from him for an eternity. God would provide a postmortem opportunity to determine whether that person's nonbelief was nonresistant or not.

---

45. This point is also made by Evans, "Can God Be Hidden and Evident," 251.

CONCLUSION

The apologetic problems of divine hiddenness are challenging. Yet, as demonstrations of the falsity or epistemic invalidity of Christian theism, they must be judged as failures. Given certain common skeptical assumptions, they might explain why skeptics find belief in God to be problematic, but they give few reasons for Christians to join them in their skepticism.

BIBLIOGRAPHY

Adams, Robert M. "Middle Knowledge and the Problem of Evil." *American Philosophical Quarterly* 14 (1977) 109–17.

Anderson, Charity. "Divine Hiddenness: Defeated Evidence." *Royal Institute of Philosophy Supplement* 81 (2017) 119–32.

———. "On Providing Evidence." *Episteme* 15.3 (2018) 245–60.

———. Review of *The Hiddenness Argument: Philosophy's New Challenge to Belief in God*, by J. L. Schellenberg. *International Journal for Philosophy of Religion* 86 (2019) 85–89.

Beilby, James. *Postmortem Opportunity*. Downers Grove, IL: InterVarsity Academic, 2021.

Coakley, Sarah. "Divine Hiddenness or Dark Intimacy? How John of the Cross Dissolves a Contemporary Philosophical Dilemma." In *Hidden Diversity and Religious Belief: New Perspectives*, edited by Adam Green and Eleonore Stump, 229–45. Cambridge: Cambridge University Press, 2016.

Craig, William Lane. "Middle Knowledge, Truth-Makers, and the 'Grounding Objection.'" *Faith and Philosophy* 18 (2001) 337–52.

———. "'No Other Name': A Middle Knowledge Perspective on the Exclusivity of Salvation through Christ." *Faith and Philosophy* 6 (1989) 172–88.

Davidson, Scott A. "Craig on the Grounding Objection to Middle Knowledge." *Faith and Philosophy* 21.3 (2004) 365–69.

Demarest, Bruce A. *General Revelation: Historical Views and Contemporary Issues*. Grand Rapids: Zondervan, 1982.

Dougherty, Trent, and Ted Poston. "Divine Hiddenness and the Nature of Belief." *Religious Studies* 43 (2007) 186–89.

Evans, C. Stephen. "Can God Be Hidden and Evident at the Same Time? Some Kierkegaardian Reflections." *Faith and Philosophy* 23 (2006) 241–53.

———. "Realism and Anti-Realism on Kierkegaard's *Concluding Unscientific Postscript*." In *The Cambridge Companion to Kierkegaard*, edited by Alastair Hanney and Gordon Marino, 154–76. Cambridge: Cambridge University Press, 1997.

Geisler, Norman. *Sin and Salvation*. Vol. 3 of *Systematic Theology*. Minneapolis: Bethany, 2004.

Haley, Alex. *Roots*. New York: Dell, 1976.

Hodge, Charles. *Systematic Theology*. 3 vols. Grand Rapids: Eerdmans, 1940.

Hudson, Hud. "An Essay on Eden." *Faith and Philosophy* 27.3 (2010) 273–86.

———. *The Fall and Hypertime*. New York: Oxford University Press, 2014.

Jordan, Jeffrey. "Divine Hiddenness and Perfect Love." *European Journal for Philosophy of Religion* 9.1 (2017), 187–202.

Lewis, C. S. *The Last Battle*. New York: Collier, 1970.

———. *Mere Christianity*. Reprint, New York: Macmillan, 1978.

Milton, John. *Paradise Lost*. Introduced by Philip Pullman. Oxford: Oxford University Press, 2005.

Nietzsche, Friedrich. *Daybreak: Thoughts on the Prejudices of Morality*. Translated by R. J. Hollingdale. New York: Cambridge University Press, 1982.

Schellenberg, J. L. *Divine Hiddenness and Human Reason*. Ithaca, NY: Cornell University Press, 1993.

———. *The Hiddenness Argument: Philosophy's New Challenge to Belief in God*. New York: Oxford University Press, 2015.

———. "The Hiddenness Argument Revisited (I)." *Religious Studies* 41 (2005) 201–15.

———. *The Wisdom to Doubt: A Justification of Religious Skepticism*. Ithaca, NY: Cornell University Press, 2007.

6

An Historical Case for the Resurrection of Jesus of Nazareth

Gary R. Habermas and Benjamin C. F. Shaw

For the past several years Gary Habermas has been working on his *magnum opus* on Jesus' resurrection.[1] The project is the culmination of fifty years of research and is projected to be four volumes on the resurrection of Jesus and related topics.[2] The first volume covers historical method and evidence, and the second focuses entirely on responding to alternative theories. The third volume is a scholarly survey of contemporary positions on major resurrection questions, while the fourth volume will address worldview, theological, and practical considerations.

The purpose of this chapter is to develop a list of recent scholarly observations, along with a few conclusions that emerged from the first volume of the four-volume study. It is likely that these texts will be the

---

1. Benjamin Shaw has been working alongside Habermas for over a decade and throughout this project (including as the editor of volume 3, of which he organized the format and structure of an outline of contemporary views on well over 150 key questions and far more critical scholarly citations surrounding resurrection studies). Ben wrote both his MA thesis and his PhD dissertation on subjects such as these. In recent years he has become a recognized published researcher himself.

2. At present, three of the four volumes have been submitted to the publisher.

largest publication(s) on Jesus' resurrection, as the first volume (*On the Resurrection: Evidences*) has recently been published at over one thousand pages.[3] Due to the length of volume one and the decades of research involved, it will be helpful to highlight some key facets, apparent and emerging trends, and lessons that have been observed throughout the process. Because of the length of this first volume, it should be obvious that only brief details can be addressed in this essay.

THE MINIMAL FACTS APPROACH

It will be important to note first the method used in *Evidences* since this was part of the research that started in the 1970s. The Minimal Facts Approach (MFA) developed by Habermas has become one of the most popular methods for discussing Jesus' resurrection. Indeed, it has even been suggested that the MFA has reached a "near exclusive use in Christian apologetics."[4] Part of the reason for its success and effectiveness is precisely because it employs only a relatively minimal amount of highly evidenced historical data, as noted in volume one. Further, even atheist and agnostic New Testament scholars virtually always agree with these facts, thereby providing a historically strong place to begin discussing the appearances of the risen Jesus.

To state this information more succinctly, the MFA provides this evidential foundation by utilizing two criteria. First, each fact must be supported by *multiple lines* of historical evidence. Second, these facts are *widely accepted* by virtually all critical scholars in relevant disciplines from diverse theological backgrounds. Of these two criteria, it has always been emphasized that "the first is by far the most crucial."[5] The reason for this is obvious. It is precisely the multiple lines of historical reasonings of the first criterion that provide the epistemic ground for the facts themselves.

---

3. Habermas, *Evidences*. One might think that this seemingly confirms the adage (and its variations) that Scripture is simple enough for children to grasp, yet deep enough for theologians and other scholars to continually study.

4. McGrew, *Hidden in Plain View*, 220–21. It may be worth noting that the MFA can extend beyond just resurrection research. See, for example, Casabianca, "Shroud," 414–23.

5. Habermas, *Evidences*, 92.

Christianity Contested

Criteria for a Minimal Fact
1. A fact must be supported by multiple lines of evidence.
2. The fact is widely agreed upon by scholars from diverse theological backgrounds in relevant research areas.

We should expect that if there were multiple lines of evidence we would also have something of a consensus upon them. Thus, in some ways, the second criterion follows from the first. Yet there is another advantage of the second criterion. It allows the discussion to begin on already agreed upon data rather than having to convince one's dialogue partner of a whole host of historical data points or to accept that these facts are only idiosyncratically held by those who already believe. In other words, it helps mitigate against claims of bias.

So, what are these facts? It should be noted at the outset that the facts presented can vary depending upon one's situation or context.[6] The most recent list of minimal facts presented by Habermas is the following:

Minimal Facts[7]
1. Jesus' death by crucifixion
2. The disciples had experiences of what they believed to be the risen Jesus
3. The early proclamation of Jesus as risen
4. The transformed lives of the disciples and of Paul
5. The conversion of James, Jesus' skeptical brother
6. The conversion of the church's persecutor, Paul

These "Minimal Facts" are derived from a longer list of "known historical facts" that contains other important historical data related to Jesus' resurrection. However, in an effort to use as much scholarly agreement as possible, the shorter list of Minimal Facts is often used instead of the longer list. This longer list is similarly well attested, but as the list of facts grow, the number of scholars accepting more and more facts will likely decrease. Thus, having both lists can be helpful, though as the number of facts increase, it may be more difficult to have equally high agreement (though still a majority). The longer list of known historical facts includes the following:

---

6. For those interested in a more detailed description as to the MFA, its criteria, and lists of facts see chapters 4–5 in Habermas, *Evidences*.

7. Found in part 3 of Habermas, *Evidences*.

AN HISTORICAL CASE FOR THE RESURRECTION OF JESUS

Known Historical Facts[8]
1. Jesus' burial
2. The disciples' despair after the crucifixion of Jesus
3. Jesus' tomb was empty
4. Jesus' resurrection was a central Christian teaching
5. Events were initially proclaimed in Jerusalem
6. Church started and grew with Sunday as the primary day of worship

The MFA has been an effective method for presenting some important and crucial facts surrounding Jesus' resurrection. Alternative theories have repeatedly had trouble providing a solid historical explanation for these facts, while Jesus' resurrection more comfortably accounts for them. As Angus Menuge recently commented regarding a debate on Jesus' resurrection, the MFA explains why "one skeptical alternative after another to the historical fact of the resurrection has been abandoned, leaving critics with shrinking cover to hide."[9]

RELIABILITY AND THE RESURRECTION

The MFA is distinct from the reliability approach to establishing Jesus' resurrection. Some prefer to show that the New Testament documents are reliable and trustworthy in their various claims. This obviously includes claims about Jesus' resurrection. These two approaches, while different, should not be understood as mutually exclusive but complementary efforts.

Indeed, some who have studied and/or utilized the MFA specifically have also argued for the reliability of the New Testament more broadly. This includes both Michael R. Licona and Ben Shaw. Both of these researchers wrote dissertations that covered aspects of the MFA. Yet, the MFA was only the beginning for us as we both have gone on to develop our own arguments regarding the general reliability of the NT.[10] Moreover, scholarship has appeared to move more conservatively regarding the reliability of the New Testament since the 1970s (when the MFA was developed). Of course, it should be obvious that a more robust case can

---

8. Found in part 3 of Habermas, *Evidences*.

9. Menuge, "Debating Christian Theism (Book Review)," 456.

10. See Licona, *Why Are There Differences?*; Shaw, *Trustworthy*. See also Licona's most recent book on the subject, *Jesus, Contradicted*.

be made when one adds additional considerations for New Testament reliability. One might think of the minimal facts as those that are the "most reliable" in the NT.

However, there are tradeoffs with these approaches. While the MFA is able to simply present a weighty case for Jesus' resurrection, it is more limited in what it is seeking to establish. By contrast, a reliability approach will yield more information but also will be more open to debate, require more unpacking, and risks getting off the topic of Jesus' resurrection by moving into discussions of reliability itself. Here we might think that context may be our best guide, but that the MFA provides the more versatile approach due to its methodology.

SCHOLARSHIP IS NOW MORE CONSERVATIVE

While both approaches have their place, it is worth noting that reliability approaches may be easier to use today than, say, in the early to mid-1900s.[11] The authors have often discussed the differences between the times when both started their own studies into the historical Jesus. For example, as Habermas developed the MFA in the 1970s, New Testament scholars like Rudolf Bultmann and Karl Barth were some of the most influential scholars. For very different reasons, these two were significantly uninterested in the historical facts surrounding the claims of the New Testament. Historical reliability was not as widely accepted among critical scholars.

The changes between the time leading up to the 1970s and the 2000s are significant. As we will see below, the second or new quest for the historical Jesus (from roughly 1953 to 1970) began to advance important considerations regarding historical reliability, especially as it relates to the criteria of authenticity. This concern similarly grew during the third quest (1980–present) along with a growing emphasis on understanding Jesus within the surrounding Jewish cultural milieu. The point here is simply to note that there was a shift occurring in New Testament studies regarding the value of history as well as the historical reliability of the NT.[12]

---

11. For an additional discussion on this and other aspects, see Beck and Shaw, "Habermas," 772–78.

12. Another change worth noting is that in the early 1990s Richard Burridge famously and convincingly argued that the Gospels were Greco-Roman *bioi*. His work has been very decisive and is now the consensus view regarding the gospel genre. This is important because it tells us something important about what the Gospel writers thought they were doing and what they were *not* doing. They were not, for example, writing fictional novels. See Burridge, *What Are the Gospels?*

AN HISTORICAL CASE FOR THE RESURRECTION OF JESUS

Then, in the 1990s, about two decades after Habermas developed the MFA, Princeton's James Charlesworth pointed out that there was widespread agreement on the reliability of the historical bedrock of the Gospels.[13] More recently, Robert Bowman and Ed Komoszewski have pointed out that despite years of research and discovery, *"there is not a single well-evidenced historical fact about Jesus that undermines the 'orthodox' view of Jesus."*[14] They are certainly correct when they then conclude that this is "no minor matter."[15]

Thus, conversations about reliability may be much easier today than they were a few years ago, especially when Habermas was beginning in the 1970s. As Habermas developed his MFA, he did not have the shoulders of this scholarship to stand on at that time. His MFA was (and is) a fruitful approach to Jesus' resurrection, but especially so with those who are more skeptical. The reliability approach is a similarly fruitful approach, and this is even more so today as a number of scholarly arguments from a diversity of angles and levels demonstrate.

The scholarly ethos of Habermas's 1970 era is thus different to that of scholarship today. While many of the arguments for reliability used today have also been found in the past, the point we are highlighting is that the scholarly trend leading into the 1970s did not, for a variety of reasons, assume the basic reliability of the New Testament as much as scholars do today.[16] We can thus see why an MFA approach would be effective in such an environment, while today we have even more arguments at our disposal.

BODILY RESURRECTION AND LINGUISTIC STUDIES

The bodily nature of Jesus' resurrection appearances has been another trend that has seen considerable positive development, especially since

---

13. Charlesworth, "Jesus Research Expands," 5–7.

14. Bowman Jr. and Komoszewski, "Historical Jesus and the Biblical Church," 23, emphasis original.

15. Bowman Jr. and Komoszewski, "Historical Jesus and the Biblical Church," 24.

16. An example of this is that although the Gospels were thought to be biographical in nature, debate about their genre was occurring in 1970s and 1980s. In fact, Burridge set out to argue against the Gospels as biographies but changed his views as he studied the evidence. Moreover, we are not arguing that nobody held to the New Testament as being reliable, only that it was not the dominant view.

the 1970s. Yet, the bodily appearance view was not absent in the decades of the 1960s and 1970s. The strongest example was Robert Gundry's crucially important volume, *Sōma in Biblical Theology*.[17] In this work Gundry analyzes the use of the word "body" (*sōma*) in the New Testament (emphasizing Paul in particular). One of his findings is that Paul's use of the Greek word *sōma* has to do with material, physical bodies, which is especially important for our understanding of a text like 1 Corinthians 15:44 ("it is sown a natural body, it is raised a spiritual body. If there is a natural body, there is also a spiritual *body*" NASB).[18] Gundry notes, for example, that Paul is "exceptionless" in his use of *sōma* as referring to a physical body.[19]

As noted above, during the 1980s, in the third quest for the historical Jesus, there was a renewed appreciation for the Jewish context of Jesus. While these aspects cannot be pursued further here, it is worth pointing out that during these years there was a slow dismantling of the influence of the history-of-religions school that sought to show that Jesus' resurrection was derived from (or similar to) other dying and rising gods.[20] Ultimately, Jesus' resurrection is best understood within Second Temple Judaism.

In 2003, 2010, and 2018 three additionally significant works were written by, respectively, N. T. Wright, Michael Licona, and John Granger Cook.[21] While Licona provides some helpful insights on how the aorist passive of ὤφθη (*ōphthē*: "appeared" [e.g., 1 Cor 15:5–8]) did, in multiple instances, refer to events in space and time, Wright and Cook focus on the Greek words ἀνίστημι (*anistēmi*: "raise up, rise" [e.g., Acts 2:24]) and ἐγείρω (*egeirō*: "arise, raise/raise up" [e.g., used multiple times throughout 1 Cor 15]) that refer to physical bodies being raised. Thus, each of these in their own ways has further contributed to the arguments regarding the physical and bodily nature of resurrection in general, including Jesus' resurrection appearances. One might even be surprised that members of the Jesus Seminar have similarly recognized these points as

---

17. Gundry, *Sōma in Biblical Theology*, 159–83. Also helpful here is Robinson, *Body*.
18. Gundry, *Sōma in Biblical Theology*, 161–83.
19. Gundry, *Sōma in Biblical Theology*, 168.
20. One example here is Smith, *Drudgery Divine*.
21. See chapters 3–8 in Wright, *Resurrection of the Son of God*; chapters 6–7 in Cook, *Empty Tomb*, with excellent summaries on pages 1, 568–69, 591–93; Licona, *Resurrection of Jesus*, esp. 400–440. Also relevant here is Ware, "Resurrection of Jesus," 475–98.

well. John Dominic Crossan and Jonathan Reed point out the resurrection was used to denote a bodily event.[22] While rejecting literal resurrection appearances themselves, they emphasize that Paul's own teaching in passages like 1 Corinthians 9:1, 15:8, and elsewhere is enough to clearly prefer his primary sources over Luke's secondary texts in Acts, thereby deciding that for Paul, Jesus appeared to him bodily. Therefore, they "bracket" Luke's "blinded-by-light sequence."[23]

Of course, if Jesus' resurrection appearances were understood as bodily events, then that has significant implications for how we understand certain texts. On this view, it makes sense that the empty tomb would have been implied in 1 Corinthians 15:3–8, in that, as the authors above point out, the Greek terms require bodily events. The physicality of these terms also complicates (undermines) alternative views that have sought to spiritualize the resurrection or turn it into a metaphor of sorts.

CULTIVATING THE CRITERIA OF AUTHENTICITY

The criteria of authenticity have to do with certain historical principles that, when met, add to the historical probability of an event occurring. So, for example, if multiple independent sources report an event, then it is more likely to have occurred. Or, if an account reports embarrassing material (an event at odds with its interests), then that, too, may add credibility to these reports. A short list of the criteria may be presented as follows:

- Multiple independent attestation
- Enemy attestation
- Embarrassing testimony
- Coherence or contextual credibility
- Criterion of dissimilarity

In the early 1950s, Ernst Käsemann gave a lecture that would help change the direction of historical Jesus research. Though he was a follower of Rudolf Bultmann, Käsemann suggested that more historical

---

22. Crossan and Reed, *In Search of Paul*, 343. See Crossan, "Resurrection of Jesus," 29–57. See also Borg and Crossan, *First Paul*, 150; cf. their own view on 151.

23. Crossan and Reed, *In Search of Paul*, 8.

information could be known about Jesus. While historians were using some criteria prior to Käsemann, there was a renewed interest and hope that these criteria could help provide historians with a more scientific and objective historical approach to studying Jesus.

Unfortunately, it appeared that some historians apparently thought that the use of the criteria would yield identical portraits of Jesus. Some may have been hoping that these criteria of authenticity would have been similar to scientific criteria and yield similar results. Yet this was emphatically not the case. Indeed, there was such a plurality of portraits that Crossan refers to this as a "bad joke" within historical Jesus research.[24]

There are a few reasons for this, and we might just briefly note a few of them here. Some may have thought that these criteria could be applied in a mathematical manner as though the criteria were a calculator that one simply input the figures and get the results. Others valued some criteria more so than others so that the weight of the evidence would then vary. There was and is not a universally agreed upon list of criteria (though there some core criteria that are found far more often than others). The criteria did not resolve the issue of interpretation that was still involved once certain events were established to have occurred.

Rather than abandon the use of criteria altogether, some have pointed out the value of the criteria along with their proper limitations.[25] Others, like Ben Meyer, have pointed out that these criteria are like proverbs. Though they are true, it requires wisdom to know how to properly apply the right proverb in the right context (as with the criteria).[26] Moreover, as Bart Ehrman has noted, the criteria help historians to better "ferret out" what is likely to have occurred from a source even if they think it is basically an unreliable text.[27] Lastly, it has also been observed that these criteria typically only add probability to a report.[28] If, for example, there is only a single report of an event, as opposed to multiple independent

---

24. Crossan, *Historical Jesus*, xxvii. Similarly, Borg, *Jesus*, 9–10.

25. One work that argues against the criteria (or, in some cases, a more limited dependence upon the criteria) is Keith and Le Donne, *Jesus*. This book has received a number of solid responses, such as those from Licona, "Is the Sky Falling," 353–68; Bock and Komoszewski, *Jesus, Skepticism*.

26. Meyer, *Critical Realism*, 141.

27. Ehrman, *How Jesus Became God*, 94.

28. The only possible exception to this is generally contextual credibility or coherency. If it is reported that the apostle Peter was riding a motorcycle, then that would count against such a report because it fails to be contextually credible. While this is an extreme example, not all are so easy to navigate.

AN HISTORICAL CASE FOR THE RESURRECTION OF JESUS

reports, that is not a mark against the single report. Rather, events that have multiple reports are simply weightier.

This begins to highlight why historians have typically found these criteria to be helpful. They assist in both MFA and reliability approaches because they provide some of the lines of argumentations used by historians. In a recent publication, Kevin Burr has highlighted how classicists use these criteria (albeit without referring to them as the criteria of authenticity), but so do those in New Testament studies that claim to question the applicability of these criteria.[29]

Accordingly, the MFA has found great benefit in these criteria because they provide widely used historical measures that add probability to these reported events having occurred historically. Reliability approaches, too, will appreciate these tools since they can add to the weight of a New Testament author who has continually shown that their claims are probable, and thus they are a generally reliable source.

SIXTEEN ADDITIONAL OBSERVATIONS AND CONSIDERATIONS

In this section, we want to briefly and concisely highlight sixteen additional observations. Some of these points we may spend a little more time on than others, but each of these sixteen facets adds its own nuance. These sixteen takeaways were some of the chief topics that emerged during the many years of study that resulted in this initial volume of resurrection trends and evidence.

(1) During the more than century-long heyday of nineteenth-century German theological liberalism, naturalistic and other challenges to beliefs in Jesus' resurrection arose and grew in popularity among critical scholars. From Friedrich Schleiermacher to David Strauss to Wilhelm Bousset, different theses and variations were suggested, went through many discussions and subsequent variations, and the majority eventually fell by the wayside.[30]

In contrast, ever since the demise of German liberalism and largely due to factors such as the influential works of Karl Barth and Rudolf Bultmann, these ideas began to fall into dispute, for more than one reason.

---

29. Burr, *Authenticating Criteria in Jesus Research*.

30. As explained in much detail in volume 2 of *On the Resurrection*. See also Brown, *History of the Quests*.

These changes were most often due to either growing fideistic efforts that eschewed historical efforts to either bolster or critique Christianity, or a growing number of conservative trends. There were exceptions to these overall inclinations, though the present popularity of the "Third Quest for the Historical Jesus" during the last third of the twentieth century until the present has largely kept these naturalistic and other similar trends at bay.

Presently, in spite of what might be considered flareups,[31] fewer natural or other alternative theses are being proposed by critical scholars. Much more common are responses such as "something happened," often with the added rider, "but we do not know exactly what occurred." A widespread Humean backdrop or perhaps some variety of agnosticism often stands in the shadows. Yet, many scholars in relevant fields of study today embrace resurrection beliefs of some species.

(2) Besides the less critical emphasis on alternative hypotheses, another recent trend is that even fewer critical scholars are actually willing to choose a single naturalistic thesis and stick with it, no matter how much pushback is forthcoming. Although not spelled out in so many words, one often gets the sense that the contrary historical data are strong enough that the critics do not wish to find themselves stuck with their chosen thesis for fear that, after an alternative theory is endorsed, the historical facts will quickly call it into question.

(3) A few decades ago, Habermas published his research that approximately 70–75 percent of critical scholars at that time had expressed their views that Jesus' burial tomb had been discovered empty a short time later.[32] The most current investigation of this scholarly count indicated that in the intervening time, the positive critical response has risen to 80 percent acceptance of the empty tomb, perhaps due at least in part to the research from the Third Quest for the Historical Jesus.[33]

It is clear that an empty tomb by itself does not require that Jesus had been raised from the dead. But as noted by N. T. Wright, this event combined with the bodily appearances form the crux of the overall case for Jesus' resurrection.[34] This especially applies to the cognate question of the nature of Jesus' appearances, as addressed below.

---

31. See Habermas, "Late Twentieth-Century Resurgence," 179–96.

32. Examples include Habermas, *Risen Jesus and Future Hope*, 23–24, 45n127; "Resurrection Research," 140–41; "Experiences of the Risen Jesus," 292.

33. See chapter 15 in Habermas, *Evidences*.

34. Wright, *Resurrection of the Son of God*, 686–96, 709–10.

(4) Which indications constitute the best overall evidences for Jesus' resurrection appearances? Views may fluctuate among commentators, but three considerations will be mentioned here. Even for the most critical scholars as a whole, Paul's testimony is nearly always taken to be the most reliable in the New Testament.[35]

The best reason for affirming Jesus' appearances to his followers is that just three years after his conversion when he met Jesus, Paul traveled to Jerusalem to dialogue with Peter and James the brother of Jesus (Gal 1:18–20, including the Greek term *historēsai* in verse 18). Scholars agree on the historicity of Paul's trip and that it occurred in AD 35–36, or just five to six years after the crucifixion. Not only was this an exceptionally early testimony,[36] but Paul interviewed two of the other direct witnesses to appearances of the resurrected Jesus in relation to the gospel message that he had been preaching (especially a second trip in Gal 2:1–10, where the apostle John was also present).

Paul's two trips to Jerusalem allowed him to hear firsthand the resurrection testimonies of the original disciples who had also observed the appearances of the risen Jesus as he stood before them after his death by crucifixion. It likewise ensured that these earliest teachings were not hearsay of some sort, in that these initial observers were the original sources of the information and agreed with Paul on the nature of the gospel message itself (Gal 2:2, 6, 9). Bart Ehrman asked the rhetorical question of how we could "get any closer to an eyewitness report" than with Paul's interview.[37]

(5) The second-best evidence for Jesus' resurrection appearances are arguably the very early creedal traditions, which are usually brief comments that were repeatedly taught orally, before being written down subsequently. Many of these teachings are usually dated even by skeptical scholars to the decade of the AD 30s, therefore predating by years the writing of the Gospels, as well as the earliest of the epistles, including Paul's. In a large majority of these cases, the central message in these usually very brief texts such as Acts 1:22–28, Romans 1:3–4 and 10:9, and

---

35. Such as agreed by Jesus Seminar member, Hoover, "Was Jesus' Resurrection an Historical Event?," 78–79.

36. The radical Jesus Seminar as a group even concluded that at least the information regarding the events recorded in 1 Corinthians 15:3–7 were probably in existence and known prior to Paul's conversion in AD 33 (Funk and the Jesus Seminar, *Acts of Jesus*, 454; cf. 533)! See detailed discussion on scholarly views in Ware, "Resurrection of Jesus," 475–98.

37. Ehrman, *Did Jesus Exist?*, 145–46; cf. 101.

1 Corinthians 15:5–7 was the gospel message content of the deity, death, and resurrection appearances of Jesus.[38]

Besides the highly valuable nature of the eyewitness testimony described in the previous point above, dozens of these generally compact sayings from this exceptionally early time period occasioned the birth of Christianity and its beginnings. Oddly enough, several of the best scholarly treatments of these texts were written decades ago.[39]

(6) The third-best evidence for Jesus' resurrection appearances may lag slightly behind the two strongest ones, but this category includes a number of criteria or rules that help scholars judge between particular historical and non-historical events or sayings. Often acknowledged as the strongest test among these standards is that of multiple independent attestation, where different types of separate benchmarks agree in attesting to the occurrence of an event or teaching of Jesus. The resurrection appearances enjoy multiple independent attestation which, again, support their historicity and do so from a variety of different angles than those above. Furthermore, like the other two considerations for historicity, these are often employed by more skeptical scholars, as well.[40] Stein states that "the cumulative effect" of several such tests can make it very difficult to dismiss certain events or teachings in the life of Jesus.[41]

(7) Of the approximately dozen appearances of the resurrected Jesus reported in the New Testament texts, there is widespread agreement that the initial appearance to "the twelve" (e.g., 1 Cor 15:5) is the best-attested of these events.[42] Depending on how the sources are counted, several sources report that Jesus appeared to his closest group of followers very shortly after his death by crucifixion. For example, Crossan[43] and the Je-

---

38. For seminal works on the creeds, see Cullmann, *Earliest Christian Confessions*; Dodd, *Apostolic Preaching*; Neufeld, *Earliest Christian Confessions*. For an analysis of Jesus' deity, death, and resurrection within the early church, see Taylor, *Jesus Before Constantine*.

39. Cullmann, *Earliest Christian Confessions*; Dodd, *Apostolic Preaching*; Neufeld, *Earliest Christian Confessions*.

40. Ehrman, *Did Jesus Exist?*, 288–93; Funk and the Jesus Seminar, *Acts of Jesus*, 25–26, 32–35. A longer list of almost a dozen of these tests is provided by Stein, *Gospels and Tradition*, 153–87.

41. Stein, *Gospels and Tradition*, 185–86.

42. Cf. Dale Allison's comment: "We need not doubt that it really happened" (*Resurrection of Jesus*, 61).

43. Crossan, *Historical Jesus*, esp. 436.

sus Seminar[44] each list several independent sources for this appearance, although they both differ somewhat from each other and even seemingly within their own treatments.

(8) Though a worthwhile topic for a dissertation, it still appears from an initial overview of the research that more critical scholars support the position that Jesus actually appeared to his disciples after his death than those researchers who deny the reality of the appearances altogether. Some of these scholars hold the view that while Jesus actually did appear, he did so in a somewhat less physical form than that depicted in the Gospel resurrection narratives. Rather, they hold that the early disciples saw Jesus in appearances that were more similar to the three accounts in the book of Acts 9, 22, and 26 that describe the appearance of Jesus to Paul on his way to Damascus.[45] However, both positions share the central affirmation that Jesus actually did appear after his death (and Luke includes both). The latter position was quite popular in the last few decades of the last century and can still be found among recent authors.

(9) As indicated above, scholarly views regarding the New Testament teaching on the nature of Jesus' appearances to his followers favor bodily appearances. It needs to be repeated here that many of these critical scholars may reject the actual appearances themselves, while determining that the New Testament taught bodily appearances. From Paul's own writings, then, the indications are that the teachings of this apostle were that Jesus appeared bodily to his followers, as generally agreed even among most of the researchers who *personally* deny Jesus' appearances entirely. This is presently the predominant interpretation of Paul's writing.

(10) The fact that at least portions of the canonical Gospel data are being treated more regularly and seriously in the literature is one contributing reason to the recent trends mentioned in this essay. In part, this is due to the recognition that there were earlier and independent sources that were utilized by each the Gospel authors. Potential examples include the "M" source being used by Matthew, the "L" source by Luke, the "Q" sayings by both Matthew and Luke, the "Signs Gospel" by John, and possibly the teachings of Peter as well as a pre-Markan passion narrative by

---

44. Funk and the Jesus Seminar, *Acts of Jesus*, 449–50, 452, 454.

45. For a description and contrast of these two types of appearances, see Crossan and Reed, *In Search of Paul*, 6–10, 341–45. Crossan and Reed are examples of the researchers who hold that the New Testament view is that Jesus appeared bodily, though they reject that position personally (8, 341–43, 345).

Mark. Obviously, if any of these or additional sources were made use of, they had to predate the Gospels themselves. If they also contained some reliable information, that could potentially increase the accuracy of various Gospel reports of Jesus' actions and teachings. As a result, this is one of the influences on various scholars who have become more inclined to use at least portions of the Gospels as assisting in reconstructing the life of the historical Jesus, especially if independent corroboration is also available for any of the material.[46]

(11) In the more than three hundred pages of material that supported the half-dozen minimal facts that are discussed in Habermas's *On the Resurrection: Evidences*,[47] an average of some fifteen to twenty major and minor considerations supported each of these six individual occurrences. As explained therein, there is admittedly some overlap in these numbers, plus other items to consider when arriving at these general counts. The number of details pointing to each fact could also differ among individual evaluators (as was also stated often in the aforementioned volume). With these nuances in mind, it nevertheless seems rather remarkable that there is anywhere near such numbers of supporting reasons on behalf of just a half-dozen ancient reports. If the stakes were not so high with regard to whether or not Jesus' resurrection appearances actually occurred, many other ancient facts would hardly be questioned at all if they were as equally well attested.

(12) One enigmatic topic is the application of Bayes's Theorem[48] to historical events and human testimony in general. Often not well understood and perhaps even more rarely embraced and applied in cases of historical events today,[49] a few scholars have waded into this topic, though the calculations cannot be discussed in detail here. Two recent philosophers, Richard Swinburne[50] and Timothy McGrew,[51] have

---

46. The skeptical Jesus Seminar included charts of potential routes regarding how some of these texts might have predated and been used in each of the Gospel texts (Funk et al., *Five Gospels*, 17–18, 128.) For a volume that discusses more than a dozen of these areas of historical and other confirmation, see Shaw, *Trustworthy*.

47. See Habermas, *Evidences*, 281–593.

48. The name is taken from English philosopher and minister Thomas Bayes (1701–1761).

49. While not being very popular today, such calculations as applied to religious questions (such as the occurrence of miracles) were quite the opposite during seventeenth- and eighteenth-century European philosophical discussions. Even David Hume was a proponent of computing the likelihoods of miracles by utilizing calculus. See Kennedy, *History of Reasonableness*, 127–67, esp. 150–51; on Hume, see 158–61, 164.

50. Swinburne, *Resurrection of God Incarnate*.

51. McGrew and McGrew, "Argument from Miracles."

developed detailed studies that apply Bayes's Theorem to the resurrection of Jesus. Swinburne concluded after his examination that even beginning with the prior knowledge of just 50/50 for God's existence,[52] the likelihood that the Jesus' resurrection occurred is still 97 percent![53] McGrew and McGrew place Jesus' resurrection at 99.9 percent. They conclude that "there is no such thing as a finite prior probability that is so low as to be 'slippery' and hence impossible to overcome by evidence."[54]

(13) It is often, even if not usually, agreed even by more skeptical critical scholars that the "high Christology" taught in the New Testament originated from the very early belief that Jesus had appeared again after his death.[55] Jesus made a number of extraordinary claims that were sometimes misunderstood at the time. But the momentous nature of the resurrection appearances led quickly and quite naturally to the realization by his followers that there would not have been a resurrection in the first place had Jesus' teachings been false or, worse yet, blasphemous. Therefore, at a very early date the appearances developed as the ultimate grounds on which the believer's most cherished theological beliefs are based.[56]

(14) An influential group of theologians took the next step beyond the previous point, arguing that the earliest Christology was in fact the very highest Christology of all![57] This view challenged the very popular, long-held notion that the most exalted canonical Christology was very likely what is found in John's Gospel, written some sixty-five years after the crucifixion of Jesus. Citing a variety of very early pre-Pauline traditions, including exalted notions such as pre-existence,[58] and remarking that neither the Fourth Gospel nor the book of Hebrews speak about Jesus in these revered terms, Caird and Hurst write, "But this will in turn lead us to an astonishing conclusion: the highest Christology of the New Testament is also its earliest."[59] Bauckham echoes this thought while

52. Swinburne, *Resurrection of God Incarnate*, 5, 31–33, 204, 211.
53. Swinburne, *Resurrection of God Incarnate*, 213–14.
54. McGrew and McGrew, "Argument from Miracles," 642.
55. Ehrman, *How Jesus Became God*, 3, 84.
56. As depicted in the exceptionally early creedal traditions (such as Rom 10:9; 4:25; 1 Cor 8:6; Phil 2:6–11; Heb 1:3), the Acts sermon summaries (as in Acts 2:22–28, 33–36; 17:30–31), as well as in the later Gospel texts (Matt 28:18–20; Luke 24:46–49; John 20:28–30).
57. Two such examples are Caird and Hurst, *New Testament Theology*, 343; Bauckham, *Jesus and the God of Israel*, x.
58. Caird and Hurst, *New Testament Theology*, 338–43.
59. Caird and Hurst, *New Testament Theology*, 343.

highlighting the ontological status of this theological claim: "The earliest Christology was already the highest Christology. I call it a Christology of divine identity."[60]

(15) Beliefs such as Jesus' resurrection appearances and a high Christology have implications for afterlife views, as well. The earliest believers who followed Jesus were persuaded not only that Jesus rose from the dead and was alive forever, but that they would rise, too, just as he did. This correlation proceeded naturally in that a resurrection would directly involve the afterlife. This is especially evident in Paul's teaching in 1 Corinthians 15, where the entire chapter moves from the early traditional testimony for Jesus' resurrection appearances, to these events being at the very center of the Christian faith, to the resurrection of believers. Given Jesus' resurrection, there was a direct line to the truths of the chief gospel message that followed, including the eternal life of God's kingdom.[61]

(16) Lastly, no matter how strong the historical and other sorts of data may be, especially when taken together as a whole,[62] the case for Jesus' resurrection definitely does not force anyone into making a faith-commitment to God. This is in keeping with the general fact that evidence does not compel belief. It must be remembered that, as in many walks of life such as religion and politics, worldviews and personal outlooks on life still too often tend to dominate the information itself. This is viewed most of all when a strong case has been made for a position, but individuals still walk away, especially if they failed to offer an alternative view that was capable of explaining all the data. Rather, further questioning may indicate that a different position is not a view that they wish to embrace, whether or not they are able to offer a cogent alternative explanation. Frequently, even emotions alone are capable of pushing individuals in other directions. This is good to keep in mind as part of the larger picture so as to maintain a balanced perspective.

---

60. Bauckham, *Jesus and the God of Israel*, x; cf. 30. Intriguingly, Bauckham dedicated this book "to co-workers in early Christology, Jimmy Dunn and Larry Hurtado." A couple of years later, Dunn responded in his book *Did the First Christians Worship Jesus?* by dedicating his volume "to Richard Bauckham and Larry Hurtado, partners in dialogue." This group of researchers, along with a few other scholars, began to be called "the high Christology club."

61. Ehrman, *Jesus: Apocalyptic Prophet*, 229–34, also, 166, 170, 217; Strawson, *Jesus and the Future Life*, esp. chapter 8, such as 223–24, also 219–21.

62. As summarized by Allison, *Resurrection of Jesus*, esp. 346, also 344, 356.

CONCLUSION

Throughout this chapter we have sought to provide some initial insights and overviews regarding one of the most extensive research projects on Jesus' resurrection. As this was a project that began decades ago, it was helpful to begin by highlighting some of the changes in the academic ethos concerning some of these facts.[63] Scholarly perceptions regarding the New Testament, for various reasons, were more negative and skeptical in the 1970s than they are today. Indeed, Bart Ehrman is more moderate in his skepticism than was a scholar like Bultmann.

In addition to highlighting some of these shifts, we also wanted to clarify the MFA as the method used in this research project. While reliability approaches have been growing in popularity, the minimal fact approach continues to be a valid approach. Areas of overlap shared by these two approaches include the bodily nature of resurrection in Second Temple Judaism and earliest Christianity along with the use of the historical criteria of authenticity.

Moreover, we were also able to highlight sixteen additional takeaways from this recent project. These were admittedly brief, but they are helpful indicators of some new and emerging trends and conclusions regarding the data surrounding Jesus' resurrection appearances.

BIBLIOGRAPHY

Allison, Dale. *The Resurrection of Jesus: Apologetics, Criticism, History.* London: T&T Clark, 2021.

Bauckham, Richard. *Jesus and the God of Israel: God Crucified and Other Studies on the New Testament's Christology of Divine Identity.* Milton Keynes, UK: Paternoster, 2008.

Beck, W. David, and Benjamin C. F. Shaw. "Gary R. Habermas: A Minimal Fact Ministry for Disciples and Doubters." In *A History of Apologetics: Biographical and Methodological Introductions*, edited by Benjamin Kelly Forrest et al., 772–78. Grand Rapids: Zondervan Academic, 2020.

Bock, Darrell, and J. Ed Komoszewski, eds. *Jesus, Skepticism, and the Problem of History: Criteria and Context in the Study of Christian Origins.* Grand Rapids: Zondervan Academic, 2019.

Borg, Marcus J. *Jesus, a New Vision: Spirit, Culture, and the Life of Discipleship.* San Francisco: HarperSan Francisco, 1987.

---

63. Undoubtedly others could have been added, such as the fact that David Hume's arguments against miracles appear to be much less influential today than in years past. This is a point noted by McGrew, "Of Miracles," 152–73.

Borg, Marcus J., and John Dominic Crossan. *The First Paul: Reclaiming the Radical Visionary Behind the Church's Conservative Icon.* New York: HarperOne, 2009.

Bowman, Robert, and J. Ed Komoszewski. "The Historical Jesus and the Biblical Church: Why the Quest Matters." In *Jesus, Skepticism, and the Problem of History: Criteria and Context in the Study of Christian Origins,* edited by Darrell Bock and J. Ed Komoszewski, 17–35. Grand Rapids: Zondervan Academic, 2019.

Brown, Colin. *A History of the Quests for the Historical Jesus.* 2 vols. Grand Rapids: Zondervan, 2022.

Burr, Kevin B. *Authenticating Criteria in Jesus Research and Beyond: An Interdisciplinary Methodology.* Biblical Interpretation Series 219. Leiden: Brill, 2023.

Burridge, Richard. *What Are the Gospels? A Comparison with Graeco-Roman Biography.* 2nd ed. Grand Rapids: Eerdmans, 2004.

Caird, G. B., and L. D. Hurst. *New Testament Theology.* Oxford: Oxford University Press, 1994.

Casabianca, Tristan. "The Shroud of Turin: A Historiographical Approach." *Heythrop Journal* 54.3 (2013) 414–23.

Charlesworth, James H. "Jesus Research Expands with Chaotic Creativity." In *Images of Jesus Today,* edited by James H. Charlesworth and Walter P. Weaver, 5–7. Valley Forge, PA: Trinity, 1994.

Cook, James Granger. *Empty Tomb, Resurrection, Apotheosis.* Tübingen: Mohr Siebeck, 2018.

Crossan, John Dominic. *The Historical Jesus: The Life of a Mediterranean Jewish Peasant.* San Francisco: Harper SanFrancisco, 1991.

———. "The Resurrection of Jesus in Its Jewish Context." *Neotestamentica* 37.1 (2003) 29–57.

Crossan, John Dominic, and Jonathan L. Reed. *In Search of Paul: How Jesus' Apostle Opposed Rome's Empire with God's Kingdom.* San Francisco: Harper SanFrancisco, 2004.

Cullmann, Oscar. *The Earliest Christian Confessions.* Edited by Gary Habermas and Benjamin Charles Shaw. Translated by J. K. S. Reid. Reprint, Eugene, OR: Wipf & Stock, 2018.

Dodd, C. H. *The Apostolic Preaching and Its Developments.* Grand Rapids: Baker, 1936.

Dunn, James D. G. *Did the First Christians Worship Jesus? The New Testament Evidence.* Louisville, KY: Westminster John Knox, 2010.

Ehrman, Bart D. *Did Jesus Exist? The Historical Argument for Jesus of Nazareth.* New York: Harper Collins, 2012.

———. *How Jesus Became God: The Exaltation of a Jewish Preacher from Galilee.* New York: HarperOne, 2014.

———. *Jesus: Apocalyptic Prophet of the New Millennium.* Oxford: Oxford University Press, 1999.

Funk, Robert W., et al. *The Five Gospels: The Search for the Authentic Words of Jesus.* San Francisco: HarperSan Francisco, 1993.

Funk, Robert W., and the Jesus Seminar. *The Acts of Jesus: The Search for the Authentic Deeds of Jesus.* New York: Harper Collins, 1998.

Gundry, Robert. *Sōma in Biblical Theology: With Emphasis on Pauline Anthropology.* Society for New Testament Studies Monograph Series 29. Cambridge: Cambridge University Press, 1976.

Habermas, Gary. *Evidences.* Vol. 1 of *On the Resurrection.* Nashville: Broadman and Holman Academic, 2024.

———. "The Late Twentieth-Century Resurgence of Naturalistic Responses to Jesus' Resurrection." *Trinity Journal* 22 NS (2001) 179–96.

———. "Resurrection Research from 1975 to the Present: What Are Critical Scholars Saying?" *Journal for the Study of the Historical Jesus* 3.2 (2005) 135–53.

———. *The Risen Jesus and Future Hope*. Lanham, MD: Rowman and Littlefield, 2003.

Hoover, Roy W. "Was Jesus' Resurrection an Historical Event? A Debate Statement with Commentary." In *The Resurrection of Jesus: A Sourcebook*, edited by Bernard Brandon Scott, 75–92. Santa Rosa, CA: Polebridge, 2008.

Keith, Chris, and Anthony Le Donne, eds. *Jesus, Criteria, and the Demise of Authenticity*. London: T&T Clark, 2012.

Kennedy, Rick. *A History of Reasonableness: Testimony and Authority in the Art of Thinking*. Rochester, NY: University of Rochester Press, 2004.

Licona, Michael R. "Is the Sky Falling in the World of Historical Jesus Research?" *Bulletin for Biblical Research* 26.3 (2016) 353–68.

———. *Jesus Contradicted: Why the Gospels Tell the Same Story Differently*. Grand Rapids: Zondervan, 2024.

———. *The Resurrection of Jesus: A New Historiographical Approach*. Downers Grove, IL: IVP Academic, 2010.

———. *Why Are There Differences in the Gospels? What We Can Learn from Ancient Biography*. New York: Oxford University Press, 2016.

McGrew, Lydia. *Hidden in Plain View: Undesigned Coincidences in the Gospels and Acts*. Tampa: Deward, 2017.

McGrew, Timothy. "Of Miracles." In *The Nature Miracles of Jesus: Problems, Perspectives, and Prospects*, edited by Graham Twelftree, 152–73. Eugene, OR: Cascade, 2017.

McGrew, Timothy, and Lydia McGrew. "The Argument from Miracles: A Cumulative Case for the Resurrection of Jesus of Nazareth." In *The Blackwell Companion to Natural Theology*, edited by William Lane Craig and J. P. Moreland, 593–662. Oxford: Blackwell, 2012.

Menuge, Angus. "Debating Christian Theism (Book Review)." *Philosophia Christi* 16.2 (2014) 451–56.

Meyer, Ben. *Critical Realism and the New Testament*. Reprint, Allison Park, PA: Wipf & Stock, 1989.

Neufeld, Vernon. *The Earliest Christian Confessions*. Grand Rapids: Eerdmans, 1963.

Robinson, John A. T. *The Body: A Study in Pauline Theology*. Chicago: Regnery, 1952.

Shaw, Benjamin C. F. *Trustworthy: Thirteen Arguments for the Reliability of the New Testament*. Downers Grove, IL: InterVarsity, 2024.

Smith, Jonathan Z. *Drudgery Divine: On the Comparison of Early Christianities and the Religions of Late Antiquity*. Chicago: University of Chicago Press, 1990.

Stein, Robert H. *Gospels and Tradition: Studies on Redaction Criticism of the Synoptic Gospels*. Grand Rapids: Baker, 1991.

Strawson, William. *Jesus and the Future Life*. London: Epworth, 1970.

Swinburne, Richard. *The Resurrection of God Incarnate*. Oxford: Oxford University Press, 2003.

Taylor, Doug E. *Jesus Before Constantine: The Church, Her Beliefs, and Her Apologetics*. Eugene, OR: Wipf & Stock, 2020.

Ware, James. "The Resurrection of Jesus in the Pre-Pauline Formula of 1 Cor 15:3–5." *New Testament Studies* 60.4 (2014) 475–98.

7

Faith and Science

Robin Collins

INTRODUCTION

IT'S COMMONLY THOUGHT THAT the success and findings of science undermine belief in God, particularly Christian theism. Many who hold this view acknowledge that theism is not strictly incompatible with science, but think it can only be defended through convoluted reasoning and special pleading. In this chapter, I attempt to uncover some of the major misconceptions underlying this claim, with each area of misconception given its own section heading. I conclude by briefly summarizing why I think the success and findings of science strongly support faith, particularly belief in God.

Since the major sections below can be read independently of each other, those pressed for time can fruitfully just read the sections of interest to them. Because of its importance, I start with the issue of evolution.

EVOLUTION

Darwin's theory of evolution probably gets top billing as the most cited reason for thinking science conflicts with religious faith. To examine this claim, I look at what I consider the major aspects of this conflict: ideas about the Bible, lack of design in nature, evolution as competition, and animal suffering, along with a couple of "big picture" ways they harmoniously fit together. I then show how Christians have plausible responses to these purported problems, and thus that they at most offer weak reasons for rejecting Christianity, though they might cause us to broaden our conception of what Christianity claims about the world.

The Bible: Many people, both atheists and religious believers, hold that the Bible and Darwin's account of origins through evolution are in conflict. They point to the early chapters of Genesis, particularly Genesis 1–2. But the seeming conflict arises only from certain *interpretations* of the early chapters of Genesis, often based on what I regard as an overly rigid idea of how we come to truth. I have spoken to or read about several young earth creationists who have advanced degrees in biology, such as paleontology, who nonetheless hold the view that one should start with interpreting Scripture *first* without any input from science, and if the text seems to conflict with standard science, one must simply reject standard science.

I believe this is a faulty hermeneutic. If one believes that both the Bible and what has been called the "Book of Nature" come from God, then it seems perfectly proper for religious believers to use the Book of Nature to help interpret Scripture, just as it is proper to use one part of the Bible to help interpret another. This means that one is justified in using the findings of science to help select between various otherwise plausible interpretations of the early chapters of Genesis. To illustrate, consider the conflict that seemed to arise between the Bible and the Copernican theory that the earth revolves around the sun and not the other way around. Literally interpreted, Scriptures such as Joshua 10:12–13, which describes Joshua stopping the sun in the sky during a battle, seemed to conflict with the apparent motion of the sun across the sky as the result of the movement of the earth, not the sun (see also Pss 19:6 and 93:1). To resolve this apparent conflict, most Christians today interpret these types of scriptures non-literally; instead, they are understood as a manner of speaking using common language about how things appear to us. We tend to use this language ("the sun rose in the East") despite our modern knowledge that technically speaking, it is the earth that is moving and not the sun.

In the case of evolution seeming to contradict the Genesis account, one should start with trying to understand the ancient literary genre of Genesis 1–3. Scholars who have done this typically claim that the early chapters of Genesis were never meant to teach us science in the modern sense, but rather to teach us deeper spiritual truths, such as that the heavenly bodies should not be seen as divinities to be worshiped, but creations of God. Interpreting Genesis 1–3 non-literally is both indicated by numerous literary markers in the text and fits the general role that narratives about pre-history played in the surrounding culture at the time of writing, namely that of providing a structure of meaning. From this view, which takes the history and the genre of the text seriously, it would be as much of a mistake to interpret the early chapters of Genesis literally as to take Jesus' parables literally.[1] The people Jesus mentions in parables were meant to illustrate spiritual principles and truths, not tell us about a particular person who lived. Understanding this does not negate the profundity of the message. The original hearers would have accepted this without a problem, and so can we. Finally, one could argue that insisting on a literal interpretation of Genesis is in part motivated by a form of a modern idolization of science in which it is implicitly assumed that the more literal discourse characteristic of much of science is the only discourse that can truly convey the nature of reality, with poetry and other literary genres being relegated to a lesser status for conveying truth.

Lack of Design: Darwin explained the apparent design of biological organisms in terms of chance processes and natural selection. To many, this made it appear that in Darwin's scheme, chance ruled the day. But let's look at this more closely. First, note that although we do have solid evidence that evolution occurred, we have *no* evidence that it was an unguided process; in fact, I would point to evidence to the contrary, that such processes were indeed perhaps guided, especially concerning the occurrence of the advanced reasoning capacities of humans. Second, contrary to what some have thought, I would say Darwin's theory did not eliminate the need for a designer but has just shown us that for some sort of design to be perceived, we have to look at a more fundamental level, such as the extreme fine-tuning of the cosmos required for evolution to occur. (See the concluding section of this essay.)

---

1. For a good defense of the literary interpretation (also sometimes referred to as the Framework view), see chapter 2 of Blocher, *In the Beginning*.

At most, Darwin showed that certain features of the world that we once attributed to design can in part be explained by chance mutations. But not everything is chance. Instead, one could take the view that God is in charge of the fundamentals in the ordering of the cosmos but has left much of the rest up to what appear to be chance processes. Among scientists themselves, we actually find considerable disagreement about the degree to which the overall structure of life was merely the result of historical accidents. For instance, the late Harvard University paleontologist Stephen J. Gould argued that if one reran the tape of life, it would turn out entirely differently. On the other hand, former Cambridge University paleontologist Simon Conway Morris says that even though chance and natural selection play a major role in evolution, the fossil record strongly suggests that because of the deeper structure of the laws of nature, evolution inevitably leads to various biological structures—such as the eye—and even to intelligent life like human beings.[2] Thus, he proposes that purpose could exist within a superficially chance-driven process.

Evolution as Competition: Now we come to big-picture considerations—what kind of story are we in? One often hears Darwinian evolution described as driven by the struggle and competition for survival, which to some religious believers might seem contrary to the idea of a loving God. This language of competition can be attributed to Darwin's being influenced by Thomas Malthus, a late eighteenth-century economist. Malthus argued that regardless of technological advances, human populations would always become limited by competition for resources.

However, describing evolution in terms of competition unduly anthropomorphizes the evolutionary process, as if it has intention. Here's a more neutral explanation of evolution: new genes or mutations that increase an organism's ability to reproduce tend to become more prevalent, eventually becoming dominant after many generations. For instance, the Delta variant of COVID-19, more contagious than the original virus, continuously increased in number compared to the original COVID-19 version, and the Omicron variant did the same relative to the Delta variant. This has made the Omicron variant the dominant variant at the time I am writing this. But it's not as though Omicron was actively striving to gain the upper hand over the Delta variant.

So are we in a story of ultimate competition? That's one story we could tell, though with considerable anthropomorphizing of nature. But

---

2. Gould, *Wonderful Life*; Conway Morris, *Life's Solution*.

if one were going to anthropomorphize evolution or look at its overall meaning, arguably cooperation and creativity play more central roles than competition. Robert Wright, for instance, has argued that the trend in evolution has been toward cooperation, from single-celled organisms to multicellular organisms, to social species (bees, ants, dogs, and so forth), and then ultimately to human beings.[3] Additionally, evolution could be considered as exhibiting something analogous to human creativity by constantly producing new adaptions, such as giraffes being selected for longer necks to access food that other animals cannot reach.

Animal Suffering: Many people feel that evolution has amplified the problem of reconciling animal suffering with a loving God. How could a loving God create a process that, for example, produces the malaria parasite, a seemingly "malicious" organism that wreaks havoc on its host? This has led some Christians to deny evolution and instead claim this suffering must be the corruption of creation as a result of the fall of Adam and Eve. However, it is hard to see how corruption could result in organisms like the malaria parasite: if the hard drive or SSD drive on your computer gets corrupted because of some sort of physical damage, that does not cause computer viruses. These viruses would have to be designed.

Similarly, just as the tiger must have the right teeth, digestive system, instincts, and so forth to find and consume its prey, and those characteristics therefore cannot plausibly be a mere corruption of an originally plant-eating animal, the malaria parasite must be well-constructed to do its dirty work.[4] So, who designed these kinds of organisms? Some Christians have suggested that Satan and his minions played a substantial role.[5] But if so, these angels would be in part the creator of much of life on earth, contrary to what the first chapter of Genesis suggests, especially Genesis 1:31, which says, "God saw everything that he had made, and indeed, it was very good" (NRSV). Or did God perhaps set in place a massive re-design program that was constructed to be activated when humans fell into sin? This not only seems unlikely but also doesn't really

---

3. Wright, *Nonzero*.

4. Notice that the malaria parasite example, and many others like it, go beyond the predator-prey relationship, which some might argue is part of God's good provision for creation. (For example, see the repetition of the goodness of creation in Genesis 1, along with Psalm 104:20–28 and Job 38:39–41.) Rather, this parasite seems more like a computer virus, serving no good purpose except damaging the computer's functioning. It is these sorts of cases many find particularly troubling.

5. For example, in chapter 9 of Lewis, *Problem of Pain*, 134–35. See also Plantinga, *Where the Conflict Really Lies*, 58–59.

solve the problem—a redesign program would be almost the same as God's directly creating the malicious organisms.

Arguably the theory of evolution actually reduces this theological problem of animal suffering since God is no longer the direct creator of "malicious" organisms. Rather, we could say they are the byproduct of God's aim of creating life via an evolutionary process that involves a large element of chance. Such a claim is much like the claim that moral evil is a byproduct of God's creating a world with free creatures. So the idea of God's using evolution to create life may actually offer a more satisfactory answer theologically.[6]

Harmonious Fit: Finally, when one looks at the big picture of the nature of the universe and how God interacts with it, there are major ways that Christian belief and evolution harmoniously fit together, a couple of which I will mention here. Christianity (and Islam) inherited from Judaism a developmental view of history, along with that of a linear view of time. For the Jews, God was acting in history to bring it to a climax with the coming of the Messiah. This fits in nicely with one of the big stories of modern science—the development of the universe from the Big Bang and the subsequent evolution of life. In contrast, every other religion and philosophy in the world that I have studied—such as Hinduism, Buddhism, and Ancient Greek philosophy—holds to the eternal existence of physical reality, typically claiming it went in infinitely repeating cycles.

Another emphasis within Christianity (and Judaism) that is congruent with evolution is that God works *within* the world to fulfill God's purposes. For example, all major Christian thinkers have denied that God merely dictated the Bible word for word—unlike, for example, what traditional Muslims claim about the Qur'an. Rather they held that God worked through our culture, history, and language in communicating to us. In fact, for Christians, the ultimate example of God's working within history can be found in the Incarnation, in which God comes into human history to redeem humanity. This suggests that God typically works within natural processes to bring about God's providential purposes, and only overrides these processes when necessary. Once we grant this, it should not be surprising to find that God might have worked through evolution to bring about our existence. This is not to deny direct divine

---

6. There are other ways Christian doctrine has been claimed to conflict with the theory of evolution. The big one under this category is the Christian doctrine of Original Sin. This is too big a topic to address here; however, I have written a book chapter on it that has since been serialized. See Collins, "Evolution and Original Sin."

interventions in the evolutionary process, but rather to suggest that this is not the way God typically operates. An example of such intervention might be what is often called the Great Leap Forward or the Creative Explosion—something that occurred around fifty thousand years ago when suddenly artifacts appeared in abundance that required symbolic thought: musical instruments, cave paintings representing mythological events, necklaces, and much more sophisticated tools than those created by our closest relatives at the time, the Neanderthals.[7]

God of Gaps and Miracles

A related reason people think science conflicts with belief in God is that they are under the mistaken impression that the only justification for belief in God is to explain events that science is not able to explain, such as cases of purported miracles, the existence of highly complex animal and plant life, and so forth. (This limited idea of God's role in the world is called the "God of the gaps," since under this idea God is invoked only to fill in gaps in scientific explanations.) Understandably, most scientists would not want to approve of a stop-gap God; that could be taken as bad science. But in fact, this stop-gap view of God's relationship to the world has been rejected by almost all major theologians and philosophers, at least in the Christian tradition. Rather, they would claim that insofar as God is invoked to serve an explanatory function (other than to explain seemingly miraculous events in answer to prayer or ones recorded in Scripture), it should only be used to explain those items that in principle fall *outside* of scientific explanation, such as why there exists a universe at all, or why it has life-permitting and science-friendly laws. Since by its nature science explains by appealing to physical entities and laws of the universe, it simply cannot explain why the universe exists or has the laws it does.

In addition, many would say it's best *not* to understand miracles as God's *intervening* in the course of nature, since this falsely assumes that the order of nature occurs independently of God, and thus something God has to override to fulfill the divine purposes. Rather, theists have always held that God sustains the order of nature, I would say in analogy to how a computer sustains a virtual reality. In a real sense, therefore, one could say that every occurrence in the world is a "miracle" in that it

---

7. See, for example, Pfeiffer, *Creative Explosion*; Longrich, "Evolution."

only occurs because of God's sustaining activity. This is something I think Christians should keep in mind instead of looking for God's special action as a sign of God's existence. And, insofar as miracles are typically defined as falling outside the normal order of nature, even if we grant that God might sometimes "intervene," I believe miracles are better understood as God's temporarily sustaining nature in a special, non-normal way.

Misunderstanding Faith and Reason

A further major part of the appearance of conflict between science and faith is a misunderstanding of the nature of faith and reason. To elaborate, I will start by looking at faith, then reason, and then more closely at the role of intuition and spiritual perception in understanding how faith and reason can work together.

Faith: Many believe that faith is opposed to science because they associate faith with belief based on authority, dogmatism, and credulity. Since scientific practice teaches us to value doubt and questioning, this often causes scientifically-minded people to be suspicious of religious faith. Particle physicist turned Anglican priest John Polkinghonre and Nobel Laureate Richard Feynman both cite this as a major reason why fellow scientists are wary of religion.[8]

But theists and Christians in particular should reject this idea of faith for two major reasons. First, responding to legitimately expressed doubts by saying that we just need to have "faith" might have been appropriate a thousand years ago in Europe when there was a single religious authority, such as the Roman Catholic Church; but today we are exposed to many, many competing authorities about non-scientific matters. So, what "authority" am I to believe? My parents? Those I grew up with? That is not a good way of finding truth: if a hundred different parents each disagree, it is very unlikely that mine would have the correct beliefs. Further, this response to doubt trains people to accept beliefs without evaluating the evidence, leading to such evils as superstition, conspiracy theories, racism, and so forth. We see this frequently in the political and cultural arena.

Second, authority-based faith is not the kind of Christian faith advocated in the New Testament. To begin, the faith of the early Christians

---

8. For Polkinghorne, see Polkinghorne and Weinberg, "Was the Universe Designed?" For Feynman, see *Meaning of It All*, 37.

involved rejecting many of the predominant ideas of the religious and secular authorities at the time. Although the early Christians believed at least in part based on what they perceived as the authority of Jesus, the Gospels never imply that Jesus requires that people believe without evidence, but rather sometimes suggest just the opposite. For example, in John 10:37–38 (NRSV) Jesus says, "If I am not doing the works of my Father, then do not believe me. But if I do them, even though you do not believe me, believe the works, so that you may know and understand that the Father is in me and I am in the Father" (also see John 5:36 and 15:24–25).

Further, in the Gospel texts Jesus gives his disciples much evidence that he was of supernatural origin, particularly in his post-resurrection appearances. Thus, if faith were merely believing without significant evidence as is commonly supposed, then the evidence Jesus gave would have greatly undermined the ability of the disciples to have faith—clearly an absurd conclusion. Further, pitting faith against certainty based on evidence conflicts with 1 Corinthians 13:13, which says that *faith*, hope, and love will remain in the heavenly state even though "we know fully, even as I have been fully known" (v. 12 NRSV). If faith will remain in the heavenly state where Christians will seemingly have complete evidence for Christian belief, it makes no sense that part of the *essence* of faith is belief without sufficient evidence, though that might be one manifestation of it in this life.

Finally, for those who accept the Hebrew Bible or Christian Scriptures as giving us examples of how to live, the two leading figures in the Hebrew Bible, Abraham and Moses, questioned what they took to be God's intentions: in the case of Abraham, the intention to destroy Sodom and Gomorrah (Gen 18:23–33), and in the case of Moses, to destroy the Israelites (Exod 32:7–14). In both cases, God is portrayed as listening to them and doing as they requested instead of what they perceived God was intending to do. This also occurs for the case of Jesus. In Matthew 15:21–28, a Canaanite woman asks Jesus to heal her daughter, and initially, Jesus seems to rebuff her. Refusing to accept "no" for an answer, she persists by offering a reason for why even those outside of Israel deserve healing. In response, Jesus says, "Great is your faith! Be it done for you as you desire" (v. 28 NRSV). So, in each of these cases, using one's reasoning and moral intuitions was rewarded. In fact, arguing with God is part of the Jewish faith, as exemplified by the word "Israel" which literally means "one who struggles with God."[9]

Reason: Another cause of the belief that science conflicts with faith lies in how we think of human reason, especially as used in science. To begin, people often falsely equate following reason with "making sense within our current framework of understanding," a view I call *false rationalism*. False rationalism often lies behind objections to Christianity based on our inability to (fully) understand central doctrines such as the Trinity and Incarnation. However, as the eminent sixteenth-century mathematician and thinker Blaise Pascal correctly noted, "The last step of reason is the recognition that there are an infinite number of things beyond it; it is merely feeble if it does not go as far as to realize that. If natural things are beyond it, what are we to say of supernatural things?"[10]

What Pascal says implies that we would expect a true religion to contain some core doctrines that are puzzling to our limited intellect, just as the presently most fundamental theories of physics—quantum mechanics and general relativity—are very puzzling. Such puzzles, however, should not be downright contradictions (since these must be false); further, they should be fruitful puzzles that both stretch our minds by helping us develop a deeper view of reality and transform us so we no longer merely conform to the standards of this world. In contrast, we would expect a religion that was merely created by human beings to lack such puzzles and conform to the (superficial) standards of this world.[11] Since part of reason is recognizing the limitations of our minds, I suggest that we should understand following *reason as following the evidence wherever it leads, instead of following one's own prejudice,*

---

9. In support of the claim that Jesus wanted us to believe on faith without questioning, sometimes people cite Jesus' statement (Matt 18:3) that we must become like little children to enter the Kingdom of God. A primary characteristic of children, however, is questioning everything—the familiar "Why Mommy?"—and being open to new ideas and experiences. Further, sometimes Jesus' statement to Doubting Thomas that "Blessed are those who have not seen and yet have come to believe" (John 20:29 NRSV) is taken to show that Jesus preferred that we believe without evidence. However, seeing something is not the same as having evidence: I do not see the earth rotating, but I have good evidence that it does.

10. Pascal, *Pensées* 188.

11. I believe the above helps us make sense of why the apostle Paul stresses that Christian teaching is often against the (superficial) standards of this world: for example, Paul says, "If any of you think you are wise by the standards of this age, you should become 'fools' so that you may become wise" (1 Cor 3:18 NIV). Such standards are typically based on mere human tradition (such as what favors the powerful, the desire for vengeance, and so forth), not by a deep spiritual insight into reality.

tradition, or being stuck in the way one always has thought. And what does this involve? It involves thinking things through, which in turn relies on various sources of information, such as sense experience, the testimony of others, memory, and intellectual, moral and spiritual intuition, which we will now explore.

Intuition: People often forget that all human reason has to be based on subjective judgments, namely our capacity for *intellectual intuition*, which I define as the capacity to recognize whether a claim is true or false, plausible or implausible, merely by putting it before our minds, without inferring it from any other claim. Through intellectual intuition we know the fundamental rules of reasoning, such as that if A = B, and B = C, then A = C. To see this, note that ultimately humans cannot get such fundamental rules from sense experience, testimony, memory, or even inference (since these rules constitute one of the beginning principles of inference). Rather, they have seemed obvious to people when they think about them. In fact, I would argue that reliance on intuitions lies at the basis of science itself, particularly when we judge which theory offers the *best explanation* of a body of data. As long recognized by philosophers, for any set of data, there are indefinitely many hypotheses that one could formulate that would consistently explain the data. This is a challenge to the objectivity of scientific inference, known as the *underdetermination of theory by data problem.*[12] This means that when deciding which theory to believe (or tentatively work with) among those that account for the extant data, we must judge which theory we take to be the best explanation of the data. There is no logical rule for doing this. Hence scientists ultimately must rely on their own (well-trained) intuitions regarding the plausibility of competing theories (and the likelihood that there are better explanations they have not thought of). Of course, we can test a theory, but, as is widely recognized, even if it fails the test, we can make seemingly *ad hoc* adjustments in the theory to save it from refutation. Consequently, at the end of the day, one is still left with the underdetermination problem. This means that one cannot avoid relying on intuitive judgments, such as those regarding the plausibility of the adjustments needed to save the theory from refutation.

In light of the fundamental role of intuition, I propose that faith can be thought of as intuitively grasping a reality that is both beyond appearances and offers us motivation and hope. As the apostle Paul says, "For

---

12. Many philosophers, both theists and non-theists, have pointed this out. For instance, see Plantinga, *Conflict*, 296–98.

we walk by faith, not by sight" (1 Cor 5:7 NRSV). This aspect of faith is common to religious faith and secular faith, and it is essential for everyday life and doing science. For example, as Einstein noted, eminent scientists such as Kepler had great faith in the rational order of the universe, something Einstein said was a crucial motivation for Kepler's scientific pursuits and which Einstein stressed was central to his own scientific theorizing.[13] In fact, we can see that this kind of faith commonly provides the vision and confidence to do anything of significance.

Spiritual perception: Further, I propose that true *Christian* faith goes beyond the above kinds of intuitive capacities, but also involves using a special capacity for spiritual perception and understanding. As noted by Eastern Orthodox theologian I. M. Andreyev, faith is the "capability of the mind, feeling, and will . . . directed to understand that which is inaccessible for the mind alone."[14] Of course, Christians would hold that this capability needs to be enlivened and regenerated by the Holy Spirit. Similarly, according to Eleonore Stump, for the great medieval theologian and philosopher Thomas Aquinas (1225–1274), Christian faith involves the capacity to perceive real moral and metaphysical goodness (whose ultimate source is God), with a corresponding movement of the will to assent to this perceived goodness; this is why faith, hope, and love go together (1 Cor 13:13). For Aquinas, perceiving and assenting to this goodness distinguishes the "faith" of the demons, who believe there is one God and tremble (Jas 2:19), from true Christian faith.[15] This idea of faith being grounded in spiritual intuition allows us to make sense of why Hebrews 11:1 says that faith is the "assurance of things hoped for" (NRSV). Such a capacity for spiritual intuition can assure us of something in an analogy to how our capacity of intellectual intuition can assure us of basic logical truths, as noted above.

If we truly have such capacities for spiritual perception, then it would be unreasonable not to use them. I propose, therefore, that at its best, Christian faith involves using all of our faculties for perceiving truth.

13. Einstein, "Religion and Science."
14. Andreyev, *Orthodox Apologetic Theology*, 65.
15. Stump, *Aquinas*, 364–65. The reason God requires faith based on part on perceived goodness is that if we could be completely certain that God exists without first turning to God because of his perceived goodness, that would render it impossible to worship God because of who God is (perfect goodness) instead of for one's own self-interest of getting on the side of power. As an analogy, seeing a police officer in one's rearview mirror would make it very difficult to obey the speed limit because it was the right thing to do.

However, we also know that our fundamental sources of information about the world—such as sense experience, memory, inferential reasoning, and so forth—can sometimes be mistaken. So we can see the need to use reason to evaluate these sources. For example, even though our sense experience tells us that the moon is larger on the horizon than when it is overhead, our reason tells us that it doesn't shrink as it rises, since this would conflict with other things we know. Similarly, we must use reason—based on our other sources of information—to evaluate the seeming deliverance of spiritual intuitions. Otherwise, faith runs the danger of becoming mere credulity. So, under this view, faith and reason work hand in hand. This idea of faith would only come directly into conflict with science if we were to take the intellectual intuitions necessary for determining what theory is the best explanation as the *only* legitimate kind of intuition. But even scientists should deny the latter: insofar as scientists make any kind of ethical value judgment at all—that science is worth pursuing, for instance—they rely on intuitions, such as what is valuable and what is not, that go beyond those required for scientific inference.[16]

Historical Conflict Thesis

It is often taken as a truism that throughout history religion has been the opponent of scientific progress. As Alister McGrath notes, however, "The idea that science and religion are in perpetual conflict is no longer taken seriously by any major historian of science."[17] Or, as evolutionary biologist H. Allen Orr says in a review of one of Richard Dawkins's books,

> The popular impression of long warfare between Church and science—in which an ignorant institution fought to keep a fledgling science from escaping the Dark Ages—is nonsense, little more than Victorian propaganda. The truth, which emerged only from the last century of scholarship, is almost entirely unknown among scientists: the medieval Church was a leading patron of science; most theologians studied "natural

---

16. Another understanding of faith that harmonizes faith with science is given in chapter 11 of Lewis, *Mere Christianity*. In this understanding, faith involves an act of will to hold onto the truths one has once perceived (via reason or some other means) in face of the temptation to do otherwise. Such an understanding seems to provide one manifestation of faith as it occurs in our earthly life.

17. McGrath, *Twilight of Atheism*, 87.

philosophy"; and the medieval curriculum was perhaps the most scientific in Western history.[18]

Similarly, historian of science Margaret Osler notes that "the entire enterprise of studying the natural world was embedded in a theological framework that emphasized divine creation, design, and providence. These themes are prominent in the writings of almost all the major seventeenth-century natural philosophers."[19]

Many of the historical episodes of conflict often cited—such as the claim that Christians burnt the great Library of Alexandria, that anatomy was banned in the Middle Ages, or that John Calvin dismissed the Copernican theory based on Scripture—have been shown to be historically false, or at the very least not based on adequate historical evidence. Others, such as the well-known house arrest by the Catholic Church of Galileo for advocating the Copernican theory, are much more complicated than often portrayed, as much a result of political factors going on at the time as a conflict between religion and science. Many of these myths trace back to the deeply flawed history promulgated by two late nineteenth-century books, one by John Draper and one by Andrew Dixon White.[20] These authors were not anti-Christian *per se*; rather, they were writing polemics against a kind of dogmatic Christianity which they perceived as holding back scientific progress. Unfortunately, these myths have stuck in the popular imagination and have been repeated by many leading popularizers of science without checking the facts. For instance, even right up to the present, popular science explicator Neil deGrasse Tyson appears unaware that, as David B. Wilson has noted,[21] White's book had been thoroughly discredited among historians by 1980. Says Tyson,

> As was thoroughly documented in the nineteenth-century tome, *A History of the Warfare of Science with Theology in Christendom*, by the historian and one time president of Cornell University Andrew D. White, history reveals a long and

---

18. Orr, "Passion for Evolution."
19. Osler, "Myth 10," 96.
20. Specifically, Draper, *History of the Conflict*; White, *History of the Warfare of Science and Theology*. For an account of the influence of these books and their flawed history, see Hutchings and Ungureanu, *Of Popes and Unicorns*.
21. Wilson, "Historiography of Science and Religion," 21–23.

combative relationship between religion and science, depending on who was in control of society at the time.[22]

Examples such as Tyson's misunderstanding, of which there are many, show that while claiming to promote the value of evidence-based belief, often scientists writing for popular audiences fail to meet their own admonitions when talking about issues outside their field. People in the technical fields of the hard sciences, especially, often have little real training in or grasp of the actual history and philosophy of science. Fortunately, there has been increasing pushback against this narrative, even among atheists.[23] Finally, as hinted at in the quotations from Orr and Osler above, according to many historians of science, the belief that the world was created by God helped give birth to modern science. Specifically, it led to the belief that the world is rationally ordered in a way that our minds could understand and the belief that it is a *free* creation of God; the latter meant that the order could not be discovered by the mind alone (as in mathematics), but required empirical studies.[24] This combination of beliefs was foundational to modern science.

Psychological Motivators for Conflict Thesis

Prominent anti-religious scientists, such as Richard Dawkins and Steven Pinker, promote both scientism (the belief that science is the only path to truth) and naturalism (the belief that there is no supernatural reality) as the only scientifically respectable beliefs to have. At the same time, they portray religious belief as being the result of irrational psychological motivations, such as the fear of death; the desire for a cosmic father-figure to take care of and console us; and the desire for everything to be simple and to eliminate the mystery from everything, leading to dogmatism and

---

22. Tyson, "Holy Wars." Tyson has also made similar statements more recently, saying on Twitter that the view that the earth was round was "lost in the dark ages," something historically entirely false (Tyson quoted in Hutchings and Ungureanu, *Popes and Unicorns*, 61).

23. For example, historian Tim O'Neill, former state president of the Australian Skeptics, has established a blog called *History for Atheists*, whose purpose is to present "articles, book reviews and critiques relating to 'New Atheist Bad History'—the misuse of history and the use of biased, erroneous or distorted pseudo history by anti-theistic atheists." See https://www.historyforatheists.com.

24. See, for example, Harrison, "Religion and the Early Royal Society," 3–22; "Christianity and the Rise of Western Science."

fundamentalism. This helps further bolster the belief in the conflict of science and faith.

There is considerable truth to some of these accusations and it is something that one often sees in the current world. However, as discussed above, I do not think this is a core aspect of the Christian faith. Further, I do not find such motivations playing a prominent role for myself or for many prominent converts to Christianity, such as C. S. Lewis or Keith Ward (former regius professor of divinity, University of Oxford). Instead, belief is largely based on the conviction that the evidence really points to the existence of God and the truth of Christianity, properly understood. However, I do not doubt that many religious believers are motivated by irrational factors such as those mentioned above. However, I would note that *some* non-evidential motivations for belief are themselves rational from a practical perspective: for example, one can have practical reasons for holding beliefs that give one hope and meaning, and help one live ethically, even if one does not otherwise have sufficient evidence to think the belief is true.[25]

Instead of defending the rationality of faith against these charges of irrationality, in this section, I will point out the often unacknowledged evidence that belief in scientism and naturalism are themselves often the result of non-rational factors.[26] This undercuts the implicit assumption often made that, since many of the scientists who promote scientism and naturalism are exceptionally brilliant in their respective fields, their pronouncements promoting these views must be based on a deep understanding of science and its practice.

Science idolatry, conceptual hegemony, and arrogance

The scientific method is undeniably powerful. But we court danger by making it an idol—the new thing we devote ourselves to that will save us, giving us all the answers. Since clearly science of itself can't give us answers to transcendent realities, scientism has led many to adopt materialism. From this frame of mind, any glimmer of transcendence—such

---

25. Among many others, an argument for this position is presented by William James, eminent American psychologist and philosopher in James, "Will to Believe."

26. Other non-rational factors not mentioned here are given by Paul Vitz, senior scholar at Divine Mercy University in Sterling, Virginia, and emeritus professor of psychology at New York University. See Vitz, *Faith of the Fatherless*. For an online essay in which he presents some of the points in the book, see his "Psychology of Atheism."

as religious experience—can be explained away as an illusion. Moreover, by definition, theistic explanations can then be discounted as real explanations because they don't fit the mold of explanations in the natural sciences. The result is what could be called "scientism fundamentalism," since in many ways it has the same psychological motivations and belief structure as religious fundamentalism: namely, a desire for everything to be simple and to eliminate mystery when it comes to ultimate questions.

Related to science idolatry is what I will call *conceptual hegemony*: seeing everything through the conceptual lens of one's own field of study. For example, molecular biologists will tend to think of the human body as just a biochemical machine; sociologists will tend to look at science as merely a system of sociological relations, often related to power and prestige; particle physicists will tend to see the world as a set of interacting particles; and so forth. In extreme cases, these experts have a difficult time even conceiving of reality apart from the lens of their field. To illustrate, I once suggested to a postdoctoral student in neuroscience that perhaps we had an immaterial mind. She responded that she could not even conceive of a mind without a brain, to which I asked her whether she knew that she had a mind before she knew what a brain is. If she did, then she could conceive of what a mind is apart from a brain. She had no good answer.

I suspect conceptual hegemony constitutes one reason belief in a God who answers prayers falls off with scientific eminence, as shown by a survey done by two theist professors in 1999. Overall, 40 percent of scientists have this belief in a God one can pray to, but this drops to 10 percent for eminent scientists, as defined by those who belong to the prestigious National Academy of Scientists.[27] Why is this? One plausible explanation was given to me by the late John Polkinghorne, a particle physicist for twenty years who became an Anglican priest. In a private conversation, he noted that to become an eminent scientist, one must spend almost all of one's time doing science. This allows little time to cultivate a religious sensitivity to a higher reality, thereby making it difficult for one to conceive of how there could be a God, let alone a God that does miracles.

Another non-rational motivation for some prominent scientists claiming that religious faith and science are in conflict is their belief that they belong to an elite group that has the true scoop on reality. This

---

27. Larson and Witham, "Scientists and Religion in America," 88–93.

leads them to think that they can authoritatively comment on areas far outside their area of expertise without studying or consulting experts in those areas. A good example of this is Stephen Hawking and Leonard Mlodinow's book, *The Grand Design*. In the introductory chapter, they tell us that, traditionally, the domain of philosophy addressed such questions as, "What is the nature of reality? Where did all this come from? Did the universe need a creator?" On the same page, the authors then go on to tell us, "Philosophy has not kept up with modern developments of science, particularly physics. Scientists have become the bearers of the torch of discovery in our quest for knowledge."[28]

They offer no evidence for this statement, neglecting to even mention the many philosophers who do philosophy of physics and have graduate degrees in both. Worse, their proposal for how science is supposed to answer these questions logically makes no sense. According to them, "Because there is a law like gravity, the universe can and will create itself from nothing in the manner described in chapter 6." They then go on, "Spontaneous creation is the reason there is something rather than nothing, why the universe exists, why we exist. It is not necessary to invoke God to light the blue torch paper and set the universe going."[29] They never address the apparent contradiction in this statement: the universe must already exist to create anything, and thus it cannot create itself out of nothing. Not even God can pull off a trick like that. Hawking and Mlodinow are not alone in making statements like this. Physicist Laurence Krauss, for example, has written an entire book based on the same idea. As summed up in the afterword by materialist biologist Richard Dawkins: "Even the last remaining trump card of the theologian, 'Why is there something rather than nothing?', shrivels up before your eyes as you read these pages."[30]

The idea behind these far-reaching claims is the controversial thesis that quantum mechanics allows the universe to arise as a quantum fluctuation out of a quantum vacuum state—a state that contains no actual (non-virtual) particles. In a review, philosopher of physics David Albert points out that the quantum vacuum state is *far from nothing*, but rather consists of physical stuff, namely the quantum fields.[31] But even if someone like Laurence Krauss is right that the quantum realm does not

28. Hawking and Mlodinow, *Grand Design*, 5.
29. Hawking and Mlodinow, *Grand Design*, 180.
30. Krauss, *Universe from Nothing*, 191.
31. Albert, "On the Origin of Everything."

itself constitute physical stuff (and so is "nothing" in that sense), he fails to recognize that his claim that physical reality is the result of quantum fluctuation would pose an even worse problem for atheists than theists. Without matter, one could not say the laws of quantum mechanics are grounded in physical stuff, since there is no physical stuff. Thus the quantum laws that give rise to physical reality must exist in some transcendent, non-physical realm, such as the mind of God, which contradicts the very naturalism they are advocating.

This arrogance shows itself in other ways too. Returning to Hawking and Mlodinow, they also make the dubious claim that "until the advent of modern physics it was generally thought that all knowledge of the world could be obtained through direct observation, that things are what they seem, as perceived through our senses. But the spectacular success of modern physics . . . has shown that this is not the case."[32] (By "modern physics" they mean quantum mechanics.) But if these authors had just thought for a moment about what they were saying, they would have realized that throughout history people have believed in a reality beyond appearances. The examples are commonplace and everywhere—in Plato, and his belief in the world of the Forms; in religions such as Christianity and Hinduism, which posit vast realms of reality beyond sense experience; and in such scientists as Nicholas Copernicus, who claimed that the earth rotates and goes around the sun rather than the other way around—contrary to appearances, we might add. Hawking and Mlodinow may be brilliant physicists, but their grasp of basic history and philosophical discourse proves weak with an offhand comment such as this. My guess is that their sense of superiority as cosmologists has made them think they have a license to make statements far outside their discipline without even having to think through what they are really saying.

Fear of religion

Besides intellectual arrogance and casual dismissal of other modes of inquiry, we come to another major non-rational motivator for scientism and its accompanying materialism, what prominent atheist philosopher Thomas Nagel calls the "fear of religion":

32. Hawking and Mlodinow, *Grand Design*, 7.

> The thought that the relation between mind and the world is something fundamental makes many people in this day and age nervous. I believe this is one manifestation of a fear of religion which has large and often pernicious consequences for modern intellectual life. . . . I speak from experience, being strongly subject to this fear myself: I want atheism to be true and am made uneasy by the fact that some of the most intelligent and well-informed people I know are religious believers. It isn't that I don't believe in God and, naturally, hope that I'm right in my belief. It's that I hope there is no God! I don't want there to be a God; I don't want the universe to be like that.[33]

Nagel then notes,

> My guess is that the cosmic authority problem is not a rare condition and that it is responsible for much of the scientism and reductionism of our time. One of the tendencies it supports is the ludicrous overuse of evolutionary biology to explain everything about life, including everything about the human mind.[34]

The leading popular Christian writer of the twentieth century, C. S. Lewis, also admitted this fear motivated him to be an atheistic materialist early in life before he became a Christian. One form fear of religion took for him was a fear of the supernatural. Lewis says, "Every man who is afraid of spooks will have a reason for wishing to be a Materialist; that creed promises to exclude the bogies."[35] Another was the fear of being exposed, of nothing being truly private. Lewis recounts that he wanted "some area, however small, of which I could say to all other beings, 'This is my business and mine only.' . . . No word in my vocabulary expressed deeper hatred than the word Interference. But Christianity placed at the centre what then seemed to me a transcendental Interferer."[36]

We also find this same fear of religion implicitly recognized by the well-known materialist philosopher of mind, John Searle, when he talks about the "terror" of non-materialistic views of the mind:

> One of the unstated assumptions behind the current batch of [materialist] views is that they represent the only scientifically acceptable alternatives to the antiscientism that went with traditional dualism, the belief in the immortality of the soul,

33. Nagel, *Last Word*, 130–31.
34. Nagel, *Last Word*, 132–33.
35. Lewis, *Surprised by Joy*, 171.
36. Lewis, *Surprised by Joy*, 166.

spiritualism, and so on. Acceptance of the current views is motivated not so much by an independent conviction of their truth as by *a terror* of what are apparently the only alternatives.[37]

Such motivations for materialism have a long history. For example, in his history of ancient and medieval philosophy, James Jordan comments that a major motivation for the widespread adoption by the ancients of the materialist philosophy of Epicurus (341–270 BCE) was that it relieved "anxiety about life beyond the grave, . . . the present life is the only one we have, and the gods leave us alone to enjoy it as best we can."[38]

CONCLUSION

I have examined many of the major non-rational motivations for the idea that science and faith are in conflict and argued that they are based on significant misconceptions. There are several other areas of purported conflict that I did not cover, but I believe that most of these also ultimately have little merit when carefully analyzed.

Since the above analysis has been a mostly defensive enterprise, one might wonder whether there are positive reasons for belief in the Christian faith. I believe that there are, particularly for belief in God. In fact, for me, the success of science and its findings provide convincing reasons for believing in God. Here I can only summarize what I find the most compelling of such reasons:

(1) *The fine-tuning for life.* The structure of the universe appears to be finely tuned for the existence of life. If it were not structured to an enormously precise degree, life could not have arisen. For example, unless the cosmological constant (or the dark-energy density) were within one part in 10^{120} of its estimated theoretical range of values, the universe would either expand or collapse too quickly for the formation of galaxies and stars, and hence for life to evolve. In the case of the initial distribution of mass and energy in the universe, it must be fine-tuned to a ridiculous 1 part in $10^{10^{123}}$ for life to exist. (You read that right, one part in ten raised to the power of ten followed by a hundred and twenty-three zeroes.) These are just two of many examples. As I and others have argued, this fine-tuning provides strong evidence for theism.[39]

---

37. Searle, *Rediscovery of Mind*, 3–4, emphasis added.
38. Jordan, *Western Philosophy*, 177.
39. For a much more extensive defense of the fine-tuning argument, see Collins,

(2) *The order, intelligibility, and discoverability of the world.* Modern science has shown us that the order of the world can be encapsulated in mathematical equations that are intelligible to the human mind. The "miraculous" intelligibilche has been noted by many prominent scientists and philosophers. For instance, Eugene Wigner, one of the major founders of quantum mechanics, our most fundamental physical theory, famously said, "The miracle of the appropriateness of the language of mathematics for the formulation of the laws of physics is a wonderful gift which we neither understand nor deserve."[40] Similarly, Albert Einstein remarked that "the most incomprehensible thing about the world is that it is comprehensible."[41] More recently, philosopher of mathematics Mark Steiner has argued in detail that the laws of the universe appear much more discoverable than can be explained by chance, concluding at the end of his book that "the world, in other words, looks 'user friendly.' This is a challenge to naturalism."[42] In this regard, I am finishing a major project showing how the fundamental parameters of physics are precisely set to optimize scientific discovery, which both tests this claim about the seemingly miraculous discoverability of nature and makes it quantitative. Elsewhere I show why such fine-tuning for discovery cannot be explained by the leading non-theist response to the fine-tuning for life, namely the multiverse hypothesis.[43]

(3) *Human reason and the success of science.* The success of science is a testament to the ability of human reason to uncover the secrets of nature. Many have argued that this ability does not make sense under typical naturalistic views of the universe. For example, atheist philosopher Thomas Nagel has argued that since the reasoning undergirding fundamental physical and cosmological theories goes far beyond what is needed for survival and reproduction, its success cannot be accounted for by unguided evolution (understood as chance variation with natural selection).[44] However, since theists claim that God is ultimately behind

"Teleological Argument." For a recent book on the topic, see Lewis and Barnes, *Fortunate Universe.*

40. Wigner, "Unreasonable Effectiveness of Mathematics."

41. Einstein, "Physics and Reality," 315. This is the English translation the original German, "Das ewig Unbegreifliche an der Welt ist ihre Begreiflichkeit."

42. Steiner, *Mathematics as a Philosophical Problem,* 176.

43. Collins, "Argument from Physical Constants," 89–107, 90–92.

44. See Nagel, *Mind and Cosmos.* Related arguments for theism based on our ability to reason have also been presented by Alvin Plantinga and Victor Reppert, who provides an extended defense of an argument offered by C. S. Lewis that naturalism is

our mental capabilities and God created the universe, it is not surprising under theism that human reason has been successful in this way. Thus, the ability of reason to uncover the secrets of nature seems to make little sense under naturalism. However, since theists claim that God is ultimately behind our mental capabilities and God created the universe, it is not surprising under theism that human reason has been successful in this way.

Because it seems to me that the reasons given for thinking science undercuts Christian faith are misguided, and it seems to me that science offers strong reasons for believing in God, in my view science offers an extremely strong support for at least belief in God.[45]

BIBLIOGRAPHY

Albert, David. "On the Origin of Everything." *New York Times*, March 23, 2012. http://www.nytimes.com/2012/03/25/books/review/a-universe-from-nothing-by-lawrence-m-krauss.html.

Andreyev, I. M. *Orthodox Apologetic Theology*. Plantina, CA: St. Herman of Alaska Brotherhood, 1995.

Blocher, Henri. *In the Beginning: The Opening Chapters of Genesis*. Westmont, IL: InterVarsity, 1984.

Collins, Robin. "The Argument from Physical Constants: The Fine-Tuning for Discoverability." In *Two Dozen (or so) Arguments for God: The Plantinga Project*, edited by Jerry L. Walls and Trent Dougherty, 89–107. New York: Oxford University Press, 2018.

———. "Evolution and Original Sin." In *Perspectives on an Evolving Creation*, edited by Keith B. Miller, 469–501. Grand Rapids: Eerdmans, 2003. https://biologos.org/articles/evolution-and-original-sin-the-historical-ideal-view.

———. "The Teleological Argument: An Exploration of the Fine-Tuning of the Universe." In *The Blackwell Companion to Natural Theology*, edited by William Lane Craig and J. P. Moreland, 202–81. Malden, MA: Wiley-Blackwell, 2009.

Conway Morris, Simon. *Life's Solution: Inevitable Humans in a Lonely Universe*. Cambridge: Cambridge University Press, 2004.

Draper, John William. *History of the Conflict between Religion and Science*. New York: Appleton, 1874.

Einstein, Albert. "Physics and Reality." *Journal of the Franklin Institute* 221.3 (1936) 349–82.

---

inconsistent with having any confidence in human reason. See chapter 10 in Plantinga, *Conflict*; Reppert, *C. S. Lewis's Dangerous Idea*.

45. I would like to thank two students at Messiah University, Justin Divelbiss and Franklin Kelly, for helpful comments on an earlier draft of this paper. I would especially like to thank my wife, Rebecca Adams, for her considerable editorial work in making this paper more focused and comprehensible.

———. "Religion and Science." *New York Times Magazine*, November 9, 1930, 1–4. Reprinted in *Ideas and Opinions*, by Albert Einstein, 36–40. New York: Crown, 1954.

Feynman, Richard. *The Meaning of It All: Thoughts of a Citizen Scientist*. Reading, MA: Perseus, 1998.

Gould, Stephen J. *Wonderful Life: The Burgess Shale and the Nature of History*. New York: Norton, 1989.

Harrison, Peter. "Christianity and the Rise of Western Science." *ABC Religion & Ethics*, May 8, 2012. https://www.abc.net.au/religion/christianity-and-the-rise-of-western-science/10100570.

———. "Religion and the Early Royal Society." *Science and Christian Belief* 22 (2010) 3–22.

Hutchings, David, and James Ungureanu. *Of Popes and Unicorns: Science, Christianity, and How the Conflict Thesis Fooled the World*. New York: Oxford University Press, 2022.

James, William. "The Will to Believe." In *The Will to Believe, and Other Essays in Popular Philosophy*. New York: Longmans, Green, 1897. https://www.loc.gov/item/04003036.

Jordan, James. *Western Philosophy: From Antiquity to the Middle Ages*. New York: Macmillan, 1987.

Krauss, Lawrence M. *A Universe from Nothing: Why There Is Something Rather Than Nothing*. New York: Simon and Shuster, 2012.

Larson, Edward J., and Larry Witham. "Scientists and Religion in America." *Scientific American* 281.3 (1999) 88–93.

Lewis, C. S. *Mere Christianity*. New York: HarperOne, 1952.

———. *The Problem of Pain*, New York: Macmillan, 1962.

———. *Surprised by Joy: The Shape of My Early Life*. New York: Harcourt, Brace, 1956.

Lewis, Geraint F., and Luke A. Barnes. *A Fortunate Universe: Life in a Finely Tuned Cosmos*. Cambridge: Cambridge University Press, 2016.

Longrich, Nick. "Evolution's 'Great Leap Forward': When Did Humans Cross the Intelligence Rubicon?" *Genetic Literacy Project*, November 4, 2020. https://geneticliteracyproject.org/2020/11/04/evolutions-great-leap-forward-when-did-humans-cross-the-intelligence-rubicon/.

McGrath, Alister. *The Twilight of Atheism: The Rise and Fall of Disbelief in the Modern World*. New York: Doubleday, 2004.

Nagel, Thomas. *The Last Word*. Oxford: Oxford University Press, 1997.

———. *Mind and Cosmos: Why the Materialist Neo-Darwinian Conception of Nature Is Almost Certainly False*. New York: Oxford University Press, 2012.

Orr, H. Allen. "A Passion for Evolution." *New York Review of Books*, February 26, 2004, 27–29.

Osler, Margaret. "Myth 10: That the Scientific Revolution Liberated Science from Religion." In *Galileo Goes to Jail and Other Myths about Science and Religion*, edited by Ronald Numbers, 90–98. Cambridge: Harvard University Press, 2010.

Pascal, Blaise. *Pensées*. Translated by A. J. Krailsheimer. Reprint, London: Penguin, 1995.

Pfeiffer, John. *The Creative Explosion: An Inquiry into the Origins of Art and Religion*. Ithaca, NY: Cornell University Press, 1985.

Plantinga, Alvin. *Where the Conflict Really Lies: Science, Religion, and Naturalism.* New York: Oxford University Press, 2011.

Polkinghorne, John, and Steven Weinberg. "Was the Universe Designed?: An Exchange." *Counterbalance,* April 15, 1999. https://counterbalance.org/cq-jpsw/index-frame.html.

Reppert, Victor. *C. S. Lewis's Dangerous Idea: In Defense of the Argument from Reason.* Downers Grove, IL: IVP Academic, 2003.

Searle, John. *The Rediscovery of Mind.* Cambridge: MIT Press, 1992.

Steiner, Mark. *Mathematics as a Philosophical Problem.* Cambridge: Harvard University Press, 1998.

Stump, Eleonore. *Aquinas.* London: Routledge, 2005.

Tyson, Neil deGrasse. "Holy Wars." *Natural History,* October 1999. https://neildegrassetyson.com/essays/1999-10-holy-wars.

Vitz, Paul. *Faith of the Fatherless: The Psychology of Atheism.* 2nd ed. San Francisco: Ignatius, 2013.

———. "The Psychology of Atheism." *Faculty Commons,* n.d. https://www.leaderu.com/truth/1truth12.html.

White, Andrew Dickson. *History of the Warfare of Science and Theology in Christendom.* New York: Appleton, 1896.

Wigner, Eugene. "The Unreasonable Effectiveness of Mathematics in the Natural Sciences." *Communications on Pure and Applied Mathematics* 13.1 (1960) 1–14.

Wilson, David B. "The Historiography of Science and Religion." In *Science & Religion: A Historical Introduction,* edited by Gary B. Ferngren, 13–29. Baltimore: Johns Hopkins University Press, 2002.

Wright, Robert. *Nonzero: The Logic of Human Destiny.* New York: Pantheon, 1999.

8

Christianity and Human Flourishing

Gregory E. Ganssle

What decides against Christianity now is our taste not our reason.
FRIEDRICH NIETZSCHE, *THE GAY SCIENCE*, 132

INTRODUCTION

APOLOGETICS IS TYPICALLY AIMED at defending the truth of Christianity. This task is crucial, and several of the chapters in this book contribute to this endeavor. What has become clear in our cultural moment, however, is that the question of the truth of the gospel is taking a back seat. The question that drives the bus is whether the Christian story is good, or whether it is good for us.

This claim is clear when one reviews the contents of this volume. Nine of the chapters discuss objections in which the particular challenge has a similar structure.[1] The structure can be summarized as follows:

---

1. These are chapters 1–3, 5, 8–12.

1. Christianity says X about issue Y.
2. To hold that X is the case about Y is to hold a view that is deeply distasteful or immoral.
3. Therefore, we ought to reject Christianity.

Notice that the arguments are not really of the form *modus tollens*. Modus tollens arguments have the form:

1. If Christianity is true, then Y is true. (p → q)
2. Y is false. (-q)
3. Therefore, Christianity is false. (Therefore, -p)

While some of the topics covered in these chapters could be framed as modus tollens arguments, in general they are not. These issues, then, are not raised as evidence that Christianity is false. They are offered to stimulate or to explain a desire to reject it.

In this chapter I shall explore one such argument. This argument is that Christianity is an obstruction to human flourishing. Christianity is actually bad for the one who holds it. This argument, like the others referred to, does not conclude that Christianity is false. The conclusion is that we do not want to hold it. I will refer to this kind of argument as the "objection from flourishing." How the argument I shall discuss differs from the varieties found in other chapters is that they often hold forth the claim that Christianity is bad for society or for minorities or for justice. I shall focus on the argument that Christianity is bad for the person who holds it. It hinders human flourishing. The process of answering this objection will raise questions about what it is in which flourishing consists. Beyond answering the objection from flourishing, a careful exploration of this topic will result in a positive argument in favor of Christianity. I shall assess this argument for Christianity, not as an argument for its truth, but as an argument for its desirability.

HISTORICAL SOURCES OF THE FLOURISHING ARGUMENT

The objection from flourishing has a long history, even if the arguments against the truth of Christianity have been more prominent. For example, Karl Marx is famous for his view that religion keeps the laboring class from revolting against the owners of the means of production. By persuading people that they will be rewarded in the next life for their humility and obedience, religion kept the workers content. Another way that religion oppresses the masses is that it influences them to focus their attention on a spiritual rescue. Thus, religion turns their attention from their present material conditions. Since, for Marx, present material conditions are the only things that exist, religion deceives the masses by getting them preoccupied with a false, spiritual world in the future. Marx's objection focuses on how religion is bad for the working class. It does seem to imply that it is bad for the individual as well. It is on an individual level, as well as the level of society, that people are distracted from the task of improving their lot by the promises of justice and happiness in the next life.

Sigmund Freud argued that religious belief is an illusion. An illusion, he thought, is not necessarily a false belief. He explains that "we call a belief an illusion when a wish-fulfillment is a prominent factor in its motivation, and in doing so we disregard its relations to reality, just as the illusion itself sets no store by verification."[2] Human beings want a sense of security in a chaotic world. The notion that God is a loving Father who cares for his children gives many this security. It is not Freud's assertion that religion is born out of wish-fulfillment that supports the objection from flourishing. It is his claim that the specific wishes of religious people are infantile.

That religious belief is infantile is shown in the similarities of a believer's thoughts, feelings, and prayers to God and a child's interactions with his father. The believer entrusts herself to the care of a good God, thinking that he will protect her by means of some mysterious divine providence. The child climbs up on his father's lap for comfort and protection, though he may not know how it is that the father exercises his agency for protection. The actions of both God and the father are mysterious, and their thoughts are far above our thoughts.

While it is appropriate for the child to seek comfort and protection from his father, there is something characteristically immature in the adult believer's trust in God. Rather than facing the complexities of life for herself, she reverts to the attitudes and behavior of the child. The religious disposition, then, hinders the believer's growth to mature

---

2. Freud, *Future of an Illusion*, 40.

adulthood. The infantile nature of religious belief reveals that such belief is an obstacle to the flourishing of the person.

Perhaps the thinker who has done the most for the argument against Christianity from human flourishing is Friedrich Nietzsche. Because his views are so influential, I shall go into them in some detail.

Nietzsche came from a long line of Lutheran ministers. In fact, his childhood was marked by religious devotion. It was while he attended Pforta, a prestigious secondary school near Naumburg, that Nietzsche lost his Christian faith. The major influence in this move was that the critical scholarly skills he was learning pushed against the devotional respect for the Bible. As he applied the linguistic and historical methodologies he learned from engaging classical texts to the Bible itself, his confidence in the content and historicity of the Scriptures was undermined. At this time, as Julian Young reports, Nietzsche recommended Karl von Hase's work, *Life of Jesus*, to his sister.[3] This book argued for a more modernized picture of the historical Jesus. In his first year in the university, Nietzsche read David Strauss's *Life of Jesus*. Strauss argued that the miracle stories reported about Jesus never happened. They were added to the text by early Christians to solidify their claims that Jesus was the Messiah from God. The works of von Hase and Strauss helped shape a new critical approach to the New Testament text. This approach was appealing to Nietzsche as a budding philologist. As Nietzsche explored this approach to the Scriptures, he knew of no serious Christian scholars who were orthodox. There was no one to offer an answer to the challenges of von Hase, Strauss, or the philological conclusions about the New Testament drawn by the faculty and students.

Throughout his life, Nietzsche continued to favor strongly the application of the "scientific" methodology of philology to the biblical texts.[4] He thought it had been demonstrated that Moses was not the author of the Pentateuch. The Old Testament had developed over centuries by compiling disparate sources from a variety of oral traditions. Because of these findings, it was no longer believable that the Mosaic law was given by God. As far as the New Testament is concerned, from the very beginning, the original followers of Jesus had badly misunderstood his

---

3. See Young, *Friedrich Nietzsche*, 29.

4. In addition to Strauss, he also studied Wellhausen's *Prolegomena*. Wellhausen was a pioneer in the Documentary Hypothesis concerning the origin of the Pentateuch with its multiple sources (i.e., the Jahwistic, Elohistic, Deuteronomistic, and Priestly sources—or, J, E, D, and P). Another influence was Renan's *Life of Jesus*.

teachings. They were so distraught at his death that, in order to make sense of the events, they searched for someone to blame. They appropriated concepts of sin, guilt, and judgment, and used these to focus the blame on the Jewish hierarchy. They put these theological concepts into the mouth of Jesus as they constructed their Gospels.

Paul further distorted the message of the historical Jesus by introducing a number of doctrines, including the doctrine of personal immortality. He manipulated these for his own power interests. Christianity became a set of beliefs rather than a way of life. These beliefs served to distinguish those on the inside from outsiders. Any person who believed wrongly was sentenced to hell. In addition, the concepts of guilt and of the need for forgiveness kept most early Christians under the burden of self-loathing. Christianity as we now have it is nothing like the actual life and teachings of Jesus. Nietzsche summarizes the message of the historical Jesus:

> Jesus could be called a "free spirit," using the phrase somewhat loosely—he does not care for solid things: the word *kills*, everything solid *kills*. The concept, the *experience* of "life" as only he knew it, repelled every type of word, formula, law, faith, or dogma. He spoke only about what was inside him most deeply: "life" or "truth" or "light" are his words for the innermost—he saw everything else, the whole of reality, the whole of nature, language itself, as having value only as a sign, a parable.[5]

Jesus did not give his followers a set of beliefs. He elucidated a kind of life that centered on reflecting on one's inner states. Nietzsche's first front in his life-long war on Christianity, then, involved an attack on the historical validity of the traditional portrait of the Scriptures, and Jesus in particular.

While this critical approach to the historical Jesus and the origins of Christianity remained important to Nietzsche, his mature criticism of Christianity concentrated on a different front altogether. These criticisms were a version of the objection from flourishing. He claimed that Christianity is fundamentally anti-Life. This objection was connected to Nietzsche's use of biblical criticism. He thought that it was the teaching of the church, as handed down, that is an obstacle to human flourishing. This teaching, however, is a distortion of the original aim of Jesus. A concern for human flourishing can be recognized in the picture of Jesus

---

5. Nietzsche, *Anti-Christ*, 32. All emphasis in Nietzsche citations are in the original.

that remains after the corruptions of Paul and others are removed. One could, like Nietzsche, hold a grudging respect for Jesus and, at the same time, be firmly opposed to Christianity.

Nietzsche often discussed flourishing using the term *life*. It is difficult to exaggerate the importance of *life* for Nietzsche. It is *the* criterion for determining whether things like traditional morality or Christianity ought to be accepted or rejected. Nietzsche poses the question about morality as follows:

> Under what conditions did man invent the value judgments good and evil? *and what value do they themselves have?* Have they up to now obstructed or promoted human flourishing? Are they a sign of distress, poverty, and the degeneration of life? Or, on the contrary, do they reveal the fullness, vitality and will of life, its courage, its confidence, its future?[6]

Nietzsche is not investigating which moral judgments, if any, are true. He wants to know how we came to make these sorts of judgments in the first place. The key issue, however, is whether our habit of making them is good for us. His evaluation is based on whether the practice of making moral judgments promotes or hinders life. Nietzsche's criticisms of Christianity in this regard are tied to his criticisms of traditional morality. Morality and Christianity stand or fall together.

How did our traditional morality develop? Nietzsche tells the story about how the notions of *good* and *bad* became transformed into the notions of *Good* and *Evil*. The original terms did not begin as *moral* assessments. They were terms of approval or disapproval, but not of *moral* approval or disapproval. There have always been strong people and weak people. The strong, he argues, equated what was good and valuable with what was like themselves. So, goodness was identified with strength, courage, decisiveness, and the exercise of power over others. What was bad was anything opposite to these qualities. Weakness, fear, and postures such as servitude were disapproved.

In a social structure such as the one described by Nietzsche, the weak were in a terrible bind. They could not become strong. They could not overpower the strong. They could not beat the strong at their own game. They had only two alternatives. They could either remain in subjection to the strong under the rules of the strong, or they could change the rules of the game. How can the weak overthrow the strong through

---

6. Nietzsche, *On the Genealogy of Morality*, 3.

a rule change? It is astounding to recognize their accomplishment. Nietzsche introduces their strategy:

> Nothing which has been done on earth against "the noble," "the mighty," "the masters," and "the rulers," is worth mentioning compared with what the *Jews* have done against them: the Jews, that priestly people, which in the last resort was able to gain satisfaction from its enemies and conquerors only through a radical revaluation of their values, that is, through an act of the most deliberate revenge.[7]

What the weak accomplished, through the Jews in particular, was the *transvaluation of values*. What was the transvaluation of values that the Jews accomplished? They turned the standards of evaluation upside down. Rather than identifying the good with the strong, the aristocrat, the beautiful, they turned the world upside down and pronounced that *good* was to be identified with the poor, the wretched, and the lowly. Evil was identified with the use of power over others. The weak (here, the Jews) could not beat the strong on their own turf; so, in their resentment, they changed the rules. They could not be strong themselves and challenge with strength the prevailing power; so, they changed the definitions and pronounced humility a virtue. Jesus was the supreme temptation. He seduced the world to adopt the Jewish values.[8]

Nietzsche proclaims that the slaves have won! The values have been transvalued, and what formerly was seen to oppose the strong and was therefore thought to be bad was now held up as virtue. He calls this move the *slaves' revolt in morality*. The weak have triumphed over the strong

---

7. Nietzsche, *On the Genealogy of Morality*, 17 (1.7).

8. Nietzsche sounds terribly anti-Semitic in some of these texts. Although he sometimes lapses into anti-Semitic rhetoric, he was, in fact, a strong critic of the anti-Semitism that was common in both intellectual and other cultural circles in Germany. For example, he opposed laws that restricted the rights of Jewish people to pursue business. He became disgusted with Wagner's persistent anti-Semitism. This reaction is part of the reason he broke with Wagner. Nietzsche's writings, though, include a lot of derogatory rhetoric. In part, I believe he caters to his readers' anti-Semitism because he wants to criticize Christianity. His audience will accept his argument more readily if they think it is against the Jews and not the Christians. Nietzsche, then, persuades his readers to accept a line of thought that ultimately undermines their Christian belief. For a response to misunderstandings about Nietzsche, including the charge of anti-Semitism, see Solomon and Higgins, *What Nietzsche Really Said*. For a strong critique of Nietzsche's stance on the Jews, see an alternative interpretation of him in Leiter, "Nietzsche's Hatred."

while remaining weak. Everyone who is weak and acts weak is morally good. Those who exercise strength and power over the weak are wrong.

The triumph of the slaves is complete. All of civilization has as its aim to *domesticate* man; to take the spirit of the strong out of him; to make him subservient. Civilization reeks of the rejection of Life. Nietzsche exclaims, "The sight of man now makes us tired—what is nihilism today if it is not *that* ? . . . We are tired of *man* . . ."[9] Nihilism for Nietzsche is the enemy. It is the emasculation of the human spirit through the slave-morality. It is anti-Life.

Traditional morality, emerging from the Judeo-Christian heritage, made virtues out of the marks of weakness and turned the marks of strength into vices. This reversal is what triggers the charge that Christianity is anti-Life. The values Christianity held forth were those most anti-Life. This charge, of course, assumes a particular view about what it is in which life consists. For Nietzsche, life is power:

> Life itself is essentially a process of appropriating, injuring, overpowering the alien and the weaker, oppressing, being harsh, imposing your own form. Incorporating, and at least, the very least, exploiting . . .[10]

Consequently, the qualities that make for a good life are those of strength:

> What is good?—Everything that enhances people's feeling of power, will to power, power itself.
> What is bad?—Everything stemming from weakness.
> What is happiness—The feeling that power is *growing*, that some resistance has been overcome.[11]

It is clear, as a result, that Christianity is supremely *anti-Life*:

> Christianity has taken the side of everything weak, base, failed, it has made an ideal out of whatever *contradicts* the preservation instincts of a strong life; it has corrupted the reason of even the most spiritual natures by teaching people to see the highest spiritual values as sinful, as deceptive, as *temptations*.[12]

Both Christianity and traditional morality hold forth what Nietzsche calls the *ascetic ideal*. The ascetic ideal is the notion that we are under

---

9. Nietzsche, *On the Genealogy of Morality*, 25 (1.12).
10. Nietzsche, *Beyond Good and Evil*, 259.
11. Nietzsche, *Anti-Christ*, 2.
12. Nietzsche, *Anti-Christ*, 5.

obligation to sacrifice our self-oriented desires for something greater. He thinks the ascetic ideal commands us to turn away from the very things that bring life and to turn towards the things that are life-denying.

Nietzsche's critique, here, is not primarily that Christianity is false. Rather, he rejects it because it is weak, trivial, and disgusting. He thinks that no one can want to be a Christian. "Our age *knows better*. . . . What used to be just sickness is indecency today—it is indecent to be a Christian these days. *And this is where my disgust begins*."[13] Nietzsche pronounces, with a hint of glee, that "what decides against Christianity now is our taste, not our reasons."[14] Nietzsche clearly puts forward the objection from flourishing.

THE NATURE OF HUMAN FLOURISHING

Given the background we have sketched, we can turn our attention to evaluating the objection from flourishing. Whether Christianity hinders human flourishing is a matter of two issues. The first issue concerns the nature of human flourishing. The second issue is what Christianity brings to this analysis of flourishing. What it means for a human being to flourish is, of course, hotly contested. Popular American sensibilities have been strongly shaped by the inalienable rights to life, liberty, and the pursuit of happiness that the Declaration of Independence proclaimed.

Even the phrase "the pursuit of happiness" requires analysis. What exactly is happiness? Charles Taylor and Carl Trueman have identified how contemporary notions of the self and of happiness have emerged over the last two centuries.[15] While Thomas Jefferson's wording in the Declaration had in mind a more classical (e.g., Aristotelian) understanding of "happiness"—a flourishing (*eudaimonia*) that emphasized the cultivation of virtuous character and pursuit of the public good (as noted below)[16]—thinkers such as Rousseau, as well as Nietzsche and Freud, have shaped how most people today think of their own flourishing. Taylor and Trueman call this widespread view "expressive individualism." In

---

13. Nietzsche, *Anti-Christ*, 38.
14. Nietzsche, *Gay Science*, 132.
15. Among his many works, see esp. Taylor, *Sources of the Self*. For Trueman, see Trueman, *Rise and Triumph*; *Strange New World*.
16. See Kittel, "Thomas Jefferson," 34–53.

this view, "each of us finds our meaning by giving expression to our own feelings and desires."[17]

The expressive individualist notion of flourishing can be seen in popular media, advertising, film, and the plethora of self-help books and products. A person's flourishing is a matter of her identity. Her identity is not merely *discovered* through self-exploration. It is *constructed* through self-exploration. A person's deeper sense of who she is and who she wants to be is both determinative of her bedrock identity and the final authority concerning how she should live. Any attempt to challenge the choices that come out of her sense of identity is taken to be a personal affront. The individual person defines her own identity. Thus, the individual person determines what life counts as a good life for her.

It is worth noting that this view of identity can be challenged. First, it is out of step with the view of human identity that was held from the Ancient Greeks into the modern period. Second, this subjective notion of human identity is, as we shall see, inherently unstable. It fluctuates with the whims and trends in popular culture. The fact that it is widely assumed and ratified throughout our current age is not evidence that it is true or that it will deliver on its promises. One ought to take a step back and consider how to discover an adequate concept of human flourishing.

There are two basic approaches one can take to the question of human flourishing, each of which is fruitful. We can call these the bottom-up approach and the top-down approach. The bottom-up approach begins its analysis with the actual desires and goals of people. This approach will distinguish between those desires that are candidates for being constitutive of our flourishing and those that are not. The desires we happen to have are not the final say in what counts for flourishing. We subject these desires and goals to careful inquiry. We begin with a hunch that some of these desires and goals will be clues to the reality about flourishing, but others will lead to faulty concepts.

The top-down approach begins with some theory. Usually, it is a theory about the nature of human beings or a theory about the ultimate structures of reality. A theory of reality will make up the worldview of the one who holds it. The theory of human nature will be a part of the person's worldview. A particular theory will provide specific resources for an account of human nature and flourishing. Whatever concept of

---

17. Trueman, *Rise and Triumph*, 46.

flourishing emerges will be consistent with the contours of the theory in question.

We can see the bottom-up approach in Aristotle. In the opening chapters of the *Nicomachean Ethics*, Aristotle wrote that everyone agrees that the highest good for a human being is happiness [*eudaimonia*] and that they "identify living well and doing well with being happy . . ."[18] There is, he points out, still a fair amount of disagreement about what happiness or the good life is. People think that different things constitute the best life, and they pursue these things accordingly.

Aristotle considers the kinds of goals or ends people commonly identify with the best life. These include pleasure, wealth, honor, and the life of contemplation. Wealth is easily shown not to be an ingredient in flourishing because wealth has no intrinsic value. Its value lies solely in what it can provide for the wealthy person. A person, then, does not really desire money. He desires the things that money can buy. Honor does not fare much better. Honor depends on the ones who bestow it on the honored person. Thus, the person of honor is dependent on others. Aristotle notes that the good for a human being must be a final end rather than an instrumental good. Furthermore, it must be self-sufficient rather than dependent.

From here, Aristotle does investigate his theory of human nature. He argues that it would be surprising if there were not an end or a function for the human person. He notes that a sculptor has a characteristic function—to produce sculptures. This is the characteristic function of the person as a sculptor. Aristotle asks whether there would not also be a function of a person simply as a human being. It would be something that each human being has the capacities to fulfill, and it would be something distinct to human beings. This end he finds in the rational nature of human beings. Excelling in our rational nature, then, is what constitutes flourishing for a human being. Our rational nature includes both theoretical rationality and practical rationality. It is more than our intellectual life. It involves our active life as well. The better life is lived with excellence in both theoretical and practical wisdom. The term "excellence" in English translations of Aristotle is generally the same as the term "virtue." In the end, Aristotle states that "human good turns out

---

18. Aristotle, *Nicomachean Ethics* 1.4 (1095a).

to be activity of the soul in accordance with virtue and if there are more than one virtue, in accordance with the best and most complete."[19]

An example of a top-down approach is that of Jean-Paul Sartre.[20] At the close of World War II, he delivered a lecture that has been published with the English title, *Existentialism and Humanism*.[21] His aim was to defend existentialism against common criticisms. He describes the starting point of existentialism as *existence precedes essence*. What Sartre meant by this summary is best seen in contrast with Augustine. Augustine held that Plato's forms were thoughts in the mind of God.[22] The forms are eternal universals that explain the nature of the particular things in the world. For example, each beautiful thing in the world is beautiful in virtue of its participating in Beauty itself.

If the forms are ideas in God's mind, they are as eternal and as unchangeable as God himself. When God created the world, he did so in accordance with his ideas. The idea of what it means to be a human being, then, was in God's mind before he created any actual human beings. The idea of a human being is God's idea of the nature of a human being. He then creates individual people in accordance with this idea. The idea in God's mind constitutes the *essence* of the human. What it is to be a human being, then, is fixed and eternal. In Augustine's view, *essence precedes existence*.

It is this picture of human nature that Sartre is rejecting. Because he thought that there is no God, he also thought that there is no prior idea of what a human being must be that constitutes a common human nature. For human beings, then, *existence precedes essence*. There are existing persons, but they do not come into the world already bearing an essence or a nature. Each person creates her own nature. People exist before they have any essence. There is more to Sartre's existentialism than his claim that there is no given human nature. This aspect of his theory, however, is both an expression of and an influence on the current expressive individualism.

Sartre's existential contribution comes in the implication of his claim that existence precedes essence. One result of this fact is that a person's

---

19. Aristotle, *Nicomachean Ethics* 1.4 (1098a).

20. The following paragraphs are drawn from my "Human Nature and Freedom," 224–38.

21. Sartre, *Existentialism and Humanism*. This book has also been titled *Existentialism as a Humanism*.

22. See Augustine, "On the Ideas," 79–81.

nature is up to that person. A person chooses his own nature. This choice is deeper than choosing a career or a spouse or a hobby. Human beings define their identities at the deepest levels. Sartre called this choice a radical freedom. There are no moral, metaphysical, or divinely-ordained boundaries limiting how someone creates herself. Her only obligation is to choose. Not to choose, that is, to allow the culture around her to mold her into its own image, whether consciously or unconsciously, is to live in bad faith. Whatever life she lives, she must choose it, and in doing so, she creates her nature.

We can see that Sartre has a top-down approach to what it means to live well. He begins with the theoretical claim about reality that there is no God and, therefore, no human nature. The end goal of a person's life, then, is to choose her nature and to live it out. The resources for flourishing that his theory provides do not include a fixed human nature, definitive moral virtues, or an objective purpose for the individual. They do include a self-determined identity and the necessity of taking responsibility for one's authentic choices.

There are two ways to engage the bottom-up and the top-down approaches. The first is to evaluate the larger theories that underlie our views of the best life. For example, Sartre's existentialism relies on the notion that there is no God. Independent arguments in favor of the existence of God, then, will count against his theory. In the same way, arguments against the existence of God will lend it some support. If a theory is supported by independent arguments, it is more secure. We can, then, draw upon the resources within the theory to mark out the contours of human flourishing.

The second way is that we can test various candidates for the best theory of human nature and flourishing against a well-grounded assessment of our desires and goals. Thus, we can see which theories have the resources to account for what seems to be our actual views of flourishing. In what follows, I shall not bring independent arguments to bear on various theories. I shall explore the kinds of desires and goals people report. From these I shall point out some promising candidates for the kind of desires that make up human flourishing. It is against these features that I shall test the claim that Christianity hinders our flourishing.

What do people want? The answer, as Aristotle observed, could be summarized with a simple statement: people want many things. Each of us has a whole array of wants, loves, and desires. While the list might be long, it is not difficult to begin to sort our desires into the ones that are more important to us and the ones that are less important. The least important desires we have might be surface-desires. These are wants that are satisfied rather easily. Sometimes, one of these desires can be met with a decent sandwich. Other times, we want a nap or a break or to complete the jigsaw puzzle we are working on. Other desires might be called vacation-desires. These may be desires to see different parts of the country or the world. Vacation-desires can also be closer to home. One of my vacation-desires is to sit on our back patio with my wife, Jeanie, and enjoy a glass of red wine. To have time for leisurely conversation is a bit like being on vacation. I love the times when we can have unhurried moments together.

These desires are meaningful to us, but they are not as important to us as some of our other desires that might be called goal-desires. These wants have more of a long-term trajectory in our lives. They may include desires to complete various goals, such as finishing a graduate degree or becoming a manager in your work. Often these are tied with the marks of accomplishment or persisting on a path towards a career or skill. There are still deeper desires than goal-desires. We want to be successful in our work, and we want it to matter. We want our children to grow into mature adults who have rich lives. We desire deeply for our relationships to be healthy. We want to be good people, who love, support, and respect others. These items are examples of our deeper desires. At the center of many of these wants is our desire to be a certain kind of person.[23]

Each of us has a core of deepest desires about who we are and who we want to be. I call these our *core identity*. Our core identity includes more than our desires. It includes our beliefs as well as assumptions about who we are. The desires that make up our core identities are deeper than our surface or vacation or goal-desires. Our core identities are formed as we inhabit certain belief and value structures over time. We begin to inhabit these beliefs and values at a very young age. In fact, we begin this process before we can speak. Our sense of being loved and of being secure has a great impact on our deepest sense of who we are. As we grow, we develop patterns of ordering our various choices, beliefs, values, goals, and interests around these deeper ones. Each time we adapt our surface beliefs and values to our deeper ones, the deeper ones become even more deeply entrenched. As a result, we become more fixed as a certain kind of

---

23. The rest of this essay follows parts of my book, *Our Deepest Desires*.

person. In a sense, we *habituate* ourselves into our core identities by the practice of ordering our other beliefs and values around them.

What constitutes our core identity is rarely in the forefront of our minds. We have to pause and think about which desires and beliefs are most central to our lives. With some careful self-reflection, however, we can see that the content of our core identities is not terribly mysterious. There are deeper desires that are widely shared and fairly easily recognized. I suggest that within the core identity of almost every person are at least the following desires. First, there is the desire for a meaningful life. Second, we share a fundamental desire for rich relationships. Third, we deeply long to be people who embody certain character traits.

The desire for a meaningful life is connected to purpose. Our meaning is a matter of there being a *point* to our existence. Is my life connected to something that is good? Or am I just wandering "lost in the cosmos," to use Walker Percy's phrase?[24] People long to make a difference with what they do. We do not want our projects to count for nothing in the end. We often hear of people wanting a job about which they can be passionate. Even in recreation, a common sentiment is the longing to "feel alive." These observations point to a persistent longing for something to come out of our lives that matters and that feels like it matters.

The question of meaning and value can be asked on both a local level and on a global level. We might distinguish between "local meaning" and "cosmic meaning." What I am calling local meaning can be illustrated by the game of Monopoly. Every time you pass "Go," it is a happy event. The $200 you receive is important. While you are playing the game, the money has meaning and value. You treat it as hard currency. You buy property and houses in order to make more money. You build your strategies around the value of the money. Within the game, the $200 matters. Once you stop playing the game, however, it all disappears. The $500 dollar bill and the $1 bill have the same real value. Monopoly money has local value and local meaning. That is, it has value internal to the game, but no value or meaning external to it.

On the local level, we can and do find meaning in the projects and people that are important to us. This meaning is a good and valuable thing. The question of meaning, however, also has a global or cosmic horizon. Here the question concerns our place in reality. Do I matter in any ultimate way? Are there purposes for my life beyond the ones I construct

---

24. Percy, *Lost in the Cosmos*.

for myself, as meaningful as these are to me? The question of cosmic meaning and value is a question that presses upon thoughtful people. Our desires for meaning and value are not limited to local meaning and value. We long for cosmic meaning and value.

The core desire for relationships is in some way connected to the longing for meaning and purpose. Our relationships are among the most important contributors to our flourishing. If our relationships are going well, our lives are going well. This observation leads to questions about the marks of fruitful and fulfilling relationships. The features we want in our relationships are clear to us. We want our relationships to be marked by trust, kindness, love, patience, peace, and joy. Each person longs for these features in all of her friendships and family relations. We want our relationships to be sources of strength and support for ourselves, and we want to be a resource for strength and support for those we care about.

Beside our deep desires for meaning and for relationships of a certain quality, we long to be people who experience and embody character. We want our own lives to reflect qualities that can and ought to be admired. The qualities we want our lives to manifest overlap with the features of the kind of relationships we want. Many of these qualities are moral virtues. We want to be good people. We want to be honest, trustworthy, and loving to those around us. The qualities we long for include more than what we might call moral virtues. We also want to have the kind of wisdom that helps us navigate our lives well. We want insight that we can bring into the many decisions we make each week. We want to be satisfied with the kind of person we are becoming.

These desires are found in the core identities of most people. As such, they can play the role of the facts against which we test various theories. The central question of this chapter is whether Christianity hinders or promotes human flourishing. Now that we have seen some of the features that are widely thought to constitute flourishing, we can subject Christianity to the test. What we will find is that the core aspirations that are part of the flourishing life are both explained well and fulfilled in the Christian story.

Central to Christianity is the fact that God created the universe, and he created human beings for his own reasons. The fact that we are made by God guarantees that each human life is both valuable and meaningful in an objective, cosmic sense. Beginning with the issue of value, regardless of how we feel about our worth, our value is given by God. The value that any human person has is not something that she has to achieve. Our value is not due to accidental or contingent factors such as our health or education or whatever good we may do in the world. Each person has intrinsic value regardless of these things because each person is made by God for God's good reasons. The point to our existence is not a matter of our accomplishing anything or of our succeeding at some task. We fit into reality because we were made by God. Thus, we matter.

We did not invent God's reasons for creating us, nor did anyone else. Therefore, these reasons cannot be erased or canceled by any human being. There is nothing that one human being can do to annul the objective and global value of another human being. We may try to ignore or to avoid the fact that a person's value is not up to us, but we cannot change this basic fact. There have been many attempts to ground human value in culture or in status or even in the state. Others try to locate the value of persons in their contribution to the broader society. If a person's worth is grounded in these kinds of things, she may either fail to gain value or her value can be rescinded. We have seen throughout history that the claim that the value of certain people can be eliminated by others has catastrophic consequences. Because our value is derived from God's purposes, however, it cannot be overruled by any human being. It is the conviction that each person has intrinsic, objective and indelible value that has grounded the commitment to universal human rights.

In the Christian story, God's purposes for us also guarantee our global meaning. There is a point to our lives, and this point is grounded in something outside of us as individuals, as communities, and even outside of our membership in the biological species. Thus, our meaning is objective, and it is independent of how we think our lives are going. Because God has purposes for us, our meaning does not depend on how we feel about our lives on any given day. We matter independently of our achievements. Our lives are meaningful simply because God has reasons for making us. We stand in relation to the fundamental meaning-maker of the universe. The point of our lives is grounded in our relationship with God, and it is real whether we can recognize it or not. We have been made and placed in this world for God's purposes. Although our accomplishments are fragile, our meaning is secure.

The teachings of Christianity also capture the kind of relationships that are crucial to human flourishing. Our care for one another is to be modeled on the love God has for human beings. God's love is revealed in the creation of all reality and in his redemption of human beings in Christ. This love sets that pattern for our relationships. We know that the best of our relationships is characterized by mutual giving. We all long for relationships in which we are known and accepted and supported, while we in turn know, accept, and support the other. There is a deep fittingness, then, between what we grasp about the best in human relationships on the one hand and God's love for human beings on the other.

Once we reflect on the quality of relationship that characterizes God's own being, we are not surprised that the content of Christian ethics centers on love and service to others. Jesus continually stretched the moral imaginations of his followers in terms of whom they were to love. He named the second most important law, the law to "love your neighbor as yourself" (Matt 22:39 ESV). Jesus pushed his followers even further: "You have heard that it was said, 'You shall love your neighbor and hate your enemy.' But I say to you, love your enemies and pray for those who persecute you" (Matt 5:43-44 ESV). The kind of love that God demonstrates is to be our model of how we ought to love, not just our family and friends, but those who are strangers and those who may be out to hurt us. To be honest, we have rarely seen anyone consistently come close to meeting the challenge of these commands. When we do witness such love, we tend to be humbled and awed.

The Christian story, then, captures many of our deepest intuitions and aspirations about relationships. It makes sense of the fact that relationships are the most important aspects of our lives. It grounds even the manner how we best relate and to whom we relate. Practicing this vision of relationship, then, results in the best quality of life for human beings.

The third longing in our core identity that we discussed is our desire to be people of character. As we have seen, this desire is related to but broader than our longings for strong relationships. The life we want is a life of moral, relational, and epistemic virtue. Christianity holds our development of virtue as central. Part of God's purposes in creating us is that we would reflect the character qualities he has. The Christian story includes the promise that our character development is not something that we pursue on our own. As we cooperate with the work of God in our lives, he builds these qualities into us. We become the people we want to be.

The common thread in the way Christianity accounts for these features of our core identity is that God created us for his own reasons. In contrast to Sartre, there is a human nature that is given to us by God. This fact guarantees that our natures are stable and secure. We are free from the tyranny of having to invent our own essence. The popular construct of human nature called expressive individualism leaves each person in the precarious position of having to carve out meaning and purpose in a world that has no cosmic meaning or purpose. Most people, frankly, do not succeed in this task. Our world is littered with mid-life crises, depression, anxiety, and hopelessness. While these symptoms are complicated, it is plausible that they are exacerbated by the sense of lostness people encounter when they consider their place in the cosmos.

Within the stable nature that is given to us by God, we can navigate our lives with confidence and with hope. God's purposes for us are for our good. They involve the cultivation of the very qualities we long for. They are expressed in the quality relationships we seek. This objective purpose and value free us from the task of having to construct our lives.

What of the historical objections from flourishing? We can see that the objections from flourishing can be easily met with the resources of Christianity. Marx, as we stated, argued that Christianity distracted oppressed people from their plight by the empty promise of reward after this life. Although Christianity does indeed promise eternal life to those who trust the work of Christ on their behalf, this promise does not have to produce distraction. In fact, the reality of the afterlife is one of the motivations for followers of Jesus to engage the world around them and to work for justice. It is essential to the Christian story that our purpose of cultivating the world must now be pursued among the "thorns and thistles" (Gen 3:18 ESV) we find in a fallen world. In other words, we have to push back the effects of evil as we bring good and true and beautiful and useful things out of this world. The task of pushing back the effects of evil takes on the form of love for the poor and oppressed throughout the Scriptures. One example will suffice. In the book of Isaiah, God reveals the kind of piety he wants:

> Is not this the fast that I choose: to loose the bonds of wickedness, to undo the straps of the yoke, to let the oppressed go free, and to break every yoke? Is it not to share your bread with the hungry and bring the homeless poor into your house; when you see the naked, to cover him, and not to hide yourself from your own flesh? (Isa 58:6–7 ESV)

Although believers do fail in their commitment to work on behalf of the oppressed, the clear teaching of Christianity is that bringing justice to the oppressed is part of the path of following Jesus. Marx's version of the objection from flourishing, then, misses the mark.

Freud's claim that religious belief is infantile can be dealt with briefly as well. The plausibility of this objection rests on the claim that there is a significant disanalogy between a child's relationship with her father and an adult's relation to God. The accusation of being immature or infantile is plausible when an adult does not take responsibility for his life or when he depends on things that he should not depend on. For example, there is a fairly common trope in films and television of a person who was a football star in high school and, ten years later, continues to ground his sense of worth in the past. His dependence on his past accomplishments or popularity reveals his immaturity. On the other hand, no one faults an adult who trusts his surgeon when he needs to have a complicated medical procedure. Some dependencies in the life of an adult are immature or infantile. Some dependencies are appropriate and rational. The question is, *to which category does belief in God belong?*

Christianity holds that we are fundamentally dependent on God. We depend on him for our coming to be, and we depend on him for our continued existence. Furthermore, as we have seen, aligning our lives with his purposes is the path to capturing the desires that make up our core identity. If it turns out that Christianity is true, this dependence reflects reality. Independence from God is the path to human impoverishment. If Christianity turns out to be false, however, then believers routinely order their lives around a significant falsehood. In this case, leaning on God for comfort, guidance, or meaning is wrong-headed. If our dependence on a God who does not exist prevents us from taking responsibility for our lives, it might be called infantile. It would be something that keeps us immature. It is clear that Freud's argument—that Christianity is a hindrance to human flourishing—relies on the assumption that Christianity is false. At the same time, the Christian argument that aligning our lives with the purposes of God is the path to flourishing requires the truth of the Christian story. As a result, Freud has not provided an argument against Christianity. He assumes that God does not exist.

A similar analysis will be applicable to Nietzsche's argument from flourishing. Nietzsche argues that Christianity requires that we give up the things that actually lead to the fullness of life. We must turn away from pride, independence, and the expression of strength. We must resist the urge to exert our will in opposition to others or to conventional moral norms. The vision of life Nietzsche holds forth is in some sense

Eudaimonistic.[25] It is a vision of the good life. The content of this vision, however, is in strong contrast to the Eudaimonistic vision of Christianity.

As we have seen, the Christian vision of life includes the pursuit of the kind of relationships that are categorized by love, patience, humility, generosity, and kindness. These are the very qualities that Nietzsche thinks hinder our flourishing. If we think about the kinds of relationships we *want*, however, we can see that Nietzsche's vision is not conducive to flourishing. As we saw, the deepest desires concerning our relationships match the Christian vision exactly. Nietzsche's vision is significantly out of step with the things that make up our core identity.

The objection to Christianity from flourishing is a common obstacle for people considering the gospel. There is a widespread notion that Christianity is bad for those who hold it. It requires a posture that hinders our pursuit of the best life. As we have seen, it has roots in some of the seminal thinkers of the past two centuries. When considered carefully, however, there is little to be said in favor of this argument. When we consider both what flourishing involves and what Christianity actually offers, we see that the Christian vision of life strongly captures most people's reflections of what makes for human flourishing. The good news is truly good news for us.

BIBLIOGRAPHY

Aristotle. *The Basic Works of Aristotle*. Edited by Richard McKeon. New York: Random, 1941.

Augustine. "On the Ideas." In *Eighty-Three Different Questions*. Translated by David L. Mosher. Fathers of the Church 70. Washington, DC: Catholic University Press, 1982.

Freud, Sigmund. *The Future of an Illusion*. Translated by James Strachey. New York: Norton, 1961.

Ganssle, Gregory. "Human Nature and Freedom in Adaptation." In *The Philosophy of Charles Kaufman*, edited by David LaRocca, 224–38. Lexington, KY: University of Kentucky Press, 2011.

———. *Our Deepest Desires: How the Christian Story Fulfills Human Aspirations*. Downers Grove, IL: InterVarsity, 2017.

Kittel, Laura. "Thomas Jefferson and the Pursuit of Happiness: Rethinking What Right Means for Us Today." In *Religious Liberty and Law*, edited by Angus Menuge, 34–53. London: Routledge, 2017.

Leiter, Brian. "Nietzsche's Hatred of 'Jew Hatred'—A Review of *Nietzsche's Jewish Problem: Between Anti-Semitism and Anti-Judaism*, by Robert C. Holub (Princeton: Princeton University Press, 2015)." *New Rambler*, December 21, 2015.

---

25. I want to thank David Horner for this observation.

https://newramblerreview.com/book-reviews/philosophy/nietzsche-s-hatred-of-jew-hatred.

Nietzsche, Friedrich. *The Anti-Christ*. In *The Anti-Christ, Ecce Homo, Twilight of the Idols and Other Writings*, edited by Aaron Ridley and Judith Norman, 1–68. Cambridge: Cambridge University Press, 2005.

———. *Beyond Good and Evil*. Edited by Rolf-Peter Horstmann and Judith Norman. Cambridge: Cambridge University Press, 2002.

———. *The Gay Science*. Edited by Bernard Williams. Cambridge: Cambridge University Press, 2011.

———. *On the Genealogy of Morality*. Edited by Keith Ansell-Pearson. Cambridge: Cambridge University Press, 1994.

Percy, Walker. *Lost in the Cosmos: The Last Self-Help Book*. New York: Farrar, Straus, and Giroux, 1983.

Renan, Ernst. *Life of Jesus*. New York: Modern Library, 1955.

Sartre, Jean-Paul. *Existentialism and Humanism*. Translated by Philip Mairet. London: Methuen, 1948.

Solomon, Robert, and Kathleen Higgins. *What Nietzsche Really Said*. New York: Shocken, 2000.

Taylor, Charles. *The Sources of the Self*. Cambridge: Harvard University Press, 1989.

Trueman, Carl. *The Rise and Triumph of the Modern Self*. Wheaton, IL: Crossway, 2020.

———. *Strange New World: How Thinkers and Activists Redefined Identity and Sparked the Sexual Revolution*. Wheaton, IL: Crossway, 2022.

Wellhausen, Julius. *Prolegomena to the History of Ancient Israel*. Durham, NC: Duke University Press, 2000.

Young, Julian. *Friedrich Nietzsche: A Philosophical Biography*. Cambridge: Cambridge University Press, 2010.

9

Gender and Christianity

Preston Sprinkle

INTRODUCTION

THE BIBLE HAS FACED criticism from various corners of mainstream culture. From its statements about women, slavery, violence, sexuality, and divine judgment, critics have much material to work with. In many of these areas, however, upon closer inspection, the Bible's seemingly outdated and oppressive views become more nuanced—if not, dare I say, progressive.

Take women, for instance. Critics race to passages like Deuteronomy 22:28–29, which seems to say that women are commanded to marry their rapist (it actually doesn't say that in the Hebrew),[1] as evidence that the Bible is profoundly misogynistic. And yet the first—and most fundamental—statement about women in the Bible says that they are created "in God's image" and equal to men (Gen 1:27). In the ancient world, only kings (men of the highest status) were described as being created in the image of the gods. Here, women are described as possessing the same

---

1. This is now well-established among biblical scholars. For a quick overview of the issues, see Richter, "Does God Really Command Women?"

status as male kings and the gods. You can't find a more humanizing statement on women in the ancient world than what we find in Genesis 1:27. The Bible's view of women is at the very least quite complicated.

There are, of course, many other difficult statements on women in the Bible (along with many other liberating ones), which I'll leave to my colleague Lynn Cohick to expound upon in chapter 10 of this book. The topic I'd like to focus on here is the topic of gender as it relates to transgender identities. This, of course, is a wide-ranging topic. A thorough treatment of all the ethical, theological, philosophical, scientific, and pastoral questions is impossible here.[2] For this chapter, I would like to focus more narrowly on questions related to human nature that the transgender conversation has exposed. For instance, what role do our sexed bodies play in determining human identity? Does sex or gender determine who we are? What's the relationship between biological sex and gender stereotypes? And how does the Bible compare with certain modern, Western, and secular responses to these questions?

Please note: these are not the only issues that Christians should wrestle with in the transgender conversation; many pastoral, relational, and quite personal questions will not be addressed in this chapter (e.g., should I use the preferred pronouns of my fifteen-year-old daughter?), which makes this chapter an incomplete, albeit important, contribution to the conversation. However, as we'll see shortly, the questions we'll wrestle with in this chapter will end up playing a foundational role in how we approach the many other important issues that come up in this conversation.

The overarching point I'd like to make is this: the Bible offers a coherent, humanizing, and scientifically sound perspective on human nature; in particular, the significance of our sexed bodies in determining human identity. I will also show, in turn, that some alternative, secular perspectives on transgender identities are more regressive than progressive, even if their narrative is pitched as the latter. This doesn't mean all our questions about the transgender conversation are directly addressed by the Bible, or that everything the Bible says about sex and gender makes perfect sense to modern readers. But taken as a whole, the Bible is (perhaps unexpectedly) more forward thinking, life-giving, scientifically sound, and liberating about human nature than many alternative perspectives today. This doesn't mean people have to believe the Bible.

---

2. For my best attempt to cover all this ground, see Sprinkle, *Embodied*.

Some might be happy (or almost required) to believe a regressive narrative about human nature. So be it. But the assumption that the Bible must be more backwards and unscientific because, well, it's the Bible, will be shown to be just that—an assumption.

But before we tease out this potentially audacious claim, there are several key terms and phrases that we need to define up front.

DEFINITIONS

I'll be using the term *transgender* in the same way that Christian psychologist Dr. Mark Yarhouse does, as "an umbrella term for the many ways in which people might experience and/or present and express (or live out) their gender identities differently from people whose sense of gender identity is congruent with their biological sex."[3] As an umbrella term, transgender can be used to capture many other identities that describe a similar experience of incongruence, such as nonbinary, genderqueer, genderfluid, and others. But some people would rather keep transgender, nonbinary, and other identities distinct. There is no uniform perspective on terminology. Some people use the shortened *trans** (with the asterisk) to capture the umbrella nature of term, and I'll do the same throughout. So, *trans** is a catch-all term that refers to anyone who experiences some kind of incongruence (psychological or social) with their biological sex.[4]

The term *transman* refers to a biological female who identifies as a man, and *transwoman* refers to a biological male who identifies as a woman. We'll discuss *intersex* in more detail later on, but a quick definition is: a person who has some atypical feature or features in their sexual anatomy, endocrine system, or (sometimes, *and*) their sex chromosomes. *Gender dysphoria* refers to the distress that some people experience over their biological sex. It's the phrase used to diagnose people suffering from this condition, while *transgender* is an identity term that some people diagnosed with gender dysphoria might use to

---

3. Yarhouse, *Understanding Gender Dysphoria*, 20.

4. With each year that passes, the term *transgender* keeps getting used with more and more diversity to include many different experiences, assumptions, and identities. We may be getting close to the point to where *transgender* simply means "someone who says they're *transgender*," which could mean almost anything the person wants it to mean. In any case, any thoughtful conversation about *transgender* identities and experiences should include a clear definition up front of what people mean by the term.

describe themselves. Not everyone who identifies as transgender would be diagnosed with gender dysphoria.[5]

The terms *sex* and *gender* are particularly tricky.[6] And any conversation on trans* identities needs to sort out exactly what people mean by these two terms. Beginning in the late 1960s and early 1970s, some scholars started using sex and gender to refer to different aspects of the human experience. Sex continued to refer to one's biological sex, but gender was used to refer to "the psychological, social, and cultural aspects of being male or female."[7] For instance, what would you say if I were to ask you, "Is pink a male or female color?" The answer is neither. Pink is a color, not a biological sex. And yet, pink has become (in the modern West at least) associated with femaleness. Every given culture has things that it *associates with* being male and female (like pink or blue), even though those characteristics aren't *intrinsic* to being male or female.

Now, gender itself is a concept that can be broken down into three sub-categories. *Gender identity* describes "one's internal sense of self as male, female, both, or neither."[8] *Gender role* describes the "social and cultural" aspects of being male or female, sometimes shorthand for "masculinity and femininity."[9] And *gender expression* has to do with the clothes, mannerisms, and interests that are expected of a male or female in any given culture. So, a human who dresses in pink and wears their hair long is resonating with a feminine gender *expression*. If they stay at home and raise their kids while their spouse is off at work, this too would

---

5. One of many perspectives within the transgender conversation is the so-called "Self-ID" perspective, which says that if someone says they're trans*, then they're trans*; they don't need some kind of medical diagnosis (i.e., gender dysphoria) to truly be trans*. Others will say the opposite; if you aren't diagnosed with gender dysphoria, then you're a "trans-trender" and not *really* trans*.

6. See my more expanded discussion of these two terms in *Embodied*, 35–48.

7. Yarhouse, *Understanding Gender Dysphoria*, 17

8. Robert Stoller was the first one, to my knowledge, to use the phrase *core gender identity*—he later shortened it to *gender identity*—to refer to a person's "fundamental sense of belonging to one sex" (Stoller, "Hermaphroditic Identity," 453).

9. The concept of *gender role* was developed by sexologist John Money, who said that "gender role . . . is defined as *everything* that one says and does to indicate that one is either male or female, or androgyne" (Money, *Sin, Science and the Sex Police*, 347). Others describe it in similar ways. Transgender writer Austen Hartke says: "*Gender roles* govern the way we're expected to act, depending on our gender" (Hartke, *Transforming*, 23). And Planned Parenthood says: "Gender roles in society means how we're expected to act, speak, dress, groom, and conduct ourselves based upon our assigned sex" (Planned Parenthood, "What Are Gender Roles and Stereotypes?").

be a feminine gender *role*. But if their internal sense of self is that of a male, then their gender *identity* is male.

To be clear, I'm neither endorsing nor disagreeing with these concepts. I'm simply telling you how these terms are commonly used. Whether you agree with any of this, it's important to understand how the conversation is taking place and what people mean by what they say. And here's one of the most confusing things in the conversation: many people still use the term *gender* interchangeably with biological sex, even people who just told you five seconds ago that sex is different from gender. Inconsistency and confusion seem to follow the term gender like a dog in heat. No conversation about gender can get very far until we define very clearly what we mean by the term and, preferably, stick to that definition.

Let's go back to *sex*, as in biological sex. While gender refers to the psychological, social, and cultural aspects of being male or female, *sex* refers to whether someone *is* male or female. Feminist philosopher Rebecca Reilly-Cooper gives a good airtight summary when she describes "female" and "male" as "general biological categories that apply to all species that reproduce sexually."[10] Evolutionary biologist Colin Wright gets even more specific:

> Biological sex . . . is connected to the distinct type of gametes (sex cells) that an organism produces, . . . males are the sex that produce small gametes (sperm) and females produce large gametes (ova). There are no intermediate gametes, which is why there is no spectrum of sex. Biological sex in humans is a binary system.[11]

So, *Homo sapiens* are a sexually dimorphic mammalian species; we require a male and a female (and the fusion of the different gametes they produce) to reproduce. Or in the words of two eminent scientists: "An organism is male or female if it is structured to perform one of the respective roles in reproduction," and "there is no other widely accepted biological classification for the sexes."[12]

This does not mean that males and females are completely different in every way. We are actually more alike than we are different. One female might be more different from another female in many ways, such as in personality, height, weight, physical strength, and so on. But when

---

10. Reilly-Cooper, "Sex."
11. Wright, "Sex Is Not a Spectrum."
12. McHugh and Mayer, "Sexuality and Gender," 90.

scientists say that biological sex is binary, this has to do primarily with categories of reproduction, specifically the two different gonads that produce different gametes required for reproduction.

Now of course, in a world where everything is debated and everyone has an internet connection, you'll find some people who disagree that humans are a sexually dimorphic species. (You'll also find whole societies who say the earth is flat and not round.) But if you look closely at the "sex is not binary" arguments, they almost always make two mistakes. They either confuse sex with gender, or they refer to intersex as proof that sex is not binary.

For instance, I just Googled "is biological sex binary" and the first article that popped up was from a website called *Sapiens*, titled "Biological Science Rejects the Sex Binary, and That's Good for Humanity."[13] To argue that biological sex is not binary, the author constantly refers to human behaviors and experiences, *not* the bare existence of two biological sexes. He (rightly!) points out the obvious point that there is "true diversity of the human *experience*" and "multitudes of ways *to be* female or male or both" and that "in a variety of species, females are *authoritarian, promiscuous,* and ... *pugnacious.*"[14] Well, of course, but these are all human behaviors and personalities and interests. Sexual dimorphism doesn't mean all females and males must look and act the same; it doesn't mean that females can't be "promiscuous." It just means that humans reproduce when the gamete of a male fuses with the gamete of a female.

The author also does what almost every "sex is not binary" person does; he uses intersex people as proof that sex is not binary. This too is a mistake, but we'll discuss intersex more thoroughly below, so table that discussion for a bit. The point is, for all its accusations of being unscientific, backwoods, and backwards, the Bible consistently agrees with what we know from science: that the mammalian species called *Homo sapiens* are sexually dimorphic.

---

13. In fact, the entire first page of articles that came up in this search *all* argue that sex is *not* binary. When I typed in the same phrase in the search engine DuckDuckGo, which, I believe, has a different algorithm, the findings were much more mixed. Several articles arguing (or simply pointing out) that humans are a sexually dimorphic species popped up.

14. Fuentes, "Biological Science Rejects the Sex Binary," emphasis added.

THE BIBLE, SEX, AND GENDER

Who are we as humans? Are we male, female, both, or neither? What role do our bodies play in making this decision? Do our chosen identities define who we are, or is there something or someone outside of us—culture, family, God, gods—who define who we are? And how do we know the answer to these fundamental questions? I'm going to suggest that the Bible gives us a reasonable and remarkably thoughtful and scientifically sound response to these and other questions related to human identity.

For clarity's sake, we can boil down our various questions to one singular question; it's not the only question, but it is a rather fundamental one. I call it the question of incongruence: *If someone experiences incongruence between their biological sex and their internal sense of self, which one determines who they are—and why?* For example: If a biological male feels or thinks or believes that they are a woman, are they a woman or a man? And *why*? If they have an internal sense that they are female and their body says they are male, then which one are they and *why*? Does the body or the mind determine whether we are male, female, both, or neither? What does the Christian Bible have to say?

To sum up my understanding of the biblical material, I'm going to make three observations of what the Bible says about human nature as it pertains to questions related to trans* identities.[15]

1. Our Sexed Bodies Are a Significant Part of Human Identity

Arguably the most significant statement about human identity comes in Genesis 1:27, where God says we are created in his image.

> God created mankind in his own image,
> *in the image of God* he created them;
> male and female he created them. (Gen 1:27)

Theologians have wrestled for years with what it means to bear "God's image," but much in these debates isn't crucial for our purposes.[16] What is clear from the text is that our sexed bodies are essential to bearing God's image.

---

15. I unpack this more thoroughly in *Embodied*, 63–77.
16. See the discussion in Middleton, *Liberating Image*, 17–34.

The Hebrew word for "image" is *tselem*, and it almost always refers to "idols" throughout the Old Testament. What are idols? They're visible representations of an invisible deity. The term basically means the physical "carved or hewn statue or copy" of a nonphysical being. In Genesis 1, this "statue or copy" is humanity, and the nonphysical being is Yahweh. "Visibility and bodiliness" are central to the meaning of the phrase "image of God."[17] As theologian Marc Cortez puts it: the image of God is "a declaration that God intended to create human persons to be the physical means through which he would manifest his own divine presence in the world."[18] Like the idols of pagan deities, we are visible representations of Yahweh on earth. Not just because we are embodied, but because of our *sexed* embodied nature. We bear God's image as male and female.[19]

We are created in God's image *as* sexed embodied humans, and therefore our biological sex is an important part of human identity, because bearing God's image is an important part of human identity.

2. Our Sexed Bodies Are Sacred

Throughout Scripture, the human body is viewed as sacred. This shouldn't be a surprise in light of the previous point. In any case, the point is beautifully illustrated in Genesis 2, where Eve is created from the side of Adam:

> So the LORD God caused the man to fall into a deep sleep; and while he was sleeping, he took one of the man's ribs and then closed up the place with flesh. Then the LORD God made a woman from the rib he had taken out of the man, and he brought her to the man. (Gen 2:21–22)

---

17. Middleton, *Liberating Image*, 25.

18. Cortez, *ReSourcing Theological Anthropology*, 109.

19. By "male" and "female," Genesis 1:27 is clearly talking about biological sex and not the modern concepts of gender identity, gender expression, or gender role. For one, the very next command to "be fruitful and multiply" (Gen 1:28) flows from the reproductive capabilities (not the internal senses of self or the gender expressions of the human pair) of the male and female of the previous verse. Moreover, "male and female" are the same terms used to describe the animals that went into the ark (Gen 6:19; 7:9), which most likely mean the biological sexes of the animals and not their gender identities. On the importance of the connection between the image of God—specifically God's "likeness" (*demut*)—and humans as male and female, see Garr, *In His Own Image and Likeness*, 167–69.

Even though "rib" is a popular translation, it's actually not the most likely meaning of the Hebrew word *tsela*. The term *tsela* occurs more than forty times in the Old Testament, and it never describes a human rib.[20] In almost every other usage, *tsela* refers to the side of a sacred piece of architecture, like the tabernacle or temple.[21] And a similar nuance is present here in Genesis 2 as well. Eve is formed from the *tsela* of Adam, implying that Adam's body, as well as Eve's, are like sacred pieces of architecture. Just as temples embody God's presence, so do human bodies.

This, of course, is exactly what Paul says in 1 Corinthians 6, where he describes the sanctity of the human body:

> Do you not know that your *bodies* are temples of the Holy Spirit, who is in *you*, whom you have received from God? *You* are not your own; *you* were bought at a price. Therefore honor God with your *bodies*. (1 Cor 6:19–20, emphasis added)

It's worth quickly noting here that Paul keeps using the terms "body" and "you" interchangeably. *You* are your *body* and your *body* is *you*. We aren't bodies *with* souls—we are *embodied souls*.[22]

Our bodies are an intrinsic part of who we are as humans. And Paul doesn't see our bodies as a morally neutral canvas or shell that we can do whatever we want with. Throughout 1 Corinthians 6, Paul is arguing against sexually immoral behavior, but he roots his commands in the sanctity of the body. It's because our sexed bodies are sacred and bought by God that we should steward our bodies according to our Creator's design. The one who sins sexually "sins against their own body" (v. 18).

---

20. See Walton, *Lost World of Adam and Eve*, 77–81.

21. In Ezekiel 41, for instance, the word *tsela* is used nine times to refer to the "side rooms" of the temple (vv. 5–11, 26).

22. Paul says the same thing in Romans, where he commands believers to "offer *yourselves* to God" (Rom 6:13, 16) and later says "offer *your bodies* as a living sacrifice, holy and pleasing to God" (Rom 12:1). There are some passages that refer to some kind of existence (typically in the afterlife) that could be taken to refer to a temporary disembodied existence (2 Cor 5:1–9; 12:2; Rev 6:9–11). It's disputed whether these passages refer to a disembodied intermediate existence (e.g., the language of 2 Cor 5:1–9 in particular can very well be taken to refer to our future resurrected state). In any case, even if they do, they refer to a temporary and abnormal human existence, one that does not resonate with God's original design of humanity nor his future promise of resurrection. For my interaction with the debate regarding the body and the soul, see my *Embodied*, 143–52.

3. Scripture Prohibits Cross-Sex Identity

Since we bear God's image as male and female, and since our sexed bodies are sacred, Scripture prohibits a male from identifying as or trying to be seen as a female, and vice versa. Now, Scripture doesn't often mention people seeking to be seen as the opposite sex, so we don't have a lot to go on. But there are a few relevant passages that prohibit attempts to blur sex distinctions, and these prohibitions are an extension of the first two points above.

Deuteronomy 22:5 prohibits cross-dressing: "A woman must not wear men's clothing, nor a man wear women's clothing, for the LORD your God detests anyone who does this." This prohibition must be understood within its own historical context. In the ancient world, "you were what you wore," as classicist Thomas McGinn puts it.[23] How you dressed signified your class, status, and your sex. Men and women wore very different kinds of clothing, as we might find today in some Muslim countries in the Middle East. The biblical prohibition for a man wearing women's clothing would be similar to prohibiting a Muslim man from wearing a *hijab*.

To be clear, then, Deuteronomy 22:5 isn't talking about a woman wearing blue jeans from the men's rack or a baggy flannel shirt. Today in the west, clothing isn't as gendered as it was back in the Old Testament times. Deuteronomy isn't simply concerned about the fabric on your body, but identifying as, and seeking to be seen as, the other sex.[24]

---

23. McGinn, *Prostitutes, Sexuality and the Law*, 162. McGinn is referring to the Roman world, but the same holds true of the context that the Old Testament was written in. In most cultures of every era, in fact, clothing carries powerful signs of class, style, modesty, status, and sex difference. According to two experts on the history of cross-dressing, "Dress traditionally has been a ubiquitous symbol of sexual differences, emphasizing social conceptions of masculinity and femininity. Cross dressing, therefore, represents a symbolic incursion into territory that crosses gender boundaries" (Bullough and Bullough, *Cross Dressing, Sex, and Gender*, viii, cited in Nili Sacher Fox, "Gender Transformation and Transgression," 51). In summary, "the prohibition of the wearing of clothes of members of the opposite sex was . . . to safeguard the division between male and female" and was rooted in God's concern for diversity and order as reflected in the creation account of Genesis 1–2 (Harland, "Menswear and Womenswear," 76).

24. Some have disputed the NIV's translation of the Hebrew phrase *keli geber* as "men's clothing," since *geber* often means "warrior" and, they say, *keli* never means "clothing." Therefore, some say that Deuteronomy 22:5 prohibits women from dressing up in a male warrior's armor and doesn't have to do with cross-dressing *per se* (see Herzer, *Bible and the Transgender Experience*, 34–37). But this reading is probably not correct for several reasons. First, while the adjective *gibbor* can mean "warrior,"

Some might dismiss Deuteronomy 22:5 since it's in the Old Testament. But there are a few New Testament passages that touch on similar points. For instance, while 1 Corinthians 11:2–16 is a notoriously difficult passage to interpret, virtually all the possible interpretations agree: the underlying principle in Paul's argument is maintaining the sex distinctions that God laid down at creation.[25] Head coverings and hair length took on a certain cultural currency in Paul's day, and most interpreters believe that those expressions of sex difference were unique to his time period and don't need to be applied to today (in Western cultures, anyway). But the theological principle that transcends culture is that sex differences should be celebrated not eradicated, and that Christians should respect the various cultural forms that this might take.

In 1 Corinthians 6:9 Paul uses the Greek word *malakoi*, which in the first century referred to men who acted like women and said they would not inherit the kingdom of God. Now, when I say "acted like women," I'm not thinking of men who cry during romcoms, but men who very much renounced their male identity. In the context of 1 Corinthians 6, Paul's referring specifically to men who were having sex with other men (or more specifically, receiving sex from other men).[26]

Romans 1:26–27 touches on a similar point. Paul here speaks negatively of same-sex sexual behavior, but the principle fueling his language is that such behavior violates the God-designed sex distinctions established at creation. Paul alludes to Genesis 1–2 in general throughout Romans 1:18–32, and even more specifically he draws from Genesis 1:27 ("male and female he created them") as the basis for his reasoning that same-sex sexual behavior is a departure from God's created design.

Deuteronomy 22:5 uses the noun *geber*, which often overlaps with the normal word for "man," *ish* (Exod 10:7, 11; 12:37). Second, the word *keli* doesn't usually refer to clothing, but it does often refer to various things associated with men, including certain ornaments, weapons, hunting equipment, gear, and, yes, also clothing (1 Sam 21:5; 1 Kgs 10:21; Gen 24:53; Num 19:18). The translation "the things of men" is probably a better and more inclusive translation of the phrase by itself. However, the parallel statement, "nor a man wear women's *clothing*" (*shimlat*) specifies an article of clothing, which suggests that the former reference to *keli geber* probably does have clothing in mind. In any case, the point made here goes much deeper than mere clothing, to the fundamental differences between men and women. Clothing is the external expression of those differences.

25. See Judith M. Gundry-Volf's extensive study of this passage, where she interacts with dozens of different ways scholars have understood this passage: "Gender and Creation in 1 Corinthians 11,2–16."

26. See my discussion in *People to Be Loved*, 106–7.

Put simply, same-sex sexual behavior is not just abstractly wrong; it is a violation of our sexed embodied distinctions as divine image-bearers.

In short, the Bible's prohibitions of cross-sex identities (through dress and sexual activity) are rooted in God's created distinctions between humans as male and female. These distinctions are to be celebrated not blurred.

THE BIBLE AND GENDER STEREOTYPES

However—and this is a very important however—the Bible's celebration of sex distinctions *does not* mean that it sanctifies gender stereotypes.[27] The fact is that most stereotypes come from culture not the Bible. Consider my earlier point about the color pink. Pink is not female, since pink is a color and not a biological sex. And yet, most people will still say pink is *feminine* even if it's not necessarily *female*. But why is pink a feminine color? Is there a verse that says this? Would it be wrong for a guy to wear pink pants and a pink shirt?

The fact that pink is considered feminine is a cultural phenomenon. It comes neither from the Bible nor biology. There's nothing in God's created design of females that's hardwired them to prefer pink over, say, blue. In fact, a hundred years ago pink was considered a *masculine* color and blue was considered feminine.[28]

Most of our gender stereotypes come from culture, not the Bible. That doesn't necessarily mean they're wrong; they're just not moral. The Bible itself is actually quite liberating when it comes to gender stereotypes. It doesn't shackle males and females with specific ways they must act and things they must be interested in. Throughout the Bible, men kiss other men (1 Sam 10:1), cry (Gen 33:4), and are called to be tenderhearted (Eph 4:32). Men are *very* emotional (the Psalms), relational (1 Sam 18:1–5), play harps, and write poetry (King David). Jesus commanded men to turn the other cheek (Matt 5:39), to love—not kill—their enemies (Matt 5:44), to weep with those who weep (Rom 12:15), to raise up and teach children (Eph 6:4), to be sensitive (Eph 4:2), kind (Prov 11:17), and peacemakers (Matt 5:9)—that is, if they truly want to be true *manly* men, biblically speaking.

---

27. The following section is a summary of chapter 5 in *Embodied*.
28. See Hartmann, "History of Pink."

Women in the Bible also disrupt stereotypes. The famed Proverbs 31 woman isn't just a domestic goddess who rises up early and "provides food for her household" (v. 15 ESV) and makes "bed coverings" and "linen garments" (vv. 22, 24 ESV). These are wonderful traits, and we should never demean them. But this "excellent wife" is also an excellent businesswoman: she sells those linen garments for a profit after she "considers a field and buys it" (vv. 24, 16). The Proverbs 31 woman is wise, hard-working, has strong arms, and fights for social justice in her spare time (v. 20).

Women do many things that weren't considered "feminine." They fight battles, win wars, and smash tent pegs through men's skulls (Judg 4:21). Some are unmarried successful businesswomen like Lydia (Acts 16:14–15). They are courageous in the face of physical danger, like the three women named Mary who stood by Jesus at the foot of the cross after the men had fled (John 19:25). Many wealthy women were disciples of Jesus and funded his ministry (Luke 8:1–3), which overturned the cultural stereotype—both then and now—that only men could be the breadwinners.

Jesus himself challenges gender stereotypes. The Jewish and Greco-Roman cultures of biblical times were steeped in expectations about how men (and women) should act. Men were expected to be hairy-chested, sexually charged, domineering men. Real men joined the military, never cried in public, never showed affection (not just lust) toward women, had sex outside of marriage, and they would never stoop so low as to honor, let alone *serve*, lower-class people—the poor, the marginalized, and children.[29] Real men were sexually active, had a wife, and fathered children. And according to the stereotype, no *real* man would wash another man's feet.

Reread that paragraph in light of what you know about Jesus.

Jesus blew apart the stereotypes of his day. Not in every way, of course. Jesus did things that would be expected of a manly man. He turned over tables in the temple and taught with authority. But he also wept over Jerusalem and compared himself to a mother hen who gathers "her chicks under her wings" (Luke 13:34). Jesus let others slap him in the face and hit him on the head, and Jesus didn't care too much about his personal rights. Jesus "challenges cultural notions of masculinity. He washes feet, touches sick people, shows compassion to sinful women,

---

29. See, for example, Williams, *Roman Homosexuality*, 137–76.

loves children, and more."[30] By challenging culturally shaped gender stereotypes, Jesus embodied the Father's vision of creating a humanity that is sexually distinct yet diverse in how they live this out.

Again, if you actually *do* resonate with certain gender stereotypes, that's perfectly fine. Men should not be shamed for liking sports; women should not be looked down upon for wanting to be stay-at-home moms. Many women and men will naturally resonate with many gender stereotypes. The point is this: while the Bible affirms and celebrates sex distinctions, it does not morally mandate that males and females must conform to gender stereotypes. Many men and women might naturally resonate with masculine and feminine traits respectively. (And there's a perennial debate about whether this is because of nature or nurture. Does testosterone make men more masculine or does society nurture them into these kinds of behaviors?) But the Bible never makes conformity to gender stereotypes a moral issue and it doesn't define whether you are a woman or man based on whether you are feminine or masculine. The Bible recognizes much more diversity in male and female experiences. A more feminine-acting man (whatever that means) is still a man; a more masculine woman is still a woman. Because being male or female isn't defined by how we feel, what kind of movies we like, or even whom we're sexually attracted to. Our male and female identities are stamped upon us, by our Creator, through our embodiment as bearers of his image.

The Bible, then, affirms one of the most basic observations about humanity, that we are a sexually dimorphic species, and yet it challenges the stereotypical boxes that most cultures try to place on God's image-bearers. This truly biblical perspective does clash with what I think has become a rather regressive view of male and female that pops up in some perspectives on transgender identities.

GENDER STEREOTYPES AND SOME TRANSGENDER IDEOLOGIES

There is no such thing as *the* transgender ideology, and you should get in the habit of never using that phrase. Referring to something called transgender ideology as some kind of singular, monolithic way of viewing the world makes about as much sense as saying there's a singular Baptist or Presbyterian or Californian ideology. Only non-Californians think all

---

30. Cortez, *ReSourcing Theological Anthropology*, 203.

Californians think the same. But once you spend a week in Fresno and another in San Francisco, you'll realize that they might as well be two different countries.

Likewise, there is a wide diversity in viewpoints among trans* people. Some say they were born in the wrong body, while others mock this idea. Some believe they *are* the sex they identify as, while others believe that their biological sex can never actually change—only the appearance of it can. Some desire to transition, while others don't, and some transition and then detransition. Some experience debilitating gender dysphoria, while other trans*-identified people don't. And on and on it goes. "If you've met one transgender person, you've met . . . one transgender person," as psychologist Mark Yarhouse likes to say. There is no singular transgender ideology, only transgender ideologies.

And some transgender ideologies give life to gender stereotypes in a way that is not only unhelpful but actually quite regressive. This often comes out when listening to how some people describe why they think they are trans*.

One transman (biological female who identifies as a man) recalls their childhood experience: "I was into sports and skateboards, but never into girls' toys, dolls, princesses or anything pink." They go on to say "My mum would say it was just a phase: 'You won't always be like this. When you get to secondary school, you'll like makeup and boys and all this other stuff.' And in my head it was so strong, the feelings, that I could never see myself being like that. . . . In my head, I felt like a boy."[31]

This transman, born female, was "into sports and skateboards, but never into *girls' toys, dolls, princesses or anything pink.*" But does this mean they weren't actually a girl? Can't girls play sports, ride skateboards, and abhor the color pink? Or do we define "girlness" by the hobbies and interests that most girls resonate with? It's hard to disentangle the phrase "I felt like a boy" from the gender stereotypes used to describe what this means.

This is actually becoming quite common among parents whose kids don't resonate with gender stereotypes. Within some ideologies, if your kid doesn't fit the stereotypes, then maybe they actually *are* another sex. One parent of a trans* child named Eva says:

> When Eva was about two years old and people said, "What a cute little boy," she would respond emphatically, "I'm not a boy.

---

31. Greenaway, "When I Was a Girl."

I'm a girl!" She showed a strong preference for female playmates, dolls, and anything pink. At daycare and at home, she always wore a towel or T-shirt on her head, which represented "long hair," as she called it.[32]

Eva is biologically male, and yet said they were a girl. Why? A strong preference for dolls, long hair, and the color pink. But this desire to be a girl (or belief that they *are* a girl) is based on stereotypes, where the meaning of "girl" becomes "a person who likes dolls, long hair, and pink."

Another parent describes their male-born child, Warner (age nine), as having "preferences for pink, sparkles, even her physical mannerism with her hands were very flamboyant, wanting to be a princess. You know, if you took her shopping, she'd go right for dresses." In Warner's words: "I never actually, like, fitted in with being a boy. I don't like the games, the hairstyles, the clothes, . . . and I always thought from the very beginning that I was a little bit feminine."[33] But it's culture, not science (nor, of course, the Bible) that says boys aren't allowed to like pink and sparkles.

One mother recently told me that her biological male teenage kid says they're a girl. When the mother asked why they think they're a girl, the kid responded: "Because I like to watch Romantic Comedies and lesbian porn." I waited for the mom to keep going on, but that was it. She was just as dumbfounded as I was. The definition of "girl," according to her teen, is someone who likes Romcoms and lesbian porn, which is ironic, since lesbian porn is actually one of the most popular kinds of porn that non-trans straight men search for, according to PornHub.[34]

Other testimonies from some trans-identified adults also relies on narrow gender stereotypes and seem quite regressive to me. One transwoman says she dresses "as a *normal* woman: lingerie, nylons, dresses, shoes, etc., and applying full makeup and perfume."[35] I'm not sure how many biological females would consider this attire "normal." My wife certainly wouldn't, but I'll let my female readers determine what constitutes "normal" female dress.

Another transwoman says:

32. Hirt-Manheimer, "Dead Son or a Living Daughter."
33. Conroy, "Transgender Kids: Who Knows Best?" The documentary discusses transgender summer camps for trans* kids at around the 18:55 mark. This scene illustrates rigid stereotypes of what it means to be a girl or a boy.
34. See Khazan, "Why Straight Men Gaze at Gay Women."
35. Lawrence, *Men Trapped in Men's Bodies*, 96.

> I had very strong desires to dress as a female on a fulltime basis and to attract attention as a sexy, feminine woman. I have worn sexy feminine fashions, especially bras, lingerie, pantyhose, short dresses, lace fashions, mini-skirts, high heels, etc., at home since my mid-twenties.[36]

Again: Lingerie, pantyhose, short dresses, mini-skirts—these are all culturally constructed stereotypes about how women should look. Some might even say they are projections of the male gaze. This is why some women rolled their eyes when Caitlyn Jenner posed on the cover of *Vanity Fair* magazine in seductive apparel. Caitlyn is free to dress however she wants, as is anyone else. But her seductive pose embodied certain cultural stereotypes about womanhood that, one might argue, were the product of lustful men projected upon women. Miranda Yardley puts it this way:

> This image of Jenner as being not "a man becoming a woman" but . . . "a man becoming a man's idea of what a woman should be" . . . an idealised body is presented clothed only in lingerie, the makeup is done to perfection, and every flaw is magically photoshopped out of existence. Pandering to the male gaze, the body language is coy, seductive, submissive. This is not liberation, this is not revolution, this is not life-affirming; this is the crass stereotyping of what it means to be a woman, meeting every reactionary, culturally conservative ideal of what a woman should be; passive, objectified, dehumanised.[37]

Yardley is a good example of why we should speak in terms of various ideologies, not one singular trans* ideology. Yardley is actually a transwoman. Again, trans* people are by no means in agreement about what it means to *be* a woman. Some seem to define womanhood by a preference for gender stereotypes, while others (like Yardley) think this is unhelpful and regressive.

This is where I think the Bible is more forward-thinking and liberating than certain kinds of trans* ideologies that almost unknowingly rely on gender stereotypes to support their ideology. "Woman" does not mean: a person who likes lingerie, high heels, pink dresses, sparkles, dolls, romcoms, and lesbian porn. A woman is an adult human female. And truly *biblical* forms of Christianity will celebrate the fact that adult human females have a wide range of interests, personalities, and behaviors.

36. Lawrence, *Men Trapped in Men's Bodies*, 96.
37. Yardley, "What Does It Mean to Be Caitlyn?"

Christianity Contested

THE BIBLE, SCIENCE, AND INTERSEX

Bible-readers haven't always had the best relationship with science, but when it comes to the trans* conversation, there's a lot more resonance than people assume. The Bible consistently says that humans are created male and female (Gen 1:27; 5:1–2); there is no third sex. And as we saw earlier, the Bible also records men acting in stereotypically masculine ways and women in feminine ways, but also records women and men who break the stereotypes.

This resonates with what we find in scientific research. As a sexually dimorphic mammalian species, male and female are the two categories of biological sex. And whether because of nature or nurture (or both), many men resonate with masculine types of behavior, and women with feminine types of behavior. But the Bible and science both agree that there will be some who don't resonate with the majority and that's perfectly fine. We shouldn't mandate that men act masculine and women act feminine. The Bible and science agree that humans are sexually dimorphic, yet also agree that females and males experience life across a beautiful diverse spectrum of likes and dislikes, interests, and behaviors.

But what about intersex?[38] Doesn't the existence of intersex persons destroy the assumption that sex is binary? "Intersex" is a popular term that's used to describe the various biological conditions (there are at least sixteen) that are more formally called "differences" or "disorders of sex development" (DSD).[39] These conditions include atypical features in a person's sex chromosomes, reproductive organs, or anatomical sex (or two of the three, or all three). It's been estimated that anywhere from 0.022 to 1.7 percent of the population has a DSD; it all depends on which conditions are classified as intersex. One important point to note is that most people with an intersex condition have a mild one; that is, they are still clearly male or female. It's been estimated, in fact, that about 99 percent of people who have an intersex condition are unambiguously male or female.[40]

Despite what it sounds like, then, "intersex" does not mean "neither male nor female," and it shouldn't be understood as some kind of third or "other" sex. *Homo sapiens* still only have two gametes, and we reproduce when the gamete of a male is fused with the gamete of a female, which

---

38. For a thorough answer to this question, see chapter 7 in *Embodied*.
39. See ISNA, "What Is Intersex?"
40. Sax, "How Common Is Intersex?"

is what it means to be sexually dimorphic. Even intersex people who do have a more severe condition don't technically embody a third sex. One of my friends has a very rare intersex condition where they have both male and female anatomy. Are they male or female or something else? My friend is actually both, male *and* female, but they are not something other than male and female. When science talks about humans as sexed mammals, there are two categories of sex: male and female. Most humans are either one or the other, but in some rare circumstances, some might embody traits from both sex categories. But there are still only two categories of biological sex.

Here again, the Bible and science agree. You may not have thought that the Bible talks about intersex people, but this is likely what Jesus had in mind when he said:

> For there are *eunuchs who were born that way*, and there are eunuchs who have been made eunuchs by others—and there are those who choose to live like eunuchs for the sake of the kingdom of heaven. The one who can accept this should accept it. (Matt 19:12 NIV)

Among the three categories of eunuchs, the first one ("eunuchs who were born that way") probably refers to what we now call intersex persons. The term eunuch referred to a number of different kinds of men, but the two things they had in common was that they were male and they were infertile, usually because of some kind of physical condition. The eunuchs "who have been made eunuchs by others" were usually castrated and therefore infertile. But the ones "born that way" most likely have some kind of physical deformity in their genitals that rendered them infertile. Many people "born eunuchs" probably had some kind of DSD and would be considered intersex today. And since they were infertile, they would have remained single, since marriage and procreation went hand in hand in the ancient world. This is why in this context Jesus uses the eunuch as an example of someone who doesn't marry.

We can make two important observations about Jesus' reference to the one born a eunuch. First, eunuchs were still biologically male, and Jesus doesn't think that the presence of eunuchs interrupts the sex binary. Just a few verses earlier, Jesus cites Genesis 1:27 as the foundation for his theological argument about marriage: "At the beginning the Creator 'made them male and female'" (Matt 19:4). This binary includes the eunuch, who was born with some kind of atypical feature in his genitals that rendered him infertile. Second, eunuchs were considered very "unmanly" by ancient standards. Being married and having kids was one mark of manhood. And eunuchs had a stigma of being feminine and not living up to the masculine ideal. Jesus doesn't care about this. Jesus doesn't let gender stereotypes determine whether someone is a *real* man or not, like many in his culture (and in ours as well). He refers to the eunuch as a model for kingdom living.

The Bible and science both affirm the sex binary, and yet also account for people with Disorders/Differences of Sex Development. Humans are sexually dimorphic. Gender stereotypes don't define you. Males and females are fully equally in worth and value. And intersex people don't need to conform to some masculine or feminine ideal.

THE QUESTION OF INCONGRUENCE

All of this prepares us to respond to the question we raised earlier: *If someone experiences incongruence between their biological sex and their internal sense of self, which one determines who they are—and why?*

Based on how the Scriptures view the sexed human body, and also based on basic human biology, I would suggest that one's biological sex determines whether a person is a man or woman, even if one's internal sense of self is different from this. And I would suggest that in many cases (not all), when someone who experiences incongruence describes what their "internal sense of self" (gender identity) is, it is almost always intertwined with gender stereotypes.

Many alternative responses to this view rely on some kind of "born in the wrong body" narrative, which lack scientific or philosophical credibility. Or they just assume that one's self-declared identity determines who you are, without any thoughtful reason why.

However, the most compelling alternative response to the question of incongruence than the one I offer is the so-called "Brain Sex Theory."[41] This theory says that for some people, the sex of their brain differs from the sex of their body. And when this is the case, the sex of their brain should win out—they *are* the sex of their brain. So, if a biological male was born with a female brain, then their body is actually wrong; they really *are* female based on their brain.

This is a fascinating theory that's worth thinking through. What if a female's "internal sense of self" as male was rooted in the fact that they

---

41. For a thorough assessment of "Brain-Sex Theory," see chapter 8 in *Embodied*.

were born with a male brain? I mean, our brains play a significant part of personhood. If you were to swap brains with your best friend, then which one would be *you*? Would your brain be you (now inhabiting your best friend's body)? Or would your body be you, now recharged with your friend's brain. Body/brain relationships are tricky.

The main problem with this theory, though, is that it's not really clear that brains are sexed. It's true that the body's production of estrogen and testosterone has an *effect* on the brain, and this is part of the reason why, for instance, little boys typically prefer rough and tumble play more than typically girls (even in primates, actually).[42] But research on the brain has not shown that the brain is sexually dimorphic like the body is.

There's actually been a raging debate among neuroscientists about the question of male and female brains. Some say they're different, while others say they're basically the same. But even the studies that argue for difference *still recognize that we're talking about generalities not absolutes.* In other words, the brain is not sexually dimorphic like our sexed bodies are. Here's a summary from one of the largest and most recent studies arguing for sex-differences in the brain:

> Overall, for every brain region that showed even large sex differences, there was always overlap between males and females, confirming that the human brain cannot—at least for the measures observed here—be described as "sexually dimorphic."[43]

Every study that I've read on sex-differences in the brain says something similar. While there might be *typical* differences between *some* aspects of the brain between *most* men and *most* women, the brain is not sexually distinct like the body is. Brain differences are kind of like height difference. Men, on average, are taller than women. But some women are taller than some men, and some men are shorter than some women. Height differences are based on generalities, not absolutes. And this appears to be the case for the brains of males and females.

The Brain Sex theory also runs into our continual problem of gender stereotypes. One prominent Brain Sex theorist suggests that transgender people have "the anatomy of one sex" but "*the emotional awareness* of the opposite sex."[44] Goodness, what does it mean to have "the emotional awareness of the opposite sex"? Does each sex come prepackaged with its

---

42. See, for instance, Hassett et al., "Sex Differences," 359–64.
43. Ritchie et al., "Sex Differences in the Adult Human Brain."
44. Diamond, "Transsexualism as an Intersex Condition."

own particular "emotional awareness"? Husbands, I dare you to tell your wife that she has the emotional awareness of a woman.

When people suggest that some people are born with the brains of the other sex, the proof for this often lies in the fact that the person resonates more with the gender stereotypes of that sex—men who cry during romcoms and women who love to watch football . . . or whatever. But our interests, mannerisms, and behaviors, while being rooted in the brain, don't determine whether we are male or female.

In short, a male whose internal sense of self is more feminine (they're nurturing, caring, wear their hair long, prefer Broadway musicals to American football, like to go to brunch) are in every way still male. And unless they are acting in some ungodly way, they should never be made to feel like there's something wrong with them, and they certainly should never think that they aren't *really* a man—not by any biblical or scientific standard, anyway.

WHICH VIEW OF HUMAN NATURE IS THE MOST COMPELLING?

As an ancient document, one might expect—and plenty have argued—that the Bible is scientifically out of touch, philosophically naïve, culturally oppressive, and ultimately demeaning toward women. And I'll be the first to admit, there are some tough passages where the burden of proof rests on the Bible-believing Christian to show that the Bible *isn't* those things. But when it comes to questions about human nature that the transgender conversation naturally raises, the Bible (not modern distortions of it) offers a compelling viewpoint to consider. Here are a few summary observations that I'll leave for your reflection.

First, the Bible agrees with one of the most basic observations about humans—we are a sexually dimorphic species. A growing number of public personalities say they disagree with this, much to the chagrin of classically liberal evolutionary biologists who understand the sex binary to be one of the most basic facts about human nature.[45] It has been interesting to watch people who accuse Christians of being science-deniers who believe in a narrative despite the facts now turn around and say

---

45. One of many examples is Dr. Colin Wright, an evolutionary biologist who's been quite outspoken about how other scholars have parroted a narrative that denies that *Homo sapiens* are sexually dimorphic. See his many articles at RealitysLastStand.com.

that biological sex is a social construct or exists on a spectrum. The Bible might contain some scientifically questionable statements. Its view that humans are created male and female is not one of them.[46]

Second, a biblical view of the human body supports the modern concern over body-positivity. A fifteen-year-old girl who's distressed over her body will find a comforting and compelling message in the Bible that says, *you bear the beautiful image of your Creator and you don't need to conform to some airbrushed standard of femininity to be valued.* The Bible won't tell her that her body really is the problem and that maybe she was born in the wrong one. Guys who are made to think they aren't "real men" because they're infertile or not muscular enough or not sexually attracted to women can receive the pleasure of God who delights in image-bearers who follow his way and who does not force cultural stereotypes upon his people. Biblical Christianity warns us against idolizing our bodies too much, yet also against valuing our bodies too little. Our bodies are good and beautiful in all their diversity, and our sexual anatomy comes in all shapes and sizes, and this diversity is to be celebrated, not shamed.

Third, biblical Christianity should not force gender stereotypes upon men or women. If you're an adult human female, then you are a woman, a womanly woman. And if you follow the ways of Christ, then you are a prized woman in the eyes of God, even if you love the Raiders and can't stand *Downton Abbey*. The Bible celebrates sex distinctions while acknowledging the wide diversity in how the two distinct sexes express themselves and live out their sexed identity in the world.

Fourth, the Bible acknowledges the existence of intersex persons and even holds them up as model citizens of the kingdom. The first-century culture shamed eunuchs and told them that they weren't "real men." I fear that in some pockets of secular culture today, the message would be the same. Many eunuchs were known for being more effeminate, in part because they couldn't father children, or perhaps their condition resulted in low testosterone production, which resulted in a more feminine appearance. There are many gender identities other than "man" that might be offered to someone like this today. But Jesus doesn't doubt the manhood of the eunuch because such a man infertile, single, and perhaps more feminine in appearance. Instead, he holds up such gender non-conforming people as model citizens of the kingdom of God.

---

46. Again, even people with a severe DSD are best described as a blend of male and female, so my phrase "male and female" here is still inclusive of intersex persons.

BIBLIOGRAPHY

Bullough, Bonnie. *Cross Dressing, Sex, and Gender*. Philadelphia: University of Pennsylvania Press, 1993.

Conroy, John, dir. "Transgender Kids: Who Knows Best?" *BBC Two*, January 12, 2017. https://www.bbc.co.uk/programmes/bo88kxbw.

Cortez, Marc. *ReSourcing Theological Anthropology: A Constructive Account of Humanity in Light of Christ*. Grand Rapids: Zondervan, 2017.

Diamond, Milton. "Transsexualism as an Intersex Condition." In *Transsexualität in Theologie und Neurowissenschaften: Ergebnisse, Kontroversen, Perspektiven*, edited by Gerhard Schreiber, 43–54. Boston: de Gruyter, 2016. https://www.hawaii.edu/pcss/biblio/articles/2015to2019/2016-transsexualism.html.

Fox, Nili Sacher. "Gender Transformation and Transgression: Contextualizing the Prohibition of Cross-Dressing in Deuteronomy 22:5." In *Mishneh Todah: Studies in Deuteronomy and Its Cultural Environment in Honor of Jeffrey H. Tigay*, edited by Nili Sacher Fox et al., 49–72. Winona Lake, IN: Eisenbrauns, 2009.

Fuentes, Agustín. "Biological Science Rejects the Sex Binary, and That's Good for Humanity." *Sapiens*, May 11, 2022. https://www.sapiens.org/biology/biological-science-rejects-the-sex-binary-and-thats-good-for-humanity.

Garr, W. Randall. *In His Own Image and Likeness: Humanity, Divinity and Monotheism*. Leiden: Brill, 2003.

Greenaway, Naomi. "'When I Was a Girl': Transgender Men Share Pictures of Themselves Before Transition and Reveal What It's REALLY Like to Change Sex." *Daily Mail*, October 13, 2015. https://www.dailymail.co.uk/femail/article-3270572/Transgender-men-share-pictures-transition-reveal-s-REALLY-like-change-sex.html.

Gundry-Volf, Judith M. "Gender and Creation in 1 Corinthians 11:2–16: A Study of Paul's Theological Method." In *Evangelium, Schriftauslegung, Kirche: Festschrift für Peter Stuhlmacher zum 65. Geburtstag*, edited by O. Hofius et al., 151–71. Göttingen: Vandenhoeck und Ruprecht, 1997.

Harland, P. J. "Menswear and Womenswear: A Study of Deuteronomy 22:5." *Expository Times* 110.3 (1998) 73–76.

Hartke, Austen. *Transforming: The Bible and the Lives of Transgender Christians*. Louisville, KY: Westminster John Knox, 2018.

Hartmann, Margaret. "The History of Pink for Girls, Blue for Boys." *Jezebel*, April 10, 2011. https://www.jezebel.com/the-history-of-pink-for-girls-blue-for-boys-5790638.

Hassett, Janice M., et al. "Sex Differences in Rhesus Monkey Toy Preferences Parallel Those of Children." *Hormones and Behavior* 54.4 (2008) 359–64.

Herzer, Linda Tatro. *The Bible and the Transgender Experience: How Scripture Supports Gender Variance*. Cleveland, OH: Pilgrim, 2016.

Hirt-Manheimer, Aron. "A Dead Son or a Living Daughter: A Conversation with the Mother of a Transgender Child." *Reform Judaism*, July 15, 2016.

Khazan, Olga. "Why Straight Men Gaze at Gay Women." *Atlantic*, March 8, 2016. https://www.theatlantic.com/health/archive/2016/03/straight-men-and-lesbian-porn/472521.

Lawrence, Anne. *Men Trapped in Men's Bodies: Narratives of Autogynephilic Transsexualism*. New York: Springer, 2013.

McGinn, Thomas A. J. *Prostitutes, Sexuality and the Law in Ancient Rome*. Oxford: Oxford University Press, 2003.

McHugh, Paul R., and Lawrence S. Mayer. "Sexuality and Gender: Findings from the Biological, Psychological, and Social Sciences." *New Atlantis* 50 (2016) 7–143.

Middleton, J. Richard. *The Liberating Image: The Imago Dei in Genesis 1*. Grand Rapids: Brazos, 2005.

Money, John. *Sin, Science, and the Sex Police*. Amherst, NY: Prometheus, 1998.

Planned Parenthood. "What Are Gender Roles and Stereotypes?" *Planned Parenthood*, n.d. www.plannedparenthood.org/learn/gender-identity/sex-gender-identity/what-are-gender-roles-and-stereotypes.

Reilly-Cooper, Rebecca. "Sex." *Sex and Gender: A Beginner's Guide* (blog), 2015. https://sexandgenderintro.com.

Richter, Sandra. "Does God Really Command Women to Marry Their Rapists? A Study of Deuteronomic Law." *Center for Hebraic Thought* (blog), November 10, 2020. https://hebraicthought.org/deuteronomic-law-women-marry-rapists.

Ritchie, Stuart J., et al. "Sex Differences in the Adult Human Brain." *Cerebral Cortex* 28.8 (2018) 2959–75.

Sax, Leonard. "How Common Is Intersex?" *Journal of Sex Research* 39.3 (2002) 174–78.

Sprinkle, Preston. *Embodied: Transgender Identities, the Church, and What the Bible Has to Say*. Colorado Springs: David C. Cook, 2021.

———. *People to Be Loved: Why Homosexuality Is Not Just an Issue*. Grand Rapids: Zondervan, 2015.

Stoller, Robert. "The Hermaphroditic Identity of Hermaphrodites." *Journal of Nervous and Mental Disease* 139 (1964) 453–57.

Walton, John H. *The Lost World of Adam and Eve: Genesis 2–3 and the Human Origins Debate*. Downers Grove, IL: IVP Academic, 2015.

Intersex Society of North America (ISNA). "What Is Intersex?" *ISNA*, n.d. https://isna.org/faq/what_is_intersex.

Williams, Craig A. *Roman Homosexuality*. 2nd ed. Oxford: Oxford University Press, 2010.

Wright, Colin. "Sex Is Not a Spectrum." *Reality's Last Stand*, February 1, 2021. https://www.realityslaststand.com/p/sex-is-not-a-spectrum.

Yardley, Miranda. "What Does It Mean to Be Caitlyn?" *#CounterCulturalGeek* (blog), June 2, 2015. https://mirandayardley.com/en/what-does-it-mean-to-be-caitlyn.

Yarhouse, Mark. *Understanding Gender Dysphoria: Narrating Transgender Issues in a Changing Culture*. Downers Grove, IL: InterVarsity Academic, 2015.

10

Christianity and Women

Lynn H. Cohick

INTRODUCTION

THE NEW TESTAMENT HAS been interpreted as restricting women, and Christianity has been said to devalue women. While it is true that the New Testament has been construed to control and contain women, these readings fail to capture the social and cultural setting in which the texts were written, and thus fail to demonstrate the positive position women held within the early church. It is the case that, down through the centuries, Christianity reflected the sexism and patriarchy of its wider social context, but this posture is not consistent with its foundational texts nor its founder, Jesus Christ.

Is Christianity good *for* women? Is it good *to* women? An honest answer has to be: not always. The church has failed to protect women from predatory men, has limited their development in social and religious spheres, and has narrowed women's scope of influence to the family. But these failures, as serious as they are, do not encompass the entire story. In this chapter, I explore the first-century world and set the New Testament writings in context. In so doing, I will show that Jesus, and the earliest followers of Jesus, encouraged and embraced the full participation of women alongside men. Throughout the chapter, I address several misconceptions about the New Testament texts on women and offer a culturally contextual interpretation that demonstrates women's active participation and authority within the nascent community. My argument begins with a brief sketch of Jewish and gentile women's first-century context. Next, I examine the sexism and gender bias that haunts our readings of the biblical text. Finally, I turn to key biblical passages on women and marriage, family, religious life, and leadership.

HISTORICAL CONTEXT: TRUTH AND FALSEHOODS

Historical reconstruction of bygone eras is never easy; reconstructing women's history from two thousand years ago is harder still. Nevertheless, using texts, inscriptions, and artifacts from daily life, we can build a reasonable picture of the average woman and her social world. The ancient evidence reveals a patriarchal culture that viewed women as inferior to men; however, the culture nuanced this perspective in significant ways that gave some women agency and influence within their family and wider community. I will demonstrate how a robust understanding of the ancient context shows the biblical text to support women's value as equal to that of men, and promotes women's voice and agency.

Women in the First-Century Jewish World

A subtle and sinister error creeps into the discussion of Christian women in the first century. It begins with the statement: Jesus is good for/to women. I firmly believe that this is a true statement; however, it is often defended against a foil of anti-Jewish descriptions of Jewish men, regularly identified as rabbis. The general argument is that Judaism in Jesus' day was strongly anti-woman and viewed wives as little better than chattel.[1] This false reconstruction is built on a deficient understanding of later rabbinic literature and an assumption that such later texts explain first-century Judea and Galilee.[2] Additionally, it relies on an unfounded assumption that menstrual purity laws and similar codes shamed women.

1. Kraemer, "Jewish Women and Christian Origins," 35–38.
2. Levine, "Bearing False Witness," 502–3.

No evidence suggests that women understood these purity expectations in this light. Men, too, had purity rites based on bodily emissions, further normalizing such practices. Categories of clean and unclean did not necessarily translate onto a grid of goodness and sin.

A more historically faithful portrayal of Second Temple Judaism reveals Jewish women participating alongside men in festivals, in following Jewish teachers of their choice, and making religious vows.[3] To take one example, women were active participants in the Essene community, as revealed in the Dead Sea Scrolls.[4] The group seems to have valued marriage and celibacy equally and accepted that women could walk with purity even as could a man. The wife is enjoined to reveal to the community's leader if her husband fails to uphold the specific codes around marital sexual relations, such as abstention during Sabbath, pregnancy, and menstrual impurity.[5] Women took oaths in this community, dedicating their lives to this form of Judaism. Jewish women owned property, divorced and remarried, provided loans, and owned businesses and shops. In Judea and Galilee, the homeland of Jews, Hellenism and Roman imperial context permeated economic and social life.[6]

Women in the Greco-Roman World

The picture of women's lives in the Greco-Roman world has also been blurred by false assumptions, including the following three notions: (1) an anachronistic view of public/private spheres, (2) a belief that men were viewed as superior to women in every instance, and (3) a woman had no agency or autonomy for decision-making. For example, many suppose that the ancient world was divided into public and private spheres that neatly mapped private to the home and belonging to women, while public

---

3. Ilan, *Integrating Women into Second Temple History*, offers excellent essays on this subject. See also Ilan, *Jewish Women in Greco-Roman Palestine*.

4. Wassen explains, "Amongst other sectarian documents that were published early, the Rule of the Congregation (1QSa) and CD [Damascus Document]—contrary to 1QS—take the presence of women and children for granted" (*Women in the Damascus Document*, 5).

5. 1QSa I 4–11; 4Q270 7 I 12b–13. See Wassen, *Women in the Damascus Document*, 140–43, 183–84; Grossman, "World of Qumran," 239–41.

6. The Babatha Archives provides evidence for these activities. See Hanson, "Widow Babatha," 85–103. For book-length treatments, see Oudshoorn, *Relationship Between Roman and Local Law*; Czajkowski, *Living Under Different Laws*; Esler, *Babatha's Orchard*.

space, including the marketplace, religious venues, and the political arena, belonged to men. Thus, women were sequestered to their homes with little public presence. A second false notion is that men were viewed superior to women in all circumstances, without regard to social class or wealth. Claims are made that girls were valued less than boys and wives were primarily esteemed for their childbearing capability. Wives were under the complete power of their husbands and had no sexual freedom, dignity, or autonomy. Third, many assume that a woman's public voice or actions were consistently regarded as immoral. It is often believed that women had no legal rights and little opportunity to make decisions about their own lives. Adding these inadequate assumptions together, the resulting picture is of a woman's voice and body absent in the community, sequestered in the home, tied to familial duties primarily. Any evidence to the contrary (and there is quite a lot!) was deemed the exception to the rule or representing a small sub-group within the wider society.

Recent developments in our understanding of ancient culture challenges such assumptions. First, women were involved in every activity in society, except as soldiers and government officials. Women participated in all levels of commerce, religious rites, and could plead their case in court, accompanied by their guardian. Women patrons supported trade guilds, religious cults, and important political figures. Second, rarely are women viewed only as women; instead, their cultural, economic, religious, social status and class come into play. A wealthy Roman woman might have more in common with a wealthy man than with a poor woman, for example. With wealth or social status came leadership expectations for both women and men. Women's civic responsibilities were tied to her loyalty to her family, and her public voice and actions could be aligned with domestic virtues.[7] Third, the question of women's agency in the ancient world has been revisited recently, challenging the scholarship of the last several decades.

The question of women's agency raises to the surface three presuppositions held by scholars in the late twentieth century when analyzing evidence about women's lives in the ancient world. First, they took for granted that women desired personal freedom and autonomy as the highest goods. Any system, institution, or tradition that seems to limit these goods was condemned. Second, and related,

---

7. Hylen writes, "Women could be praised for bold leadership as well as domestic virtue. The presence of one did not cancel out the other" (*Women in the New Testament World*, 166).

a theory of deprivation sought to explain why a woman might convert to Christianity. The theory suggests that women felt deprived of self-actualizing opportunities; in marriage, women would feel confined or trapped. Therefore, wanting more freedom, women joined the Christian group for its offer of celibate living. Third, scholars assumed that only if a woman's actions were counter-cultural could they be seen as authentic; therefore, agency could only be discerned in resistance. If a woman acted in traditional ways, then she was merely respecting the patriarchal society, failing to demonstrate her agency. For example, women who conformed to traditional modesty values were therefore dismissed as inauthentic or lacking self-determination.

There are at least two shortcomings with these presuppositions. First, scholars today suggest that cultural norms and rules are constantly negotiated and adjusted by men and women as they apply values and norms based on specific situations. Female patrons, to take one example, greatly influenced the fortunes and opportunities of their clients. This hierarchical social relationship empowered those with wealth and status, and some women benefited from this distribution of power and privilege to shape their society. Second, the claims about deprivation, modesty, and lack of agency have been rightly challenged as modern values of autonomy and self-actualization inserted into ancient culture.[8]

In sum, the historical contexts for both Jewish and gentile women reveal a complex set of dynamic norms and values in which women, alongside men, shaped their environment. Women's agency is demonstrated in decisions about their work, their religious choices, and in supervising their homes, where much social and business activity took place. Women with financial means or status clout were expected to influence their communities, as they supported their male and female clients and friends. Women were active in the marketplace and religious shrines and festivals. Jewish women heard the Scriptures with their husbands and brothers each Sabbath, and some gentile women were educated in the philosophical way of life. Sadly, poor women and men had fewer options to demonstrate agency. Even more tragic, slave women had no autonomy and social worth.

---

8. Mahmood rightly notes, "This positing of women's agency as consubstantial with resistance to relations of domination, and the concomitant naturalization of freedom as a social ideal, are not simply analytical oversights on the part of feminist authors. Rather, I would argue that their assumptions reflect a deeper tension within feminism attributable to its dual character as both an *analytical* and a *politically prescriptive* project" (*Politics of Piety*, 10).

ASSUMPTIONS ABOUT FEMALE AND MALE

Understanding the basic social and cultural landscape of women's lives situates the New Testament in context, thereby helping us hear the text as the original audience might have perceived it. But the historical context of women is not the whole context, for the presence of sexism, even misogyny, shaped the understanding and expectations of male and female, and the attending categories of masculine and feminine. The roots of negative gender assessment stretch back at least to Aristotle, who argued that the female is inferior to the male in all categories, thus norming all things to the male. He viewed the male as active and the female as passive. He spoke of three pairs that made up the ancient household: husband/wife, father/child, master/slave. Aristotle's views and categories continued to shape the household into the first century AD, the world of the earliest Christians. It seems clear that Western society is still in the grip of Aristotle's misogynistic views. It plays out in the most astonishing ways.

Female and Male, Egg and Sperm

For example, one might think that biology is a straightforward enterprise with little gender bias within its scientific studies. However, Emily Martin argues that we encode our expectations about masculine and feminine into our biology lessons about the egg and sperm. In 1999, the anthropologist wrote a fascinating paper exposing how science weaves a myth of masculinity and femininity into the very process of ovulation and fertilization.[9] She explores how cultural beliefs and gender stereotypes shape science, and discovers these stereotypes reinforce notions that female biological processes are less important than male, and that women are, *mutatis mutandis*, less admirable than men.

There are several ways in which biologists reinforce active male and passive female into the very DNA of our beings, presenting the sperm on a heroic mission to save the passive damsel in distress, Miss Egg. First, the woman's reproductive cycle is defined as fulfilling its goal when pregnancy occurs. Therefore, menstruation is seen as a failure. Additionally, because all eggs are present at the girl's birth, until one by one each month they are pushed to the uterus, they are not seen as active in the way that sperm are. Textbook authors speak excitedly that millions of

---

9. Martin, "Egg and the Sperm," 485–501.

sperm are produced each day. Martin wonders why scientists don't speak of females producing eggs (ova) each month.[10]

Second, Martin observes "how 'femininely' the egg behaves and how 'masculinely' the sperm."[11] The egg drifts passively down the fallopian tubes, the sperm actively seek the egg, traveling swiftly, purposefully, with strong tail motions. However, Martin points to biological research that shows that sperm tails are quite weak and offer no help in penetrating the egg. Indeed, the tail moves the head sideways with ten times the force of the forward thrust.

Martin's essay highlights the dangers of creating a social myth or story to explain a biological process. Jane Lehr observes, "Martin's work challenges science by drawing our attention to the situatedness of scientific researchers, the way the gendered values embedded in their cultural frame shape the scientific knowledge production processes in their laboratories."[12] Martin's analysis of language used to describe "objective" and "natural" biology exposes the depth and power of male/active vs. female/passive gender myth.

Separate but Equal?

The social myth about gender has, until recently, relied on claims of the ontological inferiority of women. "Women were characterized as less intelligent, more sinful, more susceptible to temptation, emotionally unstable, incapable of exercising leadership."[13] The consensus was that women did not belong in any leadership, either in the church or larger society, based on their flawed character and intelligence. However, within the last few decades, perhaps related to the civil rights discussions in the 1960s, very few argue against women leadership on the basis of women's ontological inferiority. I celebrate the rejection of faulty anthropology that deemed women to be ontologically inferior. On the one hand, new arguments accepting women's leadership in church and society are based on the "recognized . . . essential equality between men and women, including fundamental intellectual and moral equality."[14] On the other

---

10. Martin, "Egg and the Sperm," 488.
11. Martin, "Egg and the Sperm," 489.
12. Lehr, "Why Social Justice Educators," 27.
13. Witt, *Icons of Christ*, 29.
14. Witt, *Icons of Christ*, 29.

hand, new arguments *against* women's leadership rely, not as before on women's inherent inferiority, but on a claim that men and women play different roles.

The claim made by some Protestants is that men and women are equal in value but serve in different roles. Sometimes referred to as the complementarian position, these roles are organized in a gendered, hierarchical structure. Said another way, the roles discussed are not equal in responsibility, such as cleaning dishes and taking out the trash, or mowing the grass and weeding the garden, or grocery shopping and taking children to school. Instead, the roles are divided based on their relative weight of authority within the community, and the leadership aspect of the task. The roles of speaking with authority to the community and making key decisions are limited to men. Women's roles revolve around deferring to men's authority. Men are not excluded from any roles within the church on the basis of being male; only women *qua* women are excluded from certain roles. This new argument retains traditional exclusion of women's formal leadership and ordination, but uses new arguments to support the claims.

BIBLICAL TEXTS ON WOMEN IN MARRIAGE

We address these new arguments by focusing on several key passages that highlight major aspects of a woman's life, namely marriage and family, and worship in the church. The earliest followers of Jesus often met in homes, and we have household and sibling language pervading Paul's descriptions of church gatherings. Paul examines the three social pairs that make up the ancient household (wife/husband; child/parent; slave/owner) because he is convinced that no matter what one's social situation, one can live out the gospel. Greco-Roman society created a hierarchy within each pair, with husband over wife, parent over child, and owner over slave. Yet within the body of Christ, all are brothers and sisters, without any hierarchy of social worth. Paul spoke to each individual of the pair, and either raised them up or restricted their power, to better align with the equality in Christ that all believers share.[15] A brief description of marriage in the ancient world sets up our discussion of marriage in Ephesians and John 4, the story of the Samaritan woman.

---

15. Cohick, *Letter to the Ephesians*, 344–50, 387–402.

Family and Marriage in the Greco-Roman World

To our modern ear, perhaps one of the most stunning facts of the ancient world is that wives were not under the authority of their husbands but remained under the power or authority of their father. This social reality is connected to the father's legal authority over his children, both sons and daughters, until his death. At that point, both sons and daughters were independent and could own property in their own name.[16] The daughter could inherit family wealth. In a similar fashion, the Jewish daughter could receive gifts from her family that amounted to an inheritance.[17]

Marriage was established by the consent of bride and groom, and the state did not grant a marriage certificate. If the bride brought a dowry, its contents were written down as a legal document, describing in detail all items and money brought by the wife. The husband had free use of the dowry money, but the wife might also have her own property or wealth, separate from the dowry. If the couple divorced, the wife received back the principle of her dowry, and the husband kept any earnings he made on the money.[18]

Marriage and Ephesians 5

Most people assume that our modern marriage vows, with the wife's promise to obey her husband, go back to the first century. And in part they are correct, for almost without exception, ancient authors speak of wives obeying their husbands.[19] However, such language is not part of the biblical text.[20] Instead, the New Testament uses the word "submit." This word carries primarily negative connotations today, but in the ancient world, it was a virtue pursued by both men and women. Society was highly stratified, and it was imperative that people honored those

---

16. While a woman who was *sui iuris* owned property, she needed a guardian/tutor to sign a bill of sale for land, slaves, and certain property such as livestock. This need not be an onerous burden, as the woman often chose her guardian. See Hylen, *Women in the New Testament World*, 66–67.

17. Hanson writes of a "deed of gift" that allowed daughters to receive land or buildings ("Widow Babatha," 96–97).

18. Cohick, *Women in the World of the Earliest Christians*, 99–112.

19. The two exceptions are Plutarch, *Advice to the Bride and Groom* 33; Pseudo-Callisthenes, *Narrative, Remarkable* (*Historiae Alexandri Magni* 1.22.4) 1.22.19–20.

20. First Peter 3:6 speaks of Sarah obeying Abraham, but the call in this verse is for wives to submit to her husband.

above them. As such, a male slave or freedman would submit to a free woman's directive. Again, a free man working in a guild would defer to the guild's patron, whether the patron was a man or woman. Younger believers submit to older believers (1 Pet 5:5); believers submit to governing authorities (Rom 13:1). The assumption underlying many of these injunctions is that the one deferred to would act in the best interest of the other.

In Ephesians 5:21, every believer is asked to submit to other believers. The reason for this submission is the fear and respect every believer has for their Lord, Jesus Christ, and the reality that Christ lives in each believer. The call to submit to each other is tied grammatically to 5:18, the command to be filled with the Spirit. But how does one submit to one who is lower on the social scale as understood in the ancient world? It might at first seem like nonsense to ask a slave master to submit to her slave. But that is exactly what Paul asks when he forbids owners from threatening slaves, and when he declares that God shows no favoritism (6:9). The power invested by the culture to the slave owner is revised based on the higher demands of the gospel. God is the "master" of both owner and slave, who are equal inheritors in the kingdom of Christ and of God (5:5).[21]

English translations often include headings that separate Ephesians 5:22 from 5:21, but that does not adequately reflect the Greek grammar. Verse 5:22 lacks a verb, and so borrows the verb from the previous verse, in this case "submit." The verb, moreover, is a participle, not an imperative. While participles can carry the force of a command, it is only to the husbands that Paul uses the imperative, when he orders them to love their wife (5:25, 28, 33). The Greek grammar tells us that these two verses are tightly tied together, such that a wife's submission to her husband is related to every believer's submission to other believers. Therefore, wives submit their husbands as unto the Lord, and not as unto an autocratic ruler, for Jesus came to serve, not to be served (Mark 10:45). Jesus is described here as Savior, the one who gave his life for the sake of his beloved church (see also Eph 5:2).[22]

---

21. The analogy of a believer being a slave of God extends back through the Old Testament. However, God as a slave master pushes the analogy too far. In Eph 6:9, the term translated "master" is *kyrios*, lord.

22. The title "savior" is rarely used of Jesus in the New Testament. Cohick concludes that the juxtaposition of savior and "head" illustrates that "Christ's self-surrender unto death is part of his actions as head of the church," for the "role of savior does not emphasize 'leadership'" but "redemption and deliverance" (*Ephesians*, 357).

Why did Paul not ask husbands to submit to their wives? The short answer is that he actually *did* ask, when he commanded them to love as Christ loved. But the longer answer is that a direct command to husband to submit to wives would have sounded like nonsense. The social expectations and the legal system had no way of envisioning such submission. Paul re-shaped cultural expectations by qualifying and limiting a wife's responsibilities to her husband, and greatly expanding a husband's responsibilities to his wife.[23]

Paul speaks of the husband as "head" of his wife. In English, the metaphorical use of "head" means "leader" or "authority," but in Greek, it almost never suggested such a connotation. Instead, it referred to source or preeminence. We speak of the headwaters of a river to indicate its source. We speak of "thirty head of cattle" to mean thirty cows, using "head" as a synecdoche for the whole. In the ancient world, in the few times when head/body was used as a metaphor, the body was to sacrifice itself for the head. But in the gospel story, the opposite happens, as the head gives his life for his body.[24]

Paul commands husbands to love their wives with this self-sacrificial love of Christ. Paul's charge is incredibly counter-cultural, for the wider culture would see such sacrifice as humiliating and demeaning for the one with higher social status. Jesus' death was the supreme example of self-sacrifice. Everyone in Paul's day knew that crucifixion was not only physically excruciating, but also utterly humiliating. Jesus hung naked on a cross, stripped of clothing and his culture's view of masculinity, shamed and scorned (Heb 12:2). Paul asks that husbands show their love for their wife by modeling Christ. Interestingly, the actions listed here in Ephesians are typically seen as women's work. Jesus cleans, washes, feeds, and nurtures his body, his church (5:26–30). These are not heroic deeds, nor do they reflect someone in charge of things. The deeds involve responding to needs, being open to the other, serving humbly.

Paul declares that the husband should see his wife as his own body (5:28). Implied in this statement is that wives can see their husbands as their own body. Paul states as much explicitly to the Corinthians (1 Cor 7:2–4). The union of husband and wife does not subsume the latter into the former, as was expected in first-century culture. Instead, the unity

---

23. Cohick writes that Paul does not say "that the wife shows her submission to Christ by submitting to her husband, as if her husband were a substitute for Christ or her intermediary with Christ" (*Ephesians*, 355).

24. Lee-Barnewall, "Turning ΚΕΦΑΛΗ on Its Head," 605.

of wife and husband comes as each one loves and submits to the other in mutual respect and care. Paul reinforces the importance of unity by claiming that the marriage union points to the greater union of Christ and his church.

Marriage, Divorce, and John 4

Paul does not spend much time discussing divorce, but it was certainly a reality faced by his congregations (1 Cor 7:10–16). Jesus' words promoting marriage emphasizes the life-long commitment expected in the union (Matt 19:3–12). Most people married in the first century, and given that lives were often cut short, a man or woman might lose their partner after only a few years of marriage. Most people remarried. Some marriages ended in divorce, but it is difficult to say how many. The upper echelon traded partners to suit the changing political winds, but we have little information about whether the average family pursued divorce often.

Perhaps the most intriguing discussion about marriage in the Gospels is Jesus' conversation with the Samaritan woman (John 4:4–42).[25] Typically, she is viewed as an immoral woman who divorced five husbands and is cohabitating with her sixth lover. This explanation, however, is more the stuff of Hollywood. The interpretation reflects a sexism that fails to imagine a woman who might be interested in theological discussion and who struggles with the realities of marriage, divorce, and remarriage. I will discuss women's religious engagement below; suffice it to say that the Samaritan woman's questions to Jesus about religious truth and practice were entirely within keeping of the ancient context. Women pursued religious goals and exercised religious agency.

The nub of the issue with the Samaritan woman is her marital status.[26] Why five husbands, and how is her current situation different? She is not the immoral woman that so many have been taught, for several reasons. First, and perhaps most significantly, the text implies her reliability, for she has a positive reputation in her town. We know this because when she returns to the town from her discussion with Jesus, they believe her assessment that this man could be the Jewish messiah. The townspeople must know that this woman is an earnest seeker of the truth who bears

---

25. Cohick, *Women in the World of the Earliest Christians*, 122–28. See also Cohick, "Could This Be the Christ?," 27–42; Day, *Woman at the Well*, 5–7.

26. Cohick, "Was the Samaritan Woman Really an Adulteress?"

true testimony. It is her words, and not some imagined life change, that speaks to the townspeople. Said another way, she is not like the Gerasene demoniac whose abrupt and astonishing change in demeanor gives evidence to Jesus' healing powers.

Second, she was not condemned as immoral by Jesus (contrast Luke 7:44–50; John 8:11). In fact, he praises her for speaking the truth (John 4:16–19). Throughout John's Gospel, the term "truth" is used positively. Jesus' comments about her husbands and current situation reveals his prophetic knowledge. Jesus expressed similar knowledge of Nathanael's past, whom we meet in John 1. Nathanael immediately recognizes that only the son of God, the king of Israel, would be able to see into his heart and know his physical location (John 1:47–51). Jesus did not bring up her marital status to shame the Samaritan woman, but to show his knowledge of her past.

Third, most women in the first century were identified by their marital status and in relation to their male relatives. But we have no evidence of a woman who was married five times.[27] Such knowledge would only be known to a prophet, a messiah; it would hardly be a lucky guess.

Fourth, women could initiate divorce, but needed their legal guardian to represent them in court. We have no record of any woman filing for divorce more than once. It stretches the imagination to assume the Samaritan woman divorced five men. Additionally, it would be extremely unlikely that she was divorced by five men, especially if one postulates divorce based on her infidelity. No man would risk his honor to marry a woman charged with adultery. Some scholars suggest that she was barren, and that was why so many divorced her. But there are two flaws with that theory. First, marriages were not ended based on barrenness, for adoption of older children to carry on the family line was an option, at least for Roman families.[28] Second, it seems unlikely to me that five men in a row would roll the dice to see if this woman would produce an heir for them. It is more likely that she experienced much tragedy, becoming a widow in most of these marriages. Her fate was likely similar to Naomi's,

---

27. Queen Berenice, granddaughter of Herod the Great, was married three times and widowed twice by the age of twenty-two and divorced once. She had a longstanding love affair with Titus, who became emperor, but they never married, likely because of her Jewish ethnicity.

28. Cohick, *Women in the World of the Earliest Christians*, 131. Josephus describes the Essenes as not marrying, but adopting children and raising them according to the sect's teachings (*Jewish War* 2.120). He also notes that one subset of Essenes chose to marry, while others follow celibacy (2.61–62).

who, as we learn in the book of Ruth, lost both adult sons and her husband within ten years (Ruth 1:3–5).

Fifth, the nub of the issue is how to explain the Samaritan woman's current situation. She might be in a polygynous relationship, one that would not be embraced by Jesus, but would have been at least tolerated in her culture.[29] Or it might be that at the death of her fifth husband, his brother refused to marry her, and so she was technically unable to marry the man she was with. Perhaps she lived as a concubine, a formal relationship that does not grant privileges of marriage but requires the wife to be sexually faithful to her "husband." Often men entered into a concubinage relation because the woman was of lower social status.

In the end, the Samaritan woman's story reveals heartache and loss as well as the hope of better things to come. Based on the historical context of marriage, we see that she was not an immoral woman, a sinner hiding from God. Instead, she was a religious seeker, eager to know more about her faith and the rival claims of Jews. Her words about Jesus transformed her town, who declared that because of her testimony, they too would follow the Savior of the world (John 4:39–42).

BIBLICAL TEXTS ON WOMEN LEADERSHIP IN THE CHURCH: 1 TIMOTHY 2 & 3

The Samaritan woman's zeal for knowledge of God is not unique. Then, as now, some women (like some men) were interested in the religious life and pursued their spiritual passions, although stereotypes present women as uninterested in philosophy or theology. Gentile women were expected to honor the household gods, and they might also be a devotee of a god or goddess.[30] Gentile women (and men) made votive offerings to persuade the god to grant health, wealth, or safe childbirth. Jewish women could follow Pharisaic practices or join the Essenes.[31] And of course, women followed Jesus as disciples. For example, Jesus spoke some of the deepest theological truths, that he is the resurrection and the life, to Martha (John 11:23–27). Martha had learned, perhaps in her synagogue,

---

29. This argument assumes that the Samaritans followed Jewish custom here, which allowed bigamy. An example of a "second wife" is Babatha, a Jewish woman who lived in the early second century. For translations of Babatha's documents, see Kraemer, *Women's Religion in the Greco-Roman World*, 143–52.

30. Cohick, *Women in the World of the Earliest Christians*, 160–61, 176–83.

31. Cohick, *Women in the World of the Earliest Christians*, 199–209.

about bodily resurrection of the dead, a view held by the Pharisees, but rejected by the Sadducees. Jesus expanded on this knowledge to reveal more of himself and his mission. He clearly believed Martha capable of understanding such teachings.

Women's Religious Education

Today in the West, we take the education of women for granted. But in the ancient world, few gentile women had formal education, religious or otherwise. Parenthetically, few men other than those with wealth and the leisure that came with it, enjoyed anything above minimal education. The rare woman educated in philosophy could be viewed as promiscuous, but this bias has much to do with how education happened in the ancient world.[32] At the higher levels, students joined a teacher at his home for study. A woman living in another family's home called her honor into question. Some fathers or husbands taught their daughters or wives philosophy, which mitigated the risk of charges of impropriety. Jewish women had the advantage of hearing Scripture read each week in synagogue, and if they lived close to Jerusalem, of hearing teachings in the temple. They were educated alongside their male counterparts in the teachings and rites of Judaism.

Paul faces a situation in his predominantly gentile church in Ephesus, wherein these gentile women lacked teaching. First Timothy is a letter sent to Paul's co-worker, Timothy, that addresses this concern. Today, however, commentators pounce on the statement against women teaching rather than the command to let women learn. By focusing on the command, and establishing the historical context, we discover the importance the early church placed on both women and men learning before teaching. We turn now to examine this letter.

1 Timothy 2:1–15

The second chapter of 1 Timothy focuses on presenting the gospel message in a winsome way. In this passage, Paul envisions the community praying together, offering thanksgiving and petitions for everyone, including those outside the community who govern the city and the empire. The prayers reflect the hope that the community might live quietly with

---

32. Cohick, *Women in the World of the Earliest Christians*, 242–49.

holiness, and that nonbelievers might come to a knowledge of the truth and be saved. Men are enjoined to pray, and to do so without anger or disputing. They are to lift their hands; most likely Paul has in mind the *orans* pose, a common posture for both men and women. The Gospels note that men stand to pray (Mark 11:25; Luke 18:9–13).[33] Perhaps Paul deduces that the false teachers create dissension during worship (1 Tim 1:3–7).

As Paul turns to discuss women's attire, the majority of scholars assume a shift from the topic of men's prayer to the issue of women's modesty.[34] However, several points suggest that Paul continues to reflect on prayer in devotion to God. First, the *orans* pose was typical of women as well as men, as evidenced in the early catacomb art.[35] Additionally, this pose is linked with Pietas, and coins displayed both the goddess and imperial women dressed in the goddess's clothes.[36] It would be natural for the congregation to assume both men and women lifted holy hands in prayer.

Secondly, an ancient novel, Xenophon's *Ephesian Tale*, offers descriptions of Artemis worship, including female devotees dressed as the goddess. The text indicates the erotic appeal of braided hair and purple chiton (dress). Xenophon describes the heroine Anthia's celebration, specifically commenting on her hair, which hung loose except for a braided portion, mimicking that of the goddess. Interestingly, 1 Timothy 2:9 specifies braided hair using the cognate noun, which suggests that Paul has in mind the Artemisian festivals as a backdrop to his injunctions on proper Christian prayers. Paul's additional comments on modesty make sense, given the erotic environment of the Artemis celebrations.[37] Moreover, Paul's sanction against gold and expensive garments could be directly related to the sumptuous clothing worn in honor of the goddess. Paul uses similar terms in Acts 20:33, where he declares to the Ephesians that he has not coveted gold or clothing.

33. Fine, *Art and Judaism*, 180. The synagogue decorations in Dura Europa personify each of the twelve tribes with an *orans* male figure.

34. Towner, *Letters to Timothy and Titus*, 204.

35. Torjesen writes, "The fact that in this collection of pagan *orantes* the figure at prayer is always male makes the predominantly female *orans* of Christian art even more interesting" ("Early Christian *Orans*," 44).

36. Sutherland, "Prayer and Piety," 29–32, 367. Appendix A shows a photo of Livia (http://lobojosden.blogspot.com/2010/05/oran-orante-orans.html). This statue was found in the basilica of Otricoli.

37. *Ephesiaca* 1.3.1–2 describes Anthia and Habrocomes falling in love at Artemis's temple. He could not take his eyes off her, and Anthia put "maidenly decorum out of her mind: for what she said was for Habrocomes to hear, and she uncovered what parts of her body she could for Habrocomes to see" (Hoag, *Wealth in Ancient Ephesus*, 77).

In these ways, Paul warns believers in Ephesus to shun all behaviors that hint at pagan practices surrounding the worship of Artemis. As believers devote themselves to prayer, men lift hands to God, not raise fists at each other. Women distinguish themselves from Artemis followers by refraining from dressing as the goddess, and not succumbing to the culture's pull to display wealth as a form of piety. Paul offers guidance to new female believers, calling them to embody devotion as believers in Christ. Paul's words remind us today that devotion can be a public act, and as such, engages the public square and popular notions of piety.

1 Timothy 2:11–12

Paul states that women must learn, and that he is not letting women to teach or have authority over men. I would like to focus on the verbs from these verses: "let a woman learn," which is an imperative, "I do not permit," which is an indicative, and "to have authority over," which is an infinitive. The verb tenses are straightforward, but the sematic range of the terms has bedeviled interpreters. We will first look at the semantic range, and then focus what the text intends to do.

"Let a woman learn" seems as basic to us as women's right to vote. But even as women suffragists faced violent opposition while working to persuade both men and women of the rightness of their cause, so too the ancient world did not value education for women, except as it might enhance the lives of men. There is no pagan analog to the Bible, no equivalent to the Jewish weekly practice of worship and study. Therefore, the gentile women in the Ephesian church had little exposure to education in the Bible, and their gentile culture would not have a ready way of helping them learn Scripture. Hence Paul's command here that women should learn.

"I do not permit" can also be translated "I am not permitting." The verb tense is indicative, not imperative. Unfortunately, it is often incorrectly interpreted as a command. The more important concern is the verb's meaning. The verb occurs elsewhere in the New Testament, and in general, either grants or withholds permission based on the specific circumstances. Implied is that Paul is responding to the current situation.[38] The semantic range of the verb, and not its tense or the particular false teaching, determines Paul's meaning.

---

38. I am indebted to John H. Walton's unpublished article, "Common-Sense Lexicography and 1 Timothy 2:12–15."

Additionally, it is typically assumed that Paul is prohibiting a woman from teaching a man. However, the Greek grammar does not confirm this position. The infinitive "to teach" typically takes an accusative or perhaps a dative, but "man" in this passage is genitive, connecting it closely to "have authority over."[39] Paul may therefore be restricting women from any teaching. This could make sense based on the false teachings which are spreading in the church. Paul charges men in Ephesus who are teaching false doctrines to cease and desist (1 Tim 1:3-4, 6-7). Because Paul elsewhere praises women for teaching and assumes they will, this passage most likely restricts women from spreading *false* teaching by requiring them to first learn biblical truth. Paul applauds Priscilla for her work, including as a teacher (Acts 18:26). Paul entrusts Phoebe with the letter to the Romans, and she not only delivers the letter but also reads and interprets it to the congregation (Rom 16:1-2).[40]

We turn to the verb, "to have authority over" (*authentein*). The infinitive is difficult to translate because the verb is found nowhere else in the New Testament, and only a few times in first-century writings. Interpreters ask whether the verb carries a positive, neutral, or negative connotation, and how one might make such a determination in the specific context. Cynthia Westfall cites the church father Chrysostom, who uses this verb when cautioning a husband not to be abusive (*authenteō*) as his wife submits to him (*Hom. Col.* 27-31). Such behavior is contrasted with being a loving leader (*archōn*). Westfall rightly points out that Chrysostom reveals that a man should not commit *authenteō* against a woman, even as Paul indicates as much about a woman's actions towards a man. Westfall challenges the common assumption that "have authority over" means being senior pastor.[41] Westfall concludes that a basic semantic concept for our verb is *"the autonomous use or possession of unrestricted force."*[42] Given that the term is never used in a positive sense to describe pastoral leadership, we should not use this verse to exclude women from church ministry or offices of leadership.

---

39. Westfall, *Paul and Gender*, 288-89.

40. McKnight, *Reading Romans Backwards*, 3-5, 92; Gaventa, *When in Romans*, 9-14.

41. Westfall concludes, after studying the eighty-two examples used to support this contention, she that none show "a male doing this to another person or a group of people with a positive evaluation in a ministry or leadership context" (*Paul and Gender*, 165). She observes that the positive occurrences always reflect action towards an inanimate object, or the verb is intransitive.

42. Westfall, *Paul and Gender*, 171, emphasis original.

Rather than teach, Paul indicates that women should be *hēsychia*, translated as "quiet, still." Paul uses the noun earlier in the chapter to instruct believers, men and women, to live peaceably and honestly within the wider community as they pray for those in authority (1 Tim 2:2, see also 2 Thess 3:12; infinitive used in 1 Thess 4:11). The term describes a listening audience in Acts 22:2, and the believing wife's "gentle and quiet spirit" before her unbelieving husband (1 Pet 3:4). Twice in Acts, the term describes believers who cease to speak after realizing a new truth. In Acts 11:18, the group ceases to speak because they have no other concerns after seeing that gentiles receive the Holy Spirit, and in Acts 21:14, the believers in Caesarea Maritima, admitting they cannot dissuade Paul from his journey to Jerusalem, stop trying, and instead accept God's will. Overall, the noun and verb describe a respectful posture towards others, often with an eye to making the gospel more attractive to non-believers. The term's use here in 1 Timothy, therefore, does not imply that only women learn in quietness, or that only women should reflect the virtue of a quiet spirit.

1 Timothy 2:13–15

It is perhaps in response to the Artemis myth that Paul concludes his argument in this chapter with mention of Genesis and the creation account. The city took very seriously its responsibility to honor Artemis, for she was its founder.[43] Her image graced many of the city's coins, and her name was invoked in many official documents. The city's political business interwove seamlessly with her festivals.

We can see some points of connection between the Artemis myth and Paul's statement in 1 Timothy 2:13-15. The insistence on Adam's creation, and on Eve's deception, counters the Artemis myth of the supreme importance of the goddess's birth near Ephesus or perhaps the alternative story of the twins' birth as Artemis born first on the island of Ortygia, after which Leto traveled to Delos to give birth to Apollo.[44] If Paul had this alternate version in mind, it makes sense he would reinforce Scripture's account of the creation of Adam and Eve. Artemis must be distinguished from Eve, who with Adam sinned. Artemis was thought to save those in need and was known as the protector of women in childbirth; the bees

---

43. Trebilco, *Early Christians in Ephesus*, 29.
44. See Callimachus, *HhAp* 16, 24–25, discussed in Stephens, *Callimachus*, 102.

which decorated her skirt emphasized her special powers.[45] Artemis must be distinguished from Christ, the second Adam, who alone has the power of life and death, of deliverance from harm, including the dangers of childbirth.

Paul must reassure the Ephesians of Christ's supreme lordship, and he has an uphill battle. Not only do the believers see bi-weekly processions celebrating Artemis's greatness, but among the believers themselves lurk hypocritical liars who promote asceticism and godless myths (1 Tim 4:2, 7; see also 1:4). Read against the backdrop of the all-encompassing cult of Artemis, Paul's concerns for women's clothing and the content of their teaching makes sense. He must distance both men and women from the dangerous pagan myth that had governed their mindset and actions from childhood.

In summary, Paul commands the church in Ephesus under Timothy's guidance to teach female disciples as part of wider efforts to eliminate false teachings that both men and women were spreading. Paul had to make a special point about educating women, because the gentile believers would not have a ready image of this enterprise. Paul believes that as these (mainly gentile) women learn the proper doctrine, they will be able to teach as did Priscilla, for example (Acts 18:26). And Paul wants women (and men) to disassociate themselves from the pagan festivals that entice them back to their former way of life.

Titles and Offices in the Church

It often surprises readers to learn that the New Testament does not include any named male bishop/overseer or elder/presbyter, other than Christ, who is the bishop/overseer of our souls (1 Pet 2:25). It is also true that no women are given such title, but the import of this fact must take account of the truth that neither is any specific man so titled. A second surprise is the fluidity of the titles' meaning. Within the pages of the New Testament, we find discussions of spiritual gifts (charisms), ministry responsibilities, and offices. For example, Paul enjoins all believers to prophesy when the church comes together (1 Cor 14:5) but also seems to assume that some have a prophetic ministry (14:32, 37), and that some have an office of

---

45. Callimachus, *Hymn* (*Suda* 3.302: 859). See Strelan, *Paul, Artemis, and the Jews*, 48, 62, 114.

prophet (Eph 4:11).[46] In fact, the New Testament is frustratingly vague (from our vantage point) about the distinctions between ministry and office. Paul focuses on leadership within the community, with authority to carry out the responsibilities. I cannot emphasize enough that Paul, following the Lord Jesus, stresses self-sacrificial service as the hallmark of leadership (Mark 10:42–45; 2 Cor 4:1–12). We must keep this general picture in mind as we turn to 1 Timothy 3.

1 Timothy 3:1–13

Paul addresses two leadership titles, overseer/bishop and deacon, describing qualities of godly character that are essential for the roles (see also Titus 1:6–9). Paul does not list job duties, but rather personal virtues that characterize these leaders. For instance, while Paul states that an overseer must have obedient children, Paul is not insisting that only people with at least two children who have lived long enough to show habitual obedience could serve as overseers. Instead, he assumes, based on his culture's practices, that most people marry, and within marriage, most people have children. Therefore, one should examine family life to see if the believer cares for them.

Throughout the passage, Paul uses the indefinite pronoun "whoever." This pronoun clearly allows for both men and women to be considered for leadership. However, one phrase stands out as a possible restriction that limits the role to men. Paul speaks of a "one woman man" or more accurately, a "one wife husband," (3:2). Later in the epistle, Paul speaks of a worthy widow as one who has been "one husband woman" (5:9).[47] It is crucial for us to discover the meaning of this phrase.[48]

One option is to understand the phrase as mandating every office holder must be married. This understanding would prevent both Jesus and Paul from this office. A second option is that the phrase is restricting

---

46. Witt, *Icons of Christ*, 296.

47. In the Greek language, the same word can be translated as wife or woman, and the same word can be translated as husband or man.

48. Paul urges young "widows" to remarry, which seems at odds with his teachings in 1 Corinthians 7:25–40. However, it is possible that these young women had not been married before but had chosen a celibate life and were now struggling with the choice. In chapter 13 of his *Letter to the Smyrnaeans*, the second-century bishop of Antioch, Ignatius, speaks of virgins who are also called widows. The church created a new category for women—an unmarried woman who lives a celibate life for religious purposes, and does not reside in a family member's home.

bigamy, but Roman law forbade bigamy and assumed an implicit divorce of the first wife if a man was living with a second woman as husband and wife.[49] It is therefore highly unlikely that the Ephesians would have understood this as ruling out a practice that they did not do in the first place. A third option, and the most likely, is that the phrase speaks of marital faithfulness. The husband must remain monogamous. This expectation was already present for wives, but gentile husbands were under no such constraint. It was common for men to have mistresses and to visit prostitutes.

Because the phrase is translated literally as "one woman man," English speakers assume that Paul limits the discussion about overseers and deacons to men. More likely, however, this phrase reflects the culture's patriarchal assumption that norms to male experience. For example, the term for courage found in 1 Corinthians 16:13 can be translated as "act like men," but Paul is clearly *not* limiting his focus to male believers only. Instead, the term reflects his culture's assumption that courage is a masculine trait. Another example: if there is a group composed of all women, then the feminine noun would be used. But if there was one man present in the group, the masculine noun would be used. Therefore, given that the Greek language and culture skews general language about men and women to masculine nouns, the best understanding of the phrase "one woman man" is "marital faithfulness."

Those who argue that Paul restricts overseer and deacon to men point to 3:11, which is understood to refer to a deacon's wife. Several points weaken this claim. First, from a grammatical perspective, the adverb "likewise" points back to 3:8, and both verses point back to 3:2. This shows that the topic of deacon is front and center, not wives. If Paul had intended to speak about wives, we would also expect to find a similar verse in the discussion of overseers. Second, the moral characteristics describing women in the letter are similar or even identical to those describing these roles of overseer and deacon.[50] Paul clearly articulates his confidence that women can demonstrate the same godly characteristics as men. Third, we must ask why women are singled out in 3:11. Here is where cultural understanding plays such a role in our interpretation. In

---

49. Cicero, *Orationes philippicae* 2.69, discussed in Cohick, *Women in the World of the Earliest Christians*, 103.

50. Witt observes that Paul seems "deliberately to use similar language to describe the moral qualification of overseers/bishops and elders and the expectations for women in the church" (Witt, *Icons of Christ*, 321). See also Payne, *Man and Woman*, 445–59.

a patriarchal society that believes female is inferior to male, the default mindset of everyone would be that women lacked the qualities necessary for godly leadership. Paul tackles such bias directly by listing specifically the same basic moral characteristics expected of men.

BIBLICAL TEXTS ON WOMEN IN WORSHIP: 1 CORINTHIANS 11:2–16

Before we discuss the passage on worship, we must address the recent argument surrounding the phrase "the head of Christ is God." This claim has been explained recently as the Son is *eternally* subordinate to the Father. This interpretation assumes the term "head" (*kephalē*) means "leader" or "authority over." The traditional, classical understanding of the Trinity does not claim the Son's eternal subordination to the Father. Several key points in the argument are as follows. First, the Son in his human incarnation was subordinate to the Father. This is known as the economic subordination, with the term "economic" referring to the plan of salvation of humanity in Christ. Second, the Son is one with the Father and the Spirit in the immanent Trinity, or the ontological Trinity. The Son is eternally begotten, and the Father is eternally begetting. Unlike human fathers, God the Father has always been a father, and there was never a time when the Son was not. The Trinity is three equal persons who share in mutual love and a single, divine will. The union of three in one is not based on lines of authority, but on a single divine essence or nature.[51] In sum, the term "head" does not mean "leader" when speaking of the Son and the Father, and as we will see below, it is an unlikely meaning for the other two pairs mentioned: the man/Christ and the woman/man.

1 Corinthians 11:3

Let us turn to term "head" found in 11:3. In the English language a common metaphorical meaning of "head" is "leader" or "superior," and this is often brought into the argument, namely that man is superior in some way to woman. Yet from the earliest days in the church, commentators

---

51. Witt concludes, "To say that one divine person eternally exercises authority over or commands another divine person and that the second divine person eternally obeys and submits likely implies some version of tritheism, not Trinitarian orthodoxy" (*Icons of Christ*, 143).

have pushed against this reading because of its Trinitarian implications. For example, in the fourth century, Chrysostom (*Hom.*, 26.3) explained that "head" refers to substance, not social worth. He condemns the "heretics [who] rush upon us with a certain declaration of inferiority, which out of these words they contrive against the Son."[52] The heretics (Arians) maintain that Paul shows here the Son's subjection to the Father as being the same as a human's subjection to Christ. Chrysostom will have none of it, for such a comparison takes away Christ's full deity and wrongly suggests by simple analogy that Christ is as far from the Father as man is from Christ. Furthermore, Chrysostom notes that should Paul have wanted to stress subordination with the term "head," he would have chosen a different analogy than husband/wife—ready at hand was the slave/owner relationship. During the Council of Nicaea (325 CE), Athanasius famously declared, "There was never a time when the Son was not," to reinforce that the Son is of the same substance as the Father.

Lucy Peppiatt reminds us that Paul's analogy is limited, for man did not create woman in the way that Christ created man, and the Father did not create the Son, for the Son is eternally begotten. She rightly points back to 1 Corinthians 3:21–23, where Paul chastises the Corinthians for following human leaders and boasting based on worldly criteria. Paul declares to them that they have all things, and they are of Christ, and Christ is of God. All believers, men and women, are in Christ; through Christ's cross, God reconciles the world to himself. Paul wrestles Christ from the Corinthians' grasp, as they try to shove Christ into their social hierarchy, and rightly places Christ as the Son who, with the Father and the Spirit, draw all humanity into relationship with the Godhead.

Having shown that Paul upends social customs that reinforce hierarchy, and that Paul can use rhetorical arguments to challenge or nuance the Corinthians' beliefs, Peppiatt applies these findings to her reading of 1 Corinthians 11:4–16.

1 Corinthians 11:4–16

The typical reading of the passage understands Paul to be curbing female excesses by demanding proper submission to their authority, their husband, or perhaps father. Most believe the women have taken Paul's arguments about freedom in Christ to an extreme, beyond the scope Paul

---

52. Peppiatt, *Women and Worship at Corinth*, 88.

intended. Yet, interestingly, most churches today do not enforce what seems to be Paul's apostolic charge—namely that women should have a head covering. Beyond the general agreement that Paul restricts women in some way, or singles them out as a special concern, there is great diversity on just what Paul wants done, and what the wider culture expects. For example, it is unclear whether Paul is talking about hair styles or veils, about men's short or long hair, or uncovered head. Again, it is unclear exactly what a head covering symbolized, submission or modesty? It is not clear whether Paul addresses all women or only married women. Readers have difficulty following the logic of Paul's argument. And finally, it is not clear whether and how Paul connects his views on the creation of male and female with the honor/shame paradigm that governed the Greco-Roman society.

As we move into the text, one point must be emphasized: women were praying and prophesying. That is, women were speaking to the congregation on behalf of God (prophesying) and to God on behalf of the congregation (praying). Their thoughts were received; their words carried authority. Paul makes clear in 11:10 that they pray with authority on their head. Some translations add the words "symbol of" before authority, but this addition changes Paul's explicit language. In the surrounding verses, Paul stresses reciprocity, that woman was created from man, and men are born of women. Rather than add words to the text, let us re-examine how we might alter our interpretations to better grasp Paul's message.

Lucy Peppiatt argues that Paul weaves his rebuttal into the Corinthians' own argument, as he does elsewhere in the letter (7:1; 8:1; 12:1; 16:1; see also 6:12; 10:23, which are likely quotations from the church). She sees verses 11:4–5, 7–9, as Paul's summary of the Corinthians' views.[53] They favor head coverings for women as befits cultural decorum and maintains social honor codes (11:4–7). Peppiatt suggests that the church wrongly interpreted the creation narrative in Genesis to support their views. The church wrongly believed that the biblical creation account indicated the superiority of men/male and the inferiority of women/female. She summarizes 11:7–9 as "man fulfills a particular role in relation to God, woman in relation to man"; her question is "whether this is

---

53. Peppiatt concludes that "these verses reflect Paul's opponents' ideas and that this very Greco-Roman view of creation has infected the church at Corinth while functioning as the men's rationale to put the women in the congregation in head coverings for worship" (*Rediscovering Scripture's Vision for Women*, 66).

the correct view of creation."[54] Paul knew Genesis 1:27, which reads that both man and woman are made in God's image and likeness. Nothing is said about "glory" in the Genesis account of creation. When Paul uses "glory" he speaks primarily of God's glory, and next of the glory that will be for all believers (1 Cor 2:7), and the greater glory which each believer is being transformed to, as the Spirit works in them (2 Cor 3:18). Paul uses the specific terms "male and female" found in Genesis, and not the typical Greek terms for man and woman (Gal 3:28). Additionally, in Ephesians 5:29–31, Paul adjusts his language from "body" (*sōma*) to "flesh" (*sarx*), to accommodate the wording of Genesis 2:24, "the two become one flesh." These data points strengthen Peppiatt's claim that Paul is alluding to the Corinthians' aberrant theology in 11:7–9 and offers his own corrective in 11:10–16.[55]

Alan Padgett arrives at a similar interpretation, namely that Paul challenges the aberrant theology of the Corinthians in 11:4–7, but Padgett proposes that we start our interpretation of this passage at the end of it, where Paul offers his conclusions.[56] Padgett suggests that verses 11:15–16 are not implied questions but appeals to nature over social custom. Paul states the rather obvious fact that nature offers no guidance on the virtue of long or short hair.[57]

Both Peppiatt and Padgett offer a reading of the passage that allows for the clear statements on women's praying and prophesying with authority to stand out and guide the less-clear verses. Padgett concludes that some in Corinth insisted that women cover their heads when speaking publicly in the service, and, relatedly, they claim a man's long hair was shameful. Paul rejects their views, "basing his argument on gender balance in Christ, on what is natural, and on consensus among

---

54. Peppiatt, *Unveiling Paul's Women*, 51. See also Peppiatt, *Women and Worship at Corinth*, 76–77, where she writes, "The overwhelming evidence is that we must either accept that Paul invests a cultural practice with deep theological significance, or we must reimagine what he might be saying."

55. Peppiatt summarizes Augustine's argument that Paul was not contradicting Genesis 1:27, and that Paul affirmed what Genesis taught, namely, that men and women together show God's image. See Peppiatt, *Unveiling Paul's Women*, 50–52; Augustine, *On the Trinity* 12.

56. Padgett, *As Christ Submits to the Church*, 105–24.

57. Padgett suggests that Paul argues against a custom "based on social shame and social honor or 'glory.' It was shameful, at least in Corinth in those days, for a man to wear long hair" (*As Christ Submits to the Church*, 109).

CHRISTIANITY CONTESTED

other churches."[58] Women should have the authority to wear their hair covered or uncovered, however they please.

NAMED WOMEN IN PAUL'S CIRCLES

I have offered interpretations of key passages that focus on historical context. Fortunately, we also have evidence of how Paul enacted his teachings. I will look at several named women in Paul's circle. What we discover is that women held the same type of leadership responsibilities as men did and exercised that leadership in a group that included men.

Euodia and Syntyche (Philippians 4:2–3)

Looking first at two women in Philippi, Euodia and Syntyche, it is significant that they are named, suggesting that they are important in the community. Paul repeats his call to each of them: "I plead with Euodia and I plead with Syntyche." This implies that the women were of equal social status. Likely these women led their respective house churches, much as did Nympha (Col 4:15), Lydia (Acts 16:15, 40), and Priscilla and Aquila (Rom 16:3–5). Most commentators believe that Euodia and Syntyche were part of the leadership group of overseers/bishops and deacons mentioned by Paul (Phil 1:1).[59] Philippians is the only letter wherein Paul notes these groups specifically in his greetings. The two unusual features—noting these groups in the greeting and mentioning these women by name—likely indicate that the women belong in one of these categories.

While we can speculate as to whether Euodia and Syntyche were overseers or deacons, Paul states specifically that they are his co-workers who have labored alongside him in the work of the gospel. Other people identified as Paul's co-workers include Timothy (Rom 16:21; 1 Thess 3:2), Titus (2 Cor 8:23), Priscilla and Aquila (Rom 16:3), Apollos (1 Cor 3:9), Philemon (Phlm 1), Urbanus (Rom 16:9), Epaphroditus (Phil 2:25), and Mark, Aristarchus, Demas, Luke (Phlm 24). Within this large group, some traveled and preached, some remained in towns to disciple and lead house churches, some served as Paul's liaisons with the churches.

Paul enjoins these women to "to agree" or "be of one mind" or "think the same thing." The phrase is a repetition of the same request

---

58. Padgett, *As Christ Submits to the Church*, 112.
59. Cohick, *Philippians*, 208–11.

directed earlier to the entire church (Phil 2:2). What might these two women disagree about? Paul's evident concern suggests that the situation is serious. It is unlikely that they differed on doctrine because Paul could have weighed in on the correct answer. Most likely, Euodia and Syntyche disagreed on practice, on how to live out their faith in Christ. We might think of possible situations where through misunderstanding, miscommunication, or different assessments of need, Euodia and Syntyche came to a fork in the road. Paul asks that they join hands and go forward together in Christ.[60]

Phoebe (Romans 16:1–3)

Paul praises Phoebe as his benefactor or patron.[61] Sadly, this Greek term has been translated as "helper" in some Bibles (*prostatis*). When the term is found in its masculine form, it reflects a wealthy, influential patron. Given that many women in the broader community served as patrons at this time, there is every reason to assume Phoebe had similar influence and leadership within the church. Patronage involved social patterns of relationships that paired a patron and client in a web of social, commercial, political, and cultural connections. Phoebe likely had wealth enough to sponsor Paul's ministry and to travel to Rome with his letter. She read Romans to the house churches in Rome, which included answering questions about and interpreting Paul's letter. Additionally, she is a deacon of the church in Cenchreae, the southeastern port of Corinth. The term is often translated as "minister" when referring to Epaphras, a co-worker of Paul's who was a leader in the Colossae church (Col 1:7), and Tychicus, the one who delivered Ephesians (Eph 6:21).

Priscilla (Romans 16:3–5)

In the book of Acts, Priscilla is identified as a tent maker, along with her husband, Aquila. Paul meets this Jewish couple in Corinth, and they will travel to Ephesus to work in the church there; eventually the couple

---

60. A similar situation may be Paul's disagreement with Barnabas on the membership of their mission team (Acts 15:36–41).

61. Luke mentions three women who served Jesus out of their own financial means: Susanna, Mary of Magdala, and Joanna, whose husband was Chuza, Herod Antipas's steward (Luke 8:2–3). On the role of patron, see Osiek and MacDonald, *Woman's Place*, 194–219.

returns to Rome. They fit the pattern of married partners working together in a family business. They host a church in their homes in both Ephesus and Rome (Rom 16:3–5; 1 Cor 16:19). While ministering in Ephesus, they teach another of Paul's co-workers, Apollos, on the deeper matters of theology (Acts 18:26). I want to underline this point, as Paul restricted women in Ephesus from teaching (1 Tim 2:12). In the case of Priscilla, her knowledge of Scripture and the gospel message made any such restriction unnecessary. It is also the case that those who held church gatherings in their homes led the meeting; so Priscilla would have been regularly teaching the other believers.[62] Additionally, Paul commends both of them to the Roman church as risking their necks for his sake (Rom 16:4). In this enigmatic phrase, Paul may be suggesting that the couple was his benefactor or patron who used their social status or wealth to help him out of tight spots.

Junia (Romans 16:7)

Junia, with Andronicus, are Paul's fellow Jewish believers who experienced imprisonment for Christ. They "are outstanding among the apostles" Paul declares (Rom 16:7).[63] Church fathers, including Origen and Chrysostom, consistently understand Paul to be referring to Junia, a woman. In some older English translations, however, her name was re-configured to Junias, a man's name.[64] This was, in part, because the translators could not imagine a female apostle. It was also a legacy of Martin Luther, whose influence is strongly felt as he translated the Bible into German from Latin. He used a masculine article and identified Andronicus and Junias as "*men* of note among the apostles."[65] Yet we have no evidence of any men named Junias in the ancient world, while we have over 250 examples of women named Junia from Roman inscriptions.[66]

---

62. Osiek and MacDonald, *Woman's Place*, 157–63.

63. Cohick, *Women in the World of the Earliest Christians*, 214–17.

64. For a thorough discussion, see Epp, *Junia*.

65. McKnight, *Junia Is Not Alone*, 9. McKnight rightly points to the Greek New Testament critical editions, which up until 1927 identified Junia as female. But in 1927, "Junia" was replaced by "Junias." For about seventy years, the male name held, but in 1998, "Junia" was reinstated in the critical editions, without any mention of Junias.

66. A brief discussion of Greek and Latin naming practices underlying the text critical questions, see Cohick, *Women in the World of the Earliest Christians*, 214–16.

Recognizing the weakness of the argument over the name Junias, some modern translations have suggested that Paul states that Andronicus and Junia were highly regarded *by* the group of apostles. This argument, however, is weakened by the following evidence. The phrase "among the apostles," is typically understood as comparing two things. A parallel might be drawn from Matthew 2:6: "You Bethlehem in the land of Judah, are by no means least *among the rulers* of Judah."[67] The point is that Bethlehem is indeed numbered among the rulers of Judah.

Left to be determined is the meaning of "apostle." Paul identifies himself as apostle, and describes as apostles Timothy, Silas/Silvanus, and Epaphroditus (1 Thess 1:1; 2:7; 1 Cor 9:5-6; Phil 2:25). In the case of Epaphroditus, Paul is likely using the term in a non-technical sense of a messenger sent by the Philippians to aid Paul in his imprisonment (see also 2 Cor 8:23). The term might carry the sense of a traveling missionary and might be implied in the title for Timothy and Silas/Silvanus and perhaps others who spread the gospel message (1 Thess 2:7). But I think Paul intends something with more authority behind it as he speaks in 1 Thessalonians 2:4 that these three are men approved by God to be entrusted with the gospel. Whatever authority Paul is claiming, he includes Timothy and Silas with the same as he introduces them as apostles to the church in Thessalonica. Similarly, in Romans 16:7 Paul uses the definite article "the" in referring to this group of apostles to which Junia and Andronicus belonged. If he was intending to describe them as traveling missionaries, why not instead simply say that they were outstanding among apostles? Attending to the context, it seems best to compare Junia and Andronicus's label of apostle to that of Paul, Timothy, and Silas—as those especially called and gifted to lead the church.

What does it mean that Junia was an apostle? She got the corner office? A parking space close to the front door? A company car? For Paul, apostles were the last in line, the ones mocked, scorned, brutally treated, at times despairing of life itself (1 Cor 4:9). They had the privilege of treacherous travel, sleepless nights, beatings, imprisonments (2 Cor 6:4-10). And it seems that Junia lived up to these requirements, for Paul notes that she and Andronicus suffered imprisonment as he had, and presumably for the same reason: preaching the gospel.[68] As an apostle,

---

67. Bauckham, *Gospel Women*, 178.

68. Bauckham, *Gospel Women*, 170-72, cites several interpretations of this phrase: (1) the couple visited Paul in prison, much as did Epaphras and Aristarchus (Phlm 23; Col 4:10); (2) the couple was taken prisoner at the same time Paul was and imprisoned

she had responsibilities to preach the gospel faithfully, to train up young leaders, to shore up sagging churches and plant new ones.

This brief survey of five women highlights that Paul supported two female co-workers who led churches in Philippi. He entrusted his letter to the Romans to a woman to read and explain to the Roman house churches. He praised a married woman along with her husband for her apostolic ministry and faithful testimony that landed her in jail. From the narrative of Acts, we find Paul working alongside a married woman, who is wise and learned—to the point that she teaches another of Paul's co-workers, Apollos. This is a partial but representative list, and it demonstrates that Paul accepted, encouraged, and celebrated women's leadership activities in the church.

CONCLUSIONS

Was Christianity good for women? We have shown that the earliest communities of believers supported women's leadership and valued women's influence. Based on the gospel message of serving and loving others self-sacrificially, some aspects of the communities were highly counter-cultural, to the benefit of women. For example, the command that husbands love their wives in the self-sacrificial way of Christ, with wives having authority over their husbands' bodies, brought a mutuality to marriage unique to this time (1 Cor 7:3-4; Eph 5:25-33). Again, sexual restrictions to monogamy and sexual activity only within marriage protected slave women (and men) from exploitation (1 Cor 6:13-20; 1 Thess 4:3-8). The communities promoted education for women, following synagogue examples where reading and discussion of the Bible took place (Acts 15:21; 18:24-26; 1 Tim 2:11).[69] Women held leadership responsibilities, taught men and women, including explaining biblical texts. Women evangelized and testified, even to the point of imprisonment for the gospel. They

---

with him; (3) they suffered imprisonment for the same reasons he did—preaching the gospel, and they are perhaps even as he wrote imprisoned in Rome.

69. The counter-cultural emphasis on women's agency and voice had ramifications on definitions and expressions of masculinity within the churches. Greco-Roman definitions of masculinity included self-control and control of others, plus public action. Asikainen discusses the masculinity of marginalized groups, and contrasts voluntary and involuntary marginality, concluding, "When the Synoptic Gospels present 'feminine' service as a value, they formulate an alternative, voluntarily marginal ideal of masculinity" (*Jesus and Other Men*, 105).

worked alongside men in positions of authority in the church, serving self-sacrificially as they modeled Christ to their congregations.

I do not suggest a golden age of proto-feminism in the first century or in these early Christian communities, for women lacked equal treatment under Roman law, and received much less formal education than their brothers. Female was viewed as ontologically inferior to male. Women were not believed when they spoke of the resurrection (Luke 24:9–11), or when they declared that prayers were answered (Rhoda, Acts 12:13–16). But the aspirations of working together in the Spirit for the gospel remained. From this standpoint, we can say that Christianity, or better still, the gospel, is good for women.

BIBLIOGRAPHY

Asikainen, Susanna. *Jesus and Other Men: Ideal Masculinities in the Synoptic Gospels*. Biblical Interpretation Series 159. Leiden: Brill, 2018.
Bauckham, Richard. *Gospel Women: Studies of the Named Women in the Gospels*. Grand Rapids: Eerdmans, 2002.
Cohick, Lynn H. "'Could This Be the Christ?' The Samaritan Woman's Testimony and Jesus' Identity." In *Who Do You Say I Am?: On the Humanity of Jesus*, edited by George Kalantzis et al., 27–42. Eugene, OR: Cascade, 2020.
———. *The Letter to the Ephesians*. NICNT. Grand Rapids: Eerdmans, 2020.
———. *Philippians*. Story of God Commentary. Grand Rapids: Zondervan, 2013.
———. "Was the Samaritan Woman Really an Adulteress?" *Christianity Today*, October 2015. http://www.christianitytoday.com/ct/2015/october/was-samaritan-woman-really-adulteress.html.
———. *Women in the World of the Earliest Christians: Illuminating Ancient Ways of Life*. Grand Rapids: Baker Academic, 2009.
Czajkowski, Kimberley. *Living Under Different Laws: The Babatha and Salome Komaïse Archives*. Oxford: Oxford University Press, 2014.
Day, Janeth Norfleete. *The Woman at the Well: Interpretation of John 4:1–42 in Retrospect and Prospect*. Leiden: Brill, 2002.
Epp, Eldon Jay. *Junia: The First Woman Apostle*. Minneapolis: Fortress, 2005.
Esler, Philip F. *Babatha's Orchard: The Yadin Papyri and an Ancient Jewish Family Tale Retold*. Oxford: Oxford University Press, 2017.
Fine, Steven. *Art and Judaism in the Greco-Roman World: Toward a New Jewish Archaeology*. Cambridge: Cambridge University Press, 2005.
Gaventa, Beverly Roberts. *When in Romans: An Invitation to Linger with the Gospel According to Paul*. Grand Rapids: Baker Academic, 2016.
Grossman, Maxine. "The World of Qumran and the Sectarian Dead Sea Scrolls in Gendered Perspective." In *Early Jewish Writing*, edited by Eileen Schuller and Marie-Theres Wacker, 225–46. Atlanta: Society of Biblical Literature, 2017.
Hanson, Ann Ellis. "The Widow Babatha and the Poor Orphan Boy." In *Law in the Documents of the Judaean Desert*, edited by Ranon Katzoff and David Schaps, 85–103. Leiden: Brill, 2005.

Hoag, Gary G. *Wealth in Ancient Ephesus and the First Letter to Timothy: Fresh Insights from "Ephesiaca" by Xenophon of Ephesus*. Winona Lake, IN: Eisenbrauns, 2015.

Hylen, Susan E. *Women in the New Testament World*. Oxford: Oxford University Press, 2020.

Ilan, Tal. *Integrating Women into Second Temple History*. 1999. Reprint, Peabody, MA: Hendrickson, 2001.

———. *Jewish Women in Greco-Roman Palestine: An Inquiry into Image and Status*. 1995. Reprint, Peabody, MA: Hendrickson, 1996.

Kraemer, Ross Shepard. "Jewish Women and Christian Origins: Some Caveats." In *Women and Christian Origins*, edited by Ross Shepard Kraemer and Mary Rose D'Angelo, 35–49. Oxford: Oxford University Press, 1999.

———. *Women's Religion in the Greco-Roman World: A Sourcebook*. Oxford: Oxford University Press, 2004.

Lee-Barnewall, Michelle. "Turning ΚΕΦΑΛΗ on Its Head: The Rhetoric of Reversal in Ephesians 5:21–33." In *Christian Origins and Greco-Roman Culture: Social and Literary Contexts for the New Testament*, edited by Stanley E. Porter and Andrew W. Pitts, 599–614. Leiden: Brill, 2013.

Lehr, Jane L. "Why Social Justice Educators Must Engage Science in All of Our Classrooms." In *Six Lenses for Anti-Oppressive Education: Partial Stories, Improbable Conversations*, edited by Kevin K. Kumashiro and Bic Ngo, 17–32. New York: Peter Lang, 2007.

Levine, Amy-Jill. "Bearing False Witness: Common Errors Made about Early Judaism." In *The Jewish Annotated New Testament*, edited by Amy-Jill Levine and Marc Zvi Brettler, 759–63. Oxford: Oxford University Press, 2011.

Mahmood, Saba. *Politics of Piety: The Islamic Revival and the Feminist Subject*. 2005. Reprint, Princeton, NJ: Princeton University Press, 2012.

Martin, Emily. "The Egg and the Sperm: How Science Has Constructed a Romance Based on Stereotypical Male-Female Roles." *Signs* 16.3 (1991) 485–501.

McKnight, Scot. *Junia Is Not Alone*. Englewood, CO: Patheos, 2011.

———. *Reading Romans Backwards: A Gospel of Peace in the Midst of Empire*. Waco, TX: Baylor University Press, 2019.

Osiek, Carolyn, and Margaret Y. MacDonald. *A Woman's Place: House Churches in Earliest Christianity*. Minneapolis: Augsburg Fortress, 2006.

Oudshoorn, Jacobine G. *The Relationship Between Roman and Local Law in the Babatha and Salome Komaïse Archives: General Analysis and Three Case Studies on Law of Succession, Guardianship and Marriage*. Leiden: Brill, 2007.

Padgett, Alan G. *As Christ Submits to the Church: A Biblical Understanding of Leadership and Mutual Submission*. Grand Rapids: Baker Academic, 2011.

Payne, Philip B. *Man and Woman, One in Christ: An Exegetical and Theological Study of Paul's Letters*. Grand Rapids: Zondervan, 2009.

Peppiatt, Lucy. *Rediscovering Scripture's Vision for Women: Fresh Perspectives on Disputed Texts*. Downers Grove, IL: IVP Academic, 2019.

———. *Unveiling Paul's Women: Making Sense of 1 Corinthians 11:2–16*. Eugene, OR: Cascade, 2018.

———. *Women and Worship at Corinth: Paul's Rhetorical Arguments in 1 Corinthians*. Eugene, OR: Cascade, 2015.

Stephens, Susan A., ed. *Callimachus: The Hymns*. Oxford: Oxford University Press, 2015.

Strelan, Rick. *Paul, Artemis, and the Jews in Ephesus*. Berlin: de Gruyter, 1996.

Sutherland, Reita J. "Prayer and Piety: The *Orans*-Figure in the Christian Catacombs of Rome." MA thesis, University of Ottawa, 2013.

Torjesen, Karen Jo. "The Early Christian *Orans*: An Artistic Representation of Women's Liturgical Prayer and Prophecy." In *Women Preachers and Prophets through Two Millennia of Christianity*, edited by Beverly Mayne Kienzle and Pamela J. Walker, 42–56. Berkeley: University of California Press, 1998.

Towner, Philip H. *The Letters to Timothy and Titus*. NICNT. Grand Rapids: Eerdmans, 2006.

Trebilco, Paul. *The Early Christians in Ephesus from Paul to Ignatius*. Grand Rapids: Eerdmans, 2007.

Wassen, Cecilia. *Women in the Damascus Document*. Atlanta: Society of Biblical Literature, 2005.

Westfall, Cynthia Long. *Paul and Gender: Reclaiming the Apostle's Vision for Men and Women in Christ*. Grand Rapids: Baker Academic, 2016.

Witt, William G. *Icons of Christ: A Biblical and Systematic Theology for Women's Ordination*. Waco, TX: Baylor University Press, 2020.

11

Sexual Apologetics Through a Covenantal Lens

Paul Rhodes Eddy

INTRODUCTION

SINCE THE EARLY DAYS of the church, Christians have been encouraged to be "ready to make a defense to everyone who asks you to give an account for the hope that is in you, but with gentleness and respect" (1 Pet 3:15). Historically, however, human sexuality has not been found on the typical list of apologetic topics. A primary reason for this is that, since the fourth century, the influence of Western Christendom brought with it a broad cultural sensibility that included something of a Judeo-Christian sexual ethic. This ethic was held for roughly seventeen hundred years in the Christian West. Although many may not have followed the dictates of this sexual ethic, most knew quite well—often under penalty of law—its standards and expectations.

In recent years, along with the progressive crumbling of Christendom, this long-established Western cultural sensibility about human sexuality is crumbling too. As such, it represents but one of the many ways in which post-Christendom Christianity must wrestle with cultural dynamics in ways it has not since the pre-Christendom days of the early church. For example, as Coleman Ford has observed, the sex lives of the early Christians constituted one of the most obvious differences between them and the rest of the Roman world—and even served an "apologetic" purpose.[1] It appears that as Western culture's understanding of sexuality—including its master narrative(s), its plausibility structures, and its ethical default settings—continues to evolve, those seeking to live faithfully in their sexual lives as disciples of Jesus will be called to discern, articulate, and display an increasingly counter-cultural vision of human sexuality. Part of this calling will include the ongoing development of a compelling *Christian sexual apologetic*; that is, a missional articulation of a distinctive Christian vision of sexuality that, winsomely and persuasively, addresses the sexual questions, quandaries, and counter-narratives of the surrounding culture. Glynn Harrison puts it succinctly:

> It's time to recover our confidence that the Christian vision for sex, marriage, and family also conveys social and relational goods that can bring blessing and flourishing to all.... We shall need to open a new chapter in the history of Christian apologetics, making our case in reasoned debate and by the careful use of evidence from the social sciences.[2]

It is the purpose of this chapter to contribute to this important apologetic project. It will begin with a discussion of several visions of human sexuality at work within contemporary Western culture, along with the overlapping ethical core that grounds them. Next, a Christian vision of human sexuality will be proposed—one centered around *covenantal relationship*. Finally, a set of reflections will be offered on some of the ways in which findings from contemporary sexual science intersect with a core aspect of a Covenantal vision of sexuality, namely the value of *relational commitment*.[3]

---

1. Ford, "They Share," 25–42.
2. Harrison, *Better Story*, 173.
3. Contemporary sexual science is a complex, multi-disciplinary, and unavoidably politicized field today. Similar to other fields connected to psychology, it has been implicated in the recent "replication crisis." It is also a field whose dominant secular worldview is inherently in conflict with the Christian theistic worldview. See Fuechtner et al., *Global History*; Rind, "Sexual Science"; Sakaluk, "Replicable Sexual Science"; Slife et al., "Bias Against Theism."

Before proceeding, a brief word on use of the term *sexuality*. Broadly employed, this term can be used within Western culture today in reference to a wide range of things, including biological sex, gender identity, gender roles/norms, sexual orientation, sexual identity, and the wide variety of forms of human sexual activity. In this essay, our consideration of human sexuality will focus upon the question of the meaning and purpose(s) of *sexual intimacy/interaction*.[4]

VISIONS OF HUMAN SEXUAL INTERACTION IN CONTEMPORARY WESTERN CULTURE

There is, of course, no single "perspective" on human sexual interaction/intimacy in Western culture today. Rather, there are various perspectives that exist in a sometimes complementary, sometimes tensive, relationship with each other. In fact, one study found no fewer than 237 different motivational reasons that people report for engaging in sexual relations.[5] This section will serve to briefly summarize some of the key forces at work in the rise of modern Western understandings of sexuality, and to delineate several dominant visions of human sexual interaction that characterize contemporary Western culture, along with their shared ethical substructure.

The historical road to the contemporary Western vision(s) of human sexuality has involved many twists and turns. Key influences include several broad cultural forces at work in the modern period, such as the secularizing dynamics of the Enlightenment and its aftermath, the rise of Western individualism, capitalism, industrialization, and urbanization—each of which, in their own way, fostered a loosening of the Western cultural bonds of tradition, community, extended kinship, and the Judeo-Christian heritage.

In addition, a number of influences played a more direct role in the shaping of contemporary Western sexuality, including the rise and development of modern sexual science, the increasing technological disconnection of sex and reproduction, and the commodification of sex along with its use as a marketing tool. To this list could be added many other influential cultural forces, such as various literary/artistic persons and

---

4. The concept of sexual intimacy/interaction used in this essay includes, but is not limited to, genital intercourse.

5. Meston and Buss, "Why Humans," 477–507.

movements (e.g., the Romantic movement, the Marquis de Sade, Charles Baudelaire, Arthur Rimbaud, the Bloomsbury group, Surrealism, the Beat poets); the steady repeal of obscenity laws; the transformation of gender roles and norms over the course of the twentieth century; the rise of recreational dating; the dawn and evolution of the Hollywood film industry; the rise of the 1960s youth culture; the explosive growth of the pornography industry, and a host of other people and cultural phenomena that—directly or indirectly—contributed to a new vision of sexuality emphasizing liberation from the constraints upon the erotic imposed by religion and tradition.[6]

Out of this impressive mélange of cultural forces have emerged several visions of human sexuality by which to simplify and make sense of its powerful and complex dynamics. Some of these visions are deeply tied to a particular disciplinary perspective. For example, biologists and evolutionary psychologists typically gravitate to *a Reproductive* model of human sexual interaction, where the various subjective human motives for sex are all understood as epiphenomena arising from the more basic evolutionary impulse toward biological reproduction.[7] Conversely, scholars within the social sciences tend to favor *a Social Constructionist* model, which primarily understands human sexual encounters "as learned interactions that follow predictable sequences or 'scripts'" that have been socially constructed, dispersed, and treated as normative within a given cultural context.[8]

Other visions of human sexuality draw from broader cultural impulses. Four particularly influential ones will now be briefly discussed.[9]

1. *The Romantic Vision*: Although not necessarily religiously anchored, this vision of human sexuality views appropriate human sexual intimacy as characterized by something of the sacred. At the very least, it is to be shared with a significant other within the bounds of some sort of "committed relationship" (however temporary), and/or within the context of the experience of "love" (however vaguely defined). The Romantic vision of sex was influenced by what scholars refer to as the romantic or companionate model

6. Allyn, *Make Love*; Hekma and Giami, *Sexual Revolutions*; Rutherford, *World Made Sexy*; Trueman, *Rise and Triumph*.

7. E.g., see Buss, *Evolution*.

8. Frith and Kitzinger, "Sexual Script," 209.

9. This four-part conceptualization has been shaped by several sources, including Simon's helpful book, *Bringing Sex into Focus*, esp. chapter 1.

of marriage. Beginning in the eighteenth century, this form of marriage progressively replaced the traditional model (i.e., arranged marriages focused on the needs of the extended families) in the West.[10] As the name itself suggests, this vision of sexuality is deeply shaped by the cultural intuitions that emerged from the modern Romantic movement. This Romantic vision of sexual intimacy is reflected in the 47.8 percent of contemporary emerging adults (ages eighteen to twenty-five) in the US who report on a recent survey that "sexual activity should only occur within the context of a committed relationship."[11] Researchers have found that attitudes toward sex reflective of a Romantic vision are more often expressed by females than males.[12]

2. *The Power Dynamic Vision:* The central intuition of what we can call a Power Dynamic model of human sexual encounter is famously captured in an aphorism commonly attributed to Oscar Wilde: "Everything in the world is about sex, except sex: Sex is about power." In this view, the sexual encounter is understood as innately and unavoidably involved with *power differentials* and/or *power exchange*. From this perspective, every sexual interaction inevitably carries with it a potential threat for at least one of the parties involved. A Power Dynamic view has been adopted by a number of feminist thinkers over the years as a form of resistance and protest against centuries of male sexual use and abuse of, and sexual violence toward, women.[13]

3. *The Self-Expression Vision:* Another vision of sexual encounter is offered by a Self-Expression model. From this perspective, human sexuality is intimately bound up with self-development, self-empowerment, and self-expression. This view is quintessentially "modern" in the sense that it presupposes certain "truths" about sexuality that were simply unavailable to Western culture prior to the nineteenth century. One of these convictions is the central importance of sexuality and sexual expression to human flourishing. Thus, in the Self-Expression view, "sexual activity"

---

10. Coontz, *Marriage*, 145–60.
11. Olmstead et al., "Meanings Ascribed to Sex," 2441.
12. E.g., Olmstead et al., "Meanings Ascribed to Sex," 2441.
13. For a recent study that reflects aspects of a Power Dynamic model, see Livingston and Vik, "Empowering," 1204–26.

is often understood as "an essential human need."[14] Within some versions of this model, expressions of the importance of sex border on the mystical and transcendent, with the erotic sometimes being virtually equated with the divine.[15] Another presupposition commonly associated with this view is the fundamental importance of one's *sexual identity*—both to one's inner sense of self and to one's authentic public self-representation toward others.

4. *The Recreational Vision*: From this perspective, the language of sexual "interaction" or "encounter" is often more appropriate than sexual "intimacy." While the encounter may involve a subjective experience of intimacy on the part of one person or another, it need not. And, in fact, too deep a dive into intimacy during sexual interaction may threaten the very presuppositional heart of this perspective. An *instrumentalist* vision of sex is central to this view, which involves "the idea that sex 'is a game,' and that the sole purpose of sex is to have pleasure and excitement without the need for love or intimacy."[16] Relatedly, sexual scientists have now coined the term "sociosexuality," defined as "a personal predisposition to engage in uncommitted sex."[17]

In the Recreational view, sexual interaction is seen as a natural biological need and a normal source of human pleasure. While its underlying drive may be an evolutionary impetus toward reproduction, the goal of recreational sex is pleasure, not pregnancy and a baby. A recent study succinctly captures this view when it proclaims that "recreational sex is a popular form of leisure."[18] Thus, sexual encounters can be seen simply as forms of "erotic play."[19] This perspective is also expressed by those advocating for "sex positivity" today, defined by one research team as "the belief that all consensual expressions of sexuality are valid. . . . The sex-positive framework inherently advocates for acceptance of and attention to one's unique sexual experience."[20]

14. Irfan et al., "Sexual Abstinence," 412.
15. E.g., Lorde, "Uses of the Erotic," esp. 76–77.
16. Oosten and Vandenbosch, "Predicting," 1123.
17. Rodrigues and Lopez, "Sociosexuality," 775.
18. Lehmiller et al., "Less Sex," 295.
19. Atwood, "Sex and the Citizens," 82–96.
20. Kimmes et al., "Treatment Model," 289.

CONSENT: THE SHARED ETHICAL CORE

There are, of course, additional views and sub-views of the meaning and purpose for sexual interaction/intimacy at work within Western culture today, including economic/social-exchange theory, various psychoanalytic theories, and interactionist theories that combine and synthesize several views into a multi-faceted construct. The common ground that unites them is the presuppositional matrix of Western individualism, including a commitment to personal freedom and an approach to human sexuality that celebrates, and vigorously defends, "variability, choice or multiple options."[21] In other words, what unites the diversity of views on sex today is (to borrow a phrase from Jonathan Katz) something like a "General Theory of Sexual Relativity."[22] In a sexual atmosphere such as this, virtues include "the openness and non-judgmental attitude we often see in the developed world, gaining its fullest expression when people are asked to judge nontraditional behaviors, for which they present one word. That word is 'Whatever!'"[23]

But, of course, "Whatever!" cannot be the final ethical word in any human society that lasts more than a day. As happily simple and easy-going as "openness and non-judgmentalism" sound, such a world would quickly devolve into sexual chaos and violence. For this reason, the contemporary Western vision(s) of sexuality require a clear and unquestioned sexual ethic that tolerates no "openness" to its violation and offers only serious threat, punishment, and "judgment" to those who dare transgress its moral code. Just such a sexual ethic has been supplied by the virtually unquestioned moral law of *sexual consent*. This moral principle fits well with Western individualism and its ethical centering of individual human will and desire. Gert Hekma succinctly captures the consent principle: "No sexual relation is morally wrong as long as it is not abusive, which means that it does not go against the wishes [i.e., consent] of the partner."[24] Likewise, the "sex positivity" framework calls people to be "open-minded, non-judgmental and respectful of personal sexual autonomy, *when there is consent.*"[25] And so, the words of Miley Cyrus on her personal ethical parameters for sexual interaction capture a widely

---

21. Hatfield et al., *Love and Sex*, 228.
22. Katz, "Invention," 30.
23. Hatfield et al., *Love and Sex*, 228.
24. Hekma, "Sexual Variations," 81. See also Lang, *Consent*.
25. Ivanski and Kohut, "Sex Positivity," 216, emphasis added.

held cultural sentiment: "I am literally open to every single thing that is consenting."[26]

One sign of the consent principle's deep and rarely questioned ingression into the Western mind is the growing number of progressive/liberal expressions of Christianity that embrace it as the heart of their sexual ethic. For example, Nadia Boltz-Weber opens her book, *Shameless: A Sexual Revolution*, by proposing a sexual ethic of *consent*, no harm, mutuality, and a "concern" for human flourishing.[27]

Increasingly, however, the consent principle is being called into question as profoundly insufficient. For example, in her recent book, *Rethinking Sex*, reporter and Washington Post columnist Christine Emba boldly argues that "consent is a good ethical floor but a terrible ceiling."[28] As a number of news outlets have reported, it appears that Emba's message both resonates with and expresses the sentiments of a growing number of people in our culture—particularly among younger cohorts who are beginning to question the virtues of the unbridled "sex positivity" perspective.[29]

A CHRISTIAN COVENANTAL VISION OF HUMAN SEXUALITY

This section will be devoted to explicating a distinctively Christian vision of sexuality that is intimately bound up with covenantal relationship, specifically, *the covenant of marriage*.[30] It will begin with a call to the church for a sexual confession and repentance of sorts. Next, it will briefly mention several key components of the historic Christian worldview that will serve as a framework for the understanding of sexuality that follows. Finally, it will move to a reflection on a covenantal vision of sexual intimacy.

---

26. Petrusich, "Free to Be Miley."

27. Bolz-Weber, *Shameless*, 11–12.

28. Emba, *Rethinking Sex*. See publisher's description at https://www.penguinrandomhouse.ca/books/622579/rethinking-sex-by-christine-emba/9780593402559.

29. E.g., French, "Consent Was Never Enough"; Holden, "Gen Z Women."

30. For a defense of marriage as a covenant relationship, see parts 1–3 of Eddy, "Is Marriage a Covenant?"

Toward a Corporate Christian Reckoning about Matters of Human Sexuality

Any sexual apologetic that aspires to persuasively engage the plausibility structures of contemporary Western culture will have to begin by addressing the ways in which the church itself has so often fallen short—both in terms of theology and practice—of the type of Christian vision of sexuality worthy of the name. Toward this end, we begin with the need for the church to adopt a posture of sexual confession and repentance. A call for followers of Jesus to humbly model a truly Kingdom sexual vision and way of life as a prelude to asking others to consider doing the same, along with frank acknowledgement of the many ways in which Christians have not always lived up to their own sexual ethic over the years. Areas in which corporate confession and repentance seem called for include:

- The ways in which we, as Christians, have often adopted, both publicly and privately, a posture of sexual self-righteousness rather than humility. Instead of following the teaching of Jesus (Luke 18:9–14) and the teaching and general example reflected by the apostle Paul (1 Tim 1:15), the church has generally failed to recognize and openly acknowledge its own sexual sin and brokenness. Instead, and contrary to Jesus' clear instruction (Matt 7:1–5), we have tended to see other people's sexual sin as a "log" and our own as a mere dust speck.[31]

- The fact that, since the second century, the church—contrary to its own scriptures—has tended to foster attitudes of negativity and shame toward human sexuality.[32] This has led to a general sense that the church is not a place to talk openly and honestly about sexuality, especially about one's own sexual struggles and brokenness. As a recent book title puts it: *Sex, Jesus, and the Conversations the Church Forgot.*[33]

---

31. E.g., Kinnaman and Lyons document that among sixteen- to twenty-nine-year-olds, the number one idea associated with the word "Christian" is *anti-gay* (*UnChristian*, 25–26).

32. On the generally positive views of sexuality reflected in the Bible, see Davidson, *Flame of Yahweh*; Ellis, *Paul*; Loader, *New Testament on Sexuality*.

33. Isom, *Conversations the Church Forgot*.

- This characteristic silence of the church on sexual matters—outside of its regular commentary on the decline of sexual mores with the wider culture, or the occasional (and often awkward) youth group "sex talk"—has left many Christians without a compelling and robust vision of healthy sexuality. This fact has been documented by the Barna Group in their survey finding that, among the many young people leaving the church today, what seems to have been lacking in their church experience is any clear articulation of "how to live up to the church's expectations of chastity and sexual purity" while living within a culture that constantly offers an opposing vision.[34] As Caroline Simon wisely reminds us: "Sexual insight and sexual integrity rise and fall together."[35]

- There are significant levels of sexual moral failure within the church, even as it pronounces judgment upon the surrounding culture for the very same behaviors. From the regular cross-denominational reports of clergy sexual abuse and, often, its subsequent cover-up, to survey findings that report significant gaps between Christians' professed beliefs about sexual ethics and their actual practices, the incongruence between our sexual "talk" and our sexual "walk" is regularly put on public display.[36] For example, one recent study focusing on "deviant cyber-sexual activities" found, to the researchers' surprise, that within their survey sample of young adults, more Christians than non-Christians reported involvement in sexting.[37] This common gap between sexual profession and practice no doubt contributes to the fact that among the most common attributes that non-Christians associate Christians with are hypocrisy (50 percent), judgmentalism (49 percent), and self-righteousness (46 percent).[38]

- Bound up with the previous concerns is the tendency within much of contemporary Christianity, particularly in the US, toward the idolization of romance, sex, and marriage. Whereas early Christians tended to construe unmarried celibacy as superior to marriage,

---

34. Kinnaman, "Six Reasons." This article is reporting on findings discussed in Kinnaman, *You Lost Me*.

35. Simon, *Bringing Sex into Focus*, 12.

36. E.g., Guidepost Solutions, "Report"; Charles, "Everyone's Doing It"; and chapters 3–5 in Ayers, *After the Revolution*.

37. Klein and Cooper, "Deviant," 628.

38. Ipsos, "Jesus in America."

today many within the church have simply reversed the hierarchy. For example, among the problems associated with evangelical Christian "purity culture" has been its tendency to motivate young people to abstain from sex with the promise of future marital and sexual bliss. For those whose future marriage never came, or, when it came, was far from blissful (sexually or otherwise), the promised marital carrot was traded for the stick of harsh reality and the shame of "singleness," divorce, or a disappointing marriage.[39] By largely buying into the modern Western Romantic model of marriage, the contemporary church has provided little in the way of a robust and compelling vision of how unmarried people are to live within deep, intimate relationships beyond the horizons of sex and marriage.[40]

AN OUTLINE OF A CHRISTIAN COVENANTAL VISION OF HUMAN SEXUALITY

Setting the Theological Stage: The Triune God, the Imago Dei, and the Gift of Covenantal Relationship

A Christian perspective on sexuality will align with those who claim that the consent principle is ethically insufficient. One way of framing the issue here is in terms of the three primary anchor posts of cross-cultural human ethics, what Richard Shweder and colleagues refer to as "the 'Big Three' of morality": *individual autonomy* (focused on personal rights), *community* (focused on communal identity and values), and *divinity* (focused on sacred, divinely authorized values and principles).[41] To put the matter simply: the contemporary Western sexual ethic and its wider vision of human sexuality is anchored by only one of these three pillars: *individual autonomy*. For this very reason, its anchoring is myopic, shallow, and ethically fragile.

A robust Christian vision of sexuality will draw from all three dimensions of human ethical support, with the divinely revealed creational design for human sexuality serving as its center-post, and the values associated with individual autonomy being more securely grounded in a

---

39. Despite good intentions, evangelical purity culture fostered some damaging consequences. See Welcher, *Purity Culture*.

40. See Callaway, *Marriage Idol*; Clapp, "Singleness."

41. Shweder et al., "Big Three," 119–69.

non-negotiable principle of human dignity, value and worth that, itself, is anchored in the trans-cultural fact that every human being is created by, and in the image of, the Triune Creator God (Gen 1:26–28).

Whatever complexities and mysteries are involved in the doctrine of the Trinity, this much seems clear: the Triune nature of God reveals that at the heart of Ultimate Reality we find *a single Being of three differentiated persons in an everlasting, radically unified* agape-love relationship (with the fully flowered historic Christian dogma of the Trinity being foreshadowed by such New Testament seeds as Mark 1:9–11; John 14:25–26; 17:20–23; etc.).[42] First John 4:8 states that God is love (*agape*), suggesting an instantiation of *agape*-love so radical that it literally names the very unitive essence of the three-personed Creator God. Augustine points in this direction when he suggests that the very relationship between the Trinitarian persons is the love of God; and many other theologians have similarly embraced this intuition.[43]

From the approach of a theological interpretation of Scripture (TIS), we can say it is *this Triune, relational God* who, in the words of the opening chapter of Genesis, says:

> Let us make humanity in our image, according to our likeness. . . . So, God created humanity in his own image, in the image of God he created them; male and female he created them."
> (Gen 1:26–27)[44]

In the ancient world, a divine "image" functioned as a physical representation of a divine spirit that visibly reflected one or more qualities of that spirit. Genesis tells us that when the eternal Creator God designed a physical "image" to reflect the divine essence, *humanity* was the creaturely outcome of that creative act. And more specifically, *humanity in community*, that is, differentiated, embodied persons called to be bound as one through *agape*-love.[45] This theme is perhaps most

---

42. Feldmeier and Spieckermann, *God of the Living*, 96.

43. Augustine, *Homilies*, 108. More recently, see, e.g., Barth, *Church Dogmatics*, 2.1:272–97 (esp. 280); Oravecz, *God as Love*, 480.

44. Adopting a TIS approach *does not* equate to saying the human author of Genesis intended the "us" to signify a Trinitarian conception of God. On TIS, see Treier, *Theological Interpretation of Scripture*. That being said, some scholars have offered interesting exegetical cases for seeing Genesis 1 as pointing to plurality in the Godhead, e.g., Keiser, "Divine Plural," 131–46.

45. On the theological importance of our bodies, both for being human and for our sexuality, see Jones, *Marks*.

clearly seen in the words of Jesus' prayer to his heavenly Father, "that they [God's people] may all be one. As you, Father, are in me and I am in you ... that they may be one, as we are one" (John 17:21–22). And so, in light of the revelation of Jesus Christ—who, himself is described by the apostle Paul as the true image of God (e.g., 2 Cor 4:4; Col 1:15)—this divine image is seen to be not simply that of some generic God concept but rather *the image of the Triune God of unitive* agape-love. And so, as biblical scholar Joel Green reminds us: "The concept of the *imago Dei* [i.e., humanity created in and as the image of God] is fundamentally relational, or covenantal."[46] And this leads us to a brief consideration of *covenantal relationship*.

Reflecting the culture of its time, the language associated with covenant used in the biblical texts encompasses a fairly wide semantic range. However, in tracing the covenantal heart of God through the biblical metanarrative, a more focused vision of, and purpose for, covenant relationship emerges, one that is *centered on kinship*.[47] Based on this biblical thematic trajectory, I propose as a robust vision of covenant relationship: *a committed, community-oriented, kinship-creating relationship that is grounded in promises of faith and faithfulness, sealed with an oath and/or oath-sign, and whose primary purpose is to provide the partners with the blessings of family (i.e., identity and belonging, community and safety, loyalty and responsibility, purpose and calling, legacy and destiny)*. This definition of covenant relationship reminds us that there are only ever two ways of becoming family: birth and promise. That is, blood and covenant. We become part of a family by either being *born* into it or, alternatively, by being *promised* into it, as in the covenant of marriage or the adoption of a child. And of these two ways of creating family, only covenant can take people who are *non-family to each other* and make them family. Likewise, only covenant can take the "unfamilied" (i.e., those who have no family at all, a prime concern of God reflected in Scripture by the recurring theme of "widows and orphans") and provide them with family. The creation of family out of the absence of family is one of the miracles of covenant relationship.

Through this kinship-creating power of covenant, God enables the creation of new human-to-human family relationships (marriage,

---

46. Green, *Body*, 63.

47. A point emphasized by the late Harvard professor of Hebrew, Frank Moore Cross, in his ground-breaking essay "Kinship and Covenant." See also Hahn, *Kinship by Covenant*.

adoption, covenant friendship, etc.), all of which are, in their own way, a small "image" of the new covenant that the Triune God of *agape*-love has, through Jesus, entered with human beings in order to bring forth the eternal family of God. In sum, we can say that *covenant relationship is one of the most profound ways by which humans enter into committed,* agape-*love relationships that serve to "image" the God who is eternal* agape-*love.* This is the wider covenantal context within which we can now turn to consider the biblical vision of *the marriage covenant and the role of sexual intimacy within its kinship-creating capacity.*

Sexual Intimacy as the Covenantal "Sign" of the Marriage Covenant

From a Christian perspective, we can identify several different purposes for sexual intimacy. For example, Dennis Hollinger identifies four primary purposes for sex: consummation of a marriage, procreation, expression of love, and pleasure.[48] The final three of these purposes are widely acknowledged throughout contemporary Western culture and beyond. It is the first of these four purposes—*sexual intimacy as the divinely designed act that consummates and ratifies a marriage covenant*—that has largely been lost in modern Western culture. It is also, I propose, the most meaning-laden of these four purposes in the sense that, while the relationship between sex and the other three purposes is relatively clear and universally recognized, recognition of the ratifying nature of sexual intimacy requires a covenantal interpretive lens, which decodes its divinely intended symbolic significance and the covenant "sign" function that it serves. It is this *covenantal dimension of sexual intimacy*—one largely neglected by contemporary Western culture—that must now function as *a central pillar of a Christian sexual apologetic.* For this reason, it will be the focus of the remainder of this essay.

Both Jewish and Christian traditions have recognized marriage and sexuality as important aspects of God's design for humanity. Key to this recognition is the identification of these themes in the Genesis creation texts.[49] For the Christian tradition, the centrality of Genesis 1 and 2 for understanding the divine vision of marriage and sexuality is rooted in the

48. Hollinger, *Meaning of Sex*, 93–115.

49. On Genesis 1 and 2 as key texts in the development of ancient Jewish and Christian understandings of marriage and sexuality, see Loader, *Sexuality*, 121–22; Witte Jr., *Sacrament to Contract*, 335.

teachings of Jesus.[50] Both Mark and Matthew record an episode in which some Pharisees publicly test Jesus on the question of legitimate grounds upon which a man can divorce his wife (Mark 10:1–9; Matt 19:1–12). Jesus responds not by answering their question, but by pointing them back to the nature of marriage itself:

> "What did Moses command you?" They said, "Moses allowed a man to write a certificate of dismissal and to divorce her." But Jesus said to them, "Because of your hardness of heart he wrote this commandment for you. But from the beginning of creation, 'God made them male and female.' 'For this reason a man shall leave his father and mother and be joined to his wife, and the two shall become one flesh.' So, they are no longer two, but one flesh. Therefore, what God has joined together, let no one separate." (Mark 10:3–9)

Two aspects of Jesus' response are important for our purposes here. First, as commentators have noted, the Genesis creation account was so fundamental to Jesus' sense of God's purposes for the human sexes that he uses this text as a basis for critiquing other passages of the Torah (i.e., the teaching on divorce in Deuteronomy 24:1–4).[51] Second, in appealing to Genesis, Jesus turns their attention to God's original vision for marriage. But he does so with an unexpected hermeneutical move—one that appears to be unattested in prior Jewish biblical interpretation. Jesus begins by quoting Genesis 1:27: "From the beginning of creation, 'God made them male and female.'" But then, instead of finishing the quote by moving on to the procreative purpose clearly stated in the next verse (1:28), Jesus leaps right over it and all the way down to 2:24: "For this reason a man shall leave his father and mother and be joined to his wife, and the two shall become one flesh."

As many commentators have pointed out, Genesis 2:24 culminates a line of thought begun in 2:23, one that, by using several different phrases (i.e., "bone of my bone; flesh of my flesh," "cleave," and "one flesh") emphasizes *the kinship-producing reality of the marriage covenant*.[52]

---

50. There is much scholarly debate on the degree to which the Jesus tradition found in the Gospels reflects the actual oral teaching of the Jesus of history. I have argued elsewhere for the general historical reliability of the Synoptic Jesus tradition. See Eddy and Boyd, *Jesus Legend*. On this basis, as well as the specifics of the material on marriage and sexuality in the Synoptics, I will use "Jesus tradition" and "teachings of Jesus" interchangeably.

51. E.g., Meier, *Law and Love*, 123; Countryman, *Dirt, Greed, and Sex*, 174.

52. E.g., Brueggemann, "Flesh and Bone," 532–42; Cross, "Kinship and Covenant,"

To return to Jesus: he ends with this commentary: "So, they are no longer two, but one flesh. Therefore, what God has joined together, let no one separate" (Mark 10:8–9). With these final words, Jesus doubles down on the covenantal nature of this relationship. But not only this. William Loader reminds us that, within Second Temple Jewish literature, the Genesis 2:24 theme of "one flesh" was regularly understood as implying sexual union.[53] Thus, by the time of Jesus, an appeal to the "one flesh" of Genesis 2:24 is able to evoke a synthesis both of the covenantal and the sexual. In Loader's words, Jesus uses Genesis 2:24 "to assert that sexual union creates permanent oneness."[54] In Jesus' eyes, marriage is more than merely a contractual arrangement between two people who were joined by their parents for the betterment of their extended families—a common perception of the traditional model of arranged marriage in the ancient world. *Rather, it is a family-forming relationship in which the very lives and bodies of two people are fused into one covenantal flesh through a divinely designed and empowered process that involves sexual union.*

Following Jesus, the apostle Paul views the creation texts, particularly Genesis 2:24 and 1:27, as a guide on matters related to sexuality and marriage (quotations or likely allusions include 1 Cor 6:16; Eph 5:31; Gal 3:28; Rom 1:26–27; 1 Tim 4:3–4).[55] But what is the import of Jesus' interpreting Genesis 1:27 and Genesis 2:24 in light of each other? It appears that by juxtaposing them, Jesus is explicitly linking the divinely designed sexual dimension of humanity—i.e., "male and female" (Gen 1:27) with the purposes of the marriage covenant (Gen 2:24).[56] More specifically—and an insight confirmed by the consistent linkage of sexual intimacy with the marriage covenant throughout the rest of the New Testament—Jesus' teaching here adopts and affirms the robust scriptural thread that portrays *sexual union itself as the covenantal oath-sign that serves to inaugurate and ongoingly reaffirm the kinship-creating power of the marriage covenant.*[57]

7–8; Davidson, "Theology of Sexuality," 21; Goldingay, *Genesis*, 64–65; Hugenberger, *Marriage as a Covenant*, 164–67.

53. Loader, *New Testament on Sexuality*, 277–78.

54. Loader, "Genesis 2:24," 266. Similarly, regarding the Markan parallel, see Marcus, *Mark 8–16*, 712–13.

55. Bouteneff, *Beginnings*, 54.

56. Commentators have pointed out that, by this juxtaposition, Jesus appears to be defining the marriage covenant as a relationship divinely designed as a male-female dyad, e.g., Marcus, *Mark 8–16*, 703–13; Sprinkle, *People*, 34–36.

57. Hugenberger, *Marriage as a Covenant*, 248–79.

A brief clarifying word on covenant (oath-) signs can be helpful here. In covenantal context, a "sign" can serve both as (1) a constituent element of the inauguration of a covenant itself (i.e., "signing" the covenant), and (2) a regular reminder of the covenant, one whose symbolism is, ideally, intended to capture the essence of the covenant that is being physically represented. Being sensorily perceptible and regularly repeated are, therefore, essential qualities for an effective covenant sign, in that it is the very purpose of a covenant sign to regularly impinge upon the consciousness of the partners so as to call them back simultaneously to remembrance and renewal of the covenant itself. We see these qualities, for example, in the covenant signs chosen by God in his various covenantal relationships with humanity, i.e., the (rain)bow in the Noahic covenant (Gen 9:12–17), circumcision in the Abrahamic covenant (Gen 17:9–14), the Sabbath day of rest in the Sinai covenant (Exod 31:12–17), and the Lord's Supper in the new covenant (Luke 22:19; 1 Cor 11:25). In light of a number of biblical passages in both Testaments—succinctly crystallized in Jesus' teaching in Mark 10/Matthew 19—it appears that we can confidently add to this list *sexual union as the divinely designated oath-sign of the marriage covenant*. It is in light of Jesus' covenantal understanding of sexual intimacy—a conviction with deep roots in the Hebrew Bible—that we can understand the other distinctives of his perspective on human sexuality, including the utter seriousness with which he takes the proper use of our sexuality, and the fact that sexual integrity is measured not merely by our physical behaviors but also by our inner thought life (Matt 5:27–28).

In our contemporary context, most people recognize the spoken vows as the most significant covenant-making element of the wedding, with sexual union often going unrecognized as an essential covenant sign. However, viewed in light of the vision of sexuality articulated above, a marriage covenant is best understood as composed of two distinct, though deeply inter-related, moments: (1) the couple's speaking of public vows in the presence of a witnessing community, plus (2) the couple's private signing (consummation, ratification) of their covenantal vows through sexual union. As the divinely designated oath-sign of the marriage covenant, the significance of human sexual union transcends the realm of "mere biology" alone; it is equally located in the realm of covenantal inauguration, intimacy and responsibility. To misuse the act of sexual intimacy outside of its intended covenant context is to violate the very covenantal purpose for which it was intended. This explains, in part, the consistent seriousness with which the Bible takes human sexual encounter. As Doug Baker observes, "sexual acts" are always "covenant acts—either covenant making or covenant breaking."[58] This insight leads Monford Harris to note "the self-contradictory quality of non-covenantal sex."[59] This means that, within the divinely conditioned economy of human sexuality, to engage in sexual intimacy is, in fact, to performatively enact a covenantal, kinship-creating "I do" with our bodies. For this reason, the apostle Paul reminds his ancient Corinthian audience that to engage in sex with a prostitute—as clear an example of intentionally commercial/contractual, and thus non-covenantal, sex as one can imagine—nonetheless results in a "one flesh" relationship between the two people (1 Cor 6:15–16). Analogous to the contemporary signing ritual of "signing a check"—which is a ratifying act that serves as a promissory pledge of the existence of sufficient funds within a legitimate bank account owned by the signatory—*human sexual intimacy is divinely designed to function as a ritual "signing" act that ratifies a promissory pledge (i.e., public wedding vow) of kinship within the context of a marital covenant.* This suggests that the "only time sexual intercourse tells the truth is when it signifies that two people have united themselves as one to start a new life together."[60] Now and then, even Hollywood gets it brilliantly right. In the 2001 film, *Vanilla Sky*, Julie Gianni (Cameron Diaz) says to David Aames (Tom Cruise): "Don't you know that when you sleep with someone, your body makes a promise, whether you do or not?"

Of course, this vision of sexuality raises all sorts of metaphysical complexities and ethical quandaries about sexual encounters characterized by covenantal ignorance, sexual coercion, etc. As in most cases, things intended by God to be a good gift can, in human hands, be misunderstood or misused in an array of ways. The good news is that, even in these cases, God is revealed to be both gracious and wise, and able to provide pathways of healing, redemption, and restoration in the midst of sexual ignorance, brokenness, or out-right violation.

---

58. Baker, *Covenant and Community*, 100.
59. Harris, "Pre-Marital Sexual Experience," 144.
60. Genovesi, *Pursuit of Love*, 154.

CORRELATIONS BETWEEN A COVENANTAL VISION OF HUMAN SEXUALITY AND CONTEMPORARY SEXUAL SCIENCE

This final section will offer reflections on several points at which the Covenantal vision of sexuality resonates with findings from contemporary sexual science, particularly in contrast with the increasingly influential Recreational and Self-Expression visions of sex. Given that sexual science today is characterized by an atmosphere of "sex positivity" oriented around a synthesis of the Recreational and Self-Expression models, one would expect to find very little correlation between its research findings and a Covenantal perspective. And, in fact, many of the published conclusions of sexual science do serve to support a Recreational–Self-Expression synthesis. For example, a number of studies have concluded that casual sex among college students is not inherently correlated with negative outcomes for health and well-being.[61] Another example involves the practice of "sexting" (i.e., the digital sending or receiving of sexually explicit messages and/or images). Given that by eleventh grade, up to 50 percent of adolescents have engaged in some form of sexting, researchers adopting a sex-positive framework have concluded that sexting is now a "normative" aspect of adolescent sexual development, to be seen as "a modern-day form of flirting,"[62] and that "safe-sexting" guidelines should be added to school-based sex education curriculum.[63]

However, despite the dominant influence of the Recreational–Self-Expression synthesis, it is noteworthy that the findings of a wide range of studies are easily correlated with a Covenantal view of sexuality. Of course, researchers committed to a naturalistic/atheistic worldview will typically explain such correlations either as nothing more than the socially constructed vestiges of our Judeo-Christian past, and/or the accidental epiphenomena of our evolutionary history. However, seen in light of Christian Trinitarian theism and a Covenantal vision of sexuality, these correlations appear as unsurprising data points that resonate, to one degree or another, with the divinely designed relational anchoring function of human sexual intimacy.

Among these areas of correlation are a variety of research findings that point toward *an important connection between human sexual*

---

61. Vrangalova, "Casual Sex," 945–59.
62. Mori et al., "Prevalence of Sexting," 1111.
63. Patchin and Hinduja, "Teach Safe Sexting," 140–43.

interaction/intimacy and relational commitment. Space limitations only allow for brief comments on a few representative examples.

- A 2008 publication reported "for the first time, experimental evidence . . . that sexual interest and arousal are associated with motives to form and maintain a close relationship."[64] Specifically, this study found that "sexual priming," particularly at the subliminal level, tended to foster an increase in willingness to self-disclose, willingness to self-sacrifice for one's partner, and pursuit of positive conflict-resolution strategies.

- In a series of studies published over a decade (2013, 2017, 2021), a team of US researchers investigated the *meaning* assigned to sex by emerging adults.[65] Despite the common emphasis on the normativity of casual sex among young adults, each of these studies reported that the majority of study participants fell into the "committers" group, defined as holding the view that sex involves "a deep personal meaning and a demonstration of one's commitment to an exclusive romantic relationship."[66] A similar pattern was found in a 2018 study of Canadian university students.[67]

- A number of studies involving emerging adults have found that *commitment* is a key factor that significantly correlates with relational satisfaction and/or sexual pleasure.[68]

- Additionally, research has found that the "expression of love and commitment" prior to first sexual interaction not only serves to "enhance relationship" and "minimize regret, but it also distinguishes those relationships that terminate after first sex . . . from those relationships that remain intact."[69]

A variety of studies have found that "adolescents and young adults with casual sexual partners report more negative consequences of sex than individuals with committed partners," particularly with regard to genital

---

64. Gillath et al., "Sex Primes Love," 1057–69.
65. Olmstead et al., "Sex, Commitment," 561–71; Olmstead et al., "Meanings for Sex," 1831–42; Olmstead et al., "Meanings Ascribed to Sex," 2435–46.
66. Olmstead et al., "Meanings for Sex," 1836.
67. Netting and Reynolds, "Thirty Years," 55–68.
68. E.g., De Jong and Reis, "We Do It Best," 181–202.
69. Metts, "First Sexual Involvement," 156.

sexual activity.[70] Relatedly, early sexual debut has been linked with a number of negative outcomes.[71]

Importantly, historic Christianity emphasizes that the covenantal bond of marriage itself *is* the expression of the robust relational commitment required to support healthy sexual intimacy. Anything less is a semi-commitment or pseudo-commitment.

In conclusion, a Covenantal vision of human sexual interaction/intimacy serves as a central pillar of a compelling Christian sexual apologetic, one that contrasts in distinctive ways with the dominant visions of sexuality that guide contemporary Western culture.

BIBLIOGRAPHY

Allyn, David. *Make Love, Not War: The Sexual Revolution: An Unfettered History.* London: Routledge, 2001.

Atwood, Feona. "Sex and the Citizens: Erotic Play and the New Leisure Culture." In *The New Politics of Leisure and Pleasure*, edited by Peter Bramham and Stephen Wagg, 82–96. New York: Palgrave Macmillan, 2011.

Augustine. *Homilies on the First Epistle of John.* Translated by Boniface Ramsey. New York: New City, 2008.

Ayers, David. *After the Revolution: Sex and the Single Evangelical.* Bellingham, WA: Lexham, 2022.

Baker, Doug. *Covenant and Community: Our Role as the Image of God.* Eugene, OR: Wipf & Stock, 2008.

Barth, Karl. *Church Dogmatics.* Translated by T. H. L. Parker et al. Edinburgh: T&T Clark, 1957.

Bolz-Weber, Nadia. *Shameless: A Sexual Revolution.* New York: Convergent, 2019.

Bouteneff, Peter C. *Beginnings: Ancient Christian Readings of the Biblical Creation Narratives.* Grand Rapids: Baker Academic, 2008.

Brueggemann, Walter. "Of the Same Flesh and Bone (GN 2, 23a)." *Catholic Biblical Quarterly* 32 (1970) 532–42.

Buss, David M. *The Evolution of Desire: Strategies of Human Mating.* 4th ed. New York: Basic, 2017.

Callaway, Kutter. *Breaking the Marriage Idol: Reconstructing Our Cultural and Spiritual Norms.* Downers Grove, IL: IVP, 2018.

Clapp, Rodney. "The Superiority of Singleness." In *Families at the Crossroads: Beyond Traditional and Modern Options*, 89–113. Downers Grove, IL: InterVarsity, 1993.

Charles, Tyler. "(Almost) Everyone's Doing It." *Relevant* 53 (2011) 64–69.

Coontz, Stephanie. *Marriage, A History: How Love Conquered Marriage.* New York: Penguin, 2005.

Countryman, L. William. *Dirt, Greed, and Sex: Sexual Ethics in the New Testament and Their Implications for Today.* Philadelphia: Fortress, 1988.

---

70. E.g., Wesche et al., "Short-Term Consequences," 1614.

71. E.g., Kluger et al., "Long-Term Consequences," 662–76.

Cross, Frank Moore. "Kinship and Covenant in Ancient Israel." In *From Epic to Canon: History and Literature in Ancient Israel*, 3–21. Baltimore: Johns Hopkins University Press, 1998.

Davidson, Richard M. *Flame of Yahweh: Sexuality in the Old Testament*. Peabody, MA: Hendrickson, 2007.

———. "The Theology of Sexuality in the Beginning: Genesis 1–2." *Andrews University Seminary Studies* 26 (1988) 5–24.

De Jong, David C., and Harry T. Reis. "We Do It Best: Commitment and Positive Construals of Sex." *Journal of Social and Clinical Psychology* 34.3 (2015) 181–202.

Eddy, Paul Rhodes. "Is Marriage a Covenant? Part I." *Centrality and Supremacy of Jesus Christ* (blog), June 18, 2014. http://daviddflowers.com/2014/06/18/is-marriage-a-covenant-part-i.

———. "Is Marriage a Covenant? Part II." *Centrality and Supremacy of Jesus Christ* (blog), June 19, 2014. http://daviddflowers.com/2014/06/19/is-marriage-a-covenant-part-ii.

———. "Is Marriage a Covenant? Part III." *Centrality and Supremacy of Jesus Christ* (blog), August 25, 2014. http://daviddflowers.com/2014/08/25/is-marriage-a-covenant-part-iii.

Eddy, Paul Rhodes, and Gregory A. Boyd. *The Jesus Legend: A Case for the Historical Reliability of the Synoptic Jesus Tradition*. Grand Rapids: Baker Academic, 2007.

Ellis, J. Edward. *Paul and Ancient Views of Sexual Desire: Paul's Sexual Ethics in 1 Thessalonians 4, 1 Corinthians 7 and Romans 1*. London: T&T Clark, 2007.

Emba, Christine. *Rethinking Sex: A Provocation*. New York: Sentinel, 2022.

Feldmeier, Reinhard, and Hermann Spieckermann. *God of the Living: A Biblical Theology*. Translated by Mark E. Biddle. Waco, TX: Baylor University Press, 2011.

French, David. "Consent Was Never Enough." *Atlantic*, April 4, 2022. https://newsletters.theatlantic.com/the-third-rail/624b278a6c9086002052fdd2/sexual-consent-culture-christine-emba.

Ford, Coleman M. "'They Share Their Food but Not Their Wives': Sexual Holiness as Christian Apologetic in the Second Century." *Journal of Discipleship and Family Ministry* 5.1 (2015) 25–42.

Frith, Hannah, and Celia Kitzinger. "Reformulating Sexual Script Theory: Developing a Discursive Psychology of Sexual Negotiation." *Theory and Psychology* 11 (2001) 209–32.

Fuechtner, Veronika, et al., eds. *A Global History of Sexual Science, 1880–1960*. Oakland, CA: University of California Press, 2018.

Genovesi, Vincent J. *In Pursuit of Love: Catholic Morality and Human Sexuality*. 2nd ed. Collegeville, MN: Liturgical, 1996.

Gillath, Omri, et al. "When Sex Primes Love." *Personality and Social Psychology Bulletin* 34.8 (2008) 1057–69.

Goldingay, John. *Genesis*. Grand Rapids: Baker Academic, 2020.

Green, Joel B. *Body, Soul, and Human Life*. Grand Rapids: Baker Academic, 2008.

Guidepost Solutions. "Report of the Independent Investigation: The Southern Baptist Convention Executive Committee's Response to Sexual Abuse Allegations and an Audit of the Procedures and Actions of the Credentials Committee." May 15, 2022. https://bit.ly/3PLY8ZC.

Hahn, Scott. *Kinship by Covenant*. New Haven, CT: Yale University Press, 2009.

Harris, Monford. "Pre-Marital Sexual Experience: A Covenantal Critique." *Judaism* 19.2 (1970) 134–44.

Harrison, Glynn. *A Better Story: God, Sex and Human Flourishing*. London: Inter-Varsity, 2017.

Hatfield, Elaine, et al. *What's Next in Love and Sex: Psychological and Cultural Perspectives*. New York: Oxford University Press, 2020.

Hekma, Gert. "Sexual Variations." In *A Cultural History of Sexuality in the Modern Age*, edited by Gert Hekma, 79–104. Oxford: Berg, 2011.

Hekma, Gert, and Alain Giami, eds. *Sexual Revolutions*. New York: Palgrave, 2014.

Holden, Madeleine. "The Gen Z Women Think Sex Positivity Is Overrated." *BuzzFeed News*, July 29, 2021. https://www.buzzfeednews.com/article/madeleineholden/gen-z-sex-positivity.

Hollinger, Dennis P. *The Meaning of Sex: Christian Ethics and the Moral Life*. Grand Rapids: Baker Academic, 2009.

Hugenberger, Gordon P. *Marriage as a Covenant: Biblical Law and Ethics as Developed from Malachi*. Grand Rapids: Baker, 1998.

Ipsos. "Jesus in America." *Episcopal Church*, March 2022. https://www.episcopalchurch.org/jesus-in-america.

Irfan, Muhammad, et al. "Sexual Abstinence and Associated Factors Among Young and Middle-Aged Men: A Systematic Review." *Journal of Sexual Medicine* 17.3 (2020) 412–30.

Isom, Mo. *Sex, Jesus, and the Conversations the Church Forgot*. Grand Rapids: Baker, 2018.

Ivanski, Chantelle, and Taylor Kohut. "Exploring Definitions of Sex Positivity through Thematic Analysis." *Canadian Journal of Human Sexuality* 26.3 (2017) 216–25.

Jones, Beth Felker. *Marks of His Wounds: Gender Politics and Bodily Resurrection*. New York: Oxford University Press, 2007.

Katz, Jonathan Ned. "The Invention of Heterosexuality." *Socialist Review* 20.1 (1990) 7–34.

Keiser, Thomas A. "The Divine Plural: A Literary-Contextual Argument for Plurality in the Godhead." *Journal for the Study of the Old Testament* 34 (2009) 131–46.

Kimmes, Jonathan G., et al. "A Treatment Model for Anxiety-Related Sexual Dysfunctions Using Mindfulness Meditation Within a Sex-Positive Framework." *Sexual and Relationship Therapy* 30.2 (2015) 286–96.

Kinnaman, David. "Six Reasons Young Christians Leave Church." *Barna Group*, September 27, 2011. https://www.barna.com/research/six-reasons-young-christians-leave-church.

———. *You Lost Me: Why Young Christians are Leaving Church . . . and Rethinking Faith*. Grand Rapids: Baker, 2011.

Kinnaman, David, and Gabe Lyons. *UnChristian: What a New Generation Really Thinks About Christianity . . . and Why It Matters*. Grand Rapids: Baker, 2007.

Klein, Jennifer L., and Danielle Tolson Cooper. "Deviant Cyber-Sexual Activities in Young Adults." *Archives of Sexual Behavior* 48 (2019) 619–30.

Kluger, Kari C., et al. "Long-Term Consequences of Early Sexual Initiation on Young Adult Health." *Journal of Early Adolescence* 37.5 (2017) 662–76.

Lang, Jennifer. *Consent: The New Rules of Sex Education*. Emeryville, CA: Althea, 2018.

Lehmiller, Justin J., et al. "Less Sex, but More Sexual Diversity: Changes in Sexual Behavior during the Covid-19 Coronavirus Pandemic." *Leisure Sciences* 43.1-2 (2021) 295–304.

Livingston, Tyler N., and Tennley A. Vik. "'Empowering, Humbling, and of Course Arousing': A Qualitative Analysis of Experiences with Power in Sexual Relationships." *Sexuality & Culture* 25.2 (2021) 1204–26.

Loader, William. "Genesis 2:24 and the Jesus Tradition." In *Sexuality and Gender: Collected Essays*, 257–69. Tübingen: Mohr Siebeck, 2021.

———. *The New Testament on Sexuality*. Grand Rapids: Eerdmans, 2012.

———. *Sexuality in the New Testament: Understanding the Key Texts*. Louisville, KY: Westminster Knox, 2010.

Lorde, Audre. "Uses of the Erotic: The Erotic as Power." In *Sexuality and the Sacred: Sources for Theological Reflection*, edited by James B. Nelson and Sandra P. Longfellow, 76–79. Louisville, KY: Westminster/John Knox, 1994.

Marcus, Joel. *Mark 8–16*. New Haven, CT: Yale University Press, 2009.

Meier, John P. *Law and Love*. Vol. 4 of *A Marginal Jew: Rethinking the Historical Jesus*. New Haven, CT: Yale University Press, 2009.

Meston, Cindy M., and David M. Buss. "Why Humans Have Sex." *Archives of Sexual Behavior* 36.4 (2007) 477–507.

Metts, Sandra. "First Sexual Involvement in Romantic Relationships." In *Handbook of Sexuality in Close Relationships*, edited by John H. Harvey et al., 135–58. Mahwah, NJ: Erlbaum, 2004.

Mori, Camille, et al. "The Prevalence of Sexting Behaviors among Emerging Adults: A Meta-Analysis." *Archives of Sexual Behavior* 49.4 (2020) 1103–19.

Netting, Nancy S., and Meredith K. Reynolds. "Thirty Years of Sexual Behavior at a Canadian University." *Canadian Journal of Human Sexuality* 27.1 (2018) 55–68.

Olmstead, Spencer B., et al. "Meanings Ascribed to Sex and Commitment among College-Attending and Non-College Emerging Adults: A Replication and Extension." *Archives of Sexual Behavior* 50.6 (2021) 2435–46.

Olmstead, Spencer B., et al. "Meanings for Sex and Commitment among First Semester College Men and Women: A Mixed-Methods Analysis." *Archives of Sexual Behavior* 46.6 (2017) 1831–42.

Olmstead, Spencer B., et al. "Sex, Commitment and Casual Sex Relationships among College Men: A Mixed-Methods Analysis." *Archives of Sexual Behavior* 42.4 (2013) 561–71.

Oosten, Johanna M. F. van, and Laura Vandenbosch. "Predicting the Willingness to Engage in Non-Consensual Forwarding of Sexts: The Role of Pornography and Instrumental Notions of Sex." *Archives of Sexual Behavior* 49 (2020) 1121–32.

Oravecz, Johannes Miroslav. *God as Love: The Concept and Spiritual Aspects of Agapē in Modern Russian Religious Thought*. Grand Rapids: Eerdmans, 2014.

Patchin, Justin W., and Sameer Hinduja. "It's Time to Teach Safe Sexting." *Journal of Adolescent Health* 66 (2020) 140–43.

Petrusich, Amanda. "Free to Be Miley." *Paper*, June 9, 2015. https://web.archive.org/web/20160107201726/http://www.papermag.com/free-to-be-miley-1427581961.html.

Rind, Bruce. "Sexual Science versus Progressive Advocacy: The Need for Resistance." *Archives of Sexual Behavior* 48.6 (2019) 1649–50.

Rodrigues, David, and Diniz Lopez. "Sociosexuality, Commitment, and Sexual Desire for an Attractive Person." *Archives of Sexual Behavior* 46.3 (2017) 775–88.

Rutherford, Paul. *A World Made Sexy: Freud to Madonna*. Toronto: University of Toronto Press, 2007.

Sakaluk, John Kitchener. "Promoting Replicable Sexual Science: A Methodological Review and Call for Metascience." *Canadian Journal of Human Sexuality* 25.1 (2016) 1–8.

Shweder, Richard A., et al. "The 'Big Three' of Morality (Autonomy, Community, Divinity) and the 'Big Three' Explanations of Suffering." In *Morality and Health*, edited by Alan M. Brandt and Paul Rozin, 119–69. Florence, KY: Taylor & Frances, 1997.

Simon, Caroline J. *Bringing Sex into Focus: The Quest for Sexual Integrity*. Downers Grove, IL: IVP Academic, 2012.

Slife, Brent D., and Jeffrey S. Reber. "Is There a Pervasive Implicit Bias against Theism in Psychology?" *Journal of Theoretical and Philosophical Psychology* 29.2 (2009) 63–79.

Sprinkle, Preston. *People to Be Loved: Why Homosexuality Is Not Just an Issue*. Grand Rapids: Zondervan, 2015.

Treier, Daniel J. *Introducing Theological Interpretation of Scripture: Recovering a Christian Practice*. Grand Rapids: Baker, 2008.

Trueman, Carl R. *The Rise and Triumph of the Modern Self: Cultural Amnesia, Expressive Individualism, and the Road to Sexual Revolution*. Wheaton, IL: Crossway, 2020.

Vrangalova, Zhana. "Does Casual Sex Harm College Students' Well-Being?" *Archives of Sexual Behavior* 44 (2015) 945–59.

Welcher, Rachel Joy. *Talking Back to Purity Culture: Rediscovering Faithful Christian Sexuality*. Downers Grove, IL: IVP, 2020.

Wesche, Rose, et al. "Short-Term Consequences of Sex: Contextual Predictors and Change across College." *Archives of Sexual Behavior* 50.4 (2021) 1613–26.

Witte, John, Jr. *From Sacrament to Contract: Marriage, Religion, and Law in the Western Tradition*. Louisville, KY: Westminster John Knox, 2012.

12

Religious Apathy

Kyle Beshears and Tawa Anderson

INTRODUCTION

As NORTH AMERICA BECOMES increasingly post-Christian, the challenges to Christianity seem to multiply exponentially. Some contest Christianity based on the presence of evil and suffering in the world or the perceived character of God as revealed in the Old Testament. Others contest the Christian conception of race, gender, and sexuality. Still others contest the truth of the resurrection or the compatibility of Christianity and science.

An oft-overlooked challenge to contemporary Christianity comes from religious disinterest—what we will call *apatheism*. We contend that apatheism contests the very fabric and foundations of the faith: we cannot contend for the truth of Christianity if folks do not care about the conversation in the first place.

In this chapter, we will accomplish four tasks. First, we will explain the nature and origins of apatheism. Second, we will illuminate five areas in which apatheism contests the Christian faith. Third, we will outline philosophical reasons for rejecting apatheism. Finally, we will articulate theological arguments against apatheism. Our fundamental contention is that apatheism, when embraced, poses significant challenges to the Christian mission and that apatheism should be neither embraced nor encouraged by well-intentioned people.

WHAT IS APATHEISM?

The term *apatheism* is an intuitive combination of "apathy" and "theism" that expresses a lack of interest in God.[1] It is indifference to God-questions (GQs), those most profound philosophical inquiries that humans have pondered since time immemorial. Does God exist? If so, what is God, and what is God like? Does God act, and if so, how would we know, assuming we could comprehend God's activity in the first place? If God does not exist, what does his nonexistence mean? How does God's existence or nonexistence inform our understanding of death, i.e., what happens after we die? Theism upholds both God's existence and the importance of GQs. Atheism agrees that GQs are important but denies that God exists. Agnosticism affirms the significance of GQs but believes our responses must be held with a measure of uncertainty. Apatheism, however, finds GQs to be irrelevant. An apatheist may affirm, deny, or be uncertain about God's existence, but, in the end, God is "nothing to get too excited about," wrote Robert Nash.[2]

Nash first recognized that apatheism is not a broad disregard for religion in general, but indifference toward questions related to God's existence specifically.[3] For Nash, apathy toward GQs extinguishes "passion, emotion, or excitement regarding religious matters," which results in apatheism, a "disposition toward religion that sees it as nothing more than an individual idiosyncrasy, a matter of personal temperament or taste, only vaguely interesting in an intellectual sense."[4] Although apatheism was nascent during the Enlightenment, a term to describe the

---

1. While no universal definition of apatheism presently exists, consensus recognizes it as general indifference toward God. For various definitions, see Nash, *Religious Pluralism*, 27; Rauch, "Let It Be," 35; Budimir, "Apatheism," 88–93; Norenzayan, *Big Gods*, 188–89; Hedberg and Huzarevich, "Appraising Objections to Practical Apatheism," 3; Beshears, "Athens Without a Statue to the Unknown God," 518–20; Kraay, *Axiology of Theism*, 8; Mouzelis, *Modernity*, 75–76; Groothuis, *Christian Apologetics*, 144–45.

2. Nash, *Religious Pluralism*, 27.

3. Nash, *Religious Pluralism*, 27.

4. Nash, *Religious Pluralism*, 27.

concept was not apparently coined until the early 1970s by sociologist Stuart D. Johnson, who discerned the religious apathy that "accompanies the shift from sacred to secular orientations in the contemporary world."[5] Apatheism was popularized in 2003 by Jonathan Rauch's influential essay, "Let It Be," in which he defined it as "a disinclination to care all that much about one's own religion, and an even stronger disinclination to care about other people's [religion]."[6] Apatheism is not concerned with what you believe but *how* you believe—it is "an *attitude*, not a belief system."[7]

Here, Rauch identifies an essential distinction of apatheism that sets it apart from other "-isms" one might instinctually lump together, e.g., atheism and agnosticism. While a theist believes God exists, an atheist believes God does not exist, and an agnostic believes we cannot know with certainty whether God exists, an apatheist might believe or disbelieve God exists but simply doesn't care one way or the other. Theirs is a holistic indifference toward God in both mind and heart. They find GQs uninterestingly irrelevant and feel nothing about God one way or another.

This feature of apatheism shows how belief is more than merely the sum of our ideas concerning God. Christian theism, for example, affirms the supernatural. It confesses an eternal creator God who transcends the universe yet is immanently involved with it. Atheism, on the other hand, believes quite oppositely. It imagines a self-caused, material cosmos governed and functioning by natural laws and forces. But simply *what* is believed among Christians and atheists does not communicate *how* they believe. A Christian whose faith is animated by fervor might be described as a "true believer," and the New Atheists were notorious for their passionate convictions against theism. But the less a Christian and atheist care about GQs, the more they start to resemble one another's listlessness toward GQs, even though they answer those questions antithetically. It is possible to be an apatheistic theist and an apatheistic atheist.

In other words, apatheism exists across the spectrum of beliefs about God.[8] Again, it has less to do with *what* one believes than with *how*. Apatheism is "a general attitude of apathy or indifference regarding

---

5. Johnson, "Correctional Chaplaincy," 179.
6. Rauch, "Let It Be," 34.
7. Rauch, "Let It Be," 34, emphasis added.
8. See Beshears, *Apatheism*, 53–57.

how we answer [existence question about God]," explained philosophers Trevor Hedberg and Jordan Huzarevich.[9]

Why Does Apatheism Exist in Our Society?

Apatheism is possible in a secular society where belief in God is contestable and diverse, and the status of life is generally comfortable and very distracted.[10] As Charles Taylor has argued, belief about God in Western society became challenged and diversified due, in part, to a "mind-centered view" of meaning, i.e., value, significance, importance, and so on.[11] Centuries ago, the self was vulnerable to external processes of change by supernatural powers, and meaning was received from an enchanted world outside the mind. The meaning of God was assigned *to* us by the church. However, the self is now buffered from the disenchanted world, and the mind determines meaning. God's meaning is assigned *by* us. Some exercise this autonomy to contest God's existence, giving rise to areligious beliefs. Others choose to believe in God differently than before, leading to new religious beliefs. For Western society, belief in God is contested and diverse, whereas before it was consolidated to the orthodoxy of the church.

Ethan Shagan paralleled Taylor's insight by arguing that not only have beliefs changed throughout the centuries, but belief itself has evolved.[12] In the Middle Ages, the act of believing was categorically distinct from personal judgment and opinion. Belief was not a set of premises adopted by someone after private adjudication; instead, it was "some form of participation in the collective and indubitable credenda of the church."[13] Belief had more to do with community participation than individual pontification. During the Reformation, however, the boundary between belief, knowledge, and opinion began to collapse, and from that merger emerged the modern assumption that belief must be justified by evidence and decided on individually. The difference is subtle but significant, something discernible in the variance between believing the church and believing *in* the church. The church is either an authority that

---

9. Hedberg and Huzarevich, "Appraising Objections to Practical Apatheism," 3.
10. Beshears, *Apatheism*, 11–41.
11. Taylor, *Secular Age*.
12. Shagan, *Birth of Modern Belief*.
13. Shagan, *Birth of Modern Belief*, 62.

declares truth over us (i.e., "I believe the *church*") or it is a source from which we, the authority, draw from (i.e., "*I* believe *in* the church"). Belief is now "a second-order commitment to the autonomous judgment of the believing subject," argued Shagan; it's "simply the output of the human mind."[14] Consequently, for something to be believed, it must be justified by evidence and adjudicated individually.

Suppose it is true of Western society that the human mind is the locus of meaning, and our beliefs come after independent decision-making. In that case, apatheism occurs when a person assigns God little meaning and concludes God's existence to be irrelevant. Add to this the general comfortable and distracted lifestyle of most Westerners, and God, for them, further feels unneeded and unnoticed. Apatheism, then, exists wherever a person lacks the reason, motivation, or will to care about GQs.

What Is the Value of Apatheism?

But is apatheism to be desired, and is it even valuable? Unsurprisingly, it is our conviction that apatheism is undesirable, and in this chapter, we will highlight philosophical and theological reasons to reject apatheism as adverse to humanity. Even to the areligious, this question has no readily apparent answer, which is, perhaps, why some philosophers who look upon apatheism favorably have come to its defense. Hedberg and Huzarevich, for example, have addressed several practical arguments against apatheism to support it tacitly by substantiating its plausibility and, consequently, its adoptability. In short, they argue that because GQs have no practical significance to human morality or meaning, there is no obligation to care about them one way or the other.[15] Another writer owed God's supposed insignificance to theological "fuzziness," or non-consensus about God's nature, which leads some people to a "principled and justified lack of interest in arguments about God's possible existence."[16]

---

14. Shagan, *Birth of Modern Belief*, 247.

15. Hedberg and Huzarevich, "Appraising Objections to Practical Apatheism."

16. Lindsay, *Everybody Is Wrong About God*, 69. Lindsay, an adamant non-theist, echoed Richard Dawkins's tired concern that theism is like a cognitive virus. To simply remain apathetic about it is, from his perspective, to ignore an existential epidemic of the mind. Instead of focusing on arguments about God—the battle is won, after all, according to him—secular humanists ought to reorient discussion with theists toward the future of humanity.

Ian von Hegner was more forthright, arguing that God is a cosmic tyrant who need not be rejected by doubt or disobedience but through simple disregard to the benefit of human flourishing.[17]

Perhaps no argument is more popular at present than the one made by Jonathan Rauch, who framed apatheism as an exciting development in Western culture because of its potential to curb ideological zealotry. Rauch denounced religion as the "most divisive and volatile of social forces," evidenced by the 9/11 terrorism attacks.[18] He argued that zealotry of any kind, whether "fanatical religiosity" or "tyrannical secularism"—currently a rising concern among major non-Western powers—plagues the human condition and habitually jeopardizes human flourishing. The solution, Rauch said, is to leverage apatheism's potential for neutralizing dogmatic zeal so that societies might enjoy cultural *enkrateia*, a collective tranquility undisturbed by any enthusiasm that threatens to upset the social order. Rauch esteems apatheism as "nothing less than a major civilizational advance."[19]

In sum, apatheism is a philosophical and theological value judgment that assesses GQs as essentially meaningless and, therefore, not worth our concern. It occurs when a person believes that God is unimportant and feels that way as well, and appears in secular societies where people lack the reason, motivation, and will to care about God. Apatheism has been championed as warranted and even virtuous, a benefit to both individuals and society. But is it necessarily so?

HOW DOES APATHEISM CONTEST CHRISTIANITY?

While its benefits may be debatable, apatheism has undeniably contributed to a new cultural climate in the Western world. In the latter half of this chapter, we will argue that the impact of apatheism is predominantly negative for society *as a whole* and ought to be rejected and opposed. But first, it seems important to explicitly identify how apatheism challenges the Christian church. It is easy to intuitively "feel in my bones" that apatheism makes life more difficult for committed Christians: but *how precisely* do difficulties arise and apply?

---

17. Hegner, "Heroical Apatheism," 76–92.
18. Rauch, "Let It Be," 35.
19. Rauch, "Let It Be," 35.

Apatheism Contests Discipleship

The label "Christian" derives from the Greek *christianos*, meaning "little Christ"; disciple, meanwhile, comes from the Greek *mathētētes*, meaning "follower" or "learner." A Christian disciple, therefore, is one who follows the example and teaching of Jesus Christ, seeking to become more like him with each passing day.

When Christians adopt an apatheistic attitude toward their faith, it becomes exceedingly difficult to exhort them toward deeper discipleship. Given apatheism, what motivation exists toward a "closer walk with Thee"? To the extent that GQs are considered inconsequential, an apatheistic Christian's "faith" will probably be nominal or "cultural." Could the existence of so-called CEO (Christmas-and-Easter-only) Christians be at least partially the result of their theistic apatheism?[20] Could the prevalence of "Sunday morning Christians" be due to believers' apatheistic attitudes?[21] After all, if the existence and nature of God are relatively unimportant, then certainly any demands or expectations of that irrelevant God are themselves trivial as well.

So what if St. Paul calls us to "behave decently,... not in orgies and drunkenness, not in sexual immorality and debauchery, not in dissension and jealousy. Rather, clothe yourselves with the Lord Jesus Christ, and do not think about how to gratify the desires of the sinful nature" (Rom 13:13–14)?[22] What does it matter if Jesus himself urges us to live actively for his Kingdom principles: feeding the hungry, visiting the prisoner, clothing the naked, hosting the stranger—with the looming threat of eternal damnation if Christians disobey (Matt 25:31–46)? Who cares that the apostle James declares that "religion that God our father accepts as pure and faultless is this: to look after orphans and widows in their distress and to keep oneself from being polluted by the world" (Jas 1:27)? If God's existence and related issues are inconsequential, then the apatheist surely cannot be blamed for disregarding key precepts in biblical tradition, can they?

---

20. CEO Christians attend church rarely—perhaps only on the significant holy days of the church calendar—but continue to self-identify as Christians.

21. Sunday morning Christians may be quite faithful in their church attendance, but their behavior the rest of the week reflects "the world" (e.g., 1 John 2:16) rather than the life of Christ.

22. This passage, for what it is worth, was instrumental in the conversion of St. Augustine. See Augustine, *Confessions*, 153. All biblical citations are taken from the New International Version (1984) unless otherwise noted.

Apatheism thus serves as a distinct challenge to Christian discipleship.

Apatheism Contests Corporate Worship

While Sunday church attendance is neither the goal nor the end of the Christian life, the call to worship and gather together is central to the church.[23] We have already hinted at the phenomenon of CEO Christians. Granted, the sporadic attendance and lukewarm faith of self-identified Christians is a specter that dates back even to the first-century church and was particularly pronounced in nineteenth-century Europe.[24] The rise of apatheism has exacerbated those existing tendencies within Christendom—and the onset of COVID-19 with its resultant church shutdowns has further accelerated the trend of professing Christians who do not physically attend church.

To be sure, we celebrate the technological and theological innovations that have permitted churches to establish and maintain strong online ministries and stream worship services. At the same time, it is problematic to hear one of our deacons insist that "there is no significant difference between attending church online and attending an in-person church service." In contrast, the author of Hebrews provides this exhortation:

> Let us hold unswervingly to the hope we profess, for he who promised is faithful. And let us consider how we may spur one another on toward love and good deeds. Let us not give up meeting together, as some are in the habit of doing, but let us encourage one another—and all the more as you see the Day approaching. (Heb 10:23–25)

Many mainstream and evangelical churches have seen considerable "melt" from pre-pandemic to post-pandemic average attendance (though it should be noted that others have seen no decline, and some have even grown). Anecdotally, many professing Christians insist that attending church just isn't very important to them. Statistically, the proportion of Americans who claim that religion is very important in their

---

23. Besides Hebrews 10 (cited below), the example of the early church in the book of Acts establishes the centrality of corporate gatherings. See, e.g., Acts 2:42–47; 4:23–35; 5:41–42; 6:1–7; 9:32–43; 11:1–18, 27–30; 13:1–3.

24. Hence the harsh words for the church in Laodicea in Rev 3:14–20, and Søren Kierkegaard's withering attacks upon the "dead orthodoxy" of his state-sponsored Danish Lutheran Church.

lives has dropped from 70 percent in 1965 to 51 percent in 2018.[25] Where religious faith holds less importance, motivation to attend weekly or even monthly worship services will drop accordingly.

Apatheism thus serves as a distinct challenge to corporate worship.

Apatheism Contests Evangelism

The English term "gospel," so often attached to the news that Jesus is Savior and Lord, translates the Greek *euangelion*, which literally means "good news" and serves as the etymological root of our English term "evangelism." Evangelism, then, refers to actively communicating the good news of Jesus to others: sharing "good news of great joy that will be for all the people" (Luke 2:10). Indeed, the gospel is good news which is understood to be not only *worth* sharing with others, but *necessary* to share with others.[26]

The apostle Paul declares that the gospel of Jesus Christ is "the power of God for the salvation of everyone who believes: first for the Jew, then for the Gentile" (Rom 1:16).[27] Everywhere Paul went, he preached the good news that salvation has come by grace through faith in Jesus Christ.[28] Paul did not refrain from preaching when controversy, confrontation, opposition, and even riots ensued. On account of his preaching, Paul gets kicked out of Pisidian Antioch (Acts 13:50), mistreated and expelled in Iconium (Acts 14:5–6), stoned nearly to death in Lystra (Acts 14:19), and beaten and imprisoned in Philippi (Acts 16:19–24). His preaching sparks riots in Thessalonica (Acts 17:5–8), Berea (Acts 17:13–14), Ephesus (Acts 19:23–41), and Jerusalem (Acts 21:27–36).

25. According to Gallup polling in Brenan, "Religion Considered Important." The Pew Research Center data shows the proportion of Americans who claim religion is either "very important" or "somewhat important" to them dropped from 82 percent in 2007 to 77 percent in 2014. See "Importance of Religion in One's Life."

26. See, e.g., 1 Corinthians 9:16–18, where Paul declares: "Yet when I preach the gospel, I cannot boast, for I *am compelled* to preach. Woe to me if I do not preach the gospel! . . . What then is my reward? Just this: that in preaching the gospel I may offer it free of charge." Similarly, in 2 Corinthians 5:14, Paul insists that "Christ's love *compels* us, because we are convinced that one died for all" (emphasis added).

27. Later, Paul appeals to his readers: "Be reconciled to God. God made him who had no sin to be sin for us, so that in him we might become the righteousness of God. As God's fellow workers we urge you not to receive God's grace in vain. . . . I tell you, now is the time of God's favor, now is the day of salvation" (2 Cor 5:20—6:2).

28. "For it is by grace you have been saved, through faith—and this not from yourselves, it is the gift of God—not by works, so that no one can boast" (Eph 2:8–9).

CHRISTIANITY CONTESTED

Paul's boldness in preaching the good news is not unique—Peter and the other apostles demonstrate the same compulsion and commitment to spreading the gospel regardless of the consequences,[29] as have Christians through the ages.

But an apatheistic attitude saps evangelism in two ways. First, the Christian apatheist will lack the compulsion to share the good news of Jesus Christ. After all, their faith isn't experienced as "the best news ever"; so why should they be motivated to risk confrontation or opposition by sharing the gospel with others? Second, it will be difficult to gain the attention of the non-Christian apatheist. If GQs are seen as irrelevant, why should apatheists listen to Christians try to share the good news? The gospel will not be perceived initially as good news—indeed, it will not be "news" at all, but trivial drivel.[30]

Apatheism thus serves as a distinct challenge to Christian evangelism.

Apatheism Contests Missions

A widespread attitude of apatheism has the potential to accomplish something that neither martyrdom nor persecution could: end Christian missions. In Acts 13:2–3, the Christian church in Antioch anoints Saul (Paul) and Barnabas for the work of God, and sends them off to bring the gospel to distant cities and provinces that have not yet heard the good news of Jesus Christ. So begins a nearly two-thousand-year project of Christian missionary endeavor, which has brought the Christian faith to most every tongue and tribe and nation, and to the ends of the earth.

Apatheism threatens missions in two ways. First, the same internal challenge that apatheism poses to Christian evangelism (and, indeed, to discipleship and worship) applies also to missions. The Christian apatheist, who cannot even bring himself to share the gospel with his neighbor or friend, will neither spend his meager resources supporting missionary enterprises nor participate in such missions himself. An apatheistic faith that cannot motivate sustained growth, corporate worship, and personal evangelism will certainly not fuel transcultural missions.

---

29. See, e.g., Acts 4:1–12; 5:17–32.

30. A powerful example is provided in Rauch's article: "Even true-believing godliness today often has an apatheistic flavor. I have Christian friends who organize their lives around an intense and personal relationship with God, but who betray no sign of caring that I am an unrepentantly atheistic Jewish homosexual" (Rauch, "Let It Be," 35).

Second, an increasingly apatheistic atmosphere in contemporary society sets a backdrop against which proselytization (encouraging others to abandon their religion in favor of yours) is strongly discouraged. In such a cultural framework, Christians, regardless of their personal passion and zeal, will feel the pressure to leave others to their religious traditions and devices.

Apatheism thus serves as a distinct challenge to Christian evangelism.

Apatheism Contests Apologetics

A while back, I was with a group of friends debating the relative merits of fishing rods and lures. What is the best lure for crappie? What technique will bring in a striped bass? Is casting superior to trawling? I was, frankly, uninterested. I don't fish (though I love being on the water), and I don't have any interest in fishing debates. But, my friends insisted, one rod *is better* than another, and one lure *is better* than another, right? As they sought to give an apologetic for the truth of their fishing position, I raised my eyebrows in bemused bewilderment.

Christian apologetics is "the explanation and defense of the Christian faith,"[31] or more fully, "the rational defense of the Christian worldview as *objectively true*, rationally compelling and existentially or subjectively engaging."[32] But in the eyes and ears of an apatheist, the supposed truth-claims of the Christian apologist are entirely uninteresting. What use is it to advocate for Christianity's truthfulness if your audience has no interest in the subject matter under consideration? Can someone be persuaded of the truth of the faith if they simply do not care about the questions apologists are answering?

Apatheism thus serves as a distinct challenge to Christian apologetics.

WHY OUGHT ONE REJECT APATHEISM?

A cultural context of increasing apatheism thus challenges five core elements of vibrant Christianity: discipleship, worship, evangelism, missions, and apologetics. Necessarily, then, a believing Christian must not only reject but *actively oppose* apatheism. Proponents like Jonathan Rauch, however, contend that apatheism is a tremendous boon

---

31. Anderson, *Why Believe*, 28.
32. Groothuis, *Christian Apologetics*, 24, emphasis added.

to modern society, potentially eliminating strife and conflict caused by religious zealotry. In Rauch's mind, apatheism breeds tolerance, discourages violence, and facilitates peaceful coexistence. It is our contention, however, that the benefits of apatheism are illusory, and that non-Christians and Christians ought to reject it.

Philosophical Reasons for Rejecting Apatheism

Apatheism breeds the vice of acedia

Acedia is the theological word for apathy, and refers to "the unwillingness to pursue worthy goals . . . because of the effort involved."[33] It is our contention, following the vast weight of the world's philosophical traditions, that pursuing answers to GQs is necessary to living "an examined life" in the Socratic model.[34] Living an examined life, in turn, is part and parcel of enjoying a "good" (*eudaimonian*) life—one which is worthwhile and has the potential for contentment and fulfillment. Hence, pursuing (or at the very least caring about) answers to GQs, like one's post-mortem fate, is necessary to living a full and fulfilled human life.

Perhaps an analogy would help. Consider an imaginary friend Paul, who lives in Palm Beach, Florida. Paul has a little wooden shack on the beach where he likes to spend his weekends and holidays reading, meditating, and writing. Paul is on a sabbatical this semester, and last month was camped out in his little wooden shack, hunkered down to complete some significant projects. One morning, a state trooper knocked on his front (and only) door, telling Paul that he needed to leave. "Whatever for?" Paul asked. The state trooper informed Paul that there was a Category 5 hurricane bearing down upon the beach front, and the hurricane would make landfall later that night. It looked, the state trooper said, like every man-made structure within a mile of the beach was likely to be obliterated, including Paul's little wooden shack.

How should Paul respond to his front-door visitor? One might think that Paul should clearly abandon his little wooden shack and run to the hills. But this is not as obvious as you might think. Why? It is, of course, possible that his visitor was merely a prankster—someone from a rival philosophy department come to scare Paul away from his work

---

33. Groothuis, *Philosophy in Seven Sentences*, 45.
34. Groothuis, *Philosophy in Seven Sentences*, 35–48.

and thereby diminish his academic reputation. It is also, of course, possible that the state trooper is honest, but sincerely mistaken—that the hurricane is coming, but it will miss this beach by a wide margin, and Paul's little wooden shack will come through the minor storm unscathed. In either of those scenarios, it might not be incumbent upon Paul to run away.

But it *does* seem clear that Paul ought to at least seek to come to some conclusion regarding the impending hurricane and act in accordance with that conclusion. That is, Paul should investigate sufficiently to draw a reasonable conclusion as to whether or not he is in imminent danger: if so, he should run away; if not, he can reasonably stay where he is. But it would be irredeemably irresponsible for Paul to merely shrug his shoulders and say, "Who cares whether the state trooper is right or wrong, friend or foe, honest or deceiving. It doesn't matter to me one way or the other." To "not care" in this situation is to fail to care sufficiently about something about which one ought to care very deeply indeed! Paul is guilty of *acedia*.

Consider now what is arguably the central constellation of GQs: What happens when we die? Is there a transcendent God who will judge us?[35] Are we resurrected to eternal life or eternal damnation? Will we be reincarnated in better or worse conditions based on our conduct in this life?

As Blaise Pascal passionately writes, such questions regarding "the immortality of the soul" are "of such vital importance to us, affecting us so deeply, that one must have lost all feeling not to care about knowing the facts of the matter."[36] Such questions have occupied thoughtful humans since the very dawn of civilization, and continue to plague the minds even of angst-ridden, atheist teens.[37] An apatheist who sincerely does not care about the question of post-mortem fate is guilty of the vice of acedia. Such questions are so essential that they cannot virtuously be dodged.

We know intuitively that it is irresponsible for Paul not to care about whether a hurricane will wipe out his little wooden shack with him still

---

35. This question, in turn, requires a prior answer to similarly significant God questions like: Is there to believe that some sort of divine being exists? Is there a God? Multiple gods? Personal or impersonal? Immanent or transcendent?

36. Pascal, *Pensées* 427.

37. I was such a teen, convinced that there was no God but nonetheless deeply concerned by the philosophical questions surrounding human mortality.

inside. How much more is it irresponsible if Paul were to not care a whit about the possibility or nature of post-mortem human existence? To not care about these questions of ultimate human existence is, as Pascal says, "quite monstrous" and "incomprehensible."[38] Apatheism leads to *acedia* and should therefore be shunned by thoughtful humans pursuing a good and examined life.

Apatheism breeds the vice of misology

But perhaps I am not being fair to the apatheist. Perhaps the apatheist has, in the past, cared about the God question in mind, but given the way he has answered the question, no longer cares much about it. Consider two hypothetical apatheists.

Susan is a Christian apatheist—faithful in church, generous in her giving, disciplined in her personal spiritual practices of prayer and Bible reading, but unwilling to be drawn into disputes or disagreements about the existence and nature of God. She has her perspective and respects others' right to believe differently than her. Susan participates in neither street evangelism nor online theological disputes. She just quietly keeps her beliefs to herself and wishes that others would do the same. Susan's seventeen-year-old daughter, Mary, comes home from school one day to announce that she has become an atheist, as she believes there is no good reason to believe in the existence of God. Mary has come to see Christianity as an emotional crutch used by the weak to give them feelings of security, stability, and meaning in life. Mary is above such weaknesses and encourages her mother to renounce her Christianity and be truly free. Mary launches argument after argument against her mother's beliefs, giving her reason after reason not to believe in God. Amid the months-long storm, Susan simply smiles and nods, allowing her daughter to express her opinions and beliefs, but refusing to be drawn into any kind of conversation or dialogue about the relative reasonability of their respective beliefs. Susan is uninterested in the rational objections Mary poses to her faith and is unconcerned with Mary's newfound atheistic beliefs.

Ronald is an atheistic apatheist. Many years ago, he concluded that God does not exist and has continued to live as an intellectually and emotionally fulfilled atheist. Ronald's long-time domestic partner, Howard,

---

38. Pascal, *Pensées* 427.

has long attended a local Episcopal church, but has been as apatheistic about his faith as Ronald has been about his lack of faith. However, one Sunday, Howard comes home different, recounting a radical conversion experience that morning. Howard has come to believe that Jesus Christ is not just a source of moral guidance and admiration but is the risen Lord of life—here and hereafter. Consequently, Howard tells Ronald that he wants to orient his life around Jesus' teachings. Furthermore, Howard starts sharing with Ronald why he believes that Ronald also ought to turn his life over to God and begin following Jesus. He points out inconsistencies in Ronald's atheistic worldview, and articulates logical arguments for the existence of God and the deity of Jesus of Nazareth. Amid that months-long storm, Ronald simply smiles and nods, allowing his longtime partner to express his beliefs, arguments, and reasons without once considering how (if at all) they might affect Ronald's own worldview. Ronald is uninterested in the potential rational objections that Howard has raised for his faith, and is similarly unconcerned with Howard's newfound religious beliefs.

One might be tempted to admire Ronald and Susan. Neither of them is eager to be drawn into a fight—they are willing to let Howard and Mary adopt and articulate divergent religious beliefs without creating divisiveness or violence. But in these situations, continued apatheism does not represent a virtuous refusal to engage in religious conflict—rather, it illuminates a vicious descent into *misology*.

Ronald and Susan seem guilty of misology: a "hatred of . . . reasonable argument and dialogue,"[39] or a disinclination to be drawn into a reasonable dialogue about essential questions or perspectives. Ronald is simply insulating his position, refusing to consider the reasonable arguments and objections that Howard brings to the table. Ronald may be wrong, but he doesn't care enough to investigate the question. To do so would require hard work, dialogue, and open conversation. Similarly, Susan's self-insulation shows a distaste for pursuing truth. If her preacher said Christianity is true, that is good enough for Susan—someone else bringing reasons, logic, or evidence to the table is irrelevant. No, Susan's position will remain Susan's—she doesn't want or need to consider Mary's arguments.

Apatheism leads to precisely this sort of misology. The apatheist has his views on GQs, like life after death, but doesn't care much about what he or anyone else thinks. Hence, he will never be drawn into meaningful

---

39. Groothuis, *Philosophy in Seven Sentences*, 43.

dialogue about such questions. No logic or evidence is needed here, thank you very much—I'm quite content with what I think. The insulating and self-congratulatory nature of apatheism is indicative of vicious misology not of virtuous tolerance.

And therein lies our deep and abiding misgiving about and mistrust of apatheism. Apatheism lends itself to being used as a mask for an unthinking and insular worldview (atheistic or theistic). Let us illustrate with one last story.

I (Tawa) did my doctoral research on the historical Jesus research of John Dominic Crossan—a lovable and brilliant Irish New Testament scholar. In my dissertation, I demonstrate three deep and undefended worldview presuppositions throughout Crossan's scholarship—one of which is the conviction that human life ceases irrevocably at physical death. Crossan acknowledges that presupposition in an informal interview and letter, but never once, in all his published work, explains *how* or *why* he came to that conclusion. Post-mortem extinction is simply an unexamined worldview presupposition that drives his research and conclusions.[40] In a fan letter, Crossan is once asked whether or not he believes in life after death. Crossan's response is concise: "No, but to be honest, I do not find it a particularly important question one way or the other."[41] Crossan's answer is classic apatheism: "This is my religious belief on that particular God question, but I really don't care much about it one way or the other—someone could disagree with me, and it really wouldn't bother me. So I don't much want to talk about it, because it's unimportant to me."

If we assumed that life ceases at death, we would probably not think it's a terribly important question either. But Crossan only considers life after death a trivial question because he has *already arrived at* (or presupposed) the conclusion that there is no life after death! His naturalistic assumption leads naturally to an apatheistic attitude regarding the question. The naturalistic attitude then permits him (emotionally, if not rationally) to treat the God question itself as unimportant—and apatheism emerges.

We see the same trend at work in Jonathan Rauch's seminal article. Rauch acknowledges that he has been an atheist for several years, and eventually, he realized that he simply did not care much at all about the very question of God's existence. Again, it is easy to understand why

---

40. Anderson, "Myth of the Metaphorical Resurrection," 90–105.
41. Crossan and Watts, *Who Is Jesus?*, 131.

he would not care about God's existence, given that he does not believe in God's existence! His apatheism becomes a way of insulating himself against the need to re-consider, re-evaluate, or dialogue about his atheistic worldview. In the face of personal or public proclamations of significant reasons and evidence to believe in God, Rauch can simply play his apatheistic trump card: "I don't care much about my religious view on this matter, and I care even less about *your* view. I don't want to talk about it, I don't want to think about it, and my indifference and apathy mark me as a more civilized and peaceable fellow."

In both cases (Crossan and Rauch), apatheism is not a virtuous restraint of religious passion and zeal but rather vicious acedia or misology, a refusal to reconsider, discuss, or defend one's existing religious perspectives. In a well-known quote from a little-known address, C. S. Lewis emphasizes that "Christianity is a statement which, if false, is of no importance, and if true, of infinite importance. The one thing it cannot be is moderately important."[42] A matter of such import cannot reasonably be discarded as irrelevant or uninteresting. The apatheist who cares naught for the GQs is guilty of the vices of acedia and misology. We ought instead to strive for a virtuous life of philosophical investigation, determining whether or not God exists, whether there is life after death, and being willing (when appropriate) to engage in thoughtful conversation about such questions.

Theological Reasons for Rejecting Apatheism

Just as apatheism fosters acedia and misology, it also stifles theological pursuit, obviously as it relates to God, but perhaps less obviously, as theology relates to humanity. The most profound questions of identity, meaning, and purpose are intimately bound to theology, and we all seek answers to these questions. "Everyone's a theologian," as one systematician liked to remind us.[43] It is not a matter of *whether* one pursues theology but *how*. So, if it is the "bold and silly creature" that loves its Creator disinterestedly, as Lewis said, then what is the creature who is disinterested in the Creator altogether, offering him no morsel of attention, let alone love?[44]

42. Lewis, *God in the Dock*, 101.
43. See Sproul, *Everyone's a Theologian*.
44. Lewis, *Four Loves*, 14.

It is certainly not a motionless heart. Disinterest in the Creator does not equate to indifference *to* and *in* and *among* his creation. Quite the opposite. The more listless we are toward the Creator, the more restless we become in his creation. Indeed, restlessness is a fruit of apatheism, its great theological paradox. The more aloof we are toward the Creator, the more zealous we become toward his creation, seeking and searching for meaning in the created order without ever finding full satisfaction. The Bible defines this zeal toward creation as "idolatry," giving our time, talent, and treasure to something or someone other than God, i.e., worshiping the creation rather than the Creator (Rom 1:25).

Apatheism, then, fosters a form of idolatry, one in which a person not only rejects and ignores God but is disinterested and indifferent to him. Even Christians are susceptible here.[45] An apatheist—whether theistic, agnostic, or atheistic—is never disinterested in all things but is disinterested in the one who created and is before all things (Eph 3:9; Col 1:17).[46] He is interested in the pursuit of meaning in earthly things, but never in the one through whom all things were made, and he is restless in this pursuit.

With idolatry, all the desire within us to be seen, known, loved, and redeemed revolves around a thing—a person, object, activity, ideology, or community—rather than God. It is the golden calves of the world, those powerful yet (supposedly) controllable things that we hope will satisfy our deepest yearnings. And like Israel, who was commanded to rest in God's presence (Exod 31:12–17), the Israelites did just the opposite—they were rest*less* before the idol as they "sat down to eat and drink and rose up to play" (Exod 32:6). Israel's idol restlessness is a parable of the human condition. By being indifferent to God—after all, "who knows that has become of him?" (Exod 32:1)—we honor things while forgetting the King of Kings. We restlessly pursue fullness in the world.

John Calvin located this restlessness in the fallenness of the "flesh," in both our sensual experiences and "the higher part of the soul."[47] In other words, as restless as our flesh is to find *pleasure*, our souls are equally restless to find *purpose*. With God out of the picture (as if he

---

45. For a thoughtful analysis of acedia in the modern church, see Anizor, *Overcoming Apathy*.

46. Unlike apatheism, which expresses disinterest in God questions, disinterest in everything altogether is indicative of other illnesses of the soul. See Anizor, *Overcoming Apathy*, 45–50.

47. Calvin, *Institutes* 2.3.1.

could be), we exhaust ourselves searching for fullness in activities and ideas that we hope will satiate our senses (e.g., sex, substances, etc.) and satisfy our soul (e.g., spirituality, society, and so on). But we never find it, and, fatigued by our futile efforts, we become disappointed, anxious, and enraged at the world and those within it for failing to deliver what only God can (e.g., social media). We care too much for creation and too little for its Creator. Roaming the earth for rest, we never find it, for "here is true rest," wrote Calvin, summoning Bernard of Clairvaux: "A tranquil God tranquilizes all things; and to see him at rest, is to be at rest."[48]

There is a deeper issue, though, one discovered long before Calvin. Augustine drew attention to the hidden restlessness of the human heart. According to his well-known confessional prayer: "You have made us for yourself, and our heart is restless until it comes to rest in you."[49] Our hearts—which Calvin famously described as idol factories—dart from one idol to another in a desperate search for fullness. But we never find it because we search for the wrong thing in the wrong places. We're looking for peace, joy, and love in the world from God when we should be looking for it in the Word of God.

The solution to our restlessness is yielding to the internal sense that we are meant for more forever for the Lord Jesus Christ (Rom 11:36), to acknowledge and act on that universal "yearning for an eternal order, which God has planted in the heart of man, in the inmost recesses of his being, in the core of his personality."[50] We instinctually know that "everything which belongs to the temporal order cannot satisfy man," yet we try to find it there anyhow.[51] And so we exhaust ourselves, even to death, joining the ultimate fate of every idol we ever worshiped.

As biblical scholar G. K. Beale argued, the more we worship our idols, the more we become like them. "What people revere, they resemble, either for ruin or for restoration."[52] To worship an idol is to become *like* the idol, the tragic antithesis to being made in the image and likeness of God (Gen 1:27). We were made to image the true and living God who speaks, sees, hears, and feels, but idolatry turns us *away* from God and *into* the "gods" we worship. Just as idols have mouths and eyes and ears but cannot speak or see or hear, so too do idols lack hearts, and in

---

48. Calvin, *Institutes* 3.24.4.
49. Augustine, *Confessions* 1.1.1.
50. Bavinck, *Wonderful Works of God*, 3.
51. Bavinck, *Wonderful Works of God*, 3.
52. Beale, *We Become What We Worship*, 16.

becoming like them, we lose our purposed ability to feel affection for love's truest source. "Those who make [idols] are just like them," warned the psalmist, lifelessly unable to praise and see and hear and love God (Ps 115:8).

Apatheism is an avenue to idolatry, along with all the bitterness idolatry predictably delivers. Idols are incapable of providing what I demand from them: the kind of peace, joy, and love that is powerful and permanent enough to withstand the deepest, most powerful tragedies of life. But the peace this chaotic world offers is only ever a fermata in between the previous and the next economic collapse or pandemic or war. And to seek my greatest joy in the created order, in created things or activities or ideas or people, is to set an unavoidable appointment with future disappointment when that thing that "makes me happy," whatever or whoever it is, fails to *keep* me happy. Perhaps most bitter of all, finding all my love in a lover will inevitably fade in light of their fickleness, infidelity, failures, and death. Indeed, the "vanity of all our efforts and the cold of the yawning grave poison all our joys."[53] Any hope we have whatsoever rests on rejecting our indifference to God and receiving the rest promised by his Son: "Come to me, all who labor and are heavy laden, and I will give you rest. Take my yoke upon you, and learn from me, for I am gentle and lowly in heart, and you will find rest for your souls" (Matt 11:28–29).

But to hear this invitation, we need ears. And to have ears that hear, we cannot be like the deaf idols we worship. We must be like the beings we were created to be, image bearers reflecting God's own image. Apatheism leads humanity down the exact opposite road and ultimately to one which robs us of salvation in the afterlife, a culminating glorification for the reception of the fullness for which we were created to enjoy eternally.

CONCLUSION

Apathy is an overlooked challenge to Christianity because it hinders the faith's mission in less than obvious ways. It is evident when the faith is opposed by philosophical challenges or anti-religious secularism because these manifest in public and private debate. But indifference toward God is practically too quiet even to notice. Apatheism is a silent opposition,

---

53. Popov, "Deification in the Early Eastern Church," 81.

a dampening power that stifles discipleship, mutes corporate worship, and blunts the Christian mission. Moreover, it breeds the vices of *acedia* and *misology*, thus robbing one's ability to pursue the good life. Instead of discovering fullness in God, apatheism attempts vainly to fulfill universal human desires in idols by reorienting our zeal for the Creator into his creation. It is our contention, then, that apatheism leads to a sort of existential restlessness in creation that ultimately (and ironically) leads to spiritual and physical exhaustion and death. Only when one surrenders one's highest affection to love's highest source may we find what we are looking for.

BIBLIOGRAPHY

Anderson, Tawa J. "The Myth of the Metaphorical Resurrection." PhD diss, Southern Baptist Theological Seminary, 2011.

———. *Why Believe: Christian Apologetics for a Skeptical Age*. Nashville: B&H Academic, 2021.

Anizor, Uche. *Overcoming Apathy: Gospel Hope for Those Who Struggle to Care*. Wheaton, IL: Crossway, 2022.

Augustine. *Confessions*. Translated by Henry Chadwick. Oxford: Oxford University Press, 1992.

Bavinck, Herman. *The Wonderful Works of God*. Translated by Henry Zylstra. Glenside, PA: Westminster Seminary, 2019.

Beale, Gregory K. *We Become What We Worship: A Biblical Theology of Idolatry*. Downers Grove, IL: InterVarsity, 2008.

Beshears, Kyle. *Apatheism: How We Share When They Don't Care*. Nashville: B&H Academic, 2021.

———. "Athens Without a Statue to the Unknown God." *Themelios* 44 (2019) 517–29.

Brenan, Megan. "Religion Considered Important to 72 Percent of Americans." *Gallup*, December 24, 2018. https://news.gallup.com/poll/245651/religion-considered-important-americans.aspx.

Budimir, Milenko. "Apatheism: The New Face of Religion?" *Philosophy of Religion* 45 (2008) 88–93.

Calvin, John. *Institutes of the Christian Religion*. Translated by Henry Beveridge. Peabody, MA: Hendrickson, 2008.

Crossan, John Dominic, and Richard G. Watts. *Who Is Jesus? Answers to Your Questions about the Historical Jesus*. Louisville, KY: Westminster John Knox, 1996.

Groothuis, Douglas. *Christian Apologetics: A Comprehensive Case for Biblical Faith*. 2nd ed. Downers Grove, IL: IVP Academic, 2022.

———. *Philosophy in Seven Sentences: A Small Introduction to a Vast Topic*. Downers Grove, IL: IVP Academic, 2016.

Hedberg, Trevor, and Jordan Huzarevich, "Appraising Objections to Practical Apatheism." *Philosophia* (2016) 1–20.

Hegner, Ian von. "Heroical Apatheism: Mala Fide Bootstrapping Obligations." *Journal of Philosophy, Culture and Religion* 39 (2018) 76–92.

"Importance of Religion in One's Life." *Pew Research Center*, n.d. https://www.pewresearch.org/religious-landscape-study/database/importance-of-religion-in-ones-life.

Johnson, Stuart D. "The Correctional Chaplaincy: Sociological Perspectives in a Time of Rapid Change." *Canadian Journal of Criminology and Corrections: Revue Canadienne de Criminologie* 14 (1972) 173–80.

Kraay, Klaas J. *The Axiology of Theism*. Cambridge: Cambridge University Press, 2021.

Lewis, C. S. *The Four Loves*. London: Bles, 1960.

———. *God in the Dock*. Edited by Walter Hooper. Grand Rapids: Eerdmans, 1970.

Lindsay, James A. *Everybody Is Wrong about God*. Durham, NC: Pitchstone, 2015.

Mouzelis, Nicos. *Modernity: Religious and Ethical Perspectives*. Champaign, IL: University of Illinois Press, 2021.

Nash, Robert J. *Religious Pluralism in the Academy: Opening the Dialogue*. New York: Peter Lang, 2001.

Norenzayan, Ara. *Big Gods: How Religion Transformed Cooperation and Conflict*. Princeton: Princeton University Press, 2013.

Pascal, Blaise. *Pensées*. Edited by A. J. Krailsheimer. Rev. ed. New York: Penguin, 1995.

Popov, Ivan V. "The Idea of Deification in the Early Eastern Church." In vol. 2 of *Theosis: Deification in Christian Theology*, edited by Vladimir Kharlamov, 42–82. Eugene, OR: Pickwick, 2011.

Rauch, Jonathan. "Let It Be." *Atlantic Monthly*, May 2003, 34–35.

Shagan, Ethan H. *The Birth of Modern Belief: Faith and Judgment from the Middle Ages to the Enlightenment*. Princeton: Princeton University Press, 2019.

Sproul, R. C. *Everyone's a Theologian: An Introduction to Systematic Theology*. Orlando: Reformation Trust, 2014.

Taylor, Charles. *A Secular Age*. Cambridge: Harvard University Press, 2007.

Index

Abraham, William, 127
Accessibilism, 136–38
Adams, Rebecca, 190
Adams, Robert, 139
Albert, David, 185
Alexander, T. Desmond, 83
Allison, Dale, 160, 164
Allyn, David, 277
Almeida, Michael, 22–24
Alston, William, 19, 21, 29, 126
Anderson, Charity, 7, 122, 124, 128–29
Andreyev, I. M., 179
Anizor, Uche, 316
Apatheism, 3
apologetics, 309–18
    arguments for, 303–4, 309–11
    causes of, 302–3
    defined, 299–302
    discipleship, 305–6
    evangelism, 306–8
    missions, 308–9
    reject: philosophical reasons, 309–15
    reject: theological reasons, 315–18
    worship, 306–7
Aquinas, Thomas, 1, 101
Aristotle, 69, 203–5, 245
Armenian genocide, 10
Atwood, Feona, 279
Augustine, 204, 265, 285, 305, 317,
Avalos, Hector, 5, 70–72, 89–90

Awabdy, Mark, 58
Ayer, A. J., 113
Ayers, David, 283

Baker, David, 72–76, 79, 84–85, 291
Baptist, Edward, 72
Barnes, Luke, 189
Barth, Karl, 285
Bauckham, Richard, 163–64, 269
Bavinck, Herman, 317
Bayes's Theorem, 25–27, 162–63
Beal, Lissa Wray, 39, 47, 58
Beale, Gregory, 317
Beck, W. David, 152
Beilby, James, 5
Bergmann, Michael, 19, 23
Berlin, Ira, 72
Berman, Joshua, 69, 70, 74
Beshears, Kyle, 7
Biggar, Nigel, 65–67
Blocher, Henri, 170
Blomberg, Craig, 104
Bock, Darrell, 156
Bolz-Weber, Nadia, 281
Borg, Marcus, 155
Bousset, Wilhelm, 157
Bouteneff, Peter, 289
Bowen, Joshua, 44–45, 48, 52, 54, 57, 71, 91
Bowman, Jr., Robert, 153
Boyd, Gregory, 35, 288

INDEX

Brenan, Megan, 307
Brown, Colin, 157
Brown, Ken, 60, 91
Brueggemann, Walter, 288
Budimir, Milenko, 300
Bullough, Bonnie, 224
Bullough, Vern, 224
Burr, Kevin, 157
Burridge, Richard, 152–53
Buss, David, 276–77

Caird, G. B., 163
Callaway, Kutter, 284
Callimachus, 258–59
Calvin, John, 1, 181, 316–17
Carroll R., Daniel, 40
Casabianca, Tristan, 149
Charles, Tyler, 283
Charlesworth, James, 153
Chisholm, Roderick, 14
Chrysostom, 257–58
Cicero, 261
Clapp, Rodney, 284
Clay, Linnea, 34, 95
Clines, D. J. A., 91–92
Coakley, Sarah, 121
Cohick, Lynn, 7, 216
Collins, Robin, 6
Conroy, John, 230
Conway Morris, Simon, 171
Cook, James, 154
Coontz, Stephanie, 278
Cooper, Danielle, 283
Copan, Paul, 4, 34
Copernicus, Nicholaus, 186
CORNEA, 19, 24
Cortez, Marc, 222, 228
Countryman, L. William, 288
Craig, William Lane, 137, 139–40
Creation - God of gaps and miracles, 174–75
Cross, Frank, 286, 288
Crossan, John Dominic, 155–56, 160–61, 314
Cullmann, Oscar, 160
Czajkowski, Kimberley, 242

Darwin, Charles, 169, 171
Darwinian evolution, 6
Davidson, Richard, 282, 289
Davis, Richard, 5
Davison, Scott, 139
Dawkins, Richard, 2–4, 15, 31, 36, 180, 182, 303
Day, Janeth, 251
De Jong, David, 293
Decartes, René, 1
Demarest, Bruce, 136
Dennett, Daniel, 15, 31
Deuteronomy 20, 55–60
Diamond, Milton, 235
Divelbiss, Justin, 190
Dodd, C. H., 160
Dostoyevsky, Fyodor, 9
Dougherty, Trent, 124
Draper, Paul, 4, 15, 19, 27–30, 181
Dunn, James, 164

Eddy, Paul, 7
Ehrman, Bart, 156–60, 163–64
Einstein, Albert, 179, 189
Ellis, J. Edward, 282
Emba, Christine, 281
empty tomb, 158
Epicurus, 11, 188
epistemic hiddenness, 121–25
Epp, Eldon, 268
Esler, Philip, 242
evangelicalism, 8
Evans, C. Stephen, 131, 145
Evil, gratuitous, 16
Evil, logical problem, 4, 12–15
Evil, problem of, 2, 11
Evil, problem of: evidential, 4, 15–20, 27–30
Evolution, 169–88
exclusivism, 2, 5
exclusivism: epistemic objections, 113–15
exclusivism: objections, 104–12

Faith and reason: historical conflict thesis, 180–82

INDEX

Faith and reason: misunderstanding the relationship, 175–80
Feldmeier, Reinhard, 285
Ferry, Luc, 69
Feuerbach, Ludwig, 126
Feynman, Richard, 175
Fiction, Skylar, 71
Fine tuning, 6
Fine, Steven, 255
Firth, David, 37, 44, 47–48, 50, 54, 58
Ford, Coleman, 275
Ford, William, 51
Fox, Nili, 224
French, David, 281
Freud, Sigmund, 1, 126, 195, 201, 212
Frith, Hannah, 277
Fuechtner, Veronika, 275
Fuentes, Augustín, 220
Funk, Robert, 159–62

Gandalf, 20, 41
Ganssle, Gregory, 6, 20, 29
Garr, W. Randall, 222
Gaventa, Beverly, 257
Geisler, Norman, 137
gender, 3
    Biblical view strengths, 236–37
    cross-sex identity, 223–26
    definitions, 217–20
    human nature, 236–37
    incongruence, 234–36
    science and intersex, 232–34
    sexed bodies and human identity, 221–22
    sexed bodies sanctity, 222–23
    stereotypes, 226–28, 231
    transgender ideology, 228–31
genocide, 2, 4–5, 34–35
Genovesi, Vincent, 291
Giami, Alain, 277
Gillath, Omri, 293
God: epistemic hiddenness, 121–25
God: epistemic hiddenness: arguments evaluated, 132–33
God: epistemic hiddenness: response, 125–28
God: Soteriological hiddenness, 133–35

God: Soteriological hiddenness: responses, 136–40
Goldingay, John, 38–42, 48, 58, 69, 80, 84, 87, 91, 289
Gould. Stephen Jay, 171
Gowan, Donald, 72, 90
Green, Joel, 286
Greenaway, Naomi, 229
Groothuis, Douglas, 300, 309–10, 313
Gross, Rita, 108–9
Grossman, Maxine, 242
Gundry-Volf, Judith, 225
Gundry, Robert, 154
Guthrie, Woody, 11

Haas, G. H., 85
Habermas, Gary, 6, 104, 114
Hahn, Scott, 286
Haley, Alex, 135
Hanson, Ann, 242, 248
Harrill, J. Albert, 90
Harris, Monford, 291
Harris, Sam, 5, 15, 31, 70–71,
Harrison, Peter, 182, 275
Hartke, Austen, 218
Hartmann, Margaret, 226
Hartshorne, Charles, 114
Hassett, Janice, 235
Hatfield, Elaine, 280
Hawk, L. Daniel, 40, 46–47
Hawking, Stephen, 185–86
Hedberg, Trevor, 300, 302–3
Hegner, Ian, 304
Hekma, Gert, 277, 280
Herzer, Linda, 224
Hess, Richard, 46
Hick, John, 5, 99–100, 113–14
Hiddenness argument, evaluating, 131–32
Hiddenness of God, 2
Hiddenness of God, epistemic objections to, 125–28
Hiddenness, soteriological, 133–36
Higgins, Kathleen, 199
Hinduja, Sameer, 292
Hirt-Manheimer, Aron, 230

INDEX

Historical conflict thesis: psychological motivation, 182–83
Historical conflict thesis: role of fear of religion, 186–88
Hitchens, Christopher, 15, 31
Hoag, Gary, 255
Hodge, Charles, 136
Hoffmeier, James, 46, 55, 90
Hoffner, Jr., Harry, 73, 87
Holden, Madeleine, 281
Hollinger, Dennis, 287
Holly, Buddy, 11
Hoover, Roy, 159
Horner, David, 213
Hudson, Hud, 142
Huehnergard, John, 81
Hugenberger, Gordon, 289
human flourishing, 3, 6
human flourishing: historical background, 194–201
human flourishing: historical sources, 194–201
human flourishing: nature of, 201–13
human nature, 236–37
Hume, David, 1, 11, 114, 162
Humphreys, Colin, 45
Hurst, L. D., 163
Hurtado, Larry, 164
Hutchings, David, 181–82
Huzarevich, Jordan, 300, 302–3
Hylen, Susan, 243, 248

Ignatius, 260
Ilan, Tal, 242
inclusivism, 137–39
Irfan, Muhammad, 279
Isom, Mo, 282
Israel's warfare accounts, 42–55
Ivanski, Chantelle, 280

James, William, 183
Jefferson, Thomas, 201
Jenkins, Philip, 36
Jenner, Caitlyn, 231
Johnson, Stuart, 301
Jones, Beth, 285
Jordan, Jeffrey, 123, 188

Kaiser, Walter, 82–83
Kant, Immanuel, 1
Katz, Jonathan, 280
Keiser, Thomas, 285
Keith, Chris, 156
Kelly Franklin, 190
Kelly, Stewart, 4, 9
Kennedy, Rick, 162
Kepler, Johannes, 179
Khazan, Olga, 230
Kierkegaard, Søren, 131
Kimmes, Jonathan, 279
Kinnaman, David, 282–83
Kitchen, Kenneth, 43, 45
Kittel, Laura, 201
Kitzinger, Celia, 277
Klein, Jennifer, 283
Klein, Ralph, 55
Kluger, Kari, 294
Knitter, Paul, 100, 107–10, 112
Kohut, Taylor, 280
Komoszewski, J. Ed, 153, 156
Kraay, Klaas, 300
Kraemer, Ross, 241, 253
Krauss, Lawrence, 185

Lalleman, Hetty, 68
Lang, Jennifer, 280
Larson, Edward, 184
Lawrence, Anne, 230–31
Lee-Barnewall, Michelle, 250
Lee, Yena, 20, 29
Lehmiller, Justin, 279
Lehr, Jane, 246
Leibniz, Gottfried, 1
Leiter, Brian, 199
Levine, Amy-Jill, 241
Leviticus 25, 83–91, 383–91
Lewis, C. S., 140–42, 172, 180, 183, 187, 189, 315
libertarianism, 14
Licona, Michael, 151, 154, 156
Liebowitz, Harold, 81
Lindsay, James, 303
Livingston, Tyler, 278
Loader, William, 282, 287, 289
Locke, John, 1

INDEX

Longrich, Nick, 174
Lopez, Diniz, 279
Lorde, Audre, 279
Luther, Martin, 1, 286
Lyons, Gabe, 282

MacDonald, Margaret, 267–68
Mackie, J. L., 11–14
Mahmood, Saba, 244
Malthus, Thomas, 171
Mao, Zedong, 10
Marcus, Joel, 289
Marshall, John, 1
Martin, Emily, 245–46
Marx, Karl, 1, 126, 194–95, 211
Masson, Scott, 99
Mayer, Lawrence, 219
McCall, Thomas, 142
McCauley, Esau, 92
McConville, J. Gordon, 40
McGinn, Thomas, 224
McGrath, Alister, 180
McGrew, Lydia, 149, 162–63
McGrew, Timothy, 163, 165
McHugh, Paul, 219
McKnight, Scot, 257, 268
McLaren, Brian, 5, 99–100, 104–7, 115–17
Meier, John, 288
Menuge, Angus, 151
Meston, Cindy, 276
Metts, Sandra, 293
Meyer, Ben, 156
Meyers, Carol, 75, 86
Middleton, J. Richard, 221–22
Midgley, Mary, 118
Miller, Glenn, 46
Milton, John, 144
minimal facts approach, 149–51
miracles, 2
Mlodinow, Leonard, 185–86
Mori, Camille, 292
Mosaic Law, 70–79
Mouzelis, Nicos, 300

Nagel, Thomas, 26, 110, 186–87, 189
Naimark, Norman, 10

Nash, Robert, 300
Naylor, Peter, 58
Netting, Nancy, 293
Neufeld, Vernon, 160
Nietzsche, Friedrich, 1, 3, 6, 120, 193, 196–201, 212
Noll, Mark, 70
Norenzayan, Ara, 300
Numbers 31, 55–60

O'Neill, Tim, 182
Oeste, Gordon, 53, 55, 57
Olmstead, Spencer, 278, 293
Oosten, Johanna, 279
oppression of women, 3
Oppy, Graham, 16, 22–24
Oravecz, Johannes, 285
Origen, 268
Orr, H. Allen, 181
Osiek, Carolyn, 267–68
Osler, Margaret, 181
Otte, Richard, 29
Oudshoorn, Jacobine, 242

Padgett, Alan, 265–66
Pascal, Blaise, 177, 311–12
Patchin, Justin, 292
Payne, Philip, 261
Peppiatt, Lucy, 263–65
Percy, Walker, 207
Peterson, Michael, 12
Petrusich, Amanda, 281
Pfeiffer, John, 174
Pinker, Steven, 182
Plantinga, Alvin, 1, 10–11, 14, 18–19, 24, 27–28, 100, 113, 126, 172, 178, 189–90
Pluralism, 2, 5, 115–18
Plutarch, 248
Polkinghorne, John, 175, 184
Popov, Ivan, 318
Postmortem opportunity, 5
Postmortem opportunity: apologetics, 140–42
Postmortem opportunity: objections, 143–45
Poston, Ted, 124

INDEX

Pritchard, James, 43
Provan, Iain, 49
Pseudo-Callisthenes, 248

Rauch, Jonathan, 300–301, 304, 308
Rauser, Randall, 50
Rea, Michael, 23, 116–17
Reed, Jonathan, 155, 161
Reilly-Cooper, Rebecca, 219
Reis, Harry, 293
Renan, Ernst, 196
Reppert, Victor, 189–90
Restrictivism, 136–38
Resurrection
    additional observations, 157–64
    afterlife view of early believers, 164
    alternative hypotheses, 158
    bodily appearances, 159–60
    criteria of authenticity, 155–57
    early creedal traditions, 159–60
    early sources independent of Gospels, 161
    empty tomb, 158
    evidence does not compel belief, 164
    high Christology in New Testament, 163
    independent attestations, 160
    Jesus, 6
    linguistic studies, 153–55
    minimal facts approach, 149–51
    naturalistic challenges, 157
    Paul's testimony, 159
    reliability approach, 151–52
    supporting reasons are numerous, 162
Reynolds, Meredith, 293
Richter, Sandra, 215
Ringgren, Helmut, 77
Ritchie, Stuart, 235
Rodrigues, David, 279
Rousseau, Jean Jacques, 201
Rowe, William, 11, 15–22, 24–27, 30
Russell, Bruce, 16
Rutherford, Paul, 277

Sägesser, Caroline, 101
Sakaluk, John, 275

Sartre, Jean-Paul, 204–5
Sax, Leonard, 232
Schellenberg, J. L., 121–24, 126–28, 130, 132–33, 135, 144–45.
Schleiermacher, Friedrich, 157
Science, idolatry of, 183–86
Science and faith, 3
Searle, John, 187–88
Seibert, Eric, 35, 40
Servitude, 79–82
Sexual consent: shared ethical core, 280–81
Sexual intimacy
    covenant of marriage, 281–91
    intimacy: ethics, 284–86
    intimacy: God's design, 284–91
    intimacy: science contemporary, 292–93
    Western contemporary culture, 276–79
    Christian covenantal vision, 292–93
    Biblical perspective, 284–91
    Church witness of, 282–84
Shagan, Ethan, 302–3
Shaw, Benjamin, 6, 104, 152
Shweder, Richard, 284
Simon, Caroline, 277, 283
Skeptical Theism, 4, 19–24, 29
Slavery, 2, 5
Slavery Old Testament world view, 68–71
Slavery: Stowe, Harriet Beecher, 67
Slife, Brent, 275
Smith, James, 90, 111–13
Smith, Jonathan, 154
Solomon, Robert, 199
Solzhenitsyn, Alexander, 10
Soteriological hiddenness, 133–35
Soteriological hiddenness responses, 135–36
Sparks, Kenton, 36
Spieckermann, Hermann, 285
Spinoza, Benedict, 1
Sprinkle, Preston, 7, 216, 289
Sproul, R. C., 315
Stalin, Joseph, 10
Stein, Robert, 160

INDEX

Steiner, Mark, 189
Stephens, Susan, 258
Stoller, Robert, 218
Strauss, David, 157, 196
Strawson, William, 164
Strelan, Rick, 259
Stuart, Douglas, 79
Stump, Eleonore, 179
Sutherland, Reita, 255
Swinburne, Richard, 162

Taylor, Charles, 201, 302
Taylor, Vincent, 160
Tooley, Michael, 16
Torjesen, Karen Jo, 255
Towner, Philip, 255
Trebilco, Paul, 258
Treier, Daniel, 285
Trimm, Charlie, 36–37, 46
Trueman, Carl, 201–2, 277
Tyson, Neil deGrasse, 182

unevangelized, 5
Ungureanu, James, 181–82

Vandenbosch, Laura, 279
Vik, Tennley, 278
Vitz, Paul, 183
von Hase, Karl, 196
Vrangalova, Zhana, 292

Wagner, Richard, 199
Walton, J. Harvey, 47–50
Walton, John, 47–50, 223, 256
Ward, Keith, 183
Ware, James, 154
Wars against Canaanites, 36–42
Wassen, Cecilia, 242
Watts, Richard, 314
Webb, William, 53, 55, 57
Weinberg, Steven, 175
Welcher, Rachel, 284
Wellhausen, Julius, 196
Wenham, Gordon, 49, 83
Wesche, Rose, 294
Westfall, Cynthia, 257
White, Andrew Dickson, 181

Wiesel, Elie, 266–70
Wigner, Eugene, 189
Williams, Craig, 227
Williams, Peter, 78
Williams, Stephen, 40, 69, 75–77
Wilson, David, 181
Witham, Larry, 184
Witt, William, 246, 260–62
Witte, John, 287
Wolterstorff, Nicholas, 126
women, 7
women and Christianity:
    Aristotle and Western society,
        245–47
    cultural influence on science,
        245–46
    disciples of Jesus, 253–54
    divorce, 251–53
    early church leadership, 258–62,
        266–70
    Ephesians 5, 248–50
    historical context Greco-Roman,
        242–44, 248, 253–54
    historical context Jewish first
        century, 241–42, 248, 253–54
    obedience vs. submission, 248–50
    Paul, Apostle co-laborers, 262–65
    Paul, Apostle teaching of, 247–51,
        253–70
    Paul, Apostle to Timothy, 254–59
    religious education ancient world,
        253
    religious education Paul to
        Timothy, 254–60
    remarriage, 251–53
    Samaritan Woman, 251–53
    scripture vs. culture, 215–16,
        240–41, 253
    separate but equal, 246–47
    social status, 241–44
    titles and offices, 258–62, 266–70
    worship participation, 262–66
    women oppression, 3
World wars, 9
Worldview Old Testament, 68–71
Wright, Christopher, 71, 77
Wright, Colin, 219, 236

INDEX

Wright, N. T., 154, 158
Wright, Robert, 172
Wykstra, Stephen, 18-20

Yandell, Keith, 17, 115
Yardley, Miranda, 231

Yarhouse, Mark, 217-18, 229
Young, Julian, 196
Younger, K. Lawson, 43

Zehnder, Markus, 47

Made in the USA
Middletown, DE
17 September 2025